CCNP and CCIE Enterprise Core & CCNP Enterprise Advanced Routing Portable Command Guide

All ENCOR (350-401) and ENARSI (300-410) Commands in One Compact, Portable Resource

Scott Empson
Patrick Gargano

Cisco Press

CCNP and CCIE Enterprise Core & CCNP Enterprise Advanced Routing Portable Command Guide

Scott Empson, Patrick Gargano

Copyright© 2020 Cisco Systems, Inc.

Published by:
Cisco Press

29 2024

Library of Congress Control Number: 2019956928

ISBN-13: 978-0-13-576816-7

ISBN-10: 0-13-576816-0

Warning and Disclaimer

This book is designed to provide information about the CCNP and CCIE Enterprise Core (ENCOR 350-401) and CCNP Enterprise Advanced Routing (ENARSI 300-410) exams. Every effort has been made to make this book as complete and as accurate as possible, but no warranty or fitness is implied.

The information is provided on an "as is" basis. The authors, Cisco Press, and Cisco Systems, Inc. shall have neither liability nor responsibility to any person or entity with respect to any loss or damages arising from the information contained in this book or from the use of the discs or programs that may accompany it.

The opinions expressed in this book belong to the authors and are not necessarily those of Cisco Systems, Inc.

Trademark Acknowledgments

All terms mentioned in this book that are known to be trademarks or service marks have been appropriately capitalized. Cisco Press or Cisco Systems, Inc., cannot attest to the accuracy of this information. Use of a term in this book should not be regarded as affecting the validity of any trademark or service mark.

Special Sales

For information about buying this title in bulk quantities, or for special sales opportunities (which may include electronic versions; custom cover designs; and content particular to your business, training goals, marketing focus, or branding interests), please contact our corporate sales department at corpsales@pearsoned.com or (800) 382-3419.

For government sales inquiries, please contact governmentsales@pearsoned.com.

For questions about sales outside the U.S., please contact intlcs@pearson.com.

Editor-In-Chief
Mark Taub

**Alliances Manager,
Cisco Press**
Arezou Gol

Product Line Manager
Brett Bartow

Senior Editor
James Manly

Managing Editor
Sandra Schroeder

Development Editor
Eleanor Bru

Senior Project Editor
Lori Lyons

Copy Editor
Bill McManus

Technical Editor
Bob Vachon

Editorial Assistant
Cindy Teeters

Cover Designer
Chuti Prasertsith

Production Manager
Vaishnavi Venkatesan/
codeMantra

Composition
codeMantra

Indexer
Ken Johnson

Proofreader
Abigail Manheim

Feedback Information

At Cisco Press, our goal is to create in-depth technical books of the highest quality and value. Each book is crafted with care and precision, undergoing rigorous development that involves the unique expertise of members from the professional technical community.

Readers' feedback is a natural continuation of this process. If you have any comments regarding how we could improve the quality of this book, or otherwise alter it to better suit your needs, you can contact us through email at feedback@ciscopress.com. Please make sure to include the book title and ISBN in your message.

We greatly appreciate your assistance.

Reader Services

Register your copy at www.ciscopress.com/title/9780135768167 for convenient access to downloads, updates, and corrections as they become available. To start the registration process, go to www.ciscopress.com/register and log in or create an account*. Enter the product ISBN 9780135768167 and click Submit. When the process is complete, you will find any available bonus content under Registered Products.

*Be sure to check the box that you would like to hear from us to receive exclusive discounts on future editions of this product.

Americas Headquarters
Cisco Systems, Inc.
San Jose, CA

Asia Pacific Headquarters
Cisco Systems (USA) Pte. Ltd.
Singapore

Europe Headquarters
Cisco Systems International BV Amsterdam,
The Netherlands

Cisco has more than 200 offices worldwide. Addresses, phone numbers, and fax numbers are listed on the Cisco Website at www.cisco.com/go/offices.

Cisco and the Cisco logo are trademarks or registered trademarks of Cisco and/or its affiliates in the U.S. and other countries. To view a list of Cisco trademarks, go to this URL: www.cisco.com/go/trademarks. Third party trademarks mentioned are the property of their respective owners. The use of the word partner does not imply a partnership relationship between Cisco and any other company. (1110R)

Contents at a Glance

Table of Contents

Part III: Infrastructure Services

About the Authors

Scott Empson is an instructor in the Department of Information Systems Technology at the Northern Alberta Institute of Technology in Edmonton, Alberta, Canada, where he has taught for over 21 years. He teaches technical courses in Cisco routing and switching, along with courses in professional development and leadership. Scott created the *CCNA Command Quick Reference* in 2004 as a companion guide to the Cisco Networking Academy Program, and this guide became the *CCNA Portable Command Guide* in 2005. Other titles in the series in the areas of CCNP, Wireless, Security, Microsoft, and Linux followed beginning in 2006. Scott has a Master of Education degree along with three undergraduate degrees: a Bachelor of Arts, with a major in English; a Bachelor of Education, again with a major in English/language arts; and a Bachelor of Applied Information Systems Technology, with a major in network management. Scott lives in Edmonton, Alberta, with his wife, Trina, and two university-attending-but-still-haven't-moved-out-yet-but-hope-to-move-out-as-soon-as-possible-after-graduation-so-Dad-can-have-the-TV-room-back children, Zachariah and Shaelyn.

Patrick Gargano has been an educator since 1996, a Cisco Networking Academy Instructor since 2000, and a Certified Cisco Systems Instructor (CCSI) since 2005. He is currently based in Australia, where he is a Content Development Engineer at Skyline ATS, responsible for CCNP Enterprise course development with Learning@Cisco. He previously led the Networking Academy program at Collège La Cité in Ottawa, Canada, where he taught CCNA/CCNP-level courses, and he has also worked for Cisco Learning Partners Fast Lane UK, ARP Technologies, and NterOne.

In 2018 Patrick was awarded the Networking Academy Above and Beyond Instructor award for leading CCNA CyberOps early adoption and instructor training in Quebec, Canada. Patrick has also twice led the Cisco Networking Academy Dream Team at Cisco Live US.

Patrick's previous Cisco Press publications include the *CCNP Routing and Switching Portable Command Guide* (2014) and *31 Days Before Your CCNA Security Exam* (2016). His certifications include CCNA (R&S), CCNA Wireless, CCNA Security, CCNA CyberOps, and CCNP (R&S). He holds Bachelor of Education and Bachelor of Arts degrees from the University of Ottawa, and is completing a Master of Professional Studies in Computer Networking at Fort Hays State University (Kansas).

About the Technical Reviewer

Bob Vachon is a professor in the Computer Systems Technology program at Cambrian College in Sudbury, Ontario, Canada, where he teaches networking infrastructure courses. He has worked and taught in the computer networking and information technology field since 1984. He has collaborated on various CCNA, CCNA Security, and CCNP projects for the Cisco Networking Academy as team lead, lead author, and subject matter expert. He enjoys playing the guitar and being outdoors.

Dedications

Scott Empson: As always, this book is dedicated to Trina, Zach, and Shae. Also, this book is dedicated to Florence Empson. I couldn't have asked for a better mother. I love you. Cancer sucks.

—Scott

Patrick Gargano: To my wife Kathryn. I am grateful for your love, patience, and constant support, not only during the writing of this book but always. Thank you for taking us on this Australian adventure. Je t'aime.

To our son Sam. What a lovely, kind, interesting little person you are becoming. It is such a pleasure to have you in our lives and to share in your passions. Je t'aime, Samu.

—Patrick

Acknowledgments

Anyone who has ever had anything to do with the publishing industry knows that it takes many, many people to create a book. Our names may be on the cover, but there is no way that we can take credit for all that occurred to get this book from idea to publication. Therefore, we must thank the following:

Scott Empson: The team at Cisco Press. Once again, you amaze me with your professionalism and the ability to make me look good. James and Ellie—thank you for your continued support and belief in my little engineering journal. Thanks to the Production team: Lori, Bill, and Vaishnavi.

To our technical reviewer, Bob Vachon, thanks for keeping us on track and making sure that what we wrote is correct and relevant. I brought you on board with me all those years ago for the *CCNA Security Portable Command Guide*, and I have always enjoyed working with and collaborating with you. This time has been no different.

A big thank you goes to my co-author Patrick Gargano; you have made this a better book with your presence and your knowledge. I am truly honoured to have you as part of the Portable Command Guide family.

Patrick Gargano: I first want to thank Mary Beth Ray for welcoming me into the Cisco Press family back in 2013. I hope you enjoy a well-deserved retirement as you embrace this new, more-relaxed chapter in your life. Namaste.

James, Ellie, Lori, and Bill at Cisco Press did a fabulous job keeping the project on the rails and looking its best.

Bob, always a pleasure working with you. Your attention to detail and technical suggestions were truly appreciated.

Finally, to my good friend Scott. Like the first book we worked on together, this one has been fun and engaging. Thanks for putting up with all those early-morning and late-night calls as we dealt with the 15-hour time difference between Edmonton and Perth. For the last time, no, I don't have the winning lottery ticket numbers even though it's already tomorrow in Australia.

Command Syntax Conventions

The conventions used to present command syntax in this book are the same conventions used in the IOS Command Reference. The Command Reference describes these conventions as follows:

- **Boldface** indicates commands and keywords that are entered literally as shown. In actual configuration examples and output (not general command syntax), boldface indicates commands that are manually input by the user (such as a **show** command).

- *Italic* indicates arguments for which you supply actual values.

- Vertical bars (|) separate alternative, mutually exclusive elements.

- Square brackets ([ ]) indicate an optional element.

- Braces ({ }) indicate a required choice.

- Braces within brackets ([{ }]) indicate a required choice within an optional element.

Introduction

Welcome to the *CCNP and CCIE Enterprise Core & CCNP Enterprise Advanced Routing Portable Command Guide*, a handy resource that you can use both on the job and to study for the ENCOR 350-401 and ENARSI 300-410 exams. I truly hope that a shortened name comes along for this title soon as that is a real bother to continually type out. In order to increase sales, I suggested to Cisco Press that we call this one *Harry Potter and the CCNP ENCORE & ENARSI Portable Command Guide*, but I was quickly vetoed—the title is still too long, I guess. Who can really understand what lawyers say, anyway?

In June 2019, during his Cisco Live keynote address, Cisco Systems CEO Chuck Robbins made an announcement that turned the Cisco certification world completely around. The entire certification program is being reinvented—a new vision, new exams, new paths—including the DevNet pathway that focuses on programmability expertise and software skills. In response to this announcement, authors around the world jumped back into their respective home office/lab space (some would say we never truly left) and started the enormous task of updating the content needed to prepare for these new exams, scheduled to launch in February 2020. This book is one of many titles (at one point I heard that over 35 new titles were being worked on) created over the last 12 months to meet the demands of industry and academia in both the CCNP and CCIE certification space. After studying the new blueprints of all the new CCNP Enterprise exams, Patrick and I decided to combine outcomes from two certification exams into a single volume for this latest edition of our Portable Command Guide. Enterprise Core and Enterprise Advanced Routing are very closely related, so it made sense to create this volume for you to use to prepare for the new exams, and to use as a reference to accomplish tasks you may be undertaking in your production networks.

For those of you who have used one or more Portable Command Guides before, thank you for looking at this one. For those of you who are new to the Portable Command Guides, you are reading what is essentially a cleaned-up version of a personal engineering journal—a small notebook that can be carried around with you that contains little nuggets of information; commands that you use but then forget; IP address schemes for the parts of the network you work with only on occasion; and little reminders about concepts that you work with only once or twice a year but still need to know when those times roll around.. Having a journal of commands at your fingertips, without having to search Cisco.com (or resort to textbooks if the network is down and you are responsible for getting it back online), can be a real timesaver.

With the creation of the new CCNP Enterprise exam objectives, there is always something new to read, a new podcast to listen to, or a slideshow from Cisco Live that you want to review. To make this guide even more practical for you to use, it includes an appendix of blank pages where you can add details that you glean from these other resources, as well as add your own configurations, commands that are not in this book but are needed in your world, and so on. You can make this book your personal engineering journal, a central repository of information that won't weigh you down as you carry it from the office or cubicle to the server and infrastructure rooms in some remote part of the building or some branch office.

Who Should Read This Book?

This book is for those people preparing for the CCNP and CCIE Enterprise Core (ENCOR 350-401) exam and/or the CCNP Enterprise Advanced Routing (ENARSI 300-410) exam, whether through self-study, on-the-job training and practice, study within the Cisco Academy Program, or study through the use of a Cisco Training Partner. There are also many handy notes and tips along the way to make life a bit easier for you in this endeavor. This book is also useful in the workplace. It is small enough that you will find it easy to carry around with you. Big, heavy textbooks might look impressive on your bookshelf in your office, but can you really carry them all around with you when you are working in some server room or equipment closet somewhere?

Strategies for Exam Preparation

The strategy you use to prepare for the ENCOR and ENARSI exams might differ from strategies used by other readers, mainly based on the skills, knowledge, and experience you already have obtained. For instance, if you have attended a course offered by a Cisco Learning Partner or through the Cisco Networking Academy, you might take a different approach than someone who learned routing via on-the-job training or through self-study. Regardless of the strategy you use or the background you have, this book is designed to help you minimize the amount of time required to get to the point where you can pass the exam. For instance, there is no need for you to practice or read about EIGRP, OSPF, WLCs, or VLANs if you fully understand the topic already. However, many people like to make sure that they truly know a topic and therefore read over material that they already know. Several book features will help you gain the confidence that you need to be convinced that you know some material already, and to also help you know what topics you need to study more.

How This Book Is Organized

Although this book could be read cover to cover, we strongly advise against it, unless you really are having problems sleeping at night. The book is designed to be a simple listing of the commands that you need to understand to pass the ENCOR and ENARSI exams. Portable Command Guides contain very little theory; the series is designed to focus on the commands needed at this level of study.

This book focuses primarily on the **configure** and **troubleshoot** exam topics found in the CCNP and CCIE Enterprise Core (ENCOR 350-401) and CCNP Enterprise Advanced Routing (ENARSI 300-410) exam blueprints. Although this book covers two separate exams, commands for both are grouped logically according to this structure:

Part I: Layer 2 Infrastructure

- **Chapter 1, "VLANs":** Troubleshooting static and dynamic 802.1Q trunking protocols; troubleshooting static and dynamic EtherChannels

- **Chapter 2, "Spanning Tree Protocol":** Configuring and verifying common Spanning Tree Protocols—RSPT and MST

- **Chapter 3, "Implementing Inter-VLAN Routing":** Configuring inter-VLAN routing

Part II: Layer 3 Infrastructure

- **Chapter 4, "EIGRP":** Troubleshooting EIGRP, in both classic and named modes for IPv4 and IPv6

- **Chapter 5, "OSPF":** Configuring, verifying, and troubleshooting OSPF environments, using both classic modes and address families for IPv4 and IPv6

- **Chapter 6, "Redistribution and Path Control":** Configuring, verifying, and troubleshooting route redistribution between protocols; troubleshooting network performance issues; loop prevention mechanisms

- **Chapter 7, "BGP":** Configuring, verifying, and troubleshooting BGP, both internal and external, for IPv4 and IPv6

Part III: Infrastructure Services

- **Chapter 8, "IP Services":** Configuring and verifying NAT and PAT; configuring and verifying first-hop redundancy protocols; troubleshooting IPv4 and IPv6 DHCP

- **Chapter 9, "Device Management":** Configuring and verifying line and password protection; troubleshooting device management of console, VTY, Telnet, HTTP, SSH, TFTP, and SCP

Part IV: Infrastructure Security

- **Chapter 10, "Infrastructure Security":** Configuring and verifying device access control; configuring and verifying authentication/authorization using AAA; troubleshooting device security using Cisco IOS AAA; troubleshooting control plane policing

Part V: Network Assurance

- **Chapter 11, "Network Assurance":** Diagnosing network problems using different tools such as debug, traceroute, ping, SNMP, and syslog; configuring and verifying device monitoring; configuring and verifying NetFlow and Flexible NetFlow; configuring and verifying NTP; constructing Tcl scripts; constructing EEM applets

Part VI: Wireless

- **Chapter 12, "Wireless Security and Troubleshooting":** Configuring and verifying wireless security features such as authentication; troubleshooting WLAN configurations and wireless client connectivity issues

Part VII: Overlays and Virtualization

- **Chapter 13, "Overlay Tunnels and VRF":** Configuring and verifying DMVPN; configuring and verifying VRF

This chapter provides information about the following topics:

- Virtual LANs
  - Creating static VLANs using VLAN configuration mode
  - Assigning ports to data and voice VLANs
  - Using the **range** command
  - Dynamic Trunking Protocol (DTP)
  - Setting the trunk encapsulation and allowed VLANs
  - VLAN Trunking Protocol (VTP)
  - Verifying VTP
  - Verifying VLAN information
  - Saving VLAN information
  - Erasing VLAN information
  - Configuration example: VLANs
- Layer 2 link aggregation
  - Interface modes in EtherChannel
  - Default EtherChannel configuration
  - Guidelines for configuring EtherChannel
  - Configuring Layer 2 EtherChannel
  - Configuring Layer 3 EtherChannel
  - Configuring EtherChannel load balancing
  - Configuring LACP hot-standby ports
  - Monitoring and verifying EtherChannel
  - Configuration example: EtherChannel

Virtual LANs

A VLAN is a switched network that logically segments by function, project teams, or applications, without regard to the physical locations of the users. VLANs are the Layer 2 (L2) partitioning of a physical switch into two or more virtual switches. Ports assigned to one VLAN are in a single broadcast domain and are L2 forwarded only within that broadcast domain. Each VLAN is considered its own logical network where any traffic destined for outside the logical network must be forwarded by a router. Each

VLAN can support its own instance of spanning tree. VLANs can be extended across multiple interconnected switches by tagging the VLAN number on each Ethernet frame transmitted or received between them. This tagging of frames is supported by IEEE 802.1Q trunking.

Creating Static VLANs Using VLAN Configuration Mode

Static VLANs occur when a switch port is manually assigned by the network administrator to belong to a VLAN. Each port is associated with a specific VLAN. By default, all ports are originally assigned to VLAN 1. You create VLANs using the VLAN configuration mode.

NOTE: VLAN database mode has been deprecated in IOS Version 15.

Switch(config)# **vlan 3**	Creates VLAN 3 and enters VLAN configuration mode for further definitions
Switch(config-vlan)# **name Engineering**	Assigns a name to the VLAN. The length of the name can be from 1 to 32 characters
Switch(config-vlan)# **exit**	Applies changes, increases the VTP revision number by 1, and returns to global configuration mode **NOTE:** The VLAN is not created until you exit VLAN configuration mode
Switch(config)#	

NOTE: Use this method to add normal-range VLANs (1–1005) or extended-range VLANs (1006–4094). Configuration information for normal-range VLANs is always saved in the VLAN database, and you can display this information by entering the **show vlan** privileged EXEC command.

NOTE: The VLAN Trunking Protocol (VTP) revision number is increased by one each time a VLAN is created or changed.

NOTE: VTP Version 3 supports propagation of extended-range VLANs. VTP Versions 1 and 2 propagate only VLANs 1–1005.

NOTE: Transparent mode does not increment the VTP revision number.

Assigning Ports to Data and Voice VLANs

Switch(config)# **interface fastethernet 0/1**	Moves to interface configuration mode
Switch(config-if)# **switchport mode access**	Sets the port to access mode
Switch(config-if)# **switchport access vlan 10**	Assigns this port to data VLAN 10
Switch(config-if)# **switchport voice vlan 11**	Assigns this port to include tagged voice frames in VLAN 11

NOTE: When the **switchport mode access** command is used, the port will operate as a nontrunking single VLAN interface that transmits and receives untagged frames. An access port can belong to only one VLAN.

NOTE: When the **switchport voice** command is used together with the **switchport access** command, a pseudo-trunk is created allowing two VLANs on the port, one for voice traffic and one for all other traffic. The voice traffic is forwarded in 802.1Q tagged frames and the remaining nonvoice VLAN has no 802.1Q tagging (native VLAN). The internal mini-switch in a Cisco VoIP phone will pass untagged frames to an attached PC and forward 802.1Q tagged VoIP traffic with a differentiated services code point (DSCP) quality of service (QoS) value of EF (or Expedited Forwarding) to the switch port. In this special case, the switch port can belong to two VLANs, one for data and one for voice traffic.

Using the range Command

`Switch(config)# interface range fastethernet 0/1 - 9`	Enables you to set the same configuration parameters on multiple ports at the same time **NOTE:** Depending on the model of switch, there is a space before and after the hyphen in the **interface range** command. Be careful with your typing
`Switch(config-if-range)# switchport mode access`	Sets ports 1–9 as access ports
`Switch(config-if-range)# switchport access vlan 10`	Assigns ports 1–9 to VLAN 10
`Switch(config-if-range)# switchport voice vlan 11`	Assigns ports 1–9 to include tagged voice frames in VLAN 11

Dynamic Trunking Protocol (DTP)

`Switch(config)# interface fastethernet 0/1`	Moves to interface configuration mode
`Switch(config-if)# switchport mode dynamic desirable`	Makes the interface actively attempt to convert the link to a trunk link **NOTE:** With the **switchport mode dynamic desirable** command set, the interface becomes a trunk link if the neighboring interface is set to **trunk**, **desirable**, or **auto**
`Switch(config-if)# switchport mode dynamic auto`	Makes the interface able to convert into a trunk link **NOTE:** With the **switchport mode dynamic auto** command set, the interface becomes a trunk link if the neighboring interface is set to **trunk** or **desirable**
`Switch(config-if)# switchport nonegotiate`	Prevents the interface from generating DTP frames **NOTE:** Use the **switchport mode nonegotiate** command only when the interface switchport mode is **access** or **trunk**. You must manually configure the neighboring interface to establish a trunk link
`Switch(config-if)# switchport mode trunk`	Puts the interface into permanent trunking mode and negotiates to convert the link into a trunk link **NOTE:** With the **switchport mode trunk** command set, the interface becomes a trunk link even if the neighboring interface is not a trunk link

NOTE: The default mode is dependent on the platform. For the 2960/9200 series, the default mode is dynamic auto.

NOTE: On a 2960/9200 series switch, the default for all ports is to be an access port. However, with the default DTP mode being dynamic auto, an access port can be converted into a trunk port if that port receives DTP information from the other side of the link and that other side is set to **trunk** or **desirable**. It is therefore recommended that you hard-code all access ports as access ports with the **switchport mode access** command. This way, DTP information will not inadvertently change an access port to a trunk port. Any port set with the **switchport mode access** command ignores any DTP requests to convert the link.

NOTE: VLAN Trunking Protocol (VTP) domain names must match for a DTP to negotiate a trunk.

Setting the Trunk Encapsulation and Allowed VLANs

Depending on the series of switch that you are using, you may have a choice as to what type of trunk encapsulation you want to use: the Cisco proprietary Inter-Switch Link (ISL) or IEEE 802.1Q (dot1q).

CAUTION: Cisco ISL has been deprecated. Depending on the age and model of your Cisco switch, you may still be able to change the encapsulation type between dot1q and ISL.

CAUTION: The 2960, 2960-x, and 9200 series of switches support only dot1q trunking. Therefore, some commands such as **switchport trunk encapsulation {isl | dotq1}** are not available.

`Switch(config)#` **interface fastethernet 0/1**	Moves to interface configuration mode
`Switch(config-if)#` **switchport mode trunk**	Puts the interface into permanent trunking mode and negotiates to convert the link into a trunk link
`Switch(config-if)#` **switchport trunk encapsulation isl**	Specifies ISL encapsulation on the trunk link. This command is only available on switches that support ISL
`Switch(config-if)#` **switchport trunk encapsulation dot1q**	Specifies 802.1Q encapsulation on the trunk link. This command may not be required on newer switches
`Switch(config-if)#` **switchport trunk encapsulation negotiate**	Specifies that the interface negotiate with the neighboring interface to become either an ISL or dot1q trunk, depending on the capabilities or configuration of the neighboring interface. This command may not be required on newer switches
`Switch(config-if)#` **switchport trunk allowed vlan 10,12,18-22**	Configures the list of VLANs allowed on the trunk **NOTE:** All VLANs are allowed by default
`Switch(config-if)#` **switchport trunk allowed vlan add 44,47-49**	Configures the list of VLANs to add to the existing VLANs allowed on the trunk

Switch(config-if)# **switchport trunk allowed** **vlan remove 44,47-49**	Configures the list of VLANs to remove from the existing VLANs allowed on the trunk **NOTE:** Do not enter any spaces between comma-separated VLAN parameters or in hyphen-specified ranges

VLAN Trunking Protocol (VTP)

VTP is a Cisco proprietary protocol that allows for VLAN configuration (addition, deletion, or renaming of VLANs) to be consistently maintained across a common administrative domain.

Switch(config)# **vtp** **mode client**	Changes the switch to VTP client mode
Switch(config)# **vtp** **mode server**	Changes the switch to VTP server mode **NOTE:** By default, all Catalyst switches are in server mode
Switch(config)# **vtp** **mode transparent**	Changes the switch to VTP transparent mode
Switch(config)# **no vtp** **mode**	Returns the switch to the default VTP server mode
Switch(config)# **vtp** **domain** *domain-name*	Configures the VTP domain name. The name can be from 1 to 32 characters long and is case sensitive **NOTE:** All switches operating in VTP server or client mode must have the same domain name to ensure communication
Switch(config)# **vtp** **password** *password*	Configures a VTP password. In Cisco IOS Software Release 12.3 and later, the password is an ASCII string from 1 to 32 characters long. If you are using a Cisco IOS Software release earlier than 12.3, the password length ranges from 8 to 64 characters long **NOTE:** To communicate with each other, all switches must have the same VTP password set
Switch(config)# **vtp** **version** *number*	Sets the VTP Version to Version 1, Version 2, or Version 3 **NOTE:** VTP versions are not interoperable. All switches must use the same version (with V1 and V2). The biggest difference between Versions 1 and 2 is that Version 2 has support for Token Ring VLANs. Version 3 has added new features such as the creation of a VTP primary server, to prevent the accidental deletion of VLANs that occurred in V1 and V2. V3 also supports extended VLANs, private VLANs, Multiple Spanning Tree Protocol (MSTP), and the ability to be disabled per interface as well as globally **NOTE:** VTP Version 3 is compatible with Version 2, but not Version 1

Switch# **vtp primary**	Changes the operation state of a switch from a secondary server (the default state) to a primary server and advertises the configuration to the domain. If the switch password is configured as **hidden,** you are prompted to reenter the password. This happens only if configured in Version 2. This prompt occurs in privileged EXEC mode but not in global configuration mode
Switch# **vtp primary-server**	**NOTE:** The **vtp primary-server** [**vlan** | **mst** | **force**] commands are only available on older model switches. On newer switches running more recent IOS/IOS-XE, use the **vtp primary** [**vlan** | **mst** | **force**] command instead
Switch# **vtp primary vlan**	(Optional) Configures the device as the primary VTP server for VLANs
Switch# **vtp primary mst**	(Optional) Configures the devices as the primary VTP server for the multiple spanning tree (MST) feature
Switch# **vtp primary force**	(Optional) Configures the device to not check for conflicting devices when configuring the primary server
Switch(config)# **vtp pruning**	Enables VTP pruning **NOTE:** By default, VTP pruning is disabled. You need to enable VTP pruning on only one switch in VTP server mode

NOTE: Only VLANs included in the pruning-eligible list can be pruned. VLANs 2 through 1001 are pruning eligible by default on trunk ports. Reserved VLANs and extended-range VLANs cannot be pruned. To change which eligible VLANs can be pruned, use the interface-specific **switchport trunk pruning vlan** command:

```
Switch(config-if)# switchport trunk pruning vlan remove 4,20-30
! Removes VLANs 4 and 20-30
Switch(config-if)# switchport trunk pruning vlan except 40-50
! All VLANs are added to the pruning list except for 40-50
```

CAUTION: Due to the inherent risk in having VTP servers overwrite each other and cause VLANs to disappear, Cisco recommends as a best practice deploying VTP in transparent mode. If you are going to use a client/server model, use Version 3 and the use of a VTPv3 primary server to prevent accidental database overwrites.

Verifying VTP

Switch# **show vtp status**	Displays general information about VTP configuration
Switch# **show vtp counters**	Displays the VTP counters for the switch
Switch# **show vtp password**	Displays the VTP passwords

NOTE: If trunking has been established before VTP is set up, VTP information is propagated throughout the switch fabric almost immediately. However, because VTP information is advertised only every 300 seconds (5 minutes), unless a change has been made to force an update, it can take several minutes for VTP information to be propagated.

Verifying VLAN Information

Switch# **show vlan**	Displays VLAN information
Switch# **show vlan brief**	Displays VLAN information in brief
Switch# **show vlan id 2**	Displays information of VLAN 2 only
Switch# **show vlan name marketing**	Displays information of VLAN named marketing only
Switch# **show interfaces trunk**	Displays trunk ports, trunking modes, encapsulation, and native and allowed VLANs
Switch# **show interfaces switchport**	Displays the administrative and operational status of trunks, encapsulation, private VLAN, voice VLAN, and trunk VLAN pruning
Switch# **show interface fastethernet 0/1 trunk**	Displays the administrative and operational status of a trunking port

Saving VLAN Configurations

The stored configurations of VLANs 1 through 1005 are always saved in the VLAN database; the filename is *vlan.dat* and is stored in *flash:*. After creating or deleting a VLAN in VLAN configuration mode, the **exit** command will apply any new changes to the VLAN database.

If you are using VTP transparent mode, the configurations are also saved in the running configuration, and can be saved to the startup configuration using the **copy running-config startup-config** command.

If the VTP mode is transparent in the startup configuration, and the VLAN database and the VTP domain name from the VLAN database matches that in the startup configuration file, the VLAN database is ignored (cleared), and the VTP and VLAN configurations in the startup configuration file are used. The VLAN database revision number remains unchanged in the VLAN database.

Erasing VLAN Configurations

Switch# **delete flash:vlan.dat**	Removes entire VLAN database from flash **CAUTION:** Make sure that there is *no* space between the colon (:) and the characters *vlan.dat*. You can potentially erase the entire contents of the flash with this command if the syntax is not correct. Make sure to read the output from the switch. If you need to cancel, press Ctrl+C to escape back to privileged mode: Switch# Switch# **delete flash:vlan.dat** Delete filename [vlan.dat]? Delete flash:vlan.dat? [confirm] Switch#
Switch(config)# **interface fastethernet 0/5**	Moves to interface configuration mode

`Switch(config-if)#` `no switchport access vlan 5`	Removes port from VLAN 5 and reassigns it to VLAN 1 (the default VLAN)
`Switch(config-if)# exit`	Moves to global configuration mode
`Switch(config)# no vlan 5`	Removes VLAN 5 from the VLAN database

NOTE: When you delete a VLAN from a switch that is in VTP server mode, the VLAN is removed from the VLAN database for all switches in the VTP domain. When you delete a VLAN from a switch that is in VTP transparent mode, the VLAN is deleted only on that specific switch.

NOTE: You cannot delete the default VLANs for the different media types: Ethernet VLAN 1 and FDDI or Token Ring VLANs 1002 to 1005.

CAUTION: When you delete a VLAN, any ports assigned to that VLAN become inactive. This "inactive" state can be seen using the **show interfaces switchport** command for the port or ports in question. The ports remain associated with the VLAN (and thus inactive) until you assign those ports to a defined VLAN. Therefore, it is recommended that you reassign ports to a new VLAN or the default VLAN before you delete a VLAN from the VLAN database.

Configuration Example: VLANs

Figure 1-1 shows the network topology for the configuration that follows, which demonstrates how to configure VLANs using the commands covered in this chapter.

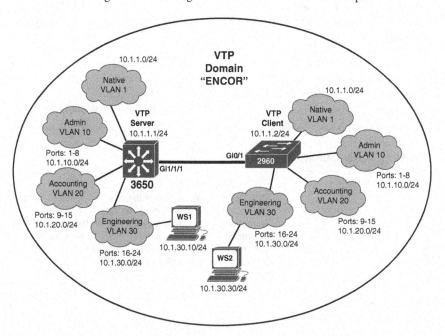

Figure 1-1   Network Topology for VLAN Configuration Example

3650 Switch

`Switch>` **`enable`**	Moves to privileged EXEC mode
`Switch#` **`configure terminal`**	Moves to global configuration mode
`Switch(config)#` **`hostname`** **`Switch3650`**	Sets the host name
`Switch3650(config)#` **`vtp`** **`mode server`**	Changes the switch to VTP server mode. Note that server is the default setting for a 3650 switch
`Switch3650(config)#` **`vtp domain`** **`ENCOR`**	Configures the VTP domain name to ENCOR
`Switch3650(config)#` **`vtp`** **`password Order66`**	Sets the VTP password to Order66
`Switch3650(config)#` **`vlan 10`**	Creates VLAN 10 and enters VLAN configuration mode
`Switch3650(config-vlan)#` **`name`** **`Admin`**	Assigns a name to the VLAN
`Switch3650(config-vlan)#` **`exit`**	Increases the revision number by 1 and returns to global configuration mode
`Switch3650(config)#` **`vlan 20`**	Creates VLAN 20 and enters VLAN configuration mode
`Switch3650(config-vlan)#` **`name`** **`Accounting`**	Assigns a name to the VLAN
`Switch3650(config-vlan)#` **`vlan 30`**	Creates VLAN 30 and enters VLAN configuration mode. You do not have to exit back to global configuration mode to execute this command **NOTE:** The VTP revision number would be incremented because VLAN 20 was created
`Switch3650(config-vlan)#` **`name`** **`Engineering`**	Assigns a name to the VLAN
`Switch3650(config-vlan)#` **`exit`**	Exiting VLAN configuration mode adds VLAN 30 to the VLAN database, which increases the revision number by 1, and returns to global configuration mode
`Switch3650(config)#` **`interface`** **`range gigabitethernet 1/0/1-8`**	Enables you to set the same configuration parameters on multiple ports at the same time
`Switch3650(config-if-range)#` **`switchport mode access`**	Sets ports 1–8 as access ports
`Switch3650(config-if-range)#` **`switchport access vlan 10`**	Assigns ports 1–8 to VLAN 10
`Switch3650(config-if-range)#` **`interface range gigabitethernet 1/0/9-15`**	Enables you to set the same configuration parameters on multiple ports at the same time

`Switch3650(config-if-range)#` `switchport mode access`	Sets ports 9–15 as access ports
`Switch3650(config-if-range)#` `switchport access vlan 20`	Assigns ports 9–15 to VLAN 20
`Switch3650(config-if-range)#` `interface range` `gigabitethernet 1/0/16-24`	Enables you to set the same configuration parameters on multiple ports at the same time
`Switch3650(config-if-range)#` `switchport mode access`	Sets ports 16–24 as access ports
`Switch3650(config-if-range)#` `switchport access vlan 30`	Assigns ports 16–24 to VLAN 30
`Switch3650(config-if-range)# exit`	Returns to global configuration mode
`Switch3650(config)# interface` `gigabitethernet 1/1/1`	Moves to interface configuration mode. Using this interface will require the installation of a Gigabit Ethernet SFP module in the appropriate uplink port
`Switch3650(config-if)#` `switchport mode trunk`	Puts the interface into permanent trunking mode and negotiates to convert the link into a trunk link
`Switch3650(config-if)# exit`	Returns to global configuration mode
`Switch3650(config)# vtp version 3`	Enables VTP Version 3
`Switch3650(config)# vtp pruning`	Enables VTP pruning on this switch
`Switch3650(config)# end`	Returns to privileged EXEC mode
`Switch3650# vtp primary` `vlan force`	Configures the 3650 to be the VTP primary server
`Switch3650# copy running-config` `startup-config`	Saves the configuration in NVRAM

2960 Switch

`Switch> enable`	Moves to privileged EXEC mode
`Switch# configure terminal`	Moves to global configuration mode
`Switch(config)# hostname` `Switch2960`	Sets the host name
`Switch2960(config)# vtp` `mode client`	Changes the switch to VTP server mode
`Switch2960(config)# vtp domain` `ENCOR`	Configures the VTP domain name to ENCOR
`Switch2960(config)# vtp password` `Order66`	Sets the VTP password to Order66
`Switch2960(config)# interface` `range fastethernet 0/1 - 8`	Enables you to set the same configuration parameters on multiple ports at the same time

`Switch2960(config-if-range)#` **`switchport mode access`**	Sets ports 1–8 as access ports
`Switch2960(config-if-range)#` **`switchport access vlan 10`**	Assigns ports 1–8 to VLAN 10
`Switch2960(config-if-range)#` **`interface range fastethernet 0/9 - 15`**	Enables you to set the same configuration parameters on multiple ports at the same time
`Switch2960(config-if-range)#` **`switchport mode access`**	Sets ports 9–15 as access ports
`Switch2960(config-if-range)#` **`switchport access vlan 20`**	Assigns ports 9–15 to VLAN 20
`Switch2960(config-if-range)#` **`interface range fastethernet 0/16 - 24`**	Enables you to set the same configuration parameters on multiple ports at the same time
`Switch2960(config-if-range)#` **`switchport mode access`**	Sets ports 16–24 as access ports
`Switch2960(config-if-range)#` **`switchport access vlan 30`**	Assigns ports 16–24 to VLAN 30
`Switch2960(config-if-range)#` **`exit`**	Returns to global configuration mode
`Switch2960(config)#` **`interface gigabitethernet 0/1`**	Moves to interface configuration mode
`Switch2960(config-if)#` **`switchport mode trunk`**	Puts the interface into permanent trunking mode and negotiates to convert the link into a trunk link
`Switch2960(config-if)#` **`exit`**	Returns to global configuration mode
`Switch2960(config)#` **`vtp version 3`**	Enables VTP Version 3 on this switch
`Switch2960(config)#` **`vtp pruning`**	Enables VTP pruning on this switch
`Switch2960(config)#` **`exit`**	Returns to privileged EXEC mode
`Switch2960#` **`copy running-config startup-config`**	Saves the configuration in NVRAM

Layer 2 Link Aggregation

EtherChannel provides fault-tolerant high-speed links between switches, routers, and servers. An EtherChannel consists of individual Fast Ethernet or Gigabit Ethernet links bundled into a single logical link. If a link within an EtherChannel fails, traffic previously carried over that failed link changes to the remaining links within the EtherChannel.

Interface Modes in EtherChannel

Mode	Protocol	Description
On	None	Forces the interface into an EtherChannel without Port Aggregation Protocol (PAgP) or Link Aggregation Control Protocol (LACP). Channel only exists if connected to another interface group also in On mode
Auto	PAgP (Cisco)	Places the interface into a passive negotiating state (will respond to PAgP packets but will not initiate PAgP negotiation)
Desirable	PAgP (Cisco)	Places the interface into an active negotiating state (will send PAgP packets to start negotiations)
Passive	LACP (IEEE)	Places the interface into a passive negotiating state (will respond to LACP packets but will not initiate LACP negotiation)
Active	LACP (IEEE)	Places the interface into an active negotiating state (will send LACP packets to start negotiations)

Default EtherChannel Configuration

Feature	Default Setting
Channel groups	None assigned
Port-channel logical interface	None defined
PAgP mode	No default
PAgP learn method	Aggregate-port learning on all ports
PAgP priority	128 on all ports
LACP mode	No default
LACP learn method	Aggregate-port learning on all ports
LACP port priority	32768 on all ports
LACP system priority	32768
LACP system ID	LACP system priority and the switch (or switch stack) MAC address
Load balancing	Load distribution on the switch is based on the source MAC address of the incoming packet

Guidelines for Configuring EtherChannel

- PAgP is Cisco proprietary and not compatible with LACP
- LACP is defined in 802.3ad
- The number of supported EtherChannels varies by switch platform model. For instance, you can create up to 6 EtherChannels on a Cisco Catalyst 2960 access layer switch, 48 EtherChannels on a Catalyst 3560 L3 switch, or up to 128 EtherChannels on a Catalyst 3650 switch

- A single PAgP EtherChannel can be made by combining anywhere from two to eight parallel links

- A single LACP EtherChannel can be made by combining up to 16 Ethernet ports of the same type. Up to eight ports can be active and up to eight ports can be in standby mode

- All ports must be identical:

    - Same speed and duplex

    - Cannot mix Fast Ethernet and Gigabit Ethernet

    - Cannot mix PAgP and LACP in a single EtherChannel

    - Can have PAgP and LACP EtherChannels on the same switch, but each EtherChannel must be exclusively PAgP or LACP

    - Must all be VLAN trunk or nontrunk operational status

- All links must be either Layer 2 or Layer 3 in a single channel group

- To create a channel in PAgP, sides must be set to one of the following:

    - Auto-Desirable

    - Desirable-Desirable

- To create a channel in LACP, sides must be set to either:

    - Active-Active

    - Active-Passive

- To create a channel without using PAgP or LACP, sides must be set to On-On

- Do *not* configure a GigaStack gigabit interface converter (GBIC) as part of an EtherChannel

- An interface that is already configured to be a Switched Port Analyzer (SPAN) destination port will not join an EtherChannel group until SPAN is disabled

- Do *not* configure a secure port as part of an EtherChannel

- When using trunk links, ensure that all trunks are in the same mode—Inter-Switch Link (ISL) or 802.1Q (dot1q)

- Interfaces with different native VLANs cannot form an EtherChannel

- When a group is first created, all ports follow the parameters set for the first port to be added to the group. If you change the configuration of one of the parameters, you must also make the changes to all ports in the group:

    - Allowed-VLAN list

    - Spanning-tree path cost for each VLAN

    - Spanning-tree port priority for each VLAN

    - Spanning-tree PortFast setting

- Do not configure a port that is an active or a not-yet-active member of an EtherChannel as an IEEE 802.1X port. If you try to enable IEEE 802.1X on an EtherChannel port, an error message will appear, and IEEE 802.1X is not enabled

- For a Layer 3 EtherChannel, assign the Layer 3 address to the port-channel logical interface, not the physical ports in the channel

Configuring Layer 2 EtherChannel

Switch(config)# **interface port-channel** {*number*}	Specifies the port-channel interface Once in the interface configuration mode, you can configure additional parameters just like for any other physical interface
Switch(config)# **interface range fastethernet 0/1 - 4**	Moves to interface range configuration mode
Switch(config-if-range)# **channel-group 1 mode on**	Creates channel group 1 as an EtherChannel and assigns interfaces FastEthernet 0/1 to 0/4 as part of it. The other end of the EtherChannel would need to be configured the same way for the link to work correctly
Switch(config-if-range)# **channel-group 1 mode desirable**	Creates channel group 1 as a PAgP channel and assigns interfaces 01 to 04 as part of it. The other end of the EtherChannel would need to be configured either as **desirable** or **auto** for the link to work correctly
Switch(config-if-range)# **channel-group 1 mode active**	Creates channel group 1 as an LACP channel and assigns interfaces 01 to 04 as part of it. The other end of the EtherChannel would need to be configured either as **active** or **passive** for the link to work correctly

NOTE: If you enter the **channel-group** command in the physical port interface mode without first setting a **port channel** command in global configuration mode, the port channel will automatically be created for you.

Configuring Layer 3 EtherChannel

L3Switch(config)# **interface port-channel** {*number*}	Creates the port-channel logical interface and moves to interface configuration mode. Valid channel numbers are 1 to 128 for a 3650 series switch. For a 2960 series switch with L3 capabilities, the valid channel numbers are 1 to 6
L3Switch(config-if)# **no switchport**	Puts the port channel into Layer 3 mode
L3Switch(config-if)# **ip address 172.16.10.1 255.255.255.0**	Assigns the IP address and netmask to the port channel
L3Switch(config-if)# **exit**	Moves to global configuration mode

L3Switch(config)# **interface range gigabitethernet 1/0/20-24**	Moves to interface range configuration mode
L3Switch(config-if)# **no switchport**	Puts the interface into Layer 3 mode
L3Switch(config-if-range)# **no ip address**	Ensures that no IP addresses are assigned on the interfaces
L3Switch(config-if-range)# **channel-group 1 mode on**	Creates channel group 1 as an EtherChannel and assigns interfaces 20 to 24 as part of it. The other end of the EtherChannel would need to be configured the same way for the link to work correctly
L3Switch(config-if-range)# **channel-group 1 mode desirable**	Creates channel group 1 as a PAgP channel and assigns interfaces 20 to 24 as part of it. The other end of the EtherChannel would need to be configured either as **desirable** or **auto** for the link to work correctly
L3Switch(config-if-range)# **channel-group 1 mode active**	Creates channel group 1 as an LACP channel and assigns interfaces 20 to 24 as part of it. The other end of the EtherChannel would need to be configured either as **active** or **passive** for the link to work correctly **NOTE:** The channel group number must match the port channel number

Configuring EtherChannel Load Balancing

L3Switch(config)# **port-channel load-balance src-mac**	Configures an EtherChannel load-balancing method. The default value varies between different switch models
	Select one of the following load-distribution methods:
	dst-ip—Specifies destination host IP address
	dst-mac—Specifies destination host MAC address of the incoming packet
	dst-mixed-ip-port—Specifies destination host IP address and the TCP/UDP port
	dst-port—Specifies destination TCP/UDP port
	extended—Specifies extended load-balance methods (combination of source and destination methods beyond those available with the standard command)

ipv6-label—Specifies the IPv6 flow label
l3-proto—Specifies the Layer 3 protocol
src-dst-ip—Specifies the source and destination host IP address
src-dst-mac—Specifies the source and destination host MAC address
src-dst-mixed-ip-port—Specifies the source and destination host IP address and TCP/UDP port
src-dst-port—Specifies the source and destination TCP/UDP port
src-ip—Specifies source host IP address
src-mac—Specifies source host MAC address (this is the default setting)
src-mixed-ip-port—Specifies the source host IP address and the TCP/UDP port
src-port—Specifies the source TCP/UDP port

Configuring LACP Hot-Standby Ports

When LACP is enabled, by default the software tries to configure the maximum number of LACP-compatible ports in a channel, up to a maximum of 16 ports. Only eight ports can be active at one time; the remaining eight links are placed into hot-standby mode. If one of the active links becomes inactive, a link in hot-standby mode becomes active in its place.

You can overwrite the default behavior by specifying the maximum number of active ports in a channel, in which case the remaining ports become hot-standby ports (if you specify only 5 active ports in a channel, the remaining 11 ports become hot-standby ports).

If you specify more than eight links for an EtherChannel group, the software automatically decides which of the hot-standby ports to make active based on LACP priority. For every link that operates in LACP, the software assigns a unique priority made up of the following (in priority order):

- LACP system priority
- System ID (the device MAC address)
- LACP port priority
- Port number

NOTE: Lower numbers are better.

`Switch(config)# interface port-channel 2`	Enters interface configuration mode for port channel 2. The range for port channels is 1 to 128
`Switch(config-if)# lacp max-bundle 3`	Specifies the maximum number of LACP ports in the port-channel bundle. The range is 1 to 8
`Switch(config-if)# port-channel min-links 3`	Specifies the minimum number of member ports (in this example, 3) that must be in the link-up state and bundled in the EtherChannel for the port-channel interface to transition to the link-up state. The range for this command is 2 to 8
`Switch(config-if)# exit`	Returns to global configuration mode
`Switch(config)# lacp system-priority 32000`	Configures the LACP system priority. The range is 1 to 65535. The default is 32768. The lower the value, the higher the system priority
`Switch(config)# interface gigabitethernet 1/0/2`	Moves to interface configuration mode
`Switch(config-if)# lacp port-priority 32000`	Configures the LACP port priority. The range is 1 to 65535. The default is 32768. The lower the value, the more likely that the port will be used for LACP transmission
`Switch(config-if)# end`	Returns to privileged EXEC mode

Monitoring and Verifying EtherChannel

`Switch# show running-config`	Displays a list of what is currently running on the device
`Switch# show running-config interface fastethernet 0/12`	Displays interface fastethernet 0/12 information
`Switch# show interfaces fastethernet 0/12 etherchannel`	Displays EtherChannel information for specified interface
`Switch# show etherchannel`	Displays all EtherChannel information
`Switch# show etherchannel 1 port-channel`	Displays port channel information
`Switch# show etherchannel summary`	Displays a summary of EtherChannel information
`Switch# show interface port-channel 1`	Displays the general status of EtherChannel 1
`Switch# show lacp neighbor`	Shows LACP neighbor information
`Switch# show pagp neighbor`	Shows PAgP neighbor information
`Switch# clear pagp 1 counters`	Clears PAgP channel group 1 information
`Switch# clear lacp 1 counters`	Clears LACP channel group 1 information

Configuration Example: EtherChannel

Figure 1-2 shows the network topology for the configuration that follows, which demonstrates how to configure EtherChannel using commands covered in this chapter.

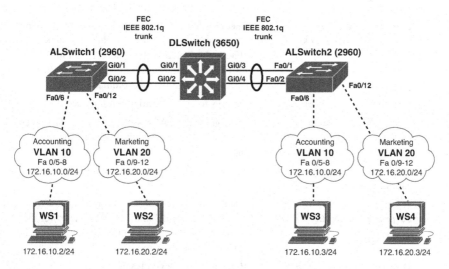

Figure 1-2 Network Topology for EtherChannel Configuration

DLSwitch (3650)

`Switch> enable`	Moves to privileged EXEC mode
`Switch# configure terminal`	Moves to global configuration mode
`Switch(config)# hostname DLSwitch`	Sets the host name
`DLSwitch(config)# no ip domain-lookup`	Turns off DNS queries so that spelling mistakes do not slow you down
`DLSwitch(config)# vtp mode server`	Changes the switch to VTP server mode
`DLSwitch(config)# vtp domain testdomain`	Configures the VTP domain name to *testdomain*
`DLSwitch(config)# vlan 10`	Creates VLAN 10 and enters VLAN configuration mode
`DLSwitch(config-vlan)# name Accounting`	Assigns a name to the VLAN
`DLSwitch(config-vlan)# exit`	Returns to global configuration mode
`DLSwitch(config)# vlan 20`	Creates VLAN 20 and enters VLAN configuration mode
`DLSwitch(config-vlan)# name Marketing`	Assigns a name to the VLAN
`DLSwitch(config-vlan)# exit`	Returns to global configuration mode

DLSwitch(config)# **interface range gigabitethernet 1/0/1-4**	Moves to interface range configuration mode
DLSwitch(config-if)# **switchport mode trunk**	Puts the interface into permanent trunking mode and negotiates to convert the link into a trunk link
DLSwitch(config-if)# **exit**	Returns to global configuration mode
DLSwitch(config)# **interface range gigabitethernet 1/0/1-2**	Moves to interface range configuration mode
DLSwitch(config-if)# **channel-group 1 mode desirable**	Creates channel group 1 and assigns interfaces 01 to 02 as part of it
DLSwitch(config-if)# **exit**	Moves to global configuration mode
DLSwitch(config)# **interface range gigabitethernet 1/0/3-4**	Moves to interface range configuration mode
DLSwitch(config-if)# **channel-group 2 mode desirable**	Creates channel group 2 and assigns interfaces 03 to 04 as part of it
DLSwitch(config-if)# **exit**	Moves to global configuration mode
DLSwitch(config)# **port-channel load-balance dst-mac**	Configures load balancing based on destination MAC address
DLSwitch(config)# **exit**	Moves to privileged EXEC mode
DLSwitch# **copy running-config startup-config**	Saves the configuration to NVRAM

ALSwitch1 (2960)

Switch> **enable**	Moves to privileged EXEC mode
Switch# **configure terminal**	Moves to global configuration mode
Switch(config)# **hostname ALSwitch1**	Sets host name
ALSwitch1(config)# **no ip domain-lookup**	Turns off DNS queries so that spelling mistakes do not slow you down
ALSwitch1(config)# **vtp mode client**	Changes the switch to VTP client mode
ALSwitch1(config)# **vtp domain testdomain**	Configures the VTP domain name to *testdomain*
ALSwitch1(config)# **interface range fastethernet 0/5 - 8**	Moves to interface range configuration mode
ALSwitch1(config-if-range)# **switchport mode access**	Sets ports 05 to 08 as access ports
ALSwitch1(config-if-range)# **switchport access vlan 10**	Assigns ports to VLAN 10
ALSwitch1(config-if-range)# **exit**	Moves to global configuration mode
ALSwitch1(config)# **interface range fastethernet 0/9 - 12**	Moves to interface range configuration mode

`ALSwitch1(config-if-range)#` `switchport mode access`	Sets ports 09 to 12 as access ports
`ALSwitch1(config-if-range)#` `switchport access vlan 20`	Assigns ports to VLAN 20
`ALSwitch1(config-if-range)# exit`	Moves to global configuration mode
`ALSwitch1(config)# interface` `range gigabitethernet 0/1 - 2`	Moves to interface range configuration mode
`ALSwitch1(config-if-range)#` `switchport mode trunk`	Puts the interface into permanent trunking mode and negotiates to convert the link into a trunk link
`ALSwitch1(config-if-range)#` `channel-group 1 mode desirable`	Creates channel group 1 and assigns interfaces 01 to 02 as part of it
`ALSwitch1(config-if-range)# exit`	Moves to global configuration mode
`ALSwitch1(config)# exit`	Moves to privileged EXEC mode
`ALSwitch1# copy running-config` `startup-config`	Saves the configuration to NVRAM

ALSwitch2 (2960)

`Switch> enable`	Moves to privileged EXEC mode
`Switch# configure terminal`	Moves to global configuration mode
`Switch(config)# hostname` `ALSwitch2`	Sets host name
`ALSwitch2(config)# no` `ip domain-lookup`	Turns off DNS queries so that spelling mistakes do not slow you down
`ALSwitch2(config)# vtp` `mode client`	Changes the switch to VTP client mode
`ALSwitch2(config)# vtp domain` `testdomain`	Configures the VTP domain name to *testdomain*
`ALSwitch2(config)# interface` `range fastethernet 0/5 - 8`	Moves to interface range configuration mode
`ALSwitch2(config-if-range)#` `switchport mode access`	Sets ports 05 to 08 as access ports
`ALSwitch2(config-if-range)#` `switchport access vlan 10`	Assigns ports to VLAN 10
`ALSwitch2(config-if-range)# exit`	Moves to global configuration mode
`ALSwitch2(config)# interface` `range fastethernet 0/9 - 12`	Moves to interface range configuration mode
`ALSwitch2(config-if-range)#` `switchport mode access`	Sets ports 09 to 12 as access ports
`ALSwitch2(config-if-range)#` `switchport access vlan 20`	Assigns ports to VLAN 20
`ALSwitch2(config-if-range)# exit`	Moves to global configuration mode

`ALSwitch2(config)# interface range gigabitethernet 0/1 - 2`	Moves to interface range configuration mode
`ALSwitch2(config-if-range)# switchport mode trunk`	Puts the interface into permanent trunking mode and negotiates to convert the link into a trunk link
`ALSwitch2(config-if-range)# channel-group 2 mode desirable`	Creates channel group 2 and assigns interfaces 01 to 02 as part of it **NOTE:** Although the local channel group number does not have to match the channel group number on a neighboring switch, the numbers are often chosen to be the same for ease of management and documentation purposes
`ALSwitch2(config-if-range)# exit`	Moves to global configuration mode
`ALSwitch2(config)# exit`	Moves to privileged EXEC mode
`ALSwitch2# copy running-config startup-config`	Saves the configuration to NVRAM

CHAPTER 2

Spanning Tree Protocol

This chapter provides information and commands concerning the following topics:

- Spanning Tree Protocol definition
- Enabling Spanning Tree Protocol
- Changing the spanning-tree mode
- Configuring the root switch
- Configuring a secondary root switch
- Configuring port priority
- Configuring the path cost
- Configuring the switch priority of a VLAN
- Configuring STP timers
- Configuring optional spanning-tree features
  - PortFast
  - BPDU Guard (2xxx/older 3xxx series)
  - BPDU Guard (3650/9xxx series)
  - BPDU Filter
  - UplinkFast
  - BackboneFast
  - Root Guard
  - Loop Guard
  - Unidirectional link detection
- Configuring and verifying port error conditions
- Enabling Rapid Spanning Tree (RSTP)
- RSTP link types
- Enabling Multiple Spanning Tree (MST)
- Verifying the extended system ID
- Verifying STP
- Troubleshooting Spanning Tree Protocol
- Configuration example: PVST+
- Spanning Tree migration example: PVST+ to Rapid PVST+

Spanning Tree Protocol Definition

The spanning-tree standards offer the same safety that routing protocols provide in Layer 3 forwarding environments to Layer 2 bridging environments. A single best path to a main bridge is found and maintained in the Layer 2 domain, and other redundant paths are managed by selective port blocking. Appropriate blocked ports begin forwarding when primary paths to the main bridge are no longer available.

There are several different spanning-tree modes and protocols:

- **Per VLAN Spanning Tree (PVST+):** This spanning-tree mode is based on the IEEE 802.1D standard and Cisco proprietary extensions. The PVST+ runs on each VLAN on the device up to the maximum supported, ensuring that each has a loop-free path through the network. PVST+ provides Layer 2 load balancing for the VLAN on which it runs. You can create different logical topologies by using the VLANs on your network to ensure that all of your links are used but that no one link is over-subscribed. Each instance of PVST+ on a VLAN has a single root device. This root device propagates the spanning-tree information associated with that VLAN to all other devices in the network. Because each device has the same information about the network, this process ensures that the network topology is maintained.

- **Rapid PVST+:** This spanning-tree mode is the same as PVST+ except that it uses a rapid convergence based on the IEEE 802.1w standard. Beginning from Cisco IOS Release 15.2(4)E, the STP default mode is Rapid PVST+. To provide rapid convergence, Rapid PVST+ immediately deletes dynamically learned MAC address entries on a per-port basis upon receiving a topology change. By contrast, PVST+ uses a short aging time for dynamically learned MAC address entries. Rapid PVST+ uses the same configuration as PVST+ and the device needs only minimal extra configuration. The benefit of Rapid PVST+ is that you can migrate a large PVST+ install base to Rapid PVST+ without having to learn the complexities of the Multiple Spanning Tree Protocol (MSTP) configuration and without having to reprovision your network. In Rapid PVST+ mode, each VLAN runs its own spanning-tree instance up to the maximum supported.

- **Multiple Spanning Tree Protocol (MSTP):** This spanning-tree mode is based on the IEEE 802.1s standard. You can map multiple VLANs to the same spanning-tree instance, which reduces the number of spanning-tree instances required to support a large number of VLANs. MSTP runs on top of the Rapid Spanning Tree Protocol (RSTP) (based on IEEE 802.1w), which provides for rapid convergence of the spanning tree by eliminating the forward delay and by quickly transitioning root ports and designated ports to the forwarding state. In a device stack, the cross-stack rapid transition (CSRT) feature performs the same function as RSTP. You cannot run MSTP without RSTP or CSRT.

NOTE: Default spanning-tree implementation for Catalyst 2950, 2960, 3550, 3560, and 3750 switches is PVST+. This is a per-VLAN implementation of 802.1D. Beginning from Cisco IOS Release 15.2(4)E, the STP default mode is Rapid PVST+ on all switch platforms.

Enabling Spanning Tree Protocol

Switch(config)# **spanning-tree vlan 5**	Enables STP on VLAN 5
Switch(config)# **no spanning-tree vlan 5**	Disables STP on VLAN 5

NOTE: Many access switches such as the Catalyst 2960, 3550, 3560, 3650, 9200, and 9300 support a maximum 128 spanning trees using any combination of PVST+ or Rapid PVST+. The 2950 model supports only 64 instances. Any VLANs created in excess of 128 spanning trees cannot have a spanning-tree instance running in them. There is a possibility of an L2 loop that could not be broken in the case where a VLAN without spanning tree is transported across a trunk. It is recommended that you use MSTP if the number of VLANs in a common topology is high.

CAUTION: Spanning tree is enabled by default on VLAN 1 and on all newly created VLANs up to the spanning-tree limit. Disable spanning tree only if you are sure there are no loops in the network topology. When spanning tree is disabled and loops are present in the topology, excessive traffic and indefinite packet duplication can drastically reduce network performance. Networks have been known to crash in seconds due to broadcast storms created by loops.

Changing the Spanning-Tree Mode

You can configure different types of spanning trees on a Cisco switch. The options vary according to the platform.

`Switch(config)# ` **`spanning-`** **`tree mode pvst`**	Enables PVST+. This is the default setting
`Switch(config)# ` **`spanning-`** **`tree mode mst`**	Enters MST mode
`Switch(config)# ` **`spanning-`** **`tree mst configuration`**	Enters MST subconfiguration mode **NOTE:** Use the command **no spanning-tree mst configuration** to clear the MST configuration
`Switch(config)# ` **`spanning-`** **`tree mode rapid-pvst`**	Enables Rapid PVST+
`Switch# ` **`clear spanning-tree`** **`detected-protocols`**	If any port on the device is connected to a port on a legacy IEEE 802.1D device, this command restarts the protocol migration process on the entire device This step is optional if the designated device detects that this device is running Rapid PVST+

Configuring the Root Switch

`Switch(config)# ` **`spanning-tree vlan 5`** **`root primary`**	Modifies the switch priority from the default 32768 to a lower value to allow the switch to become the primary root switch for VLAN 5 **NOTE:** This switch sets its priority to 24576. If any other switch has a priority set to below 24576 already, this switch sets its own priority to 4096 *less* than the lowest switch priority. If by doing this the switch has a priority of less than 1, this command fails

`Switch(config)#` `spanning-tree vlan 5` `root primary`	Configures the switch to become the root switch for VLAN 5 **NOTE:** The maximum switch topology width and the hello-time can be set within this command **TIP:** The root switch should be a backbone or distribution switch
`Switch(config)#` `spanning-tree vlan` `5 root primary` `diameter 6`	Configures the switch to be the root switch for VLAN 5 and sets the network diameter to 6 **TIP:** The **diameter** keyword defines the maximum number of switches between any two end stations. The range is from 2 to 7 switches. The default value is 7 **TIP:** The **hello-time** keyword sets the hello-interval timer to any amount between 1 and 10 seconds. The default time is 2 seconds

Configuring a Secondary Root Switch

`Switch(config)#` **`spanning-`** **`tree vlan 5 root secondary`**	Configures the switch to become the root switch for VLAN 5 should the primary root switch fail **NOTE:** This switch lowers its priority to 28672. If the root switch fails and all other switches are set to the default priority of 32768, this becomes the new root switch
`Switch(config)#` **`spanning-`** **`tree vlan 5 root secondary`** **`diameter 7`**	Configures the switch to be the secondary root switch for VLAN 5 and sets the network diameter to 7

Configuring Port Priority

`Switch(config)#` **`interface`** **`gigabitethernet 1/0/1`**	Moves to interface configuration mode
`Switch(config-if)#` **`spanning-`** **`tree port-priority 64`**	Configures the port priority for the interface that is an access port
`Switch(config-if)#` **`spanning-`** **`tree vlan 5 port-priority 64`**	Configures the VLAN port priority for an interface that is a trunk port **NOTE:** If a loop occurs, spanning tree uses the port priority when selecting an interface to put into the forwarding state. Assign a higher priority value (lower numerical number) to interfaces you want selected first and a lower priority value (higher numerical number) to interfaces you want selected last The number can be between 0 and 240 in increments of 16. The default port priority is 128

NOTE The **port priority** setting supersedes the physical port number in spanning-tree calculations.

Configuring the Path Cost

`Switch(config)# interface gigabitethernet 1/0/1`	Moves to interface configuration mode
`Switch(config-if)# spanning-tree cost 100000`	Configures the cost for the interface that is an access port. The range is 1 to 200000000; the default value is derived from the media speed of the interface
`Switch(config-if)# spanning-tree vlan 5 cost 1500000`	Configures the VLAN cost for an interface that is a trunk port. The VLAN number can be specified as a single VLAN ID number, a range of VLANs separated by a hyphen, or a series of VLANs separated by a comma. The range is 1 to 4094. For the cost, the range is 1 to 200000000; the default value is derived from the media speed of the interface **NOTE:** If a loop occurs, STP uses the path cost when trying to determine which interface to place into the forwarding state. A higher path cost means a lower-speed transmission

Configuring the Switch Priority of a VLAN

`Switch(config)# spanning-tree vlan 5 priority 12288`	Configures the switch priority of VLAN 5 to 12288

NOTE: With the **priority** keyword, the range is 0 to 61440 in increments of 4096. The default is 32768. The lower the priority, the more likely the switch will be chosen as the root switch. Only the following numbers can be used as priority values:

0	4096	8192	12288
16384	20480	24576	28672
32768	36864	40960	45056
49152	53248	57344	61440

CAUTION: Cisco recommends caution when using this command. Cisco further recommends that the **spanning-tree vlan** *x* **root primary** or the **spanning-tree vlan** *x* **root secondary** command be used instead to modify the switch priority.

Configuring STP Timers

`Switch(config)# spanning-tree vlan 5 hello-time 4`	Changes the hello-delay timer to 4 seconds on VLAN 5
`Switch(config)# spanning-tree vlan 5 forward-time 20`	Changes the forward-delay timer to 20 seconds on VLAN 5
`Switch(config)# spanning-tree vlan 5 max-age 25`	Changes the maximum-aging timer to 25 seconds on VLAN 5

NOTE: For the **hello-time** command, the range is 1 to 10 seconds. The default is 2 seconds.

For the **forward-time** command, the range is 4 to 30 seconds. The default is 15 seconds.

For the **max-age** command, the range is 6 to 40 seconds. The default is 20 seconds.

Configuring Optional Spanning-Tree Features

Although the following commands are not mandatory for STP to work, you might find these helpful to fine-tune your network.

PortFast

NOTE: By default, PortFast is disabled on all interfaces.

`Switch(config)#`
`interface`
`gigabitethernet 1/0/10`
	Moves to interface configuration mode

`Switch(config-if)#` `spanning-tree portfast`	Enables PortFast if the port is already configured as an access port

`Switch(config-if)#`
`spanning-tree portfast`
`disable`
	Disables PortFast for the interface

`Switch(config-if)#`
`spanning-tree portfast`
`edge`
	Enables the PortFast edge feature for the interface

`Switch(config-if)#`
`spanning-tree portfast`
`network`
	Enables PortFast network for the interface
	
	NOTE: Use this command on trunk ports to enable the Bridge Assurance feature, which protects against loops by detecting unidirectional links in the spanning-tree topology
	
	NOTE: Bridge Assurance is enabled globally by default

`Switch(config-if)#`
`spanning-tree portfast`
`trunk`
	Enables PortFast on a trunk port
	
	CAUTION: Use the PortFast command only when connecting a single end station to an access or trunk port. Using this command on a port connected to a switch or hub might prevent spanning tree from detecting loops
	
	NOTE: If you enable the voice VLAN feature, PortFast is enabled automatically. If you disable voice VLAN, PortFast is still enabled

`Switch(config)#`
`spanning-tree portfast`
`default`
	Globally enables PortFast on all switchports that are nontrunking
	
	NOTE: You can override the **spanning-tree portfast default** global configuration command by using the **spanning-tree portfast disable** interface configuration command

`Switch# show spanning-tree interface gigabitethernet 1/0/10 portfast`	Displays PortFast information on interface GigabitEthernet 1/0/10

BPDU Guard (2xxx/older 3xxx Series)

`Switch(config)# spanning-tree portfast bpduguard default`	Globally enables BPDU Guard on ports where **portfast** is enabled
`Switch(config)# interface range fastethernet 0/1 - 5`	Enters interface range configuration mode
`Switch(config-if-range)# spanning-tree portfast`	Enables PortFast on all interfaces in the range **NOTE:** Best practice is to enable PortFast at the same time as BPDU Guard
`Switch(config-if-range)# spanning-tree bpduguard enable`	Enables BPDU Guard on the interface **NOTE:** By default, BPDU Guard is disabled
`Switch(config-if)# spanning-tree bpduguard disable`	Disables BPDU Guard on the interface
`Switch(config)# errdisable recovery cause bpduguard`	Allows port to reenable itself if the cause of the error is BPDU Guard by setting a recovery timer
`Switch(config)# errdisable recovery interval 400`	Sets recovery timer to 400 seconds. The default is 300 seconds. The range is from 30 to 86 400 seconds
`Switch# show spanning-tree summary totals`	Verifies whether BPDU Guard is enabled or disabled
`Switch# show errdisable recovery`	Displays errdisable recovery timer information

BPDU Guard (3650/9xxx Series)

You can enable the BPDU Guard feature if your switch is running PVST+, Rapid PVST+, or MSTP.

The BPDU Guard feature can be globally enabled on the switch or can be enabled per port.

When you enable BPDU Guard at the global level on PortFast-enabled ports, spanning tree shuts down ports that are in a PortFast-operational state if any BPDU is received on them. When you enable BPDU Guard at the interface level on any port without also enabling the PortFast feature, and the port receives a BPDU, it is put in the error-disabled state.

Switch(config)# **spanning-tree portfast bpduguard default**	Enables BPDU Guard globally **NOTE:** By default, BPDU Guard is disabled
Switch(config)# **interface gigabitethernet 1/0/2**	Enters into interface configuration mode
Switch(config-if)# **spanning-tree portfast edge**	Enables the PortFast edge feature
Switch(config-if)# **end**	Returns to privileged EXEC mode

BPDU Filter

Switch(config)# **spanning-tree portfast bpdufilter default**	Globally enables BPDU filtering on PortFast-enabled port; prevents ports in PortFast from sending or receiving BPDUs
Switch(config)# **interface range gigabitethernet 1/0/1-4**	Enters interface range configuration mode
Switch(config-if-range)# **spanning-tree portfast**	Enables PortFast on all interfaces in the range
Switch(config-if-range)# **spanning-tree portfast edge**	Enables PortFast on all interfaces in the range **NOTE:** This is the command for the 3650/9300 series
Switch(config-if-range)# **spanning-tree bpdufilter enable**	Enables BPDU Filter on all interfaces in the range configured with "PortFast" **NOTE:** By default, BPDU filtering is disabled. Also, BPDU Guard has no effect on an interface if BPDU filtering is enabled **CAUTION:** Enabling BPDU filtering on an interface, or globally, is the same as disabling STP, which can result in spanning-tree loops being created but not detected
Switch# **show spanning-tree summary totals**	Displays global BPDU filtering configuration information
Switch# **show spanning-tree interface** [*interface-type, interface-number*] **detail**	Displays detailed spanning-tree interface status and configuration information of the specified interface

UplinkFast

Switch(config)# **spanning-tree uplinkfast**	Enables UplinkFast. UplinkFast provides fast convergence after a direct link failure
Switch(config)# **spanning-tree uplinkfast max-update-rate 200**	Enables UplinkFast and sets the update packet rate to 200 packets/second **NOTE:** UplinkFast cannot be set on an individual VLAN. The **spanning-tree uplinkfast** command affects all VLANs

	NOTE: For the **max-update-rate** argument, the range is 0 to 32,000 packets/ second. The default is 150. If you set the rate to 0, station-learning frames are not generated. This will cause STP to converge more slowly after a loss of connectivity
Switch# **show spanning-tree summary**	Verifies whether UplinkFast has been enabled
Switch# **show spanning-tree uplinkfast**	Displays spanning-tree UplinkFast status, which includes maximum update packet rate and participating interfaces

NOTE: UplinkFast cannot be enabled on VLANs that have been configured for switch priority.

NOTE: UplinkFast is most useful in access layer switches, or switches at the edge of the network. It is not appropriate for backbone devices.

NOTE: You can configure the UplinkFast feature for Rapid PVST+ or for the MSTP, but the feature remains disabled (inactive) until you change the spanning-tree mode to PVST+.

BackboneFast

Switch(config)# **spanning-tree backbonefast**	Enables BackboneFast. BackboneFast is initiated when a root port or blocked port receives an inferior BPDU from its designated bridge
Switch# **show spanning-tree summary**	Verifies BackboneFast has been enabled
Switch# **show spanning-tree backbonefast**	Displays spanning-tree BackboneFast status, which includes the number of root link query protocol data units (PDUs) sent/received and number of BackboneFast transitions

NOTE: You can configure the BackboneFast feature for Rapid PVST+ or for the MSTP, but the feature remains disabled (inactive) until you change the spanning-tree mode to PVST+.

NOTE: If you use BackboneFast, you must enable it on all switches in the network.

Root Guard

You can use Root Guard to limit which switch can become the root bridge. Root Guard should be enabled on all ports where the root bridge is not anticipated, such as access ports.

Switch(config)# **interface gigabitethernet 1/0/1**	Moves to interface configuration mode
Switch(config-if)# **spanning-tree guard root**	Enables Root Guard on the interface

Switch# `show spanning-tree` `inconsistentports`	Indicates whether any ports are in a root-inconsistent state
Switch# `show spanning-tree root`	Displays the status and configuration of the root bridge **NOTE:** The **show spanning-tree root** command output includes root ID for all VLANs, the associated root costs, timer settings, and root ports
Switch# `show spanning-tree`	Displays detailed spanning-tree state and configuration for each VLAN on the switch, including bridge and root IDs, timers, root costs, and forwarding status

NOTE: You cannot enable both Root Guard and Loop Guard at the same time.

NOTE: Root Guard enabled on an interface applies to all VLANs to which the interface belongs.

NOTE: Do not enable Root Guard on interfaces to be used by the UplinkFast feature.

Loop Guard

Loop Guard is used to prevent alternate or root ports from becoming designated ports due to a failure that leads to a unidirectional link. Loop Guard operates only on interfaces that are considered point to point by the spanning tree. Spanning tree determines a port to be point to point or shared from the port duplex setting. You can use Loop Guard to prevent alternate or root ports from becoming designated ports because of a failure that leads to a unidirectional link. This feature is most effective when it is enabled on the entire switched network. When Loop Guard is enabled, spanning tree does not send BPDUs on root or alternate ports.

NOTE: Both the port duplex and the spanning-tree link type can be set manually.

NOTE: You cannot enable both Loop Guard and Root Guard on the same port. The Loop Guard feature is most effective when it is configured on the entire switched network.

Switch# `show spanning-tree` `active`	Shows which ports are alternate or root ports
Switch# `show spanning-tree mst`	Shows which ports are alternate or root ports when the switch is operating in MST mode
Switch# `configure terminal`	Moves to global configuration mode
Switch(config)# `spanning-tree` `loopguard default`	Enables Loop Guard globally on the switch for those interfaces that the spanning tree identifies as point to point
Switch(config)# `interface` `gigabitethernet 1/0/1`	Moves to interface configuration mode
Switch(config-if)# `spanning-` `tree guard loop`	Enables Loop Guard on all the VLANs associated with the selected interface
Switch(config-if)# `exit`	Returns to privileged EXEC mode

`Switch# show spanning-tree summary`	Verifies whether Loop Guard has been enabled
`Switch# show spanning-tree interface detail`	Display spanning-tree link type. A link type of "point to point" is required for Loop Guard

Unidirectional Link Detection

`Switch(config)# udld enable`	Enables unidirectional link detection (UDLD) on all fiber-optic interfaces to determine the Layer 1 status of the link **NOTE:** By default, UDLD is disabled
`Switch(config)# udld aggressive`	Enables UDLD aggressive mode on all fiber-optic interfaces
`Switch(config)# interface gigabitethernet 1/0/1`	Moves to interface configuration mode
`Switch(config-if)# udld port [aggressive]`	Enables UDLD on this interface (required for copper-based interfaces) in normal or aggressive mode **NOTE:** On a fiber-optic (FO) interface, the interface command **udld port** overrides the global command **udld enable**. Therefore, if you issue the command **no udld port** on an FO interface, you will still have the globally enabled **udld enable** command to deal with
`Switch# show udld`	Displays UDLD information
`Switch# show udld interface gigabitethernet 1/0/1`	Displays UDLD information for interface Gigabit Ethernet 1/0/1
`Switch# udld reset`	Resets all interfaces shut down by UDLD **NOTE:** You can also use the **shutdown** command, followed by a **no shutdown** command in interface configuration mode, to restart a disabled interface

Configuring and Verifying Port Error Conditions

A port is "error-disabled" when the switch detects any one of a number of port violations. No traffic is sent or received when the port is in error-disabled state. The **show errdisable detect** command displays a list for the possible error-disabled reasons and whether enabled.

The **errdisable detect cause** command allows the network device administrator to enable or disable detection of individual error-disabled causes. All causes are enabled by default. All causes, except for per-VLAN error disabling, are configured to shut down the entire port.

The **errdisable recovery** command enables the network device administrator to configure automatic recovery mechanism variables. This would allow the switch port to again send and receive traffic after a configured period of time if the initial error condition is no longer present. All recovery mechanisms are disabled by default.

`Switch(config)# errdisable detect cause all`	Enables error detection for all error-disabled causes
`Switch(config)# errdisable detect cause bpduguard shutdown vlan`	Enables per-VLAN error-disable for BPDU Guard
`Switch(config)# errdisable detect cause dhcp-rate-limit`	Enables error detection for DHCP snooping
`Switch(config)# errdisable detect cause dtp-flap`	Enables error detection for Dynamic Trunk Protocol (DTP) flapping
`Switch(config)# errdisable detect cause gbic-invalid`	Enables error detection for invalid Gigabit Interface Converter (GBIC) module. **NOTE:** You can also use the **shutdown** command, followed by a **no shutdown** command in interface configuration mode, to restart a disabled interface. This error refers to an invalid small form-factor pluggable (SFP) module on the switch
`Switch(config)# errdisable detect cause inline-power`	Enables error detection for inline power
`Switch(config)# errdisable detect cause link-flap`	Enables error detection for link-state flapping
`Switch(config)# errdisable detect cause loopback`	Enables error detection for detected loopbacks
`Switch(config)# errdisable detect cause pagp-flap`	Enables error detection for the Port Aggregation Protocol (PAgP) flap error-disabled cause
`Switch(config)# errdisable detect cause security-violation shutdown vlan`	Enables voice-aware 802.1X security
`Switch(config)# errdisable detect cause sfp-config-mismatch`	Enables error detection on an SFP configuration mismatch
`Switch(config)# errdisable recovery interval 3600`	Configures errdisable recovery timer to 3600 seconds **NOTE:** The same interval is applied to all causes. The range is 30 to 86,400 seconds. The default interval is 300 seconds
`Switch(config)# errdisable recovery cause parameter`	Enables the error-disabled mechanism to recover from specific cause *parameter*. Parameters are shown below
`Switch(config)# errdisable recovery cause all`	Enables the timer to recover from all error-disabled causes

Switch(config)# **errdisable recovery cause bpduguard**	Enables the timer to recover from BPDU Guard error-disabled state
Switch(config)# **errdisable recovery cause channel-misconfig**	Enable the timer to recover from the EtherChannel misconfiguration error-disabled state
Switch(config)# **errdisable recovery cause dhcp-rate-limit**	Enables the timer to recover from the DHCP snooping error-disabled state
Switch(config)# **errdisable recovery cause dtp-flap**	Enables the timer to recover from the DTP-flap error-disabled state
Switch(config)# **errdisable recovery cause gbic-invalid**	Enables the timer to recover from the GBIC module error-disabled state **NOTE:** This error refers to an invalid SFP error-disabled state
Switch(config)# **errdisable recovery cause inline-power**	Enables the timer to recover for inline power
Switch(config)# **errdisable recovery cause link-flap**	Enables the timer to recover from the link-flap error-disabled state
Switch(config)# **errdisable recovery cause loopback**	Enables the timer to recover from a loopback error-disabled state
Switch(config)# **errdisable recovery cause pagp-flap**	Enables the timer to recover from the PAgP-flap error-disabled state
Switch(config)# **errdisable recovery cause psecure-violation**	Enables the timer to recover from a port security violation disabled state
Switch(config)# **errdisable recovery cause security-violation**	Enables the timer to recover from an IEEE 802.1X-violation disabled state
Switch(config)# **errdisable recovery cause sfp-mismatch**	Enables the timer to recover from an SFP configuration mismatch
Switch# **show errdisable detect**	Displays error-disabled detection status
Switch# **show errdisable detect	begin** *expression*	Display begins with the line that matches the *expression* **NOTE:** *expression* is the output to use as a reference point
Switch# **show errdisable detect	exclude** *expression*	Display excludes lines that match the *expression*
Switch# **show errdisable detect	include** *expression*	Display includes lines that match the *expression*
Switch# **show errdisable recovery**	Displays the error-disabled recovery timer status information

Switch# **show errdisable** **recovery** | **begin** *expression*	Display begins with the line that matches the *expression*
Switch# **show errdisable** **recovery** | **exclude** *expression*	Display excludes lines that match the *expression*
Switch# **show errdisable** **recovery** | **include** *expression*	Display includes lines that match the *expression*

Enabling Rapid Spanning Tree

Switch(config)# **spanning-tree** **mode rapid-pvst**	Enables Rapid PVST+
Switch# **clear spanning-tree** **detected-protocols**	Restarts the protocol migration process. With no arguments, the command is applied to every port of the switch
Switch# **clear spanning-tree** **detected-protocols interface** **gigabitethernet 1/0/1**	Restarts the protocol migration process on interface GigabitEthernet 1/0/1
Switch# **clear spanning-tree** **detected-protocols port-channel 1**	Restarts the protocol migration process on interface port-channel 1
Switch# **show spanning-tree**	Displays mode, root and bridge IDs, participating ports, and their spanning-tree states
Switch# **show spanning-tree** **summary**	Summarizes configured port states, including spanning-tree mode
Switch# **show spanning-tree detail**	Displays a detailed summary of spanning-tree interface information, including mode, priority, system ID, MAC address, timers, and role in the spanning tree for each VLAN and port

Rapid Spanning Tree Link Types

The link type in RSTP can predetermine the active role that the port plays as it stands by for immediate transition to a forwarding state, if certain parameters are met. These parameters are different for edge ports and non-edge ports. An *edge port* is a switch port that is never intended to be connected to another switch device. It immediately transitions to the forwarding state when enabled—similar to an STP port with the PortFast featured enabled. However, an edge port that receives a BPDU immediately loses its edge port status and becomes a normal spanning-tree port. *Non-edge ports* are ports that are intended to be connected to another switch device. Link type is automatically determined but can be overwritten with an explicit port configuration. There are two different link types for non-edge ports, as shown in Table 2-1.

Link Type	Description
Point-to-point	A port operating in full-duplex mode. It is assumed that the port is connected to a single switch device at the other end of the link
Shared	A port operating in half-duplex mode. It is assumed that the port is connected to shared media where multiple switches may exist

TABLE 2-1   RSTP Non-Edge Link Types

`Switch(config)#` **`spanning-tree mode rapid-pvst`**	Enables Rapid PVST+
`Switch(config)#` **`interface gigabitethernet 1/0/1`**	Moves to interface configuration mode
`Switch(config-if)#` **`spanning-tree link-type auto`**	Sets the link type based on the duplex setting of the interface
`Switch(config-if)#` **`spanning-tree link-type`** **`point-to-point`**	Specifies that the interface is a point-to-point link
`Switch(config-if)#` **`spanning-tree link-type shared`**	Specifies that the interface is a shared medium
`Switch(config-if)#` **`exit`**	Returns to global configuration mode

Enabling Multiple Spanning Tree

`Switch(config)#` **`spanning-tree`** **`mode mst`**	Enters MST mode
`Switch(config)#` **`spanning-tree`** **`mst configuration`**	Enters MST configuration submode
`Switch(config-mst)#` **`instance 1`** **`vlan 4`**	Maps VLAN 4 to Multiple Spanning Tree (MST) instance 1
`Switch(config-mst)#` **`instance 1`** **`vlan 1-15`**	Maps VLANs 1–15 to MST instance 1
`Switch(config-mst)#` **`instance 1`** **`vlan 10,20,30`**	Maps VLANs 10, 20, and 30 to MST instance 1 **NOTE:** For the **instance x vlan y** command, the instance must be a number between 1 and 15, and the VLAN range is 1 to 4094
`Switch(config-mst)#` **`name`** **`region12`**	Specifies the name for the MST region. The default is an empty string **NOTE:** The **name** argument can be up to 32 characters long and is case sensitive

`Switch(config-mst)# revision 4`	Specifies the revision number **NOTE:** The range for the **revision** argument is 0 to 65,535 **NOTE:** For two or more bridges to be in the same MST region, they must have the identical MST name, VLAN-to-instance mapping, and MST revision number
`Switch(config-mst)# show current`	Displays the summary of what is currently configured for the MST region
`Switch(config-mst)# show pending`	Verifies the configuration by displaying a summary of what you have configured for the MST region
`Switch(config-mst)# exit`	Applies all changes and returns to global configuration mode
`Switch(config)# spanning-tree mst 1 priority 4096`	Sets the bridge priority for the spanning tree to 4096. The priority can be a number from 0–61440 in increments of 4096 **CAUTION:** Changing spanning-tree modes can disrupt traffic because all spanning-tree instances are stopped for the old mode and restarted in the new mode **NOTE:** You cannot run both MSTP and PVST at the same time
`Switch(config)# spanning-tree mst 1 root primary`	Configures a switch as a primary root switch within MST instance 1. The primary root switch priority is 24,576
`Switch(config)# spanning-tree mst 1 root secondary`	Configures a switch as a secondary root switch within MST instance 1. The secondary root switch priority is 28,672
`Switch(config-if)# spanning-tree mst 20 port-priority 0`	Configures an interface with a port priority of 0 for MST instance 20 **NOTE:** The priority range is 0 to 240 in increments of 16, where the lower the number, the higher the priority. The default is 128. The range and increment values are platform and IOS version dependent
`Switch(config-if)# spanning-tree mst 2 cost 250`	Sets the path cost to 250 for MST instance 2 calculations. Path cost is 1 to 200,000,000, with higher values meaning higher costs
`Switch(config-if)# end`	Returns to privileged EXEC mode

Verifying the Extended System ID

Switch# **show spanning-tree summary**	Verifies that the extended system ID is enabled
Switch# **show spanning-tree bridge**	Displays the extended system ID as part of the bridge ID **NOTE:** The 12-bit extended system ID is the VLAN number for the instance of PVST+ and PVRST+ spanning tree. In MST, these 12 bits carry the instance number

Verifying STP

Switch# **show spanning-tree**	Displays STP information
Switch# **show spanning-tree active**	Displays STP information on active interfaces only
Switch# **show spanning-tree bridge**	Displays status and configuration of this bridge
Switch# **show spanning-tree detail**	Displays a detailed summary of interface information
Switch# **show spanning-tree interface gigabitethernet 1/0/1**	Displays STP information for interface giga-bitethernet 1/0/1
Switch# **show spanning-tree summary**	Displays a summary of port states
Switch# **show spanning-tree summary totals**	Displays the total lines of the STP section
Switch# **show spanning-tree vlan 5**	Displays STP information for VLAN 5
Switch# **show spanning-tree mst configuration**	Displays the MST region configuration
Switch# **show spanning-tree mst configuration digest**	Displays the message digest 5 (MD5) authen-tication digest included in the current MST configuration identifier (MSTCI)
Switch# **show spanning-tree mst 1**	Displays the MST information for instance 1
Switch# **show spanning-tree mst interface gigabitethernet 1/0/1**	Displays the MST information for interface GigabitEthernet 1/0/1
Switch# **show spanning-tree mst 1 interface gigabitethernet 1/0/1**	Displays the MST information for instance 1 on interface GigabitEthernet 1/0/1
Switch# **show spanning-tree mst 1 detail**	Shows detailed information about MST instance 1

Troubleshooting Spanning Tree Protocol

Switch# **debug spanning-tree all**	Displays all spanning-tree debugging events
Switch# **debug spanning-tree events**	Displays spanning-tree debugging topology events
Switch# **debug spanning-tree backbonefast**	Displays spanning-tree debugging BackboneFast events
Switch# **debug spanning-tree uplinkfast**	Displays spanning-tree debugging UplinkFast events
Switch# **debug spanning-tree mstp all**	Displays all MST debugging events
Switch# **debug spanning-tree switch state**	Displays spanning-tree port state changes
Switch# **debug spanning-tree pvst+**	Displays PVST+ events

Configuration Example: PVST+

Figure 2-1 shows the network topology for the configuration of PVST+ using commands covered in this chapter. Assume that other commands needed for connectivity have already been configured. For example, all inter-switch links in this topology are configured as 802.1Q trunks.

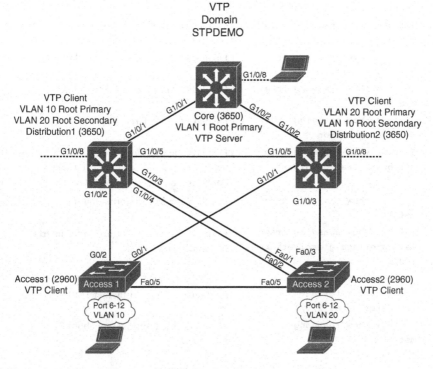

Figure 2-1 Network Topology for STP Configuration Example

Core Switch (3650)

`Switch> ` **`enable`**	Moves to privileged EXEC mode
`Switch# ` **`configure terminal`**	Moves to global configuration mode
`Switch(config)# ` **`hostname Core`**	Sets the host name
`Core(config)# ` **`no ip domain-lookup`**	Turns off Domain Name System (DNS) queries so that spelling mistakes do not slow you down
`Core(config)# ` **`vtp mode server`**	Changes the switch to VTP server mode. This is the default mode
`Core(config)# ` **`vtp domain STPDEMO`**	Configures the VTP domain name to *STPDEMO*
`Core(config)# ` **`vlan 10`**	Creates VLAN 10 and enters VLAN configuration mode
`Core(config-vlan)# ` **`name Accounting`**	Assigns a name to the VLAN
`Core(config-vlan)# ` **`exit`**	Returns to global configuration mode
`Core(config)# ` **`vlan 20`**	Creates VLAN 20 and enters VLAN configuration mode
`Core(config-vlan)# ` **`name Marketing`**	Assigns a name to the VLAN
`Core(config-vlan)# ` **`exit`**	Returns to global configuration mode
`Core(config)# ` **`spanning-tree vlan 1 root primary`**	Configures the switch to become the root switch for VLAN 1
`Core(config)# ` **`exit`**	Returns to privileged EXEC mode
`Core# ` **`copy running-config startup-config`**	Saves the configuration to NVRAM

Distribution 1 Switch (3650)

`Switch> ` **`enable`**	Moves to privileged EXEC mode
`Switch# ` **`configure terminal`**	Moves to global configuration mode
`Switch(config)# ` **`hostname Distribution1`**	Sets the host name
`Distribution1(config)# ` **`no ip domain-lookup`**	Turns off DNS queries so that spelling mistakes do not slow you down
`Distribution1(config)# ` **`vtp domain STPDEMO`**	Configures the VTP domain name to *STPDEMO*
`Distribution1(config)# ` **`vtp mode client`**	Changes the switch to VTP client mode
`Distribution1(config)# ` **`spanning-tree vlan 10 root primary`**	Configures the switch to become the root switch of VLAN 10
`Distribution1(config)# ` **`spanning-tree vlan 10 root secondary`**	Configures the switch to become the secondary root switch of VLAN 20

`Distribution1(config)# exit`	Returns to privileged EXEC mode
`Distribution1# copy running-config startup-config`	Saves the configuration to NVRAM

Distribution 2 Switch (3650)

`Switch>enable`	Moves to privileged EXEC mode
`Switch# configure terminal`	Moves to global configuration mode
`Switch(config)# hostname Distribution2`	Sets the host name
`Distribution2(config)# no ip domain-lookup`	Turns off DNS queries so that spelling mistakes do not slow you down
`Distribution2(config)# vtp domain STPDEMO`	Configures the VTP domain name to *STPDEMO*
`Distribution2(config)# vtp mode client`	Changes the switch to VTP client mode
`Distribution2(config)# spanning-tree vlan 20 root primary`	Configures the switch to become the root switch of VLAN 20
`Distribution2(config)# spanning-tree vlan 10 root secondary`	Configures the switch to become the secondary root switch of VLAN 10
`Distribution2(config)# exit`	Returns to privileged EXEC mode
`Distribution2# copy running-config startup-config`	Saves the configuration to NVRAM

Access 1 Switch (2960)

`Switch> enable`	Moves to privileged EXEC mode
`Switch# configure terminal`	Moves to global configuration mode
`Switch(config)# hostname Access1`	Sets the host name
`Access1(config)# no ip domain-lookup`	Turns off DNS queries so that spelling mistakes do not slow you down
`Access1(config)# vtp domain STPDEMO`	Configures the VTP domain name to *STPDEMO*
`Access1(config)# vtp mode client`	Changes the switch to VTP client mode
`Access1(config)# interface range fastethernet 0/6 - 12`	Moves to interface range configuration mode
`Access1(config-if-range)# switchport mode access`	Places all interfaces in switchport access mode
`Access1(config-if-range)# switchport access vlan 10`	Assigns all interfaces to VLAN 10

`Access1(config-if-range)#` `spanning-tree portfast`	Places all ports directly into forwarding mode
`Access1(config-if-range)#` `spanning-tree bpduguard enable`	Enables BPDU Guard
`Access1(config-if-range)# end`	Moves back to privileged EXEC mode
`Access1# copy running-config startup-config`	Saves the configuration to NVRAM

Access 2 Switch (2960)

`Switch> enable`	Moves to privileged EXEC mode
`Switch# configure terminal`	Moves to global configuration mode
`Switch(config)# hostname Access2`	Sets the host name
`Access2(config)# no ip domain-lookup`	Turns off DNS queries so that spelling mistakes do not slow you down
`Access2(config)# vtp domain STPDEMO`	Configures the VTP domain name to *STPDEMO*
`Access2(config)# vtp mode client`	Changes the switch to VTP client mode
`Access2(config)# interface range fastethernet 0/6 - 12`	Moves to interface range configuration mode
`Access2(config-if-range)#` `switchport mode access`	Places all interfaces in switchport access mode
`Access2(config-if-range)#` `switchport access vlan 20`	Assigns all interfaces to VLAN 20
`Access2(config-if-range)#` `spanning-tree portfast`	Places all ports directly into forwarding mode
`Access2(config-if-range)#` `spanning-tree bpduguard enable`	Enables BPDU Guard
`Access2(config-if-range)# exit`	Moves back to global configuration mode
`Access2(config)# spanning-tree vlan 1,10,20 priority 61440`	Ensures this switch does not become the root switch for VLAN 10
`Access2(config)# exit`	Returns to privileged EXEC mode
`Access2# copy running-config startup-config`	Saves config to NVRAM

Spanning-Tree Migration Example: PVST+ to Rapid-PVST+

The topology in Figure 2-1 is used for this migration example and adds to the configuration of the previous example.

Rapid-PVST+ uses the same BPDU format as 802.1D. This interoperability between the two spanning-tree protocols enables a longer conversion time in large networks without disrupting services.

The spanning-tree features UplinkFast and BackboneFast in 802.1D-based PVST+ are already incorporated in the 802.1w-based Rapid-PVST+ and are disabled when you enable Rapid-PVST+. The 802.1D-based features of PVST+ such as PortFast, BPDU Guard, BPDU Filter, Root Guard, and Loop Guard are applicable in Rapid-PVST+ mode and need not be changed.

Access 1 Switch (2960)

Access1> **enable**	Moves to privileged EXEC mode
Access1# **configure terminal**	Moves to global configuration mode
Access1 (config)# **spanning-tree mode rapid-pvst**	Enables 802.1w-based Rapid-PVST+
Access1(config)# **no spanning-tree uplinkfast**	Removes UplinkFast programming line if it exists
Access1(config)# **no spanning-tree backbonefast**	Removes BackboneFast programming line if it exists

Access 2 Switch (2960)

Access2> **enable**	Moves to privileged EXEC mode
Access2# **configure terminal**	Moves to global configuration mode
Access2(config)# **spanning-tree mode rapid-pvst**	Enables 802.1w-based Rapid-PVST+

Distribution 1 Switch (3650)

Distribution1> **enable**	Moves to privileged EXEC mode
Distribution1# **configure terminal**	Moves to global configuration mode
Distribution1(config)# **spanning-tree mode rapid-pvst**	Enables 802.1w-based Rapid-PVST+

Distribution 2 Switch (3650)

Distribution2> **enable**	Moves to privileged EXEC mode
Distribution2# **configure terminal**	Moves to global configuration mode
Distribution2(config)# **spanning-tree mode rapid-pvst**	Enables 802.1w-based Rapid-PVST+

Core Switch (3650)

Core> **enable**	Moves to privileged EXEC mode
Core# **configure terminal**	Moves to global configuration mode
Core(config)# **spanning-tree mode rapid-pvst**	Enables 802.1w-based Rapid-PVST+

CHAPTER 3

Implementing Inter-VLAN Routing

This chapter provides information and commands concerning the following topics:

- Inter-VLAN communication using an external router: router-on-a-stick
- Inter-VLAN communication tips
- Inter-VLAN communication on a multilayer switch through an SVI
  - Configuring inter-VLAN communication on an L3 switch
- Removing L2 switchport capability of an interface on an L3 switch
- Configuration example: inter-VLAN communication
- Configuration example: IPv6 inter-VLAN communication

Inter-VLAN Communication Using an External Router: Router-on-a-Stick

`Router(config)#`
`interface`
`fastethernet 0/0`
	Moves to interface configuration mode

`Router(config-if)# no` `shutdown`	Enables the interface

`Router(config-if)#`
`interface fastethernet`
`0/0.1`
	Creates subinterface 0/0.1 and moves to subinterface configuration mode

`Router(config-subif)#`
`description Management`
`VLAN 1`
	(Optional) Sets the locally significant description of the subinterface
	
	NOTE: Best practices dictate that VLAN 1 should not be used for management or native traffic. Also, consider using separate VLANs for management and native traffic

`Router(config-subif)#`
`encapsulation`
`dot1q 1 native`
	Assigns VLAN 1 to this subinterface. VLAN 1 will be the native VLAN. This subinterface uses the 802.1q tagging protocol

`Router(config-subif)#`
`ip address 192.168.1.1`
`255.255.255.0`
	Assigns the IP address and netmask

`Router(config-subif)#`
`interface fastethernet`
`0/0.10`
	Creates subinterface 0/0.10 and moves to subinterface configuration mode

`Router(config-subif)#` **`description Accounting`** **`VLAN 10`**	(Optional) Sets the locally significant description of the subinterface
`Router(config-subif)#` **`encapsulation dot1q 10`**	Assigns VLAN 10 to this subinterface. This subinterface uses the 802.1q tagging protocol
`Router(config-subif)#` **`ip address 192.168.10.1`** **`255.255.255.0`**	Assigns the IP address and netmask
`Router(config-subif)#` **`end`**	Returns to interface configuration mode

NOTE: Because the VLAN networks are directly connected to the router, routing between these networks does not require a dynamic routing protocol. However, if the router is configured with a dynamic routing protocol, then these networks should be advertised or redistributed to other routers.

NOTE: Routes to the networks associated with these VLANs appear in the routing table as directly connected networks.

NOTE: In production environments, VLAN 1 should not be used as the management VLAN because it poses a potential security risk; all ports are in VLAN 1 by default, and it is an easy mistake to add a nonmanagement user to the management VLAN.

NOTE: Instead of creating a subinterface for the native VLAN (VLAN 1 in the preceding example), it is possible to use the physical interface for native (untagged) traffic. In other words, the physical interface (FastEthernet0/0) would get IP address 192.168.1.1 255.255.255 and it would handle all VLAN 1 native untagged traffic. You would still create a subinterface for VLAN 10 as previously described.

Inter-VLAN Communication Tips

- Although most older routers (routers running IOS 12.2 and earlier) support both ISL and dot1q, some switch models support only dot1q, such as the 2960, 2960-x, 3650, and 9200 series. Check with the version of IOS you are using to determine whether ISL or dot1q is supported.

  - ISL will probably not be an option, as it has been deprecated for quite some time.

  - If you need to use ISL as your trunking protocol, use the command **encapsulation isl** *x*, where *x* is the number of the VLAN to be assigned to that subinterface.

- Recommended best practice is to use the same number as the VLAN number for the subinterface number. It is easier to troubleshoot VLAN 10 on subinterface fa0/0.10 than on fa0/0.2.

Inter-VLAN Communication on a Multilayer Switch Through a Switch Virtual Interface

NOTE: Rather than using an external router to provide inter-VLAN communication, a multilayer switch can perform the same task through the use of a switched virtual interface (SVI).

Configuring Inter-VLAN Communication on an L3 Switch

`Switch9300(config)# interface vlan 1`	Creates a virtual interface for VLAN 1 and enters interface configuration mode
`Switch9300(config-if)# ip address 172.16.1.1 255.255.255.0`	Assigns an IP address and netmask
`Switch9300(config-if)# no shutdown`	Enables the interface
`Switch9300(config)# interface vlan 10`	Creates a virtual interface for VLAN 10 and enters interface configuration mode
`Switch9300(config-if)# ip address 172.16.10.1 255.255.255.0`	Assigns an IP address and netmask
`Switch9300(config-if)# no shutdown`	Enables the interface
`Switch9300(config)# interface vlan 20`	Creates a virtual interface for VLAN 20 and enters interface configuration mode
`Switch9300(config-if)# ip address 172.16.20.1 255.255.255.0`	Assigns an IP address and netmask
`Switch9300(config-if)# no shutdown`	Enables the interface
`Switch9300(config-if)# exit`	Returns to global configuration mode
`Switch9300(config)# ip routing`	Enables routing on the switch

NOTE: For an SVI to go to up/up and be added to the routing table, the VLAN for the SVI must be created, an IP address must be assigned, and at least one interface must support it (trunk or access).

Removing L2 Switchport Capability of an Interface on an L3 Switch

`Switch9300(config)# interface gigabitethernet 0/1`	Moves to interface configuration mode
`Switch9300(config-if)# no switchport`	Creates a Layer 3 port on the switch **NOTE:** You can use the **no switchport** command on physical ports only on a Layer 3-capable switch

Configuration Example: Inter-VLAN Communication

Figure 3-1 illustrates the network topology for the configuration that follows, which shows how to configure inter-VLAN communication using commands covered in this chapter. Some commands used in this configuration are from other chapters.

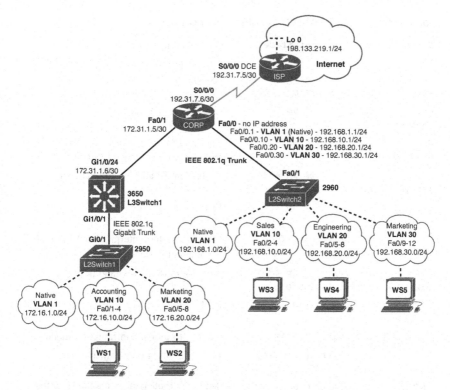

Figure 3-1 Network Topology for Inter-VLAN Communication Configuration

ISP Router

`Router> enable`	Moves to privileged EXEC mode
`Router># configure terminal`	Moves to global configuration mode
`Router(config)# hostname ISP`	Sets the host name
`ISP(config)# interface loopback 0`	Moves to interface configuration mode
`ISP(config-if)# description simulated address representing remote website`	Sets the locally significant interface description
`ISP(config-if)# ip address 198.133.219.1 255.255.255.0`	Assigns an IP address and netmask
`ISP(config-if)# interface serial 0/0/0`	Moves to interface configuration mode
`ISP(config-if)# description WAN link to the Corporate Router`	Sets the locally significant interface description
`ISP(config-if)# ip address 192.31.7.5 255.255.255.252`	Assigns an IP address and netmask

`ISP(config-if)# clock rate 4000000`	Assigns a clock rate to the interface; DCE cable is plugged into this interface
`ISP(config-if)# no shutdown`	Enables the interface
`ISP(config-if)# exit`	Returns to global configuration mode
`ISP(config-if)# router eigrp 10`	Creates Enhanced Interior Gateway Routing Protocol (EIGRP) routing process 10
`ISP(config-router)# network 198.133.219.0 0.0.0.255`	Advertises directly connected networks
`ISP(config-router)# network 192.31.7.0 0.0.0.255`	Advertises directly connected networks
`ISP(config-router)# end`	Returns to privileged EXEC mode
`ISP# copy running-config startup-config`	Saves the configuration to NVRAM

CORP Router

`Router> enable`	Moves to privileged EXEC mode
`Router># configure terminal`	Moves to global configuration mode
`Router(config)# hostname CORP`	Sets the host name
`CORP(config)# no ip domain-lookup`	Turns off Domain Name System (DNS) resolution to avoid wait time due to DNS lookup of spelling errors
`CORP(config)# interface serial 0/0/0`	Moves to interface configuration mode
`CORP(config-if)# description link to ISP`	Sets the locally significant interface description
`CORP(config-if)# ip address 192.31.7.6 255.255.255.252`	Assigns an IP address and netmask
`CORP(config-if)# no shutdown`	Enables the interface
`CORP(config)# interface fastethernet 0/1`	Moves to interface configuration mode
`CORP(config-if)# description link to L3Switch1`	Sets the locally significant interface description
`CORP(config-if)# ip address 172.31.1.5 255.255.255.252`	Assigns an IP address and netmask
`CORP(config-if)# no shutdown`	Enables the interface
`CORP(config-if)# exit`	Returns to global configuration mode
`CORP(config)# interface fastethernet 0/0`	Enters interface configuration mode
`CORP(config-if)# no shutdown`	Enables the interface
`CORP(config-if)# interface fastethernet 0/0.1`	Creates a virtual subinterface and moves to subinterface configuration mode

CORP(config-subif)# **description Management VLAN 1 - Native VLAN**	Sets the locally significant interface description
CORP(config-subif)# **encapsulation dot1q 1 native**	Assigns VLAN 1 to this subinterface. VLAN 1 is the native VLAN. This subinterface uses the 802.1q protocol
CORP(config-subif)# **ip address 192.168.1.1 255.255.255.0**	Assigns an IP address and netmask
CORP(config-subif)# **interface fastethernet 0/0.10**	Creates a virtual subinterface and moves to subinterface configuration mode
CORP(config-subif)# **description Sales VLAN 10**	Sets the locally significant interface description
CORP(config-subif)# **encapsulation dot1q 10**	Assigns VLAN 10 to this subinterface. This subinterface uses the 802.1q protocol
CORP(config-subif)# **ip address 192.168.10.1 255.255.255.0**	Assigns an IP address and netmask
CORP(config-subif)# **interface fastethernet 0/0.20**	Creates a virtual subinterface and moves to subinterface configuration mode
CORP(config-subif)# **description Engineering VLAN 20**	Sets the locally significant interface description
CORP(config-subif)# **encapsulation dot1q 20**	Assigns VLAN 20 to this subinterface. This subinterface uses the 802.1q protocol
CORP(config-subif)# **ip address 192.168.20.1 255.255.255.0**	Assigns an IP address and netmask
CORP(config-subif)# **interface fastethernet 0/0.30**	Creates a virtual subinterface and moves to subinterface configuration mode
CORP(config-subif)# **description Marketing VLAN 30**	Sets the locally significant interface description
CORP(config-subif)# **encapsulation dot1q 30**	Assigns VLAN 30 to this subinterface. This subinterface uses the 802.1q protocol
CORP(config-subif)# **ip add 192.168.30.1 255.255.255.0**	Assigns an IP address and netmask
CORP(config-subif)# **exit**	Returns to global configuration mode
CORP(config)# **router eigrp 10**	Creates EIGRP routing process 10 and moves to router configuration mode
CORP(config-router)# **network 192.168.1.0 0.0.0.255**	Advertises the 192.168.1.0 network
CORP(config-router)# **network 192.168.10.0 0.0.0.255**	Advertises the 192.168.10.0 network
CORP(config-router)# **network 192.168.20.0 0.0.0.255**	Advertises the 192.168.20.0 network

`CORP(config-router)# network` `192.168.30.0 0.0.0.255`	Advertises the 192.168.30.0 network
`CORP(config-router)# network` `172.31.0.0 0.0.255.255`	Advertises the 172.31.0.0 network
`CORP(config-router)# network` `192.31.7.0 0.0.0.3`	Advertises the 192.31.7.0 network
`CORP(config-router)# end`	Returns to privileged EXEC mode
`CORP# copy running-config` `startup-config`	Saves the configuration in NVRAM

L2Switch2 (Catalyst 2960)

`Switch> enable`	Moves to privileged EXEC mode
`Switch# configure terminal`	Moves to global configuration mode
`Switch(config)# hostname L2Switch2`	Sets the host name
`L2Switch2(config)#` `no ip domain-lookup`	Turns off DNS resolution
`L2Switch2(config)# vlan 10`	Creates VLAN 10 and enters VLAN configuration mode
`L2Switch2(config-vlan)# name Sales`	Assigns a name to the VLAN
`L2Switch2(config-vlan)# exit`	Returns to global configuration mode
`L2Switch2(config)# vlan 20`	Creates VLAN 20 and enters VLAN configuration mode
`L2Switch2(config-vlan)# name` `Engineering`	Assigns a name to the VLAN
`L2Switch2(config-vlan)#` `vlan 30`	Creates VLAN 30 and enters VLAN configuration mode. Note that you do not have to exit back to global configuration mode to execute this command
`L2Switch2(config-vlan)# name` `Marketing`	Assigns a name to the VLAN
`L2Switch2(config-vlan)# exit`	Returns to global configuration mode
`L2Switch2(config)# interface` `range fastethernet 0/2 - 4`	Enters interface range configuration mode and allows you to set the same configuration parameters on multiple ports at the same time
`L2Switch2(config-if-range)#` `switchport mode access`	Sets ports 2–4 as access ports
`L2Switch2(config-if-range)#` `switchport access vlan 10`	Assigns ports 2–4 to VLAN 10
`L2Switch2(config-if-range)#` `interface range fastethernet` `0/5 - 8`	Enters interface range configuration mode and allows you to set the same configuration parameters on multiple ports at the same time

`L2Switch2(config-if-range)#` **`switchport mode access`**	Sets ports 5–8 as access ports
`L2Switch2(config-if-range)#` **`switchport access vlan 20`**	Assigns ports 5–8 to VLAN 20
`L2Switch2(config-if-range)#` **`interface range fastethernet`** **`0/9 - 12`**	Enters interface range configuration mode and allows you to set the same configuration parameters on multiple ports at the same time
`L2Switch2(config-if-range)#` **`switchport mode access`**	Sets ports 9–12 as access ports
`L2Switch2(config-if-range)#` **`switchport access vlan 30`**	Assigns ports 9–12 to VLAN 30
`L2Switch2(config-if-range)#` **`exit`**	Returns to global configuration mode
`L2Switch2(config)#` **`interface`** **`fastethernet 0/1`**	Moves to interface configuration mode
`L2Switch2(config)#` **`description`** **`Trunk Link to CORP Router`**	Sets the locally significant interface description
`L2Switch2(config-if)#` **`switchport mode trunk`**	Puts the interface into trunking mode and negotiates to convert the link into a trunk link
`L2Switch2(config-if)#` **`exit`**	Returns to global configuration mode
`L2Switch2(config)#` **`interface vlan 1`**	Creates a virtual interface for VLAN 1 and enters interface configuration mode
`L2Switch2(config-if)#` **`ip address`** **`192.168.1.2 255.255.255.0`**	Assigns an IP address and netmask
`L2Switch2(config-if)#` **`no shutdown`**	Enables the interface
`L2Switch2(config-if)#` **`exit`**	Returns to global configuration mode
`L2Switch2(config)#` **`ip`** **`default-gateway 192.168.1.1`**	Assigns a default gateway address
`L2Switch2(config)#` **`exit`**	Returns to privileged EXEC mode
`L2Switch2#` **`copy running-config`** **`startup-config`**	Saves the configuration in NVRAM

L3Switch1 (Catalyst 3650)

`Switch>` **`enable`**	Moves to privileged EXEC mode
`Switch#` **`configure terminal`**	Moves to global configuration mode
`Switch(config)#` **`hostname L3Switch1`**	Sets the host name
`L3Switch1(config)#` **`no ip domain-lookup`**	Turns off DNS queries so that spelling mistakes do not slow you down
`L3Switch1(config)#` **`vtp mode server`**	Changes the switch to VTP server mode
`L3Switch1(config)#` **`vtp domain`** **`testdomain`**	Configures the VTP domain name to *testdomain*

`L3Switch1(config)# vlan 10`	Creates VLAN 10 and enters VLAN configuration mode
`L3Switch1(config-vlan)# name Accounting`	Assigns a name to the VLAN
`L3Switch1(config-vlan)# exit`	Returns to global configuration mode
`L3Switch1(config)# vlan 20`	Creates VLAN 20 and enters VLAN configuration mode
`L3Switch1(config-vlan)# name Marketing`	Assigns a name to the VLAN
`L3Switch1(config-vlan)# exit`	Returns to global configuration mode
`L3Switch1(config)# interface gigabitethernet 1/0/1`	Moves to interface configuration mode
`L3Switch1(config-if)# switchport trunk encapsulation dot1q`	Specifies 802.1Q tagging on the trunk link (only necessary on older model switches like the 3560 and 3750)
`L3Switch1(config-if)# switchport mode trunk`	Puts the interface into trunking mode and negotiates to convert the link into a trunk link
`L3Switch1(config-if)# exit`	Returns to global configuration mode
`L3Switch1(config)# ip routing`	Enables IP routing on this device
`L3Switch1(config)# interface vlan 1`	Creates a virtual interface for VLAN 1 and enters interface configuration mode
`L3Switch1(config-if)# ip address 172.16.1.1 255.255.255.0`	Assigns an IP address and netmask
`L3Switch1(config-if)# no shutdown`	Enables the interface
`L3Switch1(config-if)# interface vlan 10`	Creates a virtual interface for VLAN 10 and enters interface configuration mode
`L3Switch1(config-if)# ip address 172.16.10.1 255.255.255.0`	Assigns an IP address and mask
`L3Switch1(config-if)# no shutdown`	Enables the interface
`L3Switch1(config-if)# interface vlan 20`	Creates a virtual interface for VLAN 20 and enters interface configuration mode
`L3Switch1(config-if)# ip address 172.16.20.1 255.255.255.0`	Assigns an IP address and mask
`L3Switch1(config-if)# no shutdown`	Enables the interface
`L3Switch1(config-if)# exit`	Returns to global configuration mode
`L3Switch1(config)# interface gigabitethernet 1/0/24`	Enters interface configuration mode
`L3Switch1(config-if)# no switchport`	Creates a Layer 3 port on the switch
`L3Switch1(config-if)# ip address 172.31.1.6 255.255.255.252`	Assigns an IP address and netmask
`L3Switch1(config-if)# exit`	Returns to global configuration mode

`L3Switch1(config)# router` `eigrp 10`	Creates EIGRP routing process 10 and moves to router configuration mode
`L3Switch1(config-router)# network` `172.16.0.0 0.0.255.255`	Advertises the 172.16.0.0 network
`L3Switch1(config-router)# network` `172.31.0.0 0.0.255.255`	Advertises the 172.31.0.0 network
`L3Switch1(config-router)# end`	Applies changes and returns to privileged EXEC mode
`L3Switch1# copy running-config` `startup-config`	Saves configuration in NVRAM

L2Switch1 (Catalyst 2960)

`Switch> enable`	Moves to privileged EXEC mode
`Switch# configure terminal`	Moves to global configuration mode
`Switch(config)# hostname L2Switch1`	Sets the host name
`L2Switch1(config)# no ip` `domain-lookup`	Turns off DNS queries so that spelling mistakes do not slow you down
`L2Switch1(config)# vtp domain` `testdomain`	Configures the VTP domain name to *testdomain*
`L2Switch1(config)# vtp mode client`	Changes the switch to VTP client mode
`L2Switch1(config)# interface` `range fastethernet 0/1 - 4`	Enters interface range configuration mode and allows you to set the same configuration parameters on multiple ports at the same time
`L2Switch1(config-if-range)#` `switchport mode access`	Sets ports 1–4 as access ports
`L2Switch1(config-if-range)#` `switchport access vlan 10`	Assigns ports 1–4 to VLAN 10

`L2Switch1(config-if-range)#`
`interface range fastethernet`
`0/5 - 8`
	Enters interface range configuration mode and allows you to set the same configuration parameters on multiple ports at the same time

`L2Switch1(config-if-range)#` `switchport mode access`	Sets ports 5–8 as access ports
`L2Switch1(config-if-range)#` `switchport access vlan 20`	Assigns ports 5–8 to VLAN 20
`L2Switch1(config-if-range)# exit`	Returns to global configuration mode
`L2Switch1(config)# interface` `gigabitethernet 0/1`	Moves to interface configuration mode
`L2Switch1(config-if)# switchport` `mode trunk`	Puts the interface into trunking mode and negotiates to convert the link into a trunk link
`L2Switch1(config-if)# exit`	Returns to global configuration mode

L2Switch1(config)# **interface vlan 1**	Creates a virtual interface for VLAN 1 and enters interface configuration mode
L2Switch1(config-if)# **ip address 172.16.1.2 255.255.255.0**	Assigns an IP address and netmask
L2Switch1(config-if)# **no shutdown**	Enables the interface
L2Switch1(config-if)# **exit**	Returns to global configuration mode
L2Switch1(config)# **ip default-gateway 172.16.1.1**	Assigns the default gateway address
L2Switch1(config)# **exit**	Returns to privileged EXEC mode
L2Switch1# **copy running-config startup-config**	Saves the configuration in NVRAM

Configuration Example: IPv6 Inter-VLAN Communication

Figure 3-2 shows the network topology for the configuration that follows, which demonstrates how to configure IPv6 inter-VLAN communication using commands covered in this chapter. Some commands used in this configuration are from previous chapters.

NOTE: This configuration uses traditional OSPFv3 for routing. For more information on OSPFv3, see Chapter 5, "OSPF."

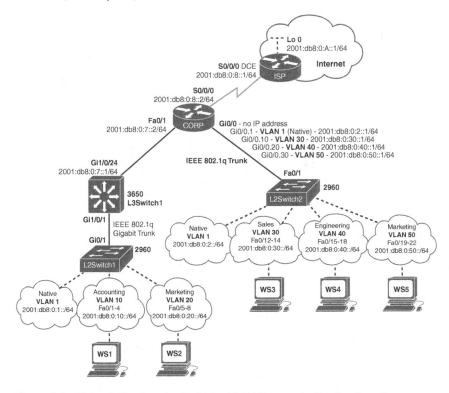

Figure 3-2 Network Topology for IPv6 Inter-VLAN Communication Configuration

ISP Router

Router(config)# **hostname ISP**	Sets the hostname
ISP(config)# **ipv6 unicast-routing**	Enables IPv6 routing
ISP(config)# **interface loopback 0**	Enters interface configuration mode
ISP(config-if)# **ipv6 address 2001:db8:0:a::1/64**	Assigns an IPv6 address
ISP(config-if)# **interface serial 0/0/0**	Enters interface configuration mode
ISP(config-if)# **clock rate 4000000**	Assigns a clock rate to the interface; DCE cable is plugged into this interface
ISP(config-if)# **ipv6 address 2001:db8:0:8::1/64**	Assigns an IPv6 address
ISP(config-if)# **no shutdown**	Turns on this interface
ISP(config-if)# **exit**	Exits into global configuration mode
ISP(config)# **ipv6 route ::/0 serial 0/0/0**	Creates a default static route to return traffic from the Internet **NOTE:** A dynamic routing protocol can also be used here
ISP(config)# **end**	Returns to privileged EXEC mode

CORP Router

Router(config)# **hostname CORP**	Sets the hostname
CORP(config)# **ipv6 unicast-routing**	Enables global IPv6 forwarding
CORP(config)# **ipv6 router ospf 1**	Enters OSPFv3 programming mode
CORP(config-rtr)# **router-id 192.168.1.1**	Assigns a router ID for the OSPFv3 process
CORP(config-rtr)# **default-information originate**	Adds any default routing information to the OSPFv3 updates
CORP(config-rtr)# **exit**	Exits to global configuration mode
CORP(config)# **interface gigabitethernet 0/0.1**	Enters subinterface programming mode
CORP(config-subif)# **encapsulation dot1q 1 native**	Assigns 802.1Q as the trunking protocol and associates VLAN 1 to this subinterface
CORP(config-subif)# **ipv6 address 2001:db8:0:2::1/64**	Assigns an IPv6 address
CORP(config-subif)# **ipv6 ospf 1 area 0**	Specifies this as an interface that will participate in OSPFv3
CORP(config-subif)# **interface gigabitethernet 0/0.30**	Enters subinterface programming mode

CORP(config-subif)# **encapsulation dot1q 30**	Assigns 802.1Q as the trunking protocol and associates VLAN 30 to this subinterface
CORP(config-subif)# **ipv6 address 2001:db8:0:30::1/64**	Assigns an IPv6 address
CORP(config-subif)# **ipv6 ospf 1 area 0**	Specifies this as an interface that will participate in OSPFv3
CORP(config-subif)# **interface gigabitethernet 0/0.40**	Enters subinterface programming mode
CORP(config-subif)# **encapsulation dot1q 40**	Assigns 802.1Q as the trunking protocol and associates VLAN 40 to this subinterface
CORP(config-subif)# **ipv6 address 2001:db8:0:40::1/64**	Assigns an IPv6 address
CORP(config-subif)# **ipv6 ospf 1 area 0**	Specifies this as an interface that will participate in OSPFv3
CORP(config-subif)# **interface gigabitethernet 0/0.50**	Enters subinterface programming mode
CORP(config-subif)# **encapsulation dot1q 50**	Assigns 802.1Q as the trunking protocol and associates VLAN 50 to this subinterface
CORP(config-subif)# **ipv6 address 2001:db8:0:50::1/64**	Assigns an IPv6 address
CORP(config-subif)# **ipv6 ospf 1 area 0**	Specifies this as an interface that will participate in OSPFv3
CORP(config-subif)# **interface gigabitethernet 0/1**	Enters interface programming mode
CORP(config-if)# **ipv6 address 2001:db8:0:7::2/64**	Assigns an IPv6 address
CORP(config-if)# **ipv6 ospf 1 area 0**	Specifies this as an interface that will participate in OSPFv3
CORP(config-if)# **interface gigabitethernet 0/0**	Enters interface programming mode
CORP(config-if)# **no shutdown**	Turns this interface on
CORP(config-if)# **interface serial 0/0/0**	Enters interface programming mode
CORP(config-if)# **ipv6 address 2001:db8:0:8::2/64**	Assigns an IPv6 address
CORP(config-if)# **no shutdown**	Turns this interface on
CORP(config-if)# **exit**	Exits to global configuration programming mode
CORP(config)# **ipv6 route ::/0 serial 0/0/0**	Creates a default static route pointing to the ISP
CORP(config)# **end**	Returns to privileged EXEC mode

L2Switch2 (Catalyst 2960)

`Switch(config)# hostname L2Switch2`	Sets the hostname
`L2Switch2(config)# sdm prefer dual-ipv4-and-ipv6 default`	Configures the Switching Database Manager (SDM) on the switch to optimize memory and operating system for both IPv4 and IPv6 Layer 3 forwarding **NOTE:** If this is a change in the SDM settings, the switch must be reloaded for this change to take effect
`L2Switch2(config)# vlan 30,40,50`	Creates VLANs 30, 40, and 50
`L2Switch2(config-vlan)# exit`	Exits VLAN configuration mode
`L2Switch2(config)# interface fastethernet 0/5`	Enters switchport interface configuration mode
`L2Switch2(config-if)# switchport mode trunk`	Sets this port to trunk unconditionally
`L2Sw2(config-if)# interface range fastethernet 0/12 - 14`	Enters switchport configuration mode for a range of switch ports
`L2Switch2(config-if-range)# switchport mode access`	Sets these ports to be access ports
`L2Switch2(config-if-range)# switchport access vlan 30`	Assigns these ports to VLAN 30
`L2Switch2(config-if-range)# interface range fastethernet 0/15 - 18`	Enters switchport configuration mode for a range of switch ports
`L2Switch2(config-if-range)# switchport mode access`	Sets these ports to be access ports
`L2Switch2(config-if-range)# switchport access vlan 40`	Assigns these ports to VLAN 20
`L2Switch2(config-if-range)# interface range fastethernet 0/19 - 22`	Enters switchport configuration mode for a range of switchports
`L2Switch2(config-if-range)# switchport mode access`	Sets these ports to be access ports
`L2Switch2(config-if-range)# switchport access vlan 50`	Assigns these ports to VLAN 50
`L2Switch2(config-if-range)# interface vlan1`	Enters interface configuration mode for the management VLAN
`L2Switch2(config-if)# ipv6 address 2001:db8:0:2::/64`	Assigns an IPv6 address
`L2Switch2(config-if)# no shutdown`	Turns this interface on
`L2Switch2(config-if)# exit`	Exits to global configuration mode

L2Switch2(config)# **ipv6 route ::/0 2001:db8:0:2::1**	Assigns a default gateway
L2Switch2(config)# **end**	Returns to privileged EXEC mode

L3Switch1 (Catalyst 3650)

Switch(config)# **hostname L3Switch1**	Sets the hostname
L3Switch1(config)# **ipv6 unicast-routing**	Enables IPv6 forwarding
L3Switch1(config)# **vlan 10,20**	Creates VLANs 10 and 20
L3Switch1(config-vlan)# **exit**	Exits VLAN configuration mode
L3Switch1(config)# **interface gigabitethernet 1/0/1**	Enters interface configuration mode
L3Switch1(config-if)# **switchport mode trunk**	Sets this port to trunk unconditionally
L3Switch1(config-if)# **ipv6 router ospf 1**	Enters OSPFv3 configuration mode
L3Switch1(config-rtr)# **router-id 192.168.1.2**	Assigns the OSPFv3 router ID
L3Switch1(config-rtr)# **exit**	Exits to global configuration mode
L3Switch1(config)# **interface gigabitethernet 1/0/24**	Enters switchport interface configuration mode
L3Switch1(config-if)# **no switchport**	Changes this Layer 2 switch port to a Layer 3 routed port
L3Switch1(config-if)# **ipv6 address 2001:db8:0:7::1/64**	Assigns an IPv6 address
L3Switch1(config-if)# **ipv6 ospf 1 area 0**	Specifies this as an interface that will participate in OSPFv3
L3Switch1(config-if)# **interface vlan1**	Enters interface configuration mode for VLAN 1
L3Switch1(config-if)# **ipv6 address 2001:db8:0:1::1/64**	Assigns an IPv6 address
L3Switch1(config-if)# **ipv6 ospf 1 area 0**	Specifies this as an interface that will participate in OSPFv3
L3Switch1(config-if)# **interface vlan10**	Enters interface configuration mode for VLAN 10
L3Switch1(config-if)# **ipv6 address 2001:db8:0:10::1/64**	Assigns an IPv6 address
L3Switch1(config-if)# **ipv6 ospf 1 area 0**	Specifies this as an interface that will participate in OSPFv3
L3Switch1(config-if)# **interface vlan20**	Enters interface configuration mode for VLAN 20
L3Switch1(config-if)# **ipv6 address 2001:db8:0:20::1/64**	Assigns an IPv6 address

| L3Switch1(config-if)# **ipv6 ospf 1 area 0** | Specifies this as an interface that will participate in OSPFv3 |
| L3Switch1(config-if)# **end** | Returns to privileged EXEC mode |

L2Switch1 (Catalyst 2960)

Switch(config)# **hostname L2Switch1**	Sets the hostname
L2Switch1(config)# **sdm prefer dual-ipv4-and-ipv6 default**	Configures the Switching Database Manager on the switch to optimize memory and operating system for both IPv4 and IPv6 Layer 3 forwarding
L2Switch1(config)# **vlan 10,20**	Creates VLANs 10 and 20
L2Switch1(config-vlan)# **exit**	Exits VLAN configuration mode
L2Switch1(config)# **interface gigabitethernet 0/1**	Enters switchport interface configuration mode
L2Switch1(config-if)# **switchport mode trunk**	Sets this port to trunk unconditionally
L2Switch1(config-if)# **interface range fastethernet 0/12 - 14**	Enters switchport configuration mode for a range of switch ports
L2Switch1(config-if-range)# **switchport mode access**	Sets these ports to be access ports
L2Switch1(config-if-range)# **switchport access vlan 10**	Assigns these ports to VLAN 10
L2Switch1(config-if-range)# **interface range fastethernet 0/15 - 18**	Enters switchport configuration mode for a range of switch ports
L2Switch1(config-if-range)# **switchport mode access**	Sets these ports to be access ports
L2Switch1(config-if-range)# **switchport access vlan 20**	Assigns these ports to VLAN 20
L2Switch1(config-if-range)# **interface vlan1**	Moves to interface configuration mode
L2Switch1(config-if)# **ipv6 address 2001:0:0:4::2/64**	Assigns an IPv6 address
L2Switch1(config-if)# **exit**	Returns to global configuration mode
L2Switch1(config)# **ipv6 route ::/0 2001:db8:0:1::1**	Assigns a default gateway
L2Switch1(config)# **end**	Returns to privileged EXEC mode

CHAPTER 4

EIGRP

This chapter provides information and commands concerning the following topics:

- Enhanced Interior Gateway Routing Protocol (EIGRP)
- Enabling EIGRP for IPv4 using classic mode configuration
- Enabling EIGRP for IPv6 using classic mode configuration
- EIGRP using named mode configuration
- EIGRP named mode subconfiguration modes
- Upgrading classic mode to named mode configuration
- EIGRP router ID
- Authentication for EIGRP
    - Configuring authentication in classic mode
    - Configuring authentication in named mode
    - Verifying and troubleshooting EIGRP authentication
- Auto-summarization for EIGRP
- IPv4 manual summarization for EIGRP
- IPv6 manual summarization for EIGRP
- Timers for EIGRP
- Passive interfaces for EIGRP
- "Pseudo" passive EIGRP interfaces
- Injecting a default route into EIGRP
    - Redistribution of a static route
    - IP default network
    - Summarize to 0.0.0.0/0
- Accepting exterior routing information: **default-information**
- Equal-cost load balancing: **maximum-paths**
- Unequal-cost load balancing: **variance**
- EIGRP Traffic Sharing
- Bandwidth use for EIGRP
- Stub routing for EIGRP

- EIGRP unicast neighbors

- EIGRP Wide Metrics

- Adjusting the EIGRP metric weights

- Verifying EIGRP

- Troubleshooting EIGRP

- Configuration example: EIGRP for IPv4 and IPv6 using named mode

Enhanced Interior Gateway Routing Protocol (EIGRP)

The Enhanced Interior Gateway Routing Protocol (EIGRP) is an enhanced version of the Interior Gateway Routing Protocol (IGRP) developed by Cisco. The convergence properties and the operating efficiency of EIGRP have improved substantially over IGRP, and IGRP is now obsolete.

The convergence technology of EIGRP is based on an algorithm called the Diffusing Update Algorithm (DUAL). The algorithm guarantees loop-free operation at every instant throughout a route computation and allows all devices involved in a topology change to synchronize. Devices that are not affected by topology changes are not involved in recomputations.

Enabling EIGRP for IPv4 Using Classic Mode Configuration

Classic mode is the original way of configuring EIGRP. In classic mode, EIGRP configurations are scattered across the router and the interface configuration modes.

`Router(config)# router eigrp 100`	Turns on the EIGRP process. 100 is the autonomous system (AS) number, which can be a number between 1 and 65,535 **NOTE:** All routers must use the same AS number to communicate with each other
`Router(config-router)# network 10.0.0.0`	Specifies which network to advertise in EIGRP
`Router(config-router)# network 10.0.0.0 0.255.255.255`	Identifies which interfaces or networks to include in EIGRP. Interfaces must be configured with addresses that fall within the wildcard mask range of the network statement. It is possible to enter a subnet mask instead of a wildcard mask; Cisco IOS is intelligent enough to recognize the difference and correct the error for you. The running configuration will only display wildcard masks

Router(config-if)# bandwidth 256	Sets the bandwidth of this interface to 256 kilobits to allow EIGRP to make a better metric calculation. Value ranges from 1–10 000 000 **NOTE:** This command is entered at the interface command prompt (config-if) and not at the router process prompt (config-router). The setting can differ for each interface to which it is applied **TIP:** The **bandwidth** command is used for metric calculations only. It does not change interface performance
Router(config-router)# eigrp log-neighbor- changes	Changes which neighbors will be displayed
Router(config-router)# eigrp log-neighbor- warnings 300	Configures the logging intervals of EIGRP neighbor warning messages to 300 seconds. The default is 10 seconds
Router(config-router)# no network 10.0.0.0 0.255.255.255	Removes the network from the EIGRP process
Router(config)# no router eigrp 100	Disables routing process 100 and removes the entire EIGRP configuration from the running configuration

TIP: There is no limit to the number of network statements (that is, **network** commands) that you can configure on a router.

TIP: The use of a wildcard mask or network mask is optional. Wildcard masks should be used when advertising subnetted networks.

TIP: If you do not use the wildcard mask, the EIGRP process assumes that all directly connected networks that are part of the overall major network will participate in the EIGRP process and that EIGRP will attempt to establish neighbor relationships from each interface that is part of that Class A, B, or C major network.

TIP: If you use the **network 172.16.1.0 0.0.0.255** command with a wildcard mask, the command specifies that only interfaces on the 172.16.1.0/24 subnet will participate in EIGRP. EIGRP automatically summarizes routes on the major network boundary when in a discontiguous IP address network topology when the **auto-summary** command is enabled.

TIP: Since Cisco IOS Software Release 15.0, EIGRP no longer automatically summarizes networks at the classful boundary by default.

Enabling EIGRP for IPv6 Using Classic Mode Configuration

No linkage exists between EIGRP for IPv4 and EIGRP for IPv6; the two are configured and managed separately. However, the commands for configuration of EIGRP for IPv4 and IPv6 using classic mode are similar, making the transition easy.

`Router(config)# ipv6 unicast-routing`	Enables the forwarding of IPv6 unicast datagrams globally on the router. This command is required before any IPv6 routing protocol can be configured
`Router(config)# interface gigabitethernet 0/0/0`	Moves to interface configuration mode
`Router(config-if)# ipv6 eigrp 100`	Enables EIGRP for IPv6 on the interface and creates the IPv6 EIGRP process
`Router(config-if)# ipv6 router eigrp 100`	Enters router configuration mode and creates an EIGRP IPv6 routing process if it does not already exist
`Router(config)# ipv6 router eigrp 100`	Creates the EIGRP IPv6 process and enters router configuration mode
`Router(config-rtr)# eigrp router-id 10.1.1.1`	Enables the use of a fixed router ID
`Router(config-rtr)# no shutdown`	Enables the EIGRP routing process. This is only necessary on older routing platforms **NOTE:** It is possible to temporarily disable the EIGRP process using the **shutdown** command

NOTE: The **eigrp router-id w.x.y.z** command is typically used when an IPv4 address is not defined on the router or when manual defining is desired.

EIGRP Using Named Mode Configuration

Named mode is the new way of configuring EIGRP; this mode allows EIGRP configurations to be entered in a hierarchical manner under the router configuration mode. Each named mode configuration can have multiple address families and autonomous system number combinations. The two most commonly used address families are IPv4 unicast and IPv6 unicast. Multicast for both IPv4 and IPv6 is also supported. The default address families for both IPv4 and IPv6 are unicast.

`Router(config)# router eigrp TEST`	Creates a named EIGRP virtual instance called *TEST* **NOTE:** The name of the virtual instance is locally significant only **NOTE:** The name does not need to match between neighbor routers **NOTE:** This command defines a single EIGRP instance that can be used for all address families. At least one address family must be defined

`Router(config-router)#`
`address-family ipv4`
`autonomous-system 1`
	Enables the IPv4 address family and starts EIGRP autonomous system 1. By default, this is a unicast address family

`Router(config-router-af)#` `network 172.16.10.0 0.0.0.255`	Enables EIGRP for IPv4 on interfaces in the 172.16.10.0 network
`Router(config-router-af)#` `network 0.0.0.0`	Enables EIGRP for IPv4 on all IPv4 enabled interfaces **NOTE:** In address family configuration mode, you can define other general parameters for EIGRP, such as **router-id** or **eigrp stub**

`Router(config-router-af)#`
`af-interface`
`gigabitethernet 0/0/0`
	Moves the router into address family interface configuration mode for interface GigabitEthernet 0/0/0

`Router(config-router-af-`
`interface)#` **summary-address**
`192.168.10.0/23`
	Configures a summary aggregate address

`Router(config)#` **router eigrp** `TEST`	Creates a named EIGRP virtual instance called *TEST*

`Router(config-router)#`
`address-family ipv6`
`autonomous-system 1`
	Enables the IPv6 address family and starts EIGRP autonomous system 1. By default, this is a unicast address family
	
	NOTE: All IPv6 enabled interfaces are automatically included in the EIGRP process

`Router(config-router-af)#` `af-interface default`	Moves the router into address family interface configuration mode for all interfaces

`Router(config-router-`
`af-interface)#` **passive-**
`interface`
	Configures all IPv6 interfaces as passive for EIGRP

`Router(config-router-` `af-interface)#` **exit**	Returns the router to address family configuration mode **NOTE:** The complete command is **exit-af-interface**, but the more commonly used shortcut of **exit** is presented here

`Router(config-router-af)#`
`af-interface`
`gigabitethernet 0/0/0`
	Moves the router into address family interface configuration mode for interface GigabitEthernet 0/0/0

`Router(config-router-af-`
`interface)#` **no passive-**
`interface`
	Removes the passive interface configuration from this interface

EIGRP Named Mode Subconfiguration Modes

EIGRP using named mode configuration gathers all EIGRP options and parameters under specific subconfiguration modes:

Mode	Commands Used in This Mode
Address family configuration mode `Router(config-router-af)#`	General configuration commands: **eigrp router-id** **eigrp stub** **metric weights** **network**
Address family interface configuration mode `Router(config-router-af-interface)#`	Interface-specific configuration commands: **authentication key-chain** **authentication mode** **bandwidth-percent** **hello-interval** **hold-time** **passive-interface** **summary-address**
Address family topology configuration mode `Router(config-router-af-topology)#`	Configuration commands that affect the topology table: **maximum-paths** **redistribute** **variance** **traffic-share** **NOTE:** From address family configuration mode, enter the **topology base** command to access topology configuration mode

Upgrading Classic Mode to Named Mode Configuration

The **eigrp upgrade-cli** command allows you to upgrade from classic mode to named mode without causing network or neighbor flaps or requiring the EIGRP process to restart. After conversion, the running configuration on the device will show only named mode configurations; you will be unable to see any classic mode configurations. This command is available only under EIGRP classic router configuration mode. You must use the **eigrp upgrade-cli** command for every classic router configuration in order to ensure that this configuration is upgraded to named mode. Therefore, if multiple classic configurations exist, you must use this command per autonomous system number. The new configurations will be present only in the running configuration; they will not be automatically saved to the startup configuration.

`Router(config-router)#` **`eigrp upgrade-cli TEST`**	Upgrades EIGRP configuration from classic mode to named mode. EIGRP virtual instance is now named *TEST*

NOTE: The **eigrp upgrade-cli** command allows you to convert only classic mode configurations to named mode and not vice versa. To revert to classic mode configurations, you can reload the router without saving the running configurations.

EIGRP Router ID

`Router(config)# router eigrp 100`	Enters EIGRP router configuration mode for AS 100
`Router(config-router)# eigrp router-id 172.16.3.3`	Manually sets the router ID to 172.16.3.3. Can be any IPv4 address except 0.0.0.0 and 255.255.255.255. If not set, the router ID will be the highest IP address of any loopback interfaces. If no loopback interfaces are configured, the router ID will be the highest IP address of your active local interface
`Router(config-router)# no eigrp router-id 172.16.3.3`	Removes the static router ID from the configuration
`Router(config)# router eigrp TEST`	Creates a named EIGRP virtual instance called TEST
`Router(config-router)# address-family ipv4 autonomous-system 1`	Enables the IPv4 address family and starts EIGRP autonomous system 1
`Router(config-router-af)# eigrp router-id 172.16.3.3`	Manually sets the router ID to 172.16.3.3

NOTE: There is no IPv6 form of the router ID. Even if a router is using IPv6 exclusively, the router ID will still be in the format of an IPv4 address.

Authentication for EIGRP

Authentication for routers using EIGRP relies on the use of predefined passwords.

NOTE: EIGRP for IPv4 and EIGRP for IPv6 use the same commands for authentication.

Configuring Authentication in Classic Mode

`Router(config)# key chain romeo`	Identifies a key chain. The name must match the name configured in interface configuration mode
`Router(config-keychain)# key 1`	Identifies the key number NOTE: The range of keys is from 0 to 2 147 483 647. The key identification numbers do not need to be consecutive. There must be at least one key defined on a key chain
`Router(config-keychain-key)# key-string shakespeare`	Identifies the key string NOTE: The string can contain from 1 to 80 uppercase and lowercase alphanumeric characters, except that the first character cannot be a number

Router(config-keychain-key)# **accept-lifetime** [**local**] *start-time* {**infinite** | *end-time* | **duration** *seconds*}	(Optional) Specifies the period during which the key can be received **local** keyword specifies time in local time zone **NOTE:** After the time is entered, you have the option to add the specific day/month/year to this command **NOTE:** The default start time and the earliest acceptable date is January 1, 1993. The default end time is an infinite time period
Router(config-keychain-key)# **send-lifetime** [**local**] *start-time* {**infinite** | *end-time* | **duration** *seconds*}	(Optional) Specifies the period during which the key can be sent **local** keyword specifies time in local time zone **NOTE:** After the time is entered, you have the option to add the specific day/month/year to this command **NOTE:** The default start time and the earliest acceptable date is January 1, 1993. The default end time is an infinite period
Router(config)# **interface gigabitethernet 0/0/0**	Enters interface configuration mode
Router(config-if)# **ip authentication mode eigrp 100 md5**	Enables message digest 5 (MD5) authentication in EIGRP packets over the interface
Router(config-if)# **ip authentication key-chain eigrp 100 romeo**	Enables authentication of EIGRP packets using **romeo** as the key chain
Router(config-if)# **exit**	Returns to global configuration mode

NOTE: For the start time and the end time to have relevance, ensure that the router knows the correct time. Recommended practice dictates that you run NTP or some other time-synchronization method if you intend to set lifetimes on keys.

Configuring Authentication in Named Mode

NOTE: EIGRP support for SHA was introduced in Cisco IOS 15 together with EIGRP using named mode configuration.

NOTE: Both MD5 and SHA can be used in either IPv4 or IPv6. Not all permutations are shown in the following example.

Router(config)# **router eigrp TEST**	Creates a named EIGRP virtual instance called *TEST*
Router(config-router)# **address-family ipv4 autonomous-system 1**	Enables the IPv4 address family and starts EIGRP AS 1
Router(config-router-af)# **af-interface gigabitethernet 0/0/0**	Moves the router into address family interface configuration mode for interface GigabitEthernet 0/0/0

`Router(config-router-af-interface)# ` **`authentication key-chain romeo`**	Identifies a key chain
`Router(config-router-af-interface)#` **`authentication mode md5`**	Enables message digest 5 (MD5) authentication in EIGRP packets over the interface
`Router(config-router-af-interface)# ` **`authentication mode hmac-sha-256`**	Enables Hashed Message Authentication Code (HMAC)-Secure Hash Algorithm (SHA-256) authentication in EIGRP packets over the interface
`Router(config-router-af-interface)# ` **`exit-af-interface`**	Exits from address family interface configuration mode
`Router(config-router-af)# ` **`exit-address-family`**	Exits address family configuration mode
`Router(config-router)# ` **`address-family ipv6 autonomous-system 1`**	Enables the IPv6 address family and starts EIGRP AS 1
`Router(config-router-af)# ` **`af-interface gigabitethernet 0/0/0`**	Moves the router into address family interface configuration mode for interface GigabitEthernet 0/0/0
`Router(config-router-af-interface)# ` **`authentication key-chain romeo`**	Identifies a key chain
`Router(config-router-af-interface)# ` **`authentication mode hmac-sha-256 0 password1`**	Enables HMAC-SHA-256 authentication in EIGRP packets over the interface
	7 – Indicates there is an explicit password encryption. A 0 indicates that there is no password encryption. 0 is the default
	The password string used is **password1**. The string can contain 1 to 32 characters, including white spaces; however, the first character cannot be a number
`Router(config-router-af-interface)# ` **`exit-af-interface`**	Exits from address family interface configuration mode
`Router(config-router-af)# ` **`exit-address-family`**	Exits address family configuration mode
`Router(config-router)# ` **`exit`**	Exits routing protocol configuration mode
`Router(config)# ` **`key chain romeo`**	Identifies a key chain. Name must match the name configured in interface configuration mode
`Router(config-keychain)# ` **`key 1`**	Identifies the key number
`Router(config-keychain-key)# ` **`key-string shakespeare`**	Identifies the key string

| Router(config-keychain-key)#
accept-lifetime start-time
{**infinite** | *end-time* |
duration *seconds*} | (Optional) Specifies the period during which the key can be received |
| Router(config-keychain-key)#
send-lifetime start-time
{**infinite** | *end-time* |
duration *seconds*} | (Optional) Specifies the period during which the key can be sent |

Verifying and Troubleshooting EIGRP Authentication

Router# **show ip eigrp neighbor**	Displays EIGRP neighbor table. Incorrect authentication configuration will prevent neighbor relationships from forming
Router# **show ipv6 eigrp neighbor**	Displays EIGRP IPv6 neighbor table. Incorrect authentication configuration will prevent neighbor relationships from forming
Router# **show key chain**	Displays key chains created on the router
Router# **debug eigrp packet**	Displays output about EIGRP packets. Incorrect key string configuration will cause failures, which will be shown in this output

Auto-Summarization for EIGRP

| Router(config-router)#
auto-summary | Enables auto-summarization for the EIGRP process

NOTE: The behavior of the **auto-summary** command is disabled by default for Cisco IOS Software Release 15 and later. Earlier software generally has automatic summarization enabled by default |
| Router(config-router)# **no auto-summary** | Disables the auto-summarization feature |

IPv4 Manual Summarization for EIGRP

| Router(config)# **interface gigabitethernet 0/0/0** | Enters interface configuration mode |
| Router(config-if)# **ip summary-address eigrp 100 10.10.0.0 255.255.0.0 75** | Enables manual summarization for EIGRP AS 100 (classic mode) on this specific interface for the given address and mask. An administrative distance of 75 is assigned to this summary route

NOTE: The *administrative-distance* argument is optional in this command. Without it, an administrative distance of 5 is automatically applied to the summary route |

| Router(config-router-af-interface)# **summary-address** 192.168.0.0 255.255.0.0 | Enables manual summarization for EIGRP using named mode configuration |

IPv6 Manual Summarization for EIGRP

Router(config)# **interface serial 0/0/0**	Moves to interface configuration mode
Router(config-if)# **ipv6 summary-address eigrp 100 2001:db8:0:1::/64**	Configures a summary address for a specified interface using classic mode There is an optional administrative distance parameter for this command This command behaves similarly to the **ip summary-address eigrp** command
Router(config-router-af-interface)# **summary-address 2001:db8::/48**	Enables manual summarization for EIGRP using named mode configuration

Timers for EIGRP

Router(config)# **interface serial 0/1/0**	Moves to interface configuration mode
Router(config-if)# **ip hello-interval eigrp 100 10**	Configures the EIGRP hello time interval for AS 100 to 10 seconds
Router(config-if)# **ip hold-time eigrp 100 30**	Configures the EIGRP hold timer interval for AS 100 to 30 seconds **NOTE:** Hold time should be set to three times the hello interval
Router(config-if)# **ipv6 hello-interval eigrp 100 10**	Configures the hello interval for EIGRP for IPv6 process 100 to be 10 seconds
Router(config-if)# **ipv6 hold-time eigrp 100 30**	Configures the hold timer for EIGRP for IPv6 process 100 to be 30 seconds
Router(config-router-af-interface)# **hello-interval 3**	Configures a hello interval of 3 seconds for EIGRP using named mode configuration
Router(config-router-af-interface)# **hold-time 9**	Configures a hold time of 9 seconds for EIGRP using named mode configuration

NOTE: EIGRP hello and hold timers do not have to match between neighbors to successfully establish a neighbor relationship. However, the reciprocating hello interval should be within the defined hold time.

NOTE: The AS number in these commands must match the AS number of EIGRP on the router for these changes to take effect.

TIP: It is recommended that you match the timers between neighbors; otherwise, you may experience flapping neighbor relationships or network instability.

Passive Interfaces for EIGRP

`Router(config)# router eigrp 110`	Starts the EIGRP routing process
`Router(config-router)# network 10.0.0.0 0.0.0.255`	Specifies a network to advertise in the EIGRP routing process
`Router(config-router)# passive-interface gigabitethernet 0/0/0`	Prevents the sending of hello packets out the GigabitEthernet 0/0/0 interface. No neighbor adjacency is formed
`Router(config-router)# passive-interface default`	Prevents the sending of hello packets out all interfaces
`Router(config-router)# no passive-interface serial 0/1/0`	Enables hello packets to be sent out interface Serial 0/0/1, thereby allowing neighbor adjacencies to form
`Router(config)# ipv6 router eigrp 110`	Starts the EIGRP for IPv6 routing process
`Router(config-rtr)# passive-interface gigabitethernet 0/0/0`	Prevents the sending of hello packets out the GigabitEthernet 0/0/0 interface. No neighbor adjacency is formed
`Router(config-rtr)# passive-interface default`	Prevents the sending of hello packets out all interfaces
`Router(config-rtr)# no passive-interface serial 0/1/0`	Enables hello packets to be sent out interface Serial 0/1/0, thereby allowing neighbor adjacencies to form
`Router(config-router-af)# af-interface gigabitethernet 0/0/0`	Enters address-family interface configuration mode for GigabitEthernet 0/0/0
`Router(config-router-af-interface)# passive-interface`	Prevents the sending of hello packets out of the GigabitEthernet 0/0/0 interface
`Router(config-router-af)# af-interface default`	Enters address-family default interface configuration mode
`Router(config-router-af-interface)# passive-interface`	Prevents the sending of hello packets out all interfaces

"Pseudo" Passive EIGRP Interfaces

A passive interface cannot send EIGRP hellos, which prevents adjacency relationships with link partners. An administrator can create a "pseudo" passive EIGRP interface by using a route filter that suppresses all routes from the EIGRP routing update. A neighbor relationship will form, but no routes will be sent out a specific interface.

`Router(config)# router` `eigrp 100`	Starts the EIGRP routing process
`Router(config-router)#` `network 10.0.0.0 0.0.0.255`	Specifies a network to advertise in the EIGRP routing process

`Router(config-router)#`
`distribute-list 5 out`
`serial 0/1/0`
	Creates an outgoing distribute list for interface Serial 0/1/0 and refers to ACL 5

`Router(config-router)# exit`	Returns to global configuration mode
`Router(config)# access-list` `5 deny any`	Matches and drops packets from any source. This ACL, when used in the earlier **distribute-list** command, will prevent EIGRP 100 routing packets from being sent out of Serial 0/1/0

Injecting a Default Route into EIGRP: Redistribution of a Static Route

`Router(config)# ip route` `0.0.0.0 0.0.0.0 serial 0/1/0`	Creates a static default route to send all traffic with a destination network not in the routing table out interface Serial 0/1/0 **NOTE:** Adding a static route (for example, **ip route 0.0.0.0 0.0.0.0 gigabitethernet 1/1**) will cause the route to be inserted into the routing table only when the interface is up
`Router(config)# router eigrp` `100`	Creates EIGRP routing process 100
`Router(config-router)#` `redistribute static`	Advertises into EIGRP any static routes that are configured on the router
`Router(config)# router eigrp` `TEST`	Enters EIGRP using named mode configuration

`Router(config-router)#`
`address-family ipv4`
`autonomous-system 10`
	Enters the IPv4 address family for AS 10

`Router(config-router-af)#` `topology base`	Enters address-family topology subconfiguration mode

`Router(config-router-af-`
`topology)# redistribute`
`static`
	Advertises static routes into the EIGRP process

NOTE: Use this method when you want to draw all traffic to unknown destinations to a default route at the core of the network.

NOTE: This method is effective for advertising default connections to the Internet, but it will also redistribute all static routes into EIGRP.

Injecting a Default Route into EIGRP: ip default-network

`Router(config)# router eigrp 100`	Creates EIGRP routing process 100
`Router(config-router)# network 192.168.100.0 0.0.0.255`	Specifies which network to advertise in EIGRP
`Router(config-router)# exit`	Returns to global configuration mode
`Router(config)# ip route 0.0.0.0 0.0.0.0 192.168.100.5`	Creates a static default route to send all traffic with a destination network not in the routing table to next-hop address 192.168.100.5
`Router(config)# ip default-network 192.168.100.0`	Defines a route to the 192.168.100.0 network as a candidate default route

NOTE: For EIGRP to propagate the route, the network specified by the **ip default-network** command must be known to EIGRP. This means that the network must be an EIGRP-derived network in the routing table, or the static route used to generate the route to the network must be redistributed into EIGRP, or advertised into these protocols using the **network** command.

TIP: In a complex topology, many networks can be identified as candidate defaults. Without any dynamic protocols running, you can configure your router to choose from several candidate default routes based on whether the routing table has routes to networks other than 0.0.0.0/0. The **ip default-network** command enables you to configure robustness into the selection of a gateway of last resort. Rather than configuring static routes to specific next hops, you can have the router choose a default route to a particular network by checking in the routing table.

TIP: The **network 0.0.0.0** command enables EIGRP for all interfaces on the router.

Injecting a Default Route into EIGRP: Summarize to 0.0.0.0/0

`Router(config)# router eigrp 100`	Creates EIGRP routing process 100
`Router(config-router)# network 192.168.100.0`	Specifies which network to advertise in EIGRP
`Router(config-router)# exit`	Returns to global configuration mode
`Router(config)# interface serial 0/1/0`	Enters interface configuration mode
`Router(config-if)# ip address 192.168.100.1 255.255.255.0`	Assigns the IP address and subnet mask to the interface
`Router(config-if)#ip summary-address eigrp 100 0.0.0.0 0.0.0.0 75`	Enables manual summarization for EIGRP AS 100 on this specific interface for the given address and mask. An optional administrative distance of 75 is assigned to this summary route

NOTE: Summarizing to a default route is effective only when you want to provide remote sites with a default route, and not propagate the default route toward the core of your network.

NOTE: Because summaries are configured per interface, you do not need to worry about using distribute lists or other mechanisms to prevent the default route from being propagated toward the core of your network.

Accepting Exterior Routing Information: default-information

`Router(config)# router` `eigrp 100`	Creates routing process 100
`Router(config-router)#` `default-information in`	Allows exterior or default routes to be received by the EIGRP process AS 100. This is the default action; exterior routes are always accepted, and default information is passed between EIGRP processes when redistribution occurs
`Router(config-router)#` `no default-information in`	Suppresses exterior or default routing information

Equal-cost Load Balancing: maximum-paths

`Router(config)# router` `eigrp 100`	Creates routing process 100
`Router(config-router)#` `network 10.0.0.0`	Specifies which network to advertise in EIGRP
`Router(config-router)#` `maximum-paths 6`	Sets the maximum number of parallel routes that EIGRP will support to six routes
`Router(config)# ipv6 router` `eigrp 100`	Creates routing process 100 for EIGRP for IPv6
`Router(config-rtr)#` `maximum-paths 6`	Sets the maximum number of parallel routes that EIGRP for IPv6 will support to six routes
`Router(config-router-af)#` `topology base`	Enters address-family topology subconfiguration mode for EIGRP using named mode
`Router(config-router-af-` `topology)# maximum-paths 6`	Sets the maximum number of parallel routes that EIGRP using named mode configuration will support to six routes

NOTE: With the **maximum-paths** router configuration command, up to 32 equal-cost entries can be in the routing table for the same destination. The default is 4.

NOTE: Setting **maximum-path** to 1 disables load balancing.

Unequal-cost Load Balancing: variance

`Router(config)# router eigrp 100`	Creates EIGRP routing process for AS 100
`Router(config-router)# network 10.0.0.0 0.0.0.255`	Specifies which network to advertise in EIGRP
`Router(config-router)# variance n`	Instructs the router to include routes with a metric less than or equal to n times the minimum metric route for that destination, where n is the number specified by the **variance** command
`Router(config)# ipv6 router eigrp 100`	Creates IPv6 EIGRP routing process for AS 100
`Router(config-rtr)# variance n`	Instructs the router to include routes with a metric less than or equal to n times the minimum metric route for that destination, where n is the number specified by the **variance** command
`Router(config-router-af-topology)# variance n`	Sets the variance for EIGRP using named mode configuration. This command is entered under address family topology subconfiguration mode

NOTE: If a path is not a feasible successor, it is not used in load balancing.

NOTE: EIGRP variance can be set to a number between 1 and 128.

EIGRP Traffic Sharing

EIGRP not only provides unequal cost path load balancing, but also intelligent load balancing such as traffic sharing. To control how traffic is distributed among routes when there are multiple routes for the same destination network that have different costs, use the **traffic-share balanced** command. With the **balanced** keyword, the router distributes traffic proportionally to the ratios of the metrics that are associated with different routes. This is the default setting. Similarly, when you use the **traffic-share** command with the **min** keyword, the traffic is sent only across the minimum-cost path, even when there are multiple paths in the routing table. This is identical to the forwarding behavior without use of the **variance** command. However, if you use the **traffic-share min** command and the **variance** command, even though traffic is sent over the minimum-cost path only, all feasible routes get installed into the routing table, which decreases convergence times.

`Router(config)# router eigrp 100`	Creates EIGRP routing process for AS 100
`Router(config-router)# traffic-share balanced`	Sets the EIGRP traffic share feature to load balance proportionally to the ratios of the metrics. This is the default value

Router(config-router)# **traffic-share min across- interfaces**	Sets the EIGRP traffic share feature to only send traffic across the minimum cost path
Router(config-router-af- topology)# **traffic-share balanced** Router(config-router-af- topology)# **traffic-share min across-interfaces**	Sets the traffic share feature for EIGRP using named mode configuration **NOTE:** These commands are entered under address family topology subconfiguration mode

Bandwidth Use for EIGRP

Router(config)# **interface serial 0/1/0**	Enters interface configuration mode
Router(config-if)# **bandwidth 256**	Sets the bandwidth of this interface to 256 kilobits to allow EIGRP to make a better metric calculation
Router(config-if)# **ip bandwidth-percent eigrp 50 100**	Configures the percentage of bandwidth that may be used by EIGRP on an interface 50 is the EIGRP AS number 100 is the percentage value $100\% \times 256 = 256$ kbps
Router(config-if)# **ipv6 bandwidth-percent eigrp 100 75**	Configures the percentage of bandwidth (75%) that may be used by EIGRP 100 for IPv6 on the interface
Router(config-router-af- interface)# **bandwidth- percent 25**	Configures the percentage of bandwidth (25%) that may be used by EIGRP under the address-family interface subconfiguration mode

NOTE: By default, EIGRP is set to use only up to 50 percent of the bandwidth of an interface to exchange routing information. Values greater than 100 percent can be configured. This configuration option might prove useful if the bandwidth is set artificially low for other reasons, such as manipulation of the routing metric or to accommodate an oversubscribed multipoint Frame Relay configuration.

NOTE: The **ip bandwidth-percent** command relies on the value set by the **bandwidth** command.

Stub Routing for EIGRP

Router(config)# **router eigrp 100**	Creates routing process 100
Router(config-router)# **eigrp stub**	Configures the router to send updates containing its connected and summary routes only **NOTE:** Only the stub router needs to have the **eigrp stub** command enabled

`Router(config-router)# ` **`eigrp`** `stub` **`connected`**	Permits the EIGRP stub routing feature to send only connected routes **NOTE:** If the connected routes are not covered by a **network** statement, it might be necessary to redistribute connected routes with the **redistribute connected** command **TIP:** The **connected** option is enabled by default
`Router(config-router)# ` **`eigrp`** `stub` **`static`**	Permits the EIGRP stub routing feature to send static routes **NOTE:** Without this option, EIGRP will not send static routes, including internal static routes that normally would be automatically redistributed. It will still be necessary to redistribute static routes with the **redistribute static** command
`Router(config-router)# ` **`eigrp`** `stub` **`summary`**	Permits the EIGRP stub routing feature to send summary routes **NOTE:** Summary routes can be created manually, or through automatic summarization at a major network boundary if the **auto-summary** command is enabled **TIP:** The summary option is enabled by default
`Router(config-router)# ` **`eigrp`** `stub` **`receive-only`**	Restricts the router from sharing any of its routes with any other router in that EIGRP autonomous system
`Router(config-router)# ` **`eigrp`** `stub` **`redistributed`**	Advertises redistributed routes, if redistribution is configured on the stub router using the **redistribute** command
`Router(config)# ` **`ipv6 router`** `eigrp 100`	Enters router configuration mode and creates an EIGRP IPv6 routing process
`Router(config-rtr)# ` **`eigrp`** `stub`	Configures a router as a stub using EIGRP
`Router(config-router-af)# ` **`eigrp stub`**	Configures the router to send updates containing its connected and summary routes only **NOTE:** This command is entered under the EIGRP address family when using named mode configuration

NOTE: You can use the optional arguments (**connected**, **redistributed**, **static**, and **summary**) as part of the same command on a single line:

```
Router(config-router)# eigrp stub connected static summary
redistributed
```

You cannot use the keyword **receive-only** with any other option because it prevents any type of route from being sent.

NOTE: The same keywords in the **eigrp stub** command that work with EIGRP for IPv4 will also work with EIGRP for IPv6: **connected** | **summary** | **static** | **redistributed** | **receive-only**

EIGRP Unicast Neighbors

R2(config)# **router eigrp 100**	Enables EIGRP routing for AS 100
R2(config-router)# **network 192.168.1.0 0.0.0.255**	Identifies which networks to include in EIGRP
R2(config-router)# **neighbor 192.168.1.101 gigabitethernet 0/0/0**	Identifies a specific neighbor with which to exchange routing information. Instead of using multicast packets to exchange information, unicast packets will now be used on the interface on which this neighbor resides. If there are other neighbors on this same interface, **neighbor** statements must also be configured for them; otherwise, no EIGRP packets will be exchanged with them
Router(config-router-af)# **neighbor 172.16.1.2 gigabitethernet 0/0/1**	When using EIGRP named mode configuration, the **neighbor** command is entered under the address family

EIGRP Wide Metrics

The EIGRP composite metric (calculated using the bandwidth, delay, reliability, and load) is not scaled correctly for high-bandwidth interfaces or EtherChannels, resulting in incorrect or inconsistent routing behavior. The lowest delay that can be configured for an interface is 10 microseconds. As a result, high-speed interfaces, such as 10 Gigabit Ethernet (GE) interfaces, or high-speed interfaces channeled together (GE EtherChannel) will appear to EIGRP as a single GE interface. This may cause undesirable equal-metric load balancing. To resolve this issue, the EIGRP Wide Metrics feature supports 64-bit metric calculations and Routing Information Base (RIB) scaling that provide the ability to support interfaces (either directly or via channeling techniques like EtherChannels) up to approximately 4.2 terabits.

NOTE: The 64-bit metric calculations work only in EIGRP using named mode configurations. EIGRP classic mode uses 32-bit metric calculations. With the calculation of larger bandwidths, EIGRP can no longer fit the computed metric into a 4-byte unsigned long value that is needed by the Cisco RIB. To set the RIB scaling factor for EIGRP, use the **metric rib-scale** command. When you configure the **metric rib-scale** command, all EIGRP routes in the RIB are cleared and replaced with the new metric values.

NOTE: The EIGRP Wide Metrics feature also introduces K6 as an additional K value for future use.

Adjusting the EIGRP Metric Weights

Use the **metric weights** command to adjust the default behavior of EIGRP routing and metric computations.

`Router(config)# router eigrp 100`	Enables EIGRP routing for AS 100
`Router(config-rtr)# metric weights tos k1 k2 k3 k4 k5`	Changes the default K-values used in metric calculation. These are the default values: tos=0, k1=1, k2=0, k3=1, k4=0, k5=0
`Router(config)# ipv6 router eigrp 100`	Enters router configuration mode and creates an EIGRP IPv6 routing process
`Router(config-rtr)# metric weights tos k1 k2 k3 k4 k5`	Changes the default K-values used in metric calculation. These are the default values: tos=0, k1=1, k2=0, k3=1, k4=0, k5=0
`Router(config)# router eigrp CISCO`	Enters router configuration mode and creates an EIGRP process using named mode
`Router(config-router)# address-family ipv4 unicast autonomous-system 100`	Enters IPv4 unicast address family mode
`Router(config-router-af)# metric weights tos k1 k2 k3 k4 k5 k6`	Changes the default K-values used in metric calculation. These are the default values: tos=0, k1=1, k2=0, k3=1, k4=0, k5=0, k6=0
`Router(config-router-af)# metric rib-scale 128`	Sets scaling value for RIB installation. The default value is 128, and the range is from 1 to 255

NOTE: *tos* is a reference to the original Interior Gateway Routing Protocol (IGRP) intention to have IGRP perform type-of-service routing. Because this was never adopted into practice, the *tos* field in this command is always set to zero (0).

NOTE: With default settings in place, the metric of EIGRP is reduced to the slowest bandwidth plus the sum of all the delays of the exit interfaces from the local router to the destination network.

TIP: For two routers to form a neighbor relationship in EIGRP, the K-values must match.

CAUTION: Unless you are very familiar with what is occurring in your network, it is recommended that you do not change the K-values.

Verifying EIGRP

`Router# clear ip route *`	Deletes all routes from the IPv4 routing table
`Router# clear ip route 172.16.10.0`	Clears this specific route from the IPv4 routing table

`Router# clear ipv6 route *`	Deletes all routes from the IPv6 routing table **NOTE:** Clearing all routes from the routing table will cause high CPU utilization rates as the routing table is rebuilt
`Router# clear ipv6 route` `2001:db8:c18:3::/64`	Clears this specific route from the IPv6 routing table
`Router# clear ipv6 traffic`	Resets IPv6 traffic counters
`Router# show ip eigrp` `neighbors`	Displays the neighbor table
`Router# show ip eigrp` `neighbors detail`	Displays a detailed neighbor table **TIP:** The **show ip eigrp neighbors detail** command will verify whether a neighbor is configured as a stub router
`Router# show ip eigrp` `interfaces`	Shows info for each interface
`Router# show ip eigrp` `interfaces detail`	Shows more detailed information for each interface, such as timers and percent bandwidth
`Router# show ip eigrp` `interface serial 0/0/0`	Shows info for a specific interface
`Router# show ip eigrp` `interface 100`	Shows info for interfaces running process 100
`Router# show ip eigrp` `topology`	Displays the topology table **TIP:** The **show ip eigrp topology** command shows where your feasible successors are
`Router# show ip eigrp` `topology all-links`	Displays all entries in the EIGRP topology table, including nonfeasible-successor sources
`Router# show ip eigrp` `traffic`	Shows the number and type of packets sent and received
`Router# show ip interface`	Displays the status of interfaces configured for IPv4
`Router# show ip interface` `brief`	Displays a summarized status of interfaces configured for IPv4
`Router# show ip protocols`	Shows the parameters and current state of the active routing protocol process
`Router# show ip route`	Shows the complete routing table
`Router# show ip route eigrp`	Shows a routing table with only EIGRP entries
`Router# show ipv6 eigrp` `interfaces`	Displays IPv6 info for each interface
`Router# show ipv6 eigrp` `interface serial 0/0/0`	Displays IPv6 info for specific interface
`Router# show ipv6 eigrp` `interface 100`	Displays IPv6 info for interfaces running process 100

Router# **show ipv6 eigrp neighbors**	Displays the EIGRP IPv6 neighbor table
Router# **show ipv6 eigrp neighbors detail**	Displays a detailed EIGRP IPv6 neighbor table
Router# **show ipv6 eigrp topology**	Displays the EIGRP IPv6 topology table
Router# **show ipv6 interface**	Displays the status of interfaces configured for IPv6
Router# **show ipv6 interface brief**	Displays a summarized status of interfaces configured for IPv6
Router# **show ipv6 neighbors**	Displays IPv6 neighbor discovery cache information
Router# **show ipv6 protocols**	Displays the parameters and current state of the active IPv6 routing protocol processes
Router# **show ipv6 route**	Displays the current IPv6 routing table
Router# **show ipv6 route eigrp**	Displays the current IPv6 routing table with only EIGRP routes
Router# **show ipv6 route summary**	Displays a summarized form of the current IPv6 routing table
Router# **show ipv6 routers**	Displays IPv6 router advertisement information received from other routers
Router# **show ipv6 traffic**	Displays statistics about IPv6 traffic

Troubleshooting EIGRP

Router# **debug eigrp fsm**	Displays events/actions related to EIGRP feasible successor metrics (FSM) **NOTE:** FSM is sometimes referred to as the Finite State Machine
Router# **debug eigrp packets**	Displays events/actions related to EIGRP packets
Router# **debug eigrp neighbors**	Displays events/actions related to your EIGRP neighbors
Router# **debug ip eigrp**	Displays events/actions related to EIGRP protocol packets
Router# **debug ip eigrp notifications**	Displays EIGRP event notifications
Router# **debug ipv6 eigrp**	Displays information about the EIGRP for IPv6 protocol
Router# **debug ipv6 neighbor 2001:db8:c18:3::1**	Displays information about the specified EIGRP for IPv6 neighbor
Router# **debug ipv6 neighbor notification**	Displays EIGRP for IPv6 events and notifications in the console of the router

Router# **debug ipv6 neighbor summary**	Displays a summary of EIGRP for IPv6 routing information
Router# **debug ipv6 packet**	Displays debug messages for IPv6 packets
	TIP: Send your **debug** output to a syslog server to ensure that you have a copy of it in case your router is overloaded and needs to reboot
Router# **debug ipv6 routing**	Displays debug messages for IPv6 routing table updates and route cache updates

Configuration Example: EIGRP for IPv4 and IPv6 Using Named Mode

Figure 4-1 shows the network topology for the configuration that follows, which shows how to configure EIGRP using commands covered in this chapter. The example assumes the IPv6 unicast routing is already enabled on R1, R2 and R3.

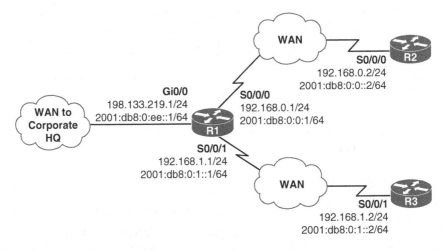

Figure 4-1 Network Topology for EIGRP Configuration

R1 Router

R1> **enable**	Enters privileged EXEC mode
R1# **configure terminal**	Moves to global configuration mode
R1(config)# **router eigrp ConfigEG**	Creates a named EIGRP virtual instance called *ConfigEG*
R1(config-router)# **address-family ipv4 autonomous-system 1**	Enables the IPv4 address family and starts EIGRP autonomous system 1
R1(config-router-af)# **network 198.133.219.0 0.0.0.255**	Enables EIGRP for IPv4 on interfaces in the 198.133.219.0 network

`R1(config-router-af)# network` `192.168.0.0 0.0.0.255`	Enables EIGRP for IPv4 on interfaces in the 192.168.0.0/24 network
`R1(config-router-af)# network` `192.168.1.0 0.0.0.255`	Enables EIGRP for IPv4 on interfaces in the 192.168.1.0/24 network

`R1(config-router-af)#`
`af-interface`
`gigabitethernet 0/0`
	Moves the router into address-family interface configuration mode for interface GigabitEthernet 0/0

`R1(config-router-af-`
`interface)# summary-address`
`192.168.0.0/23`
	Configures a summary aggregate address for the two serial prefixes
	NOTE: The command **summary-address 192.168.0.0 255.255.254.0** is also a valid entry here

`R1(config-router-af-` `interface)# exit`	Returns to address-family configuration mode
`R1(config-router-af)# exit`	Returns to EIGRP router configuration mode **NOTE:** The complete command is **exit-address-family**

`R1(config-router)# address-`
`family ipv6 autonomous-`
`system 1`
	Enables the IPv6 address family and starts EIGRP autonomous system 1. All IPv6 enabled interfaces are included in the EIGRPv6 process

`R1(config-router-af)# exit`	Returns to EIGRP router configuration mode
`R1(config-router)# exit`	Returns to global configuration mode
`R1(config)# exit`	Returns to privileged EXEC mode
`R1# copy running-config` `startup-config`	Copies the running configuration to NVRAM

R2 Router

`R2> enable`	Enters privileged EXEC mode
`R2# configure terminal`	Moves to global configuration mode
`R2(config)# router eigrp` `ConfigEG`	Creates a named EIGRP virtual instance called *ConfigEG*

`R2(config-router)# address-`
`family ipv4 autonomous-`
`system 1`
	Enables the IPv4 address family and starts EIGRP autonomous system 1

`R2(config-router-af)# network` `192.168.0.0`	Enables EIGRP for IPv4 on interfaces in the 192.168.0.0 network
`R2(config-router-af)# exit`	Returns to EIGRP router configuration mode **NOTE:** The complete command is **exit-address-family**

`R2(config-router)# address-`
`family ipv6 autonomous-`
`system 1`
	Enables the IPv6 address family and starts EIGRP autonomous system 1. All IPv6 enabled interfaces are included in the EIGRPv6 process

R2(config-router-af)# **exit**	Returns to EIGRP router configuration mode
R2(config-router)# **exit**	Returns to global configuration mode
R2(config)# **exit**	Returns to privileged EXEC mode
R2# **copy running-config startup-config**	Copies the running configuration to NVRAM

R3 Router

R3> **enable**	Enters privileged EXEC mode
R3# **configure terminal**	Moves to global configuration mode
R3(config)# **router eigrp ConfigEG**	Creates a named EIGRP virtual-instance called *ConfigEG*
R3(config-router)# **address-family ipv4 autonomous-system 1**	Enables the IPv4 address family and starts EIGRP autonomous system 1
R3(config-router-af)# **network 192.168.1.0**	Enables EIGRP for IPv4 on interfaces in the 192.168.1.0 network
R3(config-router-af)# **exit**	Returns to EIGRP router configuration mode **NOTE:** The complete command is **exit-address-family**
R3(config-router)# **address-family ipv6 autonomous-system 1**	Enables the IPv6 address family and starts EIGRP autonomous system 1. All IPv6 enabled interfaces are included in the EIGRPv6 process
R3(config-router-af)# **exit**	Returns to EIGRP router configuration mode
R3(config-router)# **exit**	Returns to global configuration mode
R3(config)# **exit**	Returns to privileged EXEC mode
R3# **copy running-config startup-config**	Copies the running configuration to NVRAM

This chapter provides information about the following topics:

- Comparing OSPFv2 and OSPFv3
- Configuring OSPFv2
- Configuring multiarea OSPFv2
- Using wildcard masks with OSPFv2 areas
- Configuring traditional OSPFv3
  - Enabling OSPFv3 for IPv6 on an interface
  - OSPFv3 and stub/NSSA areas
  - Interarea OSPFv3 route summarization
  - Enabling an IPv4 router ID for OSPFv3
  - Forcing an SPF calculation
- OSPFv3 address families
  - Configuring the IPv6 address family in OSPFv3
  - Configuring the IPv4 address family in OSPFv3
  - Applying parameters in address family configuration mode
- Authentication for OSPF
  - Configuring OSPFv2 authentication: simple password
  - Configuring OSPFv2 cryptographic authentication: MD5
  - Configuring OSPFv2 cryptographic authentication: SHA-256
  - Configuring OSPFv3 authentication and encryption
  - Verifying OSPFv2 and OSPFv3 authentication
- Optimizing OSPF parameters
  - Loopback interfaces
  - Router ID
  - DR/BDR elections
  - Passive interfaces
  - Modifying cost metrics
  - OSPF reference bandwidth

- - OSPF LSDB overload protection
  - Timers
  - IP MTU
- Propagating a default route
- Route summarization
  - Interarea route summarization
  - External route summarization
- OSPF route filtering
  - Using the **filter-list** command
  - Using the **area range not-advertise** command
  - Using the **distribute-list in** command
  - Using the **summary-address not-advertise** command
- OSPF special area types
  - Stub areas
  - Totally stubby areas
  - Not-so-stubby areas
  - Totally NSSA
- Virtual Links
  - Configuration example: virtual links
- Verifying OSPF configuration
- Troubleshooting OSPF
- Configuration example: single-area OSPF
- Configuration example: multiarea OSPF
- Configuration example: traditional OSPFv3
- Configuration example: OSPFv3 with address families

Comparing OSPFv2 and OSPFv3

Open Shortest Path First (OSPF) was developed in the 1980s and was standardized in 1989 as RFC 1131. The current version of OSPF, OSPFv2, was standardized in 1998 as RFC 2328. Now that router technology has dramatically improved, and with the arrival of IPv6, rather than modify OSPFv2 for IPv6, it was decided to create a new version of OSPF (OSPFv3), not just for IPv6, but for other newer technologies as well. OSPFv3 was standardized in 2008 as RFC 5340.

In most Cisco documentation, if you see something refer to OSPF, it is assumed to be referring to OSPFv2, and working with the IPv4 protocol stack.

The earliest release of the OSPFv3 protocol worked with IPv6 exclusively; if you needed to run OSPF for both IPv4 and IPv6, you had to have OSPFv2 and OSPFv3 running concurrently. Newer updates to OSPFv3 allow for OSPFv3 to handle both IPv4 and IPv6 address families.

Configuring OSPF

`Router(config)# router ospf 123`	Starts OSPF process 123. The process ID is any positive integer value between 1 and 65,535. The process ID is not related to the OSPF area. The process ID merely distinguishes one process from another within the device
	NOTE: The process ID number of one router does not have to match the process ID of any other router. Unlike Enhanced Interior Gateway Routing Protocol (EIGRP), matching this number across all routers does not ensure that network adjacencies will form
`Router(config-router)# network 172.16.10.0 0.0.0.255 area 0`	OSPF advertises interfaces, not networks. It uses the wildcard mask to determine which interfaces to advertise. Read this line to say, "Any interface with an address of 172.16.10.*x* is to run OSPF and be put into area 0"
`Router(config-router)# log-adjacency-changes detail`	Configures the router to send a syslog message when there is a change of state between OSPF neighbors
	TIP: Although the **log-adjacency-changes** command is on by default, only up/down events are reported unless you use the **detail** keyword
`Router(config)# interface gigabitethernet 0/0`	Moves to interface configuration mode
`Router(config-if)# ip ospf 123 area 0`	Enables OSPF area 0 directly on this interface
	NOTE: Because this command is configured directly on the interface, it takes precedence over the **network area** command entered in router configuration mode

CAUTION: Running two different OSPF processes does not create multiarea OSPF; it merely creates two separate instances of OSPF that do not communicate with each other. To create multiarea OSPF, you use two separate **network** statements and advertise two different links into different areas. See the following section for examples.

Configuring Multiarea OSPF

To create multiarea OSPF, you use two separate **network** statements and advertise two different links into different areas. You can also enable two different areas on two different interfaces to achieve the same result.

`Router(config)# router ospf 1`	Starts OSPF process 1
`Router(config-router)# network 172.16.10.0 0.0.0.255 area 0`	Read this line to say, "Any interface with an address of 172.16.10.*x* is to run OSPF and be put into area 0"

Router(config-router)# **network** **10.10.10.1 0.0.0.0 area 51**	Read this line to say, "Any interface with an exact address of 10.10.10.1 is to run OSPF and be put into area 51"
Router(config)# **interface gigabitethernet 0/0**	Moves to interface configuration mode
Router(config-if)# **ip ospf 1 area 0**	Enables OSPF area 0 directly on this interface **NOTE:** Because this command is configured directly on the interface, it takes precedence over the **network area** command entered in router configuration mode
Router(config-if)# **interface gigabitethernet 0/1**	Moves to interface configuration mode
Router(config-if)# **ip ospf 1 area 51**	Enables OSPF area 51 directly on this interface

Using Wildcard Masks with OSPF Areas

When compared to an IP address, a wildcard mask identifies what addresses are matched to run OSPF and to be placed into an area:

- A 0 (zero) in a wildcard mask means to check the corresponding bit in the address for an exact match.

- A 1 (one) in a wildcard mask means to ignore the corresponding bit in the address—can be either 1 or 0.

Example 1: 172.16.0.0 0.0.255.255

172.16.0.0 = 10101100.00010000.00000000.00000000

0.0.255.255 = 00000000.00000000.11111111.11111111

Result = 10101100.00010000.*xxxxxxxx.xxxxxxxx*

172.16.*x.x* (anything between 172.16.0.0 and 172.16.255.255 matches the example statement)

TIP: An octet in the wildcard mask of all 0s means that the octet has to match the address exactly. An octet in the wildcard mask of all 1s means that the octet can be ignored.

Example 2: 172.16.8.0 0.0.7.255

172.16.8.0 = 10101100.00010000.00001000.00000000

0.0.0.7.255 = 00000000.00000000.00000111.11111111

Result = 10101100.00010000.00001*xxx.xxxxxxxx*

00001*xxx* = 00001*000* to 00001*111* = 8–15

xxxxxxxx = 00000000 to 11111111 = 0–255

Anything between 172.16.8.0 and 172.16.15.255 matches the example statement

Router(config-router)# **network 172.16.10.1 0.0.0.0 area 0**	Read this line to say, "Any interface with an exact address of 172.16.10.1 is to run OSPF and be put into area 0"
Router(config-router)# **network 172.16.0.0 0.0.255.255 area 0**	Read this line to say, "Any interface with an address of 172.16.*x.x* is to run OSPF and be put into area 0"
Router(config-router)# **network 0.0.0.0 255.255.255.255 area 0**	Read this line to say, "Any interface with any address is to run OSPF and be put into area 0"

TIP: If you have problems determining which wildcard mask to use to place your interfaces into an OSPF area, use the **ip ospf** *process ID* **area** *area number* command directly on the interface.

Router(config)# **interface gigabitethernet 0/0**	Moves to interface configuration mode
Router(config-if)# **ip ospf 1 area 51**	Places this interface into area 51 of OSPF process 1
Router(config-if)# **interface gigabitethernet 0/1**	Moves to interface configuration mode
Router(config-if)# **ip ospf 1 area 0**	Places this interface into area 0 of OSPF process 1

TIP: If you assign interfaces to OSPF areas without first using the **router ospf** *x* command, the router creates the router process for you, and it shows up in **show running-config** output.

Configuring Traditional OSPFv3

OSPFv3 is a routing protocol for IPv4 and IPv6. Much of OSPFv3 is the same as in OSPFv2. OSPFv3, which is described in RFC 5340, expands on OSPFv2 to provide support for IPv6 routing prefixes and the larger size of IPv6 addresses. OSPFv3 also supports IPv6 and IPv4 unicast address families.

Enabling OSPF for IPv6 on an Interface

| Router(config)# **ipv6 unicast-routing** | Enables the forwarding of IPv6 unicast datagrams globally on the router

NOTE: This command is required before any IPv6 routing protocol can be configured |
|---|---|
| Router(config)# **interface gigabitethernet 0/0** | Moves to interface configuration mode |
| Router(config-if)# **ipv6 address 2001:db8:0:1::1/64** | Configures a global IPv6 address on the interface and enables IPv6 processing on the interface |

`Router(config-if)# ipv6` `ospf 1 area 0`	Enables traditional OSPFv3 process 1 on the interface and places this interface into area 0 **NOTE:** The OSPFv3 process is created automatically when OSPFv3 is enabled on an interface **NOTE:** The **ipv6 ospf** *x* **area** *y* command has to be configured on each interface that will take part in OSPFv3 **NOTE:** If a router ID has not been created first, the router may return a "NORTRID" warning (no router ID) stating that the process could not pick a router ID. It will then tell you to manually configure a router ID
`Router(config-if)# ipv6` `ospf priority 30`	Assigns a priority number to this interface for use in the designated router (DR) election. The priority can be a number from 0 to 255. The default is 1. A router with a priority set to 0 is ineligible to become the DR or the backup DR (BDR)
`Router(config-if)# ipv6` `ospf cost 20`	Assigns a cost value of 20 to this interface. The cost value can be an integer value from 1 to 65 535

`Router(config-if)#`
`ipv6 ospf neighbor`
`fe80::a8bb:ccff:fe00:c01`
	Configures a neighbor for use on nonbroadcast multiaccess (NBMA) networks
	
	NOTE: Only link-local addresses may be used in this command

OSPFv3 and Stub/NSSA Areas

`Router(config)#` `ipv6 router ospf`	Creates the OSPFv3 process if it has not already been created, and moves to router configuration mode
`Router(config-rtr)#` `area 1 stub`	The router is configured to be part of a stub area
`Router(config-rtr)#` `area 1 stub no-summary`	The router is configured to be in a totally stubby area. Only the ABR requires this **no-summary** keyword
`Router(config-rtr)#` `area 1 nssa`	The router is configured to be in an NSSA
`Router(config-rtr)#` `area 1 nssa no summary`	The router is configured to be in a totally stubby, NSSA area. Only the ABR requires the **no summary** keyword

Interarea OSPFv3 Route Summarization

`Router(config)# ipv6 router ospf 1`	Creates the OSPFv3 process if it has not already been created, and moves to router configuration mode
`Router(config-rtr)# area 1 range` `2001:db8::/48`	Summarizes area 1 routes to the specified summary address, at an area boundary, before injecting them into a different area

Enabling an IPv4 Router ID for OSPFv3

`Router(config)# ipv6 router ospf 1`	Creates the OSPFv3 process if it has not already been created, and moves to router configuration mode.
`Router(config-rtr)# router-id 192.168.254.255`	Creates an IPv4 32-bit router ID for this router. **NOTE:** In OSPFv3 for IPv6, it is possible that no IPv4 addresses will be configured on any interface. In this case, the user must use the **router-id** command to configure a router ID before the OSPFv3 process will be started. If an IPv4 address does exist when OSPFv3 for IPv6 is enabled on an interface, that IPv4 address is used for the router ID. If more than one IPv4 address is available, a router ID is chosen using the same rules as for OSPF Version 2.

Forcing an SPF Calculation

`Router# clear ipv6 ospf 1 process`	The OSPF database is cleared and repopulated, and then the SPF algorithm is performed.
`Router# clear ipv6 ospf 1 force-spf`	The OSPF database is not cleared; just an SPF calculation is performed.

CAUTION: As with OSPFv2, clearing the OSPFv3 database and forcing a recalculation of the shortest path first (SPF) algorithm is processor intensive and should be used with caution.

OSPFv3 Address Families

The OSPFv3 address families feature is supported as of Cisco IOS Release 15.1(3)S and Cisco IOS Release 15.2(1)T. Cisco devices that run software older than these releases and third-party devices will not form neighbor relationships with devices running the address families feature for the IPv4 address family because they do not set the address family bit. Therefore, those devices will not participate in the IPv4 address family SPF calculations and will not install the IPv4 OSPFv3 routes in the IPv6 RIB.

NOTE: Devices running OSPFv2 will not communicate with devices running OSPFv3 for IPv4.

NOTE: To use the IPv4 unicast address families (AFs) in OSPFv3, you must enable IPv6 on a link, although the link may not be participating in IPv6 unicast AF.

NOTE: With the OSPFv3 address families feature, users may have two processes per interface, but only one process per AF. If the AF is IPv4, an IPv4 address must first be configured on the interface, but IPv6 must be enabled on the interface.

Configuring the IPv6 Address Family in OSPFv3

`Router(config)# router ospfv3 1`	Enables OSPFv3 router configuration mode for the IPv4 or IPv6 address family

`Router(config-router)#`
`address-family ipv6 unicast`
 	
`Router(config-router-af)#`
	Enters IPv6 address family configuration mode for OSPFv3
	
	Notice the prompt change

`Router(config)# interface` `gigabitethernet 0/0`	Enters interface configuration mode for the GigabitEthernet 0/0 interface
`Router(config-if)# ospfv3 1` `ipv6 area 0`	Places the interfaces in area 0 for the IPv6 address family

Configuring the IPv4 Address Family in OSPFv3

`Router(config)# router ospfv3 1`	Enables OSPFv3 router configuration mode for the IPv4 or IPv6 address family

`Router(config-router)#`
`address-family ipv4 unicast`
 	
`Router(config-router-af)#`
	Enters IPv4 address family configuration mode for OSPFv3
	
	Notice the prompt change

`Router(config)# interface` `gigabitethernet 0/0`	Enters interface configuration mode for the GigabitEthernet 0/0 interface
`Router(config-if)# ospfv3 1` `ipv4 area 0`	Places the interfaces in area 0 for the IPv4 address family

Applying Parameters in Address Family Configuration Mode

`Router(config-router-af)# area 1` `range 2001:db8:0:0::0/56`	Summarizes area 1 routes to the specified summary address, at an area boundary, before injecting them into a different area
`Router(config-router-af)#` `default area 1`	Resets OSPFv3 area 1 parameters to their default values
`Router(config-router-af)# area 0` `range 172.16.0.0 255.255.0.0`	Summarizes area 0 routes to specified summary address, before injecting them into a different area
`Router(config-router-af)#` `default-metric 10`	Sets default metric values for IPv4 and IPv6 routes redistributed into the OSPFv3 routing protocol
`Router(config-router-af)#` `maximum-paths 4`	Sets the maximum number of equal-cost routes that a process for OSPFv3 routing can support **NOTE:** The maximum number of paths you can set is platform dependent
`Router(config-router-af)#` `summary-prefix 2001:0:0:10::/60`	Configures an IPv6 summary prefix. This is done on an Autonomous System Border Router (ASBR)

NOTE: Other commands that are available in AF mode include the following:

area nssa

area stub

passive-interface

router-id

Authentication for OSPF

Authentication for routers using OSPF relies on the use of predefined passwords.

Configuring OSPFv2 Authentication: Simple Password

`Router(config)# router ospf 1`	Starts OSPF process 1
`Router(config-router)# area 0 authentication`	Enables simple authentication; password will be sent in clear text for the entire area
`Router(config-router)# exit`	Returns to global configuration mode
`Router(config)# interface gigabitethernet 0/0`	Moves to interface configuration mode
`Router(config-if)# ip ospf authentication`	Another way to enable authentication if it has not been set up in router configuration mode shown earlier
`Router(config-if)# ip ospf authentication-key cleartxt`	Sets key (password) to *cleartxt* **NOTE:** The password can be any continuous string of characters that can be entered from the keyboard, up to eight characters in length. To be able to exchange OSPF information, all neighboring routers on the same network must have the same password

Configuring OSPFv2 Cryptographic Authentication: MD5

`Router(config)# router ospf 13`	Starts OSPF process 13
`Router(config-router)# area 0 authentication message-digest`	Enables authentication with MD5 password encryption for the entire area **NOTE:** MD5 authentication can also be enabled directly on the interface using the **ip ospf authentication message-digest** command in interface configuration mode
`Router(config-router)# exit`	Returns to global configuration mode
`Router(config)# interface gigabitethernet 0/0`	Moves to interface configuration mode
`Router(config-if)# ip ospf authentication message-digest`	Provides another way to enable authentication if it has not been set up in router configuration mode shown earlier

Router(config-if)# ip ospf message-digest-key 1 md5 secret	**1** is the key ID. This value must be the same as that of your neighboring router
	md5 indicates that the MD5 hash algorithm will be used
	secret is the key (password) and must be the same as that of your neighboring router

TIP: It is recommended that you keep no more than one key per interface. Every time you add a new key, you should remove the old key to prevent the local system from continuing to communicate with a hostile system that knows the old key.

NOTE: If the **service password-encryption** command is not used when configuring OSPF authentication, the key will be stored as plain text in the router configuration. If you use the **service password-encryption** command, there will be an encryption type of 7 specified before the encrypted key.

Configuring OSPFv2 Cryptographic Authentication: SHA-256

Starting with Cisco IOS Release 15.4(1)T, OSPFv2 supports SHA hashing authentication using key chains. Cisco refers to this feature as OSPFv2 Cryptographic Authentication. The feature prevents unauthorized or invalid routing updates in a network by authenticating OSPFv2 protocol packets using HMAC-SHA-256 algorithms.

Router(config)# **key chain samplechain**	Specifies the key chain name and enters key-chain configuration mode
Router(config-keychain)# **key 1**	Specifies the key identifier and enters key-chain key configuration mode. The range is from 1 to 255
Router(config-keychain-key)# **key-string ThisIsASampleKey54321**	Specifies the key string
Router(config-keychain-key)# **cryptographic-algorithm hmac-sha-256**	Configures the key with the specified cryptographic algorithm. Options for SHA are platform dependent but can include SHA-1, SHA-256, SHA-384, and SHA-512
Router(config-keychain-key)# **send-lifetime local 10:00:00 15 October 2019 infinite**	Sets the time period during which an authentication key on a key chain is valid to be sent during key exchange with another device
Router(config-keychain-key)# **exit**	Exits key-chain key configuration mode and returns to key-chain configuration mode
Router(config-keychain)# **exit**	Exits key-chain configuration mode and returns to global configuration mode
Router(config)# **interface gigabitethernet 0/0**	Enters interface configuration mode
Router(config-if)# **ip ospf authentication key-chain samplechain**	Specifies the key chain for the interface

Configuring OSPFv3 Authentication and Encryption

TIP: OSPFv3 requires the use of IPsec to enable authentication. Crypto images are therefore needed for authentication, as they are the only images that include the IPsec application programming interface (API) needed for use with OSPFv3.

NOTE: Authentication and encryption do not need to be done on both the interface and on the area, but rather only in one location. The following section shows both methods.

NOTE: RFC 7166 adds non-IPsec cryptographic authentication to OSPFv3. It is now possible to use the SHA encryption method previously described thanks to the addition of a new Authentication Trailer (AT) to OSPFv3 packets. The command to apply the key chain to an interface for use with OSPFv3 is **ospfv3 x authentication key-chain**. The key chain can also be applied to an entire area with the **area x authentication key-chain** router configuration command.

Router(config)# **interface gigabitethernet 0/0**	Moves to interface configuration mode
Router(config-if)# **ipv6 ospf authentication ipsec spi 500 md5 1234567890abcdef1234567890abcdef**	Applies authentication policy to the interface. **spi** (security policy index) is analogous to key numbers in a key chain but is communicated via the Authentication Header (AH). The SPI is a number between 256 and 4 294 967 295 **md5** = using the MD5 hash algorithm. SHA1 is also an option **NOTE:** The key string length is precise; it must be 32 hex digits for MD5 or 40 for SHA1
Router(config-if)# **ospfv3 authentication ipsec spi 500 md5 1234567890abcdef1234567890abcdef**	Alternative way of applying authentication policy to the interface
Router(config-if)# **ipv6 ospf encryption ipsec spi 256 esp aes-cbc 128 12345678901234567890 1234567890AB sha1 12345678901234 567890123456789012345678 90**	Specifies the encryption type for the interface to AES-128 and the authentication type to SHA
Router(config-if)# **ospfv3 encryption ipsec spi 257 esp aes-cbc 128 12345678901234567890 1234567890AB md5 123456789012345 678901234567890AB**	Alternative way of specifying the encryption type for the interface. In this example, AES-128 is enabled for encryption and MD5 is enabled for authentication
Router(config-if)# **exit**	Returns to global configuration mode
Router(config)# **router ospfv3 1**	Moves to routing protocol configuration mode

`Router(config-router)# ` **`area 0`** `authentication ipsec spi sha1 12 3456789012345678901234567890123 4567890`	Applies authentication policy to an entire area
`Router(config-router)# ` **`area 0`** `encryption ipsec spi 300 esp aes-cbc 128 12345678901234567890 1234567890AB sha1 12345678901234 5678901234567890123456789 0`	Enables AES-128 encryption and SHA authentication for the entire area
`Router(config-router)# ` **`exit`**	Returns to global configuration mode

Verifying OSPFv2 and OSPFv3 Authentication

`Router# ` **`show ip ospf neighbor`**	Displays OSPF neighbor table. Incorrect authentication configuration will prevent neighbor relationships from forming
`Router# ` **`show ip route ospf`**	Displays the OSPF routes in the routing table. Incorrect authentication configuration will prevent routes from being inserted into the routing table
`Router# ` **`show ospfv3 neighbor`**	Displays the OSPFv3 neighbor table
`Router# ` **`show ipv6 route ospf`**	Displays the OSPFv3 routes in the routing table
`Router# ` **`show ip ospf`** `interface gigabitethernet 0/0`	Verifies authentication setup on a specific interface
`Router# ` **`show crypto ipsec sa`** `interface gigabitethernet 0/0`	Displays IPsec security associations on a specific interface
`Router# ` **`debug ip ospf adj`**	Displays information about OSPF adjacencies and authentication for IPv4
`Router# ` **`debug ipv6 ospf adj`**	Displays information about OSPF adjacencies and authentication for IPv6

Optimizing OSPF Parameters

The following sections are optional but may be required in your tuning of OSPF for your network.

Loopback Interfaces

`Router(config)# ` `interface loopback 0`	Creates a virtual interface named Loopback 0 and then moves the router to interface configuration mode
`Router(config-if)# ip` `address 192.168.100.1` `255.255.255.255`	Assigns the IP address to the interface **NOTE:** Loopback interfaces are always "up and up" and do not go down unless manually shut down. This makes loopback interfaces great for use as an OSPF router ID

Router ID

`Router(config)# router ospf 1`	Starts OSPF process 1
`Router(config-router)# router-id 10.1.1.1`	Sets the router ID to 10.1.1.1. If this command is used on an OSPF router process that is already active (has neighbors), the new router ID is used at the next reload or at a manual OSPF process restart
`Router(config-router)# no router-id 10.1.1.1`	Removes the static router ID from the configuration. If this command is used on an OSPF router process that is already active (has neighbors), the old router ID behavior is used at the next reload or at a manual OSPF process restart
`Router(config-router-af)# router-id 10.1.1.1`	Sets the router ID to 10.1.1.1 in address family configuration mode **NOTE:** This works for either IPv4 or IPv6 address-family configuration mode, and also under the global OSPFv3 process. When entered there, the command applies to both address families

NOTE: To choose the router ID at the time of OSPF process initialization, the router uses the following criteria in this specific order:

1. Use the router ID specified in the **router-id** *w.x.y.z* command.
2. Use the highest IP address of all active loopback interfaces on the router.
3. Use the highest IP address among all active nonloopback interfaces.

NOTE: To have the manually configured router ID take effect, you must clear the OSPF routing process with the **clear ip ospf process** command.

NOTE: There is no IPv6 form of router ID. All router IDs are 32-bit numbers in the form of an IPv4 address. Even if a router is running IPv6 exclusively, the router ID is still in the form of an IPv4 address.

DR/BDR Elections

`Router(config)# interface gigabitethernet 0/0`	Enters interface configuration mode
`Router(config-if)# ip ospf priority 50`	Changes the OSPF interface priority to 50 **NOTE:** The assigned priority can be between 0 and 255. A priority of 0 makes the router ineligible to become a designated router (DR) or backup designated router (BDR). The highest priority wins the election and becomes the DR; the second highest priority becomes the BDR. A priority of 255 guarantees at least a tie in the election—assuming another router is also set to 255. If all routers have the same priority, regardless of the priority number, they tie. Ties are broken by the highest router ID. The default priority setting is 1 **TIP:** Do not assign the same priority value to more than one router

Router(config-if)# **ipv6 ospf priority 100**	Changes the interface priority to 100 for traditional OSPFv3
Router(config-if)# **ospfv3 1 priority 100**	Changes the interface priority to 100 for all OSPFv3 address families. It is possible to assign different priority values for each address family (IPv4 or IPv6)

Passive Interfaces

Router(config)# **router ospf 1**	Starts OSPF process 1
Router(config-router)# **network 172.16.10.0 0.0.0.255 area 0**	Read this line to say, "Any interface with an address of 172.16.10.*x* is to be put into area 0"
Router(config-router)# **passive-interface gigabitethernet 0/0**	Disables the sending of any OSPF packets on this interface
Router(config-router)# **passive-interface default**	Disables the sending of any OSPF packets out all interfaces
Router(config-router)# **no passive-interface serial 0/0/1**	When entered following the **passive interface default** command, enables OSPF packets to be sent out interface Serial 0/0/1, thereby allowing neighbor adjacencies to form
Router(config-router-af)# **passive-interface gigabitethernet 0/0**	Disables the sending of any OSPF packets on this interface for a specific OSPFv3 address family. It is possible to apply the **passive-interface** command under the global OSPFv3 process or under each address family

Modifying Cost Metrics

Router(config)# **interface serial 0/0/0**	Enters interface configuration mode
Router(config-if)# **bandwidth 128** Or	If you change the bandwidth, OSPF will recalculate the cost of the link **NOTE:** The cost of a link is determined by dividing the reference bandwidth by the interface bandwidth
Router(config-if)# **ip ospf cost 1564**	Changes the cost to a value of 1564 The bandwidth of the interface is a number between 1 and 10 000 000. The unit of measurement is kilobits per second (Kbps). The cost is a number between 1 and 65 535. The cost has no unit of measurement; it is just a number
Router(config-if)# **ospfv3 1 cost 5000**	The OSPFv3 interface cost can be modified globally for all address families or for a specific address family

OSPF Reference Bandwidth

`Router(config)# router` `ospf 1`	Starts OSPF process 1

`Router(config-router)#`
`auto-cost reference-`
`bandwidth 1000`
	Changes the reference bandwidth that OSPF uses to calculate the cost of an interface
	
	NOTE: The range of the reference bandwidth is 1 to 4 294 967 294. The default is 100. The unit of measurement is megabits per second (Mbps)
	
	NOTE: The value set by the **ip ospf cost** command overrides the cost resulting from the **auto-cost** command
	
	TIP: If you use the command **auto-cost reference-bandwidth** *reference-bandwidth*, you need to configure all the routers to use the same value. Failure to do so will result in routers using a different reference cost to calculate the shortest path, resulting in potential suboptimum routing paths

OSPF LSDB Overload Protection

`Router(config)# router` `ospf 1`	Starts OSPF process 1
`Router(config-router)#` `max-lsa 12000`	Limits the number of non-self-generated LSAs that this process can receive to 12 000. This number can be between 1 and 4 294 967 294

NOTE: If other routers are configured incorrectly, causing, for example, a redistribution of a large number of prefixes, large numbers of LSAs can be generated. This can drain local CPU and memory resources. With the **max-lsa** *x* feature enabled, the router keeps count of the number of received (non-self-generated) LSAs that it keeps in its LSDB. An error message is logged when this number reaches a configured threshold number, and a notification is sent when it exceeds the threshold number.

If the LSA count still exceeds the threshold after 1 minute, the OSPF process takes down all adjacencies and clears the OSPF database. This is called the *ignore state*. In the ignore state, no OSPF packets are sent or received by interfaces that belong to the OSPF process. The OSPF process will remain in the ignore state for the time that is defined by the **ignore-time** parameter. If the OSPF process remains normal for the time that is defined by the **reset-time** parameter, the ignore state counter is reset to 0.

Timers

`Router(config-if)# ip ospf` `hello-interval timer 20`	Changes the hello interval timer to 20 seconds
`Router(config-if)# ip ospf` `dead-interval 80`	Changes the dead interval timer to 80 seconds
`Router(config-if)# ospfv3` `1 ipv4 hello-interval 3`	Changes the hello interval to 3 seconds for the OSPFv3 IPv4 address family. It is possible to modify the hello interval for the global OSPFv3 process or for individual address families

`Router(config-if)# ospfv3` `1 ipv6 dead-interval 12`	Changes the dead interval to 12 seconds for the OSPFv3 IPv6 address family. It is possible to modify the dead interval for the global OSPFv3 process or for individual address families **NOTE:** Hello and dead interval timers must match for routers to become neighbors

NOTE: The default hello timer is 10 seconds on multiaccess and point-to-point segments. The default hello timer is 30 seconds on nonbroadcast multiaccess (NBMA) segments such as Frame Relay, X.25, or ATM.

NOTE: The default dead interval timer is 40 seconds on multiaccess and point-to-point segments. The default hello timer is 120 seconds on NBMA segments such as Frame Relay, X.25, or ATM.

NOTE: If you change the hello interval timer, the dead interval timer will automatically be adjusted to four times the new hello interval timer.

IP MTU

The IP maximum transmission unit (MTU) parameter determines the maximum size of a packet that can be forwarded without fragmentation.

`Router(config)# interface` `gigabitethernet 0/0`	Moves to interface configuration mode
`Router(config-if)# ip mtu` `1400`	Changes the MTU size to 1400 bytes. The range of this command is 68 to 1500 bytes

CAUTION: The MTU size must match between all OSPF neighbors on a link. If OSPF routers have mismatched MTU sizes, they will not form a neighbor adjacency.

Propagating a Default Route

`Router(config)# ip route`
`0.0.0.0 0.0.0.0`
`serial 0/0/0`
	Creates a default route

`Router(config)# router` `ospf 1`	Starts OSPF process 1

`Router(config-router)#`
`default-information`
`originate`
	Sets the default route to be propagated to all OSPF routers

`Router(config-router)#`
`default-information`
`originate always`
	The **always** option will propagate a default "quad-0" route even if this router does not have a default route itself
	
	NOTE: The **default-information originate** command or the **default-information originate always** command is usually configured on the "entrance" or "gateway" router, the router that connects your network to the outside world—the Autonomous System Boundary Router (ASBR)

`Router(config-router-af)#`
`default-information`
`originate`
	Sets the default route to be propagated to all OSPFv3 routers for a specific address family
	NOTE: This works for either IPv4 or IPv6 address-family configuration mode

`Router(config-router-af)#`
`default-information`
`originate always`
	Sets the default route to be propagated to all OSPFv3 routers for a specific address family even if this router does not have a default route itself
	NOTE: This works for either IPv4 or IPv6 address-family configuration mode

Route Summarization

In OSPF, there are two different types of summarization:

- Interarea route summarization
- External route summarization

Interarea Route Summarization

NOTE: Interarea route summarization is to be configured on an ABR only.

NOTE: By default, ABRs do *not* summarize routes between areas.

`Router(config)# router` `ospf 1`	Starts OSPF process 1

`Router(config-router)#`
`area 1 range 192.168.64.0`
`255.255.224.0`
	Summarizes area 1 routes to the specified summary address, before injecting them into a different area

`Router(config-router-af)#`
`area 1 range 192.168.64.0`
`255.255.224.0`
	Summarizes area 1 routes to the specified summary address, before injecting them into a different area using the OSPFv3 IPv4 address family

`Router(config-router-af)#`
`area 1 range`
`2001:db8:0:10::/60`
	Summarizes area 1 routes to the specified summary address, before injecting them into a different area using the OSPFv3 IPv6 address family

External Route Summarization

NOTE: External route summarization is to be configured on an ASBR only.

NOTE: By default, ASBRs do *not* summarize routes.

`Router(config)# router` `ospf 1`	Starts OSPF process 1

`Router(config-router)#`
`summary-address`
`192.168.64.0 255.255.224.0`
	Advertises a single route for all the redistributed routes that are covered by a specified network address and netmask

`Router(config-router-af)#` **`summary-prefix`** **`192.168.64.0 255.255.224.0`**	Advertises a single route for all the redistributed routes that are covered by a specified network address and netmask in OSPFv3 IPv4 address family configuration mode
`Router(config-router-af)#` **`summary-prefix`** **`2001:db8:0:10::/60`**	Advertises a single route for all the redistributed routes that are covered by a specified network address and netmask in OSPFv3 IPv6 address family configuration mode

OSPF Route Filtering

This section covers four methods of applying route filtering to OSPF:

- Using the **filter-list** command
- Using the **area range not-advertise** command
- Using the **distribute-list in** command
- Using the **summary-address not-advertise** command

Using the filter-list Command

`ABR(config)#` **`ip prefix-list`** **`MyPFList permit 172.16.0.0/16`** **`le 32`**	Defines a prefix list called *MyPFList* that permits all 172.16.0.0 prefixes with a mask between /16 and /32
`ABR(config)#` **`router ospf 202`**	Enters OSPF process 202
`ABR(config-router)#` **`area 1`** **`filter-list prefix MyPFList out`**	Uses a prefix list called *MyPFList* to filter Type-3 LSAs coming out of area 1
`ABR(config-router)#` **`area 1`** **`filter-list prefix MyPFList in`**	Uses a prefix list called *MyPFList* to filter Type-3 LSAs going into area 1

Using the area range not-advertise Command

`ABR(config)#` **`router ospf 202`**	Enters OSPF process 202
`ABR(config-router)#` **`area 1`** **`range 10.1.1.0 255.255.255.0`** **`not-advertise`**	Filters the 10.1.1.0/24 prefix from being advertised out of area 1 as a Type-3 Summary LSA

Using the distribute-list in Command

`ABR(config)#` **`access-list 1`** **`permit 192.168.1.0 0.0.0.255`**	Defines an ACL that permits the 192.168.1.0/24 prefix
`ABR(config)#` **`router ospf 202`**	Enters OSPF process 202
`ABR(config-router)#` **`distribute-list 1 in`**	Allows the router to only learn the 192.168.1.0/24 prefix **NOTE:** The inbound logic does not filter inbound LSAs; it instead filters the routes that SPF chooses to add to its own local routing table

NOTE: It is also possible to use a prefix list or a route map with the **distribute-list** command instead of an ACL.

Using the summary-address not-advertise Command

`ASBR(config)# router ospf 202`	Enters OSPF process 202
`ASBR(config-router)# summary-address 172.17.10 255.255.255.0 not-advertise`	Filters the 172.17.10/24 prefix from being advertised into the OSPF network as a Type-5 External LSA **NOTE:** This command is only applied to an ASBR

NOTE: Recall that the **summary-address** command is replaced by the **summary-prefix** command under OSPFv3.

OSPF Special Area Types

This section covers four different special areas with respect to OSPF:

- Stub areas
- Totally stubby areas
- Not-so-stubby areas (NSSAs)
- Totally NSSA

Stub Areas

`ABR(config)# router ospf 1`	Starts OSPF process 1
`ABR(config-router)# network 172.16.10.0 0.0.0.255 area 0`	Read this line to say, "Any interface with an address of 172.16.10.x is to run OSPF and be put into area 0"
`ABR(config-router)# network 172.16.20.0 0.0.0.255 area 51`	Read this line to say, "Any interface with an address of 172.16.20.x is to run OSPF and be put into area 51"
`ABR(config-router)# area 51 stub`	Defines area 51 as a stub area
`ABR(config-router)# area 51 default-cost 10`	Defines the cost of a default route sent into the stub area. Default is 1 **NOTE:** This is an optional command
`ABR(config-router-af)# area 51 stub`	Defines area 51 as a stub area in OSPFv3 address-family configuration mode **NOTE:** The command works for both IPv4 and IPv6 address families
`Internal(config)# router ospf 1`	Starts OSPF process 1
`Internal(config-router)# network 172.16.20.0 0.0.0.255 area 51`	Read this line to say, "Any interface with an address of 172.16.20.x is to run OSPF and be put into area 51"

Internal(config-router)# **area 51 stub**	Defines area 51 as a stub area **NOTE:** All routers in the stub area must be configured with the **area** x **stub** command, including the Area Border Router (ABR)
Internal(config-router-af)# **area 51 stub**	Defines area 51 as a stub area in OSPFv3 address-family configuration mode **NOTE:** The command works for both IPv4 and IPv6 address families

Totally Stubby Areas

ABR(config)# **router ospf 1**	Starts OSPF process 1
ABR(config-router)# **network** **172.16.10.0 0.0.0.255** **area 0**	Read this line to say, "Any interface with an address of 172.16.10.x is to run OSPF and be put into area 0"
ABR(config-router)# **network** **172.16.20.0 0.0.0.255** **area 51**	Read this line to say, "Any interface with an address of 172.16.20.x is to run OSPF and be put into area 51"
ABR(config-router)# **area 51** **stub no-summary**	Defines area 51 as a totally stubby area
ABR(config-router-af)# **area 51 stub no-summary**	Defines area 51 as a totally stubby area in OSPFv3 address-family configuration mode **NOTE:** The command works for both IPv4 and IPv6 address families
Internal(config)# **router** **ospf 1**	Starts OSPF process 1
Internal(config-router)# **network 172.16.20.0** **0.0.0.255 area 51**	Read this line to say, "Any interface with an address of 172.16.20.x is to run OSPF and be put into area 51"
Internal(config-router)# **area 51 stub**	Defines area 51 as a stub area **NOTE:** Whereas all internal routers in the area are configured with the **area** x **stub** command, the ABR is configured with the **area** x **stub no-summary** command
Internal(config-router-af)# **area 51 stub**	Defines area 51 as a stub area in OSPFv3 address-family configuration mode **NOTE:** The command works for both IPv4 and IPv6 address families

Not-So-Stubby Areas (NSSA)

ABR(config)# **router ospf 1**	Starts OSPF process 1
ABR(config-router)# **network** **172.16.10.0 0.0.0.255** **area 0**	Read this line to say, "Any interface with an address of 172.16.10.x is to run OSPF and be put into area 0"

`ABR(config-router)# ` **`network`** `172.16.20.0 0.0.0.255` `area 1`	Read this line to say, "Any interface with an address of 172.16.20.x is to run OSPF and be put into area 1"
`ABR(config-router)# ` **`area 1`** `nssa`	Defines area 1 as an NSSA
`ABR(config-router-af)#` **`area 1 nssa`**	Defines area 1 as an NSSA in OSPFv3 address-family configuration mode **NOTE:** The command works for both IPv4 and IPv6 address families
`Internal(config)# ` **`router`** **`ospf 1`**	Starts OSPF process 1
`Internal(config-router)#` **`network 172.16.20.0`** **`0.0.0.255 area 1`**	Read this line to say, "Any interface with an address of 172.16.20.x is to run OSPF and be put into area 1"
`Internal(config-router)#` **`area 1 nssa`**	Defines area 1 as an NSSA **NOTE:** All routers in the NSSA stub area must be configured with the **area** x **nssa** command
`Internal(config-router-af)#` **`area 1 nssa`**	Defines area 1 as an NSSA in OSPFv3 address-family configuration mode **NOTE:** The command works for both IPv4 and IPv6 address families

Totally NSSA

`ABR(config)# ` **`router ospf 1`**	Starts OSPF process 1
`ABR(config-router)# ` **`network`** `172.16.10.0 0.0.0.255` `area 0`	Read this line to say, "Any interface with an address of 172.16.10.x is to run OSPF and be put into area 0"
`ABR(config-router)# ` **`network`** `172.16.20.0 0.0.0.255` `area 11`	Read this line to say, "Any interface with an address of 172.16.20.x is to run OSPF and be put into area 11"
`ABR(config-router)# ` **`area 11`** **`nssa no-summary`**	Defines area 11 as a totally NSSA
`ABR(config-router-af)#` **`area 11 nssa no-summary`**	Defines area 11 as a totally NSSA in OSPFv3 address-family configuration mode **NOTE:** The command works for both IPv4 and IPv6 address families
`Internal(config)# ` **`router`** **`ospf 1`**	Starts OSPF process 1
`Internal(config-router)#` **`network 172.16.20.0`** **`0.0.0.255 area 11`**	Read this line to say, "Any interface with an address of 172.16.20.x is to run OSPF and be put into area 11"

Internal(config-router)# **area 11 nssa**	Defines area 11 as an NSSA **NOTE:** Whereas all internal routers in the area, including the ASBR, are configured with the **area** *x* **nssa** command, the ABR is configured with the **area** *x* **nssa no-summary** command
Internal(config-router-af)# **area 11 nssa**	Defines area 11 as a totally NSSA in OSPFv3 address-family configuration mode **NOTE:** The command works for both IPv4 and IPv6 address families

Virtual Links

In OSPF, all areas must be connected to a backbone area. If there is a break in backbone continuity, or the backbone is purposefully partitioned, you can establish a virtual link. The two endpoints of a virtual link are ABRs. The virtual link must be configured in both routers. The configuration information in each router consists of the other virtual endpoint (the other ABR) and the non-backbone area that the two routers have in common (called the transit area). A virtual link is a temporary solution to a topology problem.

NOTE: Virtual links cannot be configured through stub areas.

NOTE: One of these two routers must be connected to the backbone.

NOTE: The routers establishing the virtual link do not have to be directly connected.

Configuration Example: Virtual Links

Figure 5-1 shows the network topology for the configuration that follows, which demonstrates how to create a virtual link.

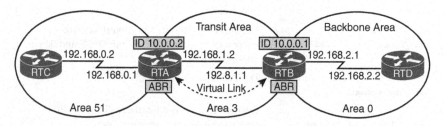

Figure 5-1 Virtual Areas: OSPF

RTA(config)# **router ospf 1**	Starts OSPF process 1
RTA(config-router)# **router-id 10.0.0.2**	Sets the router ID to 10.0.0.2
RTA(config-router)# **network** **192.168.0.0 0.0.0.255** **area 51**	Read this line to say, "Any interface with an address of 192.168.0.*x* is to run OSPF and be put into area 51"
RTA(config-router)# **network** **192.168.1.0 0.0.0.255** **area 3**	Read this line to say, "Any interface with an address of 192.168.1.*x* is to run OSPF and be put into area 3"

RTA(config-router)# **area 3 virtual-link 10.0.0.1**	Creates a virtual link with RTB
RTB(config)# **router ospf 1**	Starts OSPF process 1
RTB(config-router)# **router-id 10.0.0.1**	Sets the router ID to 10.0.0.1
RTB(config-router)# **network 192.168.1.0 0.0.0.255 area 3**	Read this line to say, "Any interface with an address of 192.168.1.*x* is to run OSPF and be put into area 3"
RTB(config-router)# **network 192.168.2.0 0.0.0.255 area 0**	Read this line to say, "Any interface with an address of 192.168.2.*x* is to run OSPF and be put into area 0"
RTB(config-router)# **area 3 virtual-link 10.0.0.2**	Creates a virtual link with RTA

NOTE: According to RFC 5838, OSPFv3 only supports virtual links for the IPv6 address family. Virtual links are not supported for the IPv4 address family.

Verifying OSPF Configuration

Router# **show ip protocols**	Displays parameters for all protocols running on the router
Router# **show ip route**	Displays a complete IP routing table
Router# **show ip route ospf**	Displays the OSPF routes in the routing table
Router# **show ip route ospfv3**	Displays the OSPFv3 routes in the routing table
Router# **show ip ospf**	Displays basic information about OSPF routing processes
Router# **show ip ospf border-routers**	Displays border and boundary router information
Router# **show ip ospf database**	Displays the contents of the OSPF database
Router# **show ip ospf database asbr-summary**	Displays Type-4 LSAs
Router# **show ip ospf database external**	Displays Type-5 LSAs
Router# **show ip ospf database nssa-external**	Displays NSSA external link states
Router# **show ip ospf database network**	Displays network LSAs
Router# **show ip ospf database router self-originate**	Displays locally generated LSAs
Router# **show ip ospf database summary**	Displays a summary of the OSPF database

Router# **show ip ospf interface**	Displays OSPF info as it relates to all interfaces
Router# **show ip ospf interface gigabitethernet 0/0**	Displays OSPF information for interface GigabitEthernet 0/0
Router# **show ip ospf neighbor**	Lists all OSPF neighbors and their states
Router# **show ip ospf neighbor detail**	Displays a detailed list of neighbors
Router# **show ipv6 interface**	Displays the status of interfaces configured for IPv6
Router# **show ipv6 interface brief**	Displays a summarized status of interfaces configured for IPv6
Router# **show ipv6 neighbors**	Displays IPv6 neighbor discovery cache information
Router# **show ipv6 ospf**	Displays general information about the OSPFv3 routing process
Router# **show ipv6 ospf border-routers**	Displays the internal OSPF routing table entries to an ABR or ASBR
Router# **show ipv6 ospf database**	Displays OSPFv3-related database information
Router# **show ipv6 ospf database database-summary**	Displays how many of each type of LSA exist for each area in the database
Router# **show ipv6 ospf interface**	Displays OSPFv3-related interface information
Router# **show ipv6 ospf neighbor**	Displays OSPFv3-related neighbor information
Router# **show ipv6 ospf virtual-links**	Displays parameters and the current state of OSPFv3 virtual links
Router# **show ipv6 protocols**	Displays the parameters and current state of the active IPv6 routing protocol processes
Router# **show ipv6 route**	Displays the current IPv6 routing table
Router# **show ipv6 route summary**	Displays a summarized form of the current IPv6 routing table
Router# **show ipv6 routers**	Displays IPv6 router advertisement information received from other routers
Router# **show ipv6 traffic**	Displays statistics about IPv6 traffic
Router# **show ip ospf virtual-links**	Displays information about virtual links
Router# **show ospfv3 database**	Displays the OSPFv3 database
Router# **show ospfv3 neighbor**	Displays OSPFv3 neighbor information on a per-interface basis

Troubleshooting OSPF

Router# **clear ip route** *	Clears the entire routing table, forcing it to rebuild
Router# **clear ip route a.b.c.d**	Clears a specific route to network a.b.c.d
Router# **clear ipv6 route** *	Deletes all routes from the IPv6 routing table
Router# **clear ipv6 route 2001:db8:c18:3::/64**	Clears this specific route from the IPv6 routing table
Router# **clear ipv6 traffic**	Resets IPv6 traffic counters
Router# **clear ip ospf counters**	Resets OSPF counters
Router# **clear ip ospf process**	Resets the *entire* OSPF process, forcing OSPF to re-create neighbors, database, and routing table
Router# **clear ip ospf 13 process**	Resets OSPF process 13, forcing OSPF to re-create neighbors, database, and routing table
Router# **clear ipv6 ospf process**	Resets the *entire* OSPFv3 process, forcing OSPFv3 to re-create neighbors, database, and routing table
Router# **clear ipv6 ospf 13 process**	Resets OSPFv3 process 13, forcing OSPF to re-create neighbors, database, and routing table
Router# **debug ip ospf events**	Displays *all* OSPF events
Router# **debug ip ospf adjacency**	Displays various OSPF states and DR/BDR election between adjacent routers
Router# **debug ipv6 ospf adjacency**	Displays debug messages about the OSPF adjacency process
Router# **debug ipv6 packet**	Displays debug messages for IPv6 packets
Router# **debug ip ospf packet**	Displays information about each OSPF packet received
Router# **debug ipv6 routing**	Displays debug messages for IPv6 routing table updates and route cache updates
Router# **undebug all**	Turns off all **debug** commands

Configuration Example: Single-Area OSPF

Figure 5-2 shows the network topology for the configuration that follows, which demonstrates how to configure single-area OSPF using the commands covered in this chapter.

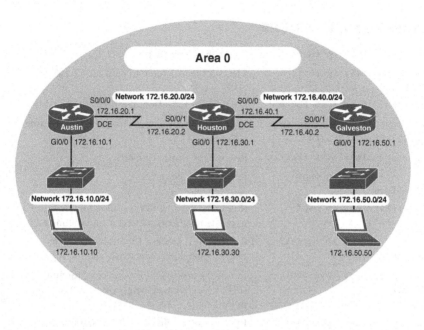

Figure 5-2   Network Topology for Single-Area OSPF Configuration

Austin Router

`Austin(config)# router ospf 1`	Starts OSPF process 1

`Austin(config-router)#`
`network 172.16.10.0 0.0.0.255`
`area 0`
	Read this line to say, "Any interface with an address of 172.16.10.*x* is to run OSPF and be put into area 0"

`Austin(config-router)#`
`network 172.16.20.0 0.0.0.255`
`area 0`
	Read this line to say, "Any interface with an address of 172.16.20.*x* is to run OSPF and be put into area 0"

`Austin(config-router)# <CTRL> z`	Returns to privileged EXEC mode
`Austin# copy running-config` `startup-config`	Saves the configuration to NVRAM
OR	
`Austin(config)# interface` `gigabitethernet 0/0`	Moves to interface configuration mode
`Austin(config-if)# ip ospf 1` `area 0`	Enables OSPF area 0 on this interface
`Austin(config-if)# interface` `serial 0/0/0`	Moves to interface configuration mode
`Austin(config-if)# ip ospf 1` `area 0`	Enables OSPF area 0 on this interface
`Austin(config-if)# <CTRL> z`	Returns to privileged EXEC mode
`Austin# copy running-config` `startup-config`	Saves the configuration to NVRAM

Houston Router

`Houston(config)# router ospf 1`	Starts OSPF process 1

`Houston(config-router)#`
`network 172.16.0.0 0.0.255.255`
`area 0`
	Read this line to say, "Any interface with an address of 172.16.x.x is to run OSPF and be put into area 0." One statement will now advertise all three interfaces

`Houston(config-router)#` `<CTRL> z`	Returns to privileged EXEC mode
`Houston# copy running-config` `startup-config`	Saves the configuration to NVRAM
OR	
`Houston(config)# interface` `gigabitethernet 0/0`	Moves to interface configuration mode
`Houston(config-if)# ip ospf 1` `area 0`	Enables OSPF area 0 on this interface
`Houston(config-if)# interface` `serial 0/0/0`	Moves to interface configuration mode
`Houston(config-if)# ip ospf 1` `area 0`	Enables OSPF area 0 on this interface
`Houston(config)# interface` `serial 0/0/1`	Moves to interface configuration mode
`Houston(config-if)# ip ospf 1` `area 0`	Enables OSPF area 0 on this interface
`Houston(config-if)#  <CTRL> z`	Returns to privileged EXEC mode
`Houston# copy running-config` `startup-config`	Saves the configuration to NVRAM

Galveston Router

`Galveston(config)# router` `ospf 1`	Starts OSPF process 1

`Galveston(config-router)#`
`network 172.16.40.2 0.0.0.0`
`area 0`
	Read this line to say, "Any interface with an exact address of 172.16.40.2 is to run OSPF and be put into area 0"
	
	This is the most precise way to place an exact address into the OSPF routing process

`Galveston(config-router)#`
`network 172.16.50.1 0.0.0.0`
`area 0`
	Read this line to say, "Any interface with an exact address of 172.16.50.1 is to be put into area 0"

`Galveston(config-router)#` `<CTRL> z`	Returns to privileged EXEC mode
`Galveston# copy running-config` `startup-config`	Saves the configuration to NVRAM
OR	
`Galveston(config)# interface` `gigabitethernet 0/0`	Moves to interface configuration mode

`Galveston(config-if)#` **`ip ospf`** **`1 area 0`**	Enables OSPF area 0 on this interface
`Galveston(config-if)#` **`interface serial 0/0/1`**	Moves to interface configuration mode
`Galveston(config-if)#` **`ip ospf`** **`1 area 0`**	Enables OSPF area 0 on this interface
`Galveston(config-if)#` **`<CTRL> z`**	Returns to privileged EXEC mode
`Galveston#` **`copy running-config`** **`startup-config`**	Saves the configuration to NVRAM

Configuration Example: Multiarea OSPF

Figure 5-3 shows the network topology for the configuration that follows, which demonstrates how to configure multiarea OSPF using the commands covered in this chapter.

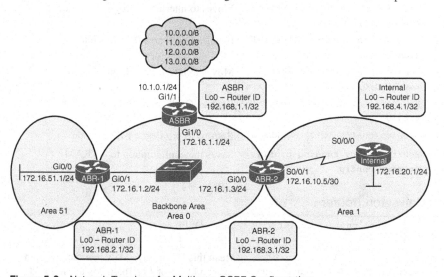

Figure 5-3 Network Topology for Multiarea OSPF Configuration

ASBR Router

`Router>` **`enable`**	Moves to privileged EXEC mode
`Router#` **`configure terminal`**	Moves to global configuration mode
`Router(config)#` **`hostname ASBR`**	Sets the router host name
`ASBR(config)#` **`interface`** **`loopback 0`**	Enters loopback interface mode
`ASBR(config-if)#` **`ip address`** **`192.168.1.1 255.255.255.255`**	Assigns an IP address and netmask
`ASBR(config-if)#` **`description`** **`Router ID`**	Sets a locally significant description

ASBR(config-if)# **exit**	Returns to global configuration mode
ASBR(config)# **ip route 0.0.0.0 0.0.0.0 10.1.0.2 gigabitethernet 1/1**	Creates default route. Using both an exit interface and next-hop address on a GigabitEthernet interface prevents recursive lookups in the routing table
ASBR(config)# **ip route 11.0.0.0 255.0.0.0 null0**	Creates a static route to a null interface. In this example, these routes represent a simulated remote destination
ASBR(config)# **ip route 12.0.0.0 255.0.0.0 null0**	Creates a static route to a null interface. In this example, these routes represent a simulated remote destination
ASBR(config)# **ip route 13.0.0.0 255.0.0.0 null0**	Creates a static route to a null interface. In this example, these routes represent a simulated remote destination
ASBR(config)# **interface gigabitethernet 1/0**	Enters interface configuration mode
ASBR(config-if)# **ip ospf 1 area 0**	Enables OSPF area 0 on this interface. Also creates the OSPF routing process
ASBR(config)# **exit**	Returns to global configuration mode
ASBR(config)# **router ospf 1**	Enters OSPF configuration mode
ASBR(config-router)# **default-information originate**	Sets the default route to be propagated to all OSPF routers
ASBR(config-router)# **redistribute static**	Redistributes static routes into the OSPF process. This turns the router into an ASBR because static routes are not part of OSPF, and the definition of an ASBR is a router that sits between OSPF and another routing process—in this case, static routing
ASBR(config-router)# **exit**	Returns to global configuration mode
ASBR(config)# **exit**	Returns to privileged EXEC mode
ASBR# **copy running-config startup-config**	Saves the configuration to NVRAM

ABR-1 Router

Router> **enable**	Moves to privileged EXEC mode
Router# **configure terminal**	Moves to global configuration mode
Router(config)# **hostname ABR-1**	Sets the router host name
ABR-1(config)# **interface loopback 0**	Enters loopback interface mode
ABR-1(config-if)# **ip address 192.168.2.1 255.255.255.255**	Assigns an IP address and netmask
ABR-1(config-if)# **description Router ID**	Sets a locally significant description

`ABR-1(config-if)# exit`	Returns to global configuration mode
`ABR-1(config)# interface` `gigabitethernet 0/1`	Enters interface configuration mode
`ABR-1(config-if)# ip ospf 1` `area 0`	Enables OSPF on this interface and creates the OSPF routing process
`ABR-1(config-if)# ip ospf` `priority 200`	Sets the priority for the DR/BDR election process. This router will win and become the DR
`ABR-1(config-if)# exit`	Returns to global configuration mode
`ABR-1(config)# interface` `gigabitethernet 0/0`	Enters interface configuration mode
`ABR-1(config-if)# ip ospf 1` `area 51`	Enables OSPF on this interface
`ABR-1(config-if)# exit`	Returns to global configuration mode
`ABR-1(config)# exit`	Returns to privileged EXEC mode
`ABR-1# copy running-config` `startup-config`	Saves the configuration to NVRAM

ABR-2 Router

`Router> enable`	Moves to privileged EXEC mode
`Router# configure terminal`	Moves to global configuration mode
`Router(config)# hostname ABR-2`	Sets the router host name
`ABR-2(config)# interface` `loopback 0`	Enters loopback interface mode
`ABR-2(config-if)# ip address` `192.168.3.1 255.255.255.255`	Assigns an IP address and netmask
`ABR-2(config-if)# description` `Router ID`	Sets a locally significant description
`ABR-2(config-if)# exit`	Returns to global configuration mode
`ABR-2(config)# interface` `gigabitethernet 0/0`	Enters interface configuration mode
`ABR-2(config-if)# ip ospf 1` `area 0`	Places this interface into OSPF area 0 and enables the OSPF routing process
`ABR-2(config-if)# ip ospf` `priority 100`	Sets the priority for the DR/BDR election process. This router will become the BDR to ABR-1's DR
`ABR-2(config)# interface` `serial 0/0/0`	Enters interface configuration mode
`ABR-2(config-if)# ip ospf 1` `area 1`	Places this interface into OSPF area 0 and enables the OSPF routing process
`ABR-2(config-if)# exit`	Returns to global configuration mode
`ABR-2(config)# router ospf 1`	Enters OSPF process 1

ABR-2(config-router)# **area 1 stub**	Makes area 1 a stub area. Type-4 and Type-5 LSAs are blocked and not sent into area 1. A default route is injected into the stub area, pointing to the ABR
ABR-2(config-router)# **exit**	Returns to global configuration mode
ABR-2(config)# **exit**	Returns to privileged EXEC mode
ABR-2# **copy running-config startup-config**	Saves the configuration to NVRAM

Internal Router

Router> **enable**	Moves to privileged EXEC mode
Router# **configure terminal**	Moves to global configuration mode
Router(config)# **hostname Internal**	Sets the router host name
Internal(config)# **interface loopback 0**	Enters loopback interface mode
Internal(config-if)# **ip address 192.168.4.1 255.255.255.255**	Assigns an IP address and netmask
Internal(config-if)# **description Router ID**	Sets a locally significant description
Internal(config)# **interface serial 0/0/0**	Enters interface configuration mode
Internal(config-if)# **ip ospf 1 area 1**	Places this interface into OSPF area 1 and enables the OSPF routing process
Internal(config)# **interface gigabitethernet 0/0**	Enters interface configuration mode
Internal(config-if)# **ip ospf 1 area 1**	Places this interface into OSPF area 1
Internal(config-if)# **exit**	Returns to global configuration mode
Internal(config)# **router ospf 1**	Enters OSPF process 1
Internal(config-router)# **area 1 stub**	Makes area 1 a stub area
Internal(config-router)# **exit**	Returns to global configuration mode
Internal(config)# **exit**	Returns to privileged EXEC mode
Internal# **copy running-config startup-config**	Saves the configuration to NVRAM

Configuration Example: Traditional OSPFv3

Figure 5-4 shows the network topology for the configuration that follows, which demonstrates how to configure traditional OSPFv3 using the commands covered in this chapter.

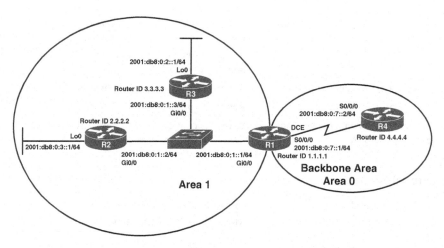

Figure 5-4 Network Topology for Traditional OSPFv3 Configuration

R3 Router

R3(config)# **ipv6 unicast-routing**	Enables the forwarding of IPv6 unicast datagrams globally on the router. This command is required before any IPv6 routing protocol can be configured
R3(config)# **ipv6 router ospf 1**	Moves to OSPFv3 router configuration mode
R3(config-rtr)# **router-id 3.3.3.3**	Sets a manually configured router ID
R3(config-rtr)# **exit**	Returns to global configuration mode
R3(config)# **interface gigabitethernet 0/0**	Moves to interface configuration mode
R3(config-if)# **ipv6 address 2001:db8:0:1::3/64**	Configures a global IPv6 address on the interface and enables IPv6 processing on the interface
R3(config-if)# **ipv6 ospf 1 area 1**	Enables OSPFv3 on the interface and places this interface into area 1
R3(config-if)# **no shutdown**	Enables the interface
R3(config-if)# **interface loopback 0**	Moves to interface configuration mode
R3(config-if)# **ipv6 address 2001:db8:0:2::1/64**	Configures a global IPv6 address on the interface and enables IPv6 processing on the interface
R3(config-if)# **ipv6 ospf 1 area 1**	Enables OSPFv3 on the interface and places this interface into area 1
R3(config-if)# **exit**	Moves to global configuration mode
R3(config)# **exit**	Moves to privileged EXEC mode
R3# **copy running-config startup-config**	Saves the configuration to NVRAM

R2 Router

R2(config)# **ipv6 unicast-routing**	Enables the forwarding of IPv6 unicast datagrams globally on the router. This command is required before any IPv6 routing protocol can be configured
R2(config)# **ipv6 router ospf 1**	Moves to OSPFv3 router configuration mode
R2(config-rtr)# **router-id 2.2.2.2**	Sets a manually configured router ID
R2(config-rtr)# **exit**	Returns to global configuration mode
R2(config)# **interface gigabitethernet 0/0**	Moves to interface configuration mode
R2(config-if)# **ipv6 address 2001:db8:0:1::2/64**	Configures a global IPv6 address on the interface and enables IPv6 processing on the interface
R2(config-if)# **ipv6 ospf 1 area 1**	Enables OSPFv3 on the interface and places this interface into area 1
R2(config-if)# **no shutdown**	Enables the interface
R2(config-if)# **interface loopback 0**	Moves to interface configuration mode
R2(config-if)# **ipv6 address 2001:db8:0:3::1/64**	Configures a global IPv6 address on the interface and enables IPv6 processing on the interface
R2(config-if)# **ipv6 ospf 1 area 1**	Enables OSPFv3 on the interface and places this interface into area 1
R2(config-if)# **no shutdown**	Enables the interface
R2(config-if)# **exit**	Moves to global configuration mode
R2(config)# **exit**	Moves to privileged EXEC mode
R2# **copy running-config startup-config**	Saves the configuration to NVRAM

R1 Router

R1(config)# **ipv6 unicast-routing**	Enables the forwarding of IPv6 unicast datagrams globally on the router. This command is required before any IPv6 routing protocol can be configured
R1(config)# **ipv6 router ospf 1**	Moves to OSPFv3 router configuration mode
R1(config-rtr)# **router-id 1.1.1.1**	Sets a manually configured router ID
R1(config-rtr)# **exit**	Returns to global configuration mode
R1(config)# **interface gigabitethernet 0/0**	Moves to interface configuration mode
R1(config-if)# **ipv6 address 2001:db8:0:1::1/64**	Configures a global IPv6 address on the interface and enables IPv6 processing on the interface

`R1(config-if)# ipv6 ospf 1 area 1`	Enables OSPFv3 on the interface and places this interface into area 1
`R1(config-if)# no shutdown`	Enables the interface
`R1(config-if)# interface serial 0/0/0`	Moves to interface configuration mode
`R1(config-if)# ipv6 address 2001:db8:0:7::1/64`	Configures a global IPv6 address on the interface and enables IPv6 processing on the interface
`R1(config-if)# ipv6 ospf 1 area 0`	Enables OSPFv3 on the interface and places this interface into area 0
`R1(config-if)# clock rate 4000000`	Assigns a clock rate to this interface
`R1(config-if)# no shutdown`	Enables the interface
`R1(config-if)# exit`	Moves to global configuration mode
`R1(config)# exit`	Moves to privileged EXEC mode
`R1# copy running-config startup-config`	Saves the configuration to NVRAM

R4 Router

`R4(config)# ipv6 unicast-routing`	Enables the forwarding of IPv6 unicast datagrams globally on the router. This command is required before any IPv6 routing protocol can be configured
`R4(config)# ipv6 router ospf 1`	Moves to OSPFv3 router configuration mode
`R4(config-rtr)# router-id 4.4.4.4`	Sets a manually configured router ID
`R4(config-rtr)# exit`	Returns to global configuration mode
`R4(config)# interface serial 0/0/0`	Moves to interface configuration mode
`R4(config-if)# ipv6 address 2001:db8:0:7::2/64`	Configures a global IPv6 address on the interface and enables IPv6 processing on the interface
`R4(config-if)# ipv6 ospf 1 area 0`	Enables OSPFv3 on the interface and places this interface into area 1
`R4(config-if)# no shutdown`	Enables the interface
`R4(config-if)# exit`	Moves to global configuration mode
`R4(config)# exit`	Moves to privileged EXEC mode
`R4# copy running-config startup-config`	Saves the configuration to NVRAM

Configuration Example: OSPFv3 with Address Families

Figure 5-5 shows the network topology for the configuration that follows, which demonstrates how to configure OSPFv3 address families using the commands covered in this chapter.

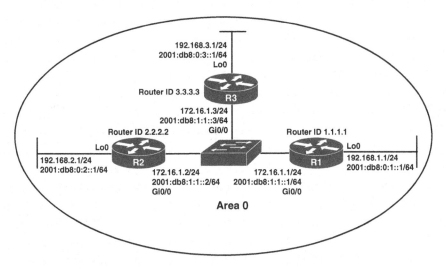

Figure 5-5   Network Topology for OSPFv3 Address Families Configuration

R1 Router

R1(config)# **ipv6 unicast-routing**	Enables the forwarding of IPv6 unicast data-grams globally on the router. This command is required before any IPv6 routing protocol can be configured
R1(config)# **interface loopback 0**	Moves to interface configuration mode
R1(config-if)# **ip address 192.168.1.1 255.255.255.0**	Assigns an IP address and netmask
R1(config-if)# **ipv6 address 2001:db8:0:1::1/64**	Configures a global IPv6 address on the interface and enables IPv6 processing on the interface
R1(config-if)# **interface gigabitethernet 0/0**	Moves to interface configuration mode
R1(config-if)# **ip address 172.16.1.1 255.255.255.0**	Assigns an IP address and netmask
R1(config-if)# **ipv6 address 2001:db8:1:1::1/64**	Configures a global IPv6 address on the interface and enables IPv6 processing on the interface
R1(config-if)# **no shutdown**	Enables the interface
R1(config-if)# **exit**	Returns to global configuration mode
R1(config)# **router ospfv3 1**	Enables OSPFv3 router configuration mode for the IPv4 or IPv6 address family
R1(config-router)# **log-adjacency-changes**	Configures the router to send a syslog message when an OSPFv3 neighbor goes up or down

R1(config-router)# **router-id 1.1.1.1**	Configures a fixed router ID
R1(config-router)# **address-family ipv6 unicast**	Enters IPv6 address family configuration mode for OSPFv3
R1(config-router-af)# **passive-interface loopback 0**	Prevents interface loopback 0 from exchanging any OSPF packets, including hello packets
R1(config-router-af)# **address-family ipv4 unicast**	Enters IPv4 address family configuration mode for OSPFv3
R1(config-router-af)# **passive-interface loopback 0**	Prevents interface loopback 0 from exchanging any OSPF packets, including hello packets
R1(config-router-af)# **exit**	Returns to OSPFv3 router configuration mode
R1(config-router)# **exit**	Returns to global configuration mode
R1(config)# **interface loopback 0**	Moves to interface configuration mode
R1(config-if)# **ospfv3 1 ipv6 area 0**	Enables OSPFv3 instance 1 with the IPv6 address family in area 0
R1(config-if)# **ospfv3 1 ipv4 area 0**	Enables OSPFv3 instance 1 with the IPv4 address family in area 0
R1(config-if)# **interface gigabitethernet 0/0**	Moves to interface configuration mode
R1(config-if)# **ospfv3 1 ipv6 area 0**	Enables OSPFv3 instance 1 with the IPv6 address family in area 0
R1(config-if)# **ospfv3 1 ipv4 area 0**	Enables OSPFv3 instance 1 with the IPv4 address family in area 0
R1(config-if)# **exit**	Returns to global configuration mode
R1(config)# **exit**	Returns to privileged EXEC mode
R1# **copy running-config startup-config**	Copies the running configuration to NVRAM

R2 Router

R2(config)# **ipv6 unicast-routing**	Enables the forwarding of IPv6 unicast datagrams globally on the router. This command is required before any IPv6 routing protocol can be configured
R2(config)# **interface loopback 0**	Moves to interface configuration mode
R2(config-if)# **ip address 192.168.2.1 255.255.255.0**	Assigns an IP address and netmask
R2(config-if)# **ipv6 address 2001:db8:0:2::1/64**	Configures a global IPv6 address on the interface and enables IPv6 processing on the interface

R2(config-if)# **interface gigabitethernet 0/0**	Moves to interface configuration mode
R2(config-if)# **ip address 172.16.1.2 255.255.255.0**	Assigns an IP address and netmask
R2(config-if)# **ipv6 address 2001:db8:1:1::2/64**	Configures a global IPv6 address on the interface and enables IPv6 processing on the interface
R2(config-if)# **no shutdown**	Enables the interface
R2(config-if)# **exit**	Returns to global configuration mode
R2(config)# **router ospfv3 1**	Enables OSPFv3 router configuration mode for the IPv4 or IPv6 address family
R2(config-router)# **log-adjacency-changes**	Configures the router to send a syslog message when an OSPFv3 neighbor goes up or down
R2(config-router)# **router-id 2.2.2.2**	Configures a fixed router ID
R2(config-router)# **address-family ipv6 unicast**	Enters IPv6 address family configuration mode for OSPFv3
R2(config-router-af)# **passive-interface loopback 0**	Prevents interface loopback 0 from exchanging any OSPF packets, including hello packets
R2(config-router-af)# **address-family ipv4 unicast**	Enters IPv4 address family configuration mode for OSPFv3
R2(config-router-af)# **passive-interface loopback 0**	Prevents interface loopback 0 from exchanging any OSPF packets, including hello packets
R2(config-router-af)# **exit**	Returns to OSPFv3 router configuration mode
R2(config-router)# **exit**	Returns to global configuration mode
R2(config)# **interface loopback 0**	Moves to interface configuration mode
R2(config-if)# **ospfv3 1 ipv6 area 0**	Enables OSPFv3 instance 1 with the IPv6 address family in area 0
R2(config-if)# **ospfv3 1 ipv4 area 0**	Enables OSPFv3 instance 1 with the IPv4 address family in area 0
R2(config-if)# **interface gigabitethernet 0/0**	Moves to interface configuration mode
R2(config-if)# **ospfv3 1 ipv6 area 0**	Enables OSPFv3 instance 1 with the IPv6 address family in area 0
R2(config-if)# **ospfv3 1 ipv4 area 0**	Enables OSPFv3 instance 1 with the IPv4 address family in area 0
R2(config-if)# **exit**	Returns to global configuration mode
R2(config)# **exit**	Returns to privileged EXEC mode
R2# **copy running-config startup-config**	Copies the running configuration to NVRAM

R3 Router

`R3(config)# ipv6 unicast-routing`	Enables the forwarding of IPv6 unicast datagrams globally on the router. This command is required before any IPv6 routing protocol can be configured
`R3(config)# interface loopback 0`	Moves to interface configuration mode
`R3(config-if)# ip address 192.168.3.1 255.255.255.0`	Assigns an IP address and netmask
`R3(config-if)# ipv6 address 2001:db8:0:3::1/64`	Configures a global IPv6 address on the interface and enables IPv6 processing on the interface
`R3(config-if)# interface gigabitethernet 0/0`	Moves to interface configuration mode
`R3(config-if)# ip address 172.16.1.3 255.255.255.0`	Assigns an IP address and netmask
`R3(config-if)# ipv6 address 2001:db8:1:1::3/64`	Configures a global IPv6 address on the interface and enables IPv6 processing on the interface
`R3(config-if)# no shutdown`	Enables the interface
`R3(config-if)# exit`	Returns to global configuration mode
`R3(config)# router ospfv3 1`	Enables OSPFv3 router configuration mode for the IPv4 or IPv6 address family
`R3(config-router)# log-adjacency-changes`	Configures the router to send a syslog message when an OSPFv3 neighbor goes up or down
`R3(config-router)# router-id 3.3.3.3`	Configures a fixed router ID
`R3(config-router)# address-family ipv6 unicast`	Enters IPv6 address family configuration mode for OSPFv3
`R3(config-router-af)# passive-interface loopback 0`	Prevents interface loopback 0 from exchanging any OSPF packets, including hello packets
`R3(config-router-af)# address-family ipv4 unicast`	Enters IPv4 address family configuration mode for OSPFv3
`R3(config-router-af)# passive-interface loopback 0`	Prevents interface loopback 0 from exchanging any OSPF packets, including hello packets
`R3(config-router-af)# exit`	Returns to OSPFv3 router configuration mode
`R3(config-router)# exit`	Returns to global configuration mode
`R3(config)# interface loopback 0`	Moves to interface configuration mode
`R3(config-if)# ospfv3 1 ipv6 area 0`	Enables OSPFv3 instance 1 with the IPv6 address family in area 0

`R3(config-if)#` **`ospfv3 1 ipv4`** **`area 0`**	Enables OSPFv3 instance 1 with the IPv4 address family in area 0
`R3(config-if)#` **`interface`** **`gigabitethernet 0/0`**	Moves to interface configuration mode
`R3(config-if)#` **`ospfv3 1 ipv6`** **`area 0`**	Enables OSPFv3 instance 1 with the IPv6 address family in area 0
`R3(config-if)#` **`ospfv3 1 ipv4`** **`area 0`**	Enables OSPFv3 instance 1 with the IPv4 address family in area 0
`R3(config-if)#` **`exit`**	Returns to global configuration mode
`R3(config)#` **`exit`**	Returns to privileged EXEC mode
`R3#` **`copy running-config`** **`startup-config`**	Copies the running configuration to NVRAM

CHAPTER 6

Redistribution and Path Control

This chapter provides information about the following redistribution and path control topics:

- Defining seed and default metrics
- Redistributing connected networks
- Redistributing static routes
- Redistributing subnets into OSPF
- Assigning E1 or E2 routes in OSPF
- Redistributing OSPF internal and external routes
- Configuration example: route redistribution for IPv4
- Configuration example: route redistribution for IPv6
- Verifying route redistribution
- Route filtering using the **distribute-list** command
  - Configuration example: inbound and outbound distribute list route filters
  - Configuration example: controlling redistribution with outbound distribute lists
  - Verifying route filters
- Route filtering using prefix lists
  - Configuration example: using a distribute list that references a prefix list to control redistribution
  - Verifying prefix lists
- Using route maps with route redistribution
  - Configuration example: route maps
- Manipulating redistribution using route tagging
- Changing administrative distance
- Path control with policy-based routing
- Verifying policy-based routing
- Configuration example: PBR with route maps
- Cisco IOS IP SLA
  - Configuring Authentication for IP SLA
  - Monitoring IP SLA Operations

- PBR with Cisco IOS IP SLA

  - **Step 1:** Define Probe(s)

  - **Step 2:** Define Tracking Object(s)

  - **Step 3a:** Define the Action on the Tracking Object(s)

  - **Step 3b:** Define Policy Routing Using the Tracking Object(s)

  - **Step 4:** Verify IP SLA Operations

Defining Seed and Default Metrics

`Router(config)# router eigrp 100`	Starts the EIGRP routing process
`Router(config-router)# network 172.16.0.0`	Specifies which network to advertise in EIGRP
`Router(config-router)# redistribute ospf 1`	Redistributes routes learned from OSPF into EIGRP

`Router(config-router)# default-metric 1000 100 250 1 1500`
Or
`Router(config-router)# redistribute ospf 1 metric 1000 100 255 1 1500`
	The metrics assigned to these learned routes will be calculated using the following components:
	1000 = Bandwidth in Kbps
	100 = Delay in tens of microseconds
	255 = Reliability out of 255
	1 = Load out of 255
	1500 = Maximum transmission unit (MTU) size
	The **metric** keyword in the second option assigns a starting EIGRP metric that is calculated using the following components: 1000, 100, 255, 1 1500

NOTE: The values used in this command constitute the seed metric for these OSPF routes being redistributed into EIGRP. The seed metric is the initial value of an imported route and it must be consistent with the destination protocol.

NOTE: The default seed metrics are as follows:

- Connected: 1
- Static: 1
- RIP: Infinity
- EIGRP: Infinity
- OSPF: 20 for all except for BGP, which is 1
- BGP: BGP metric is set to IGP metric value

NOTE: If both the **metric** keyword in the **redistribute** command and the **default-metric** command are used, the value of the **metric** keyword in the **redistribute** command takes precedence.

TIP: If a value is not specified for the **metric** option, and no value is specified using the **default-metric** command, the default metric value is 0, except for OSPF, where the default cost is 20. RIP and EIGRP must have the appropriate metrics assigned to any redistributed routes; otherwise, redistribution will not work. BGP will use the IGP metric, while both connected networks and static routes will receive an initial default value of 1.

TIP: The **default-metric** command is useful when routes are being redistributed from more than one source because it eliminates the need for defining the metrics separately for each redistribution.

TIP: Redistributed routes between EIGRP processes do not need metrics configured. Redistributed routes are tagged as EIGRP external routes and will appear in the routing table with a code of D EX.

Redistributing Connected Networks

`Router(config)# router ospf 1`	Starts the OSPF routing process
`Router(config-router)# redistribute connected`	Redistributes all directly connected networks **NOTE:** It is not necessary to redistribute networks that are already configured under the routing protocol **NOTE:** The **connected** keyword refers to routes that are established automatically by virtue of having IP enabled on an interface. For routing protocols such as OSPF, Intermediate System-to-Intermediate System (IS-IS), and EIGRP, these routes are redistributed as external to the autonomous system
`Router(config-router)# redistribute connected metric 50`	Redistributes all directly connected networks and assigns them a starting metric of 50 **NOTE:** The **redistribute connected** command is *not* affected by the **default-metric** command

Redistributing Static Routes

`Router(config)# ip route 10.1.1.0 255.255.255.0 serial 0/0/0`	Creates a static route for network 10.1.1.0/24 exiting out of interface Serial 0/0/0
`Router(config)# router eigrp 10`	Starts the EIGRP routing process
`Router(config-router)# redistribute static`	Redistributes static routes on this router into the EIGRP routing process

Redistributing Subnets into OSPF

`Router(config)# router` `ospf 1`	Starts the OSPF routing process

`Router(config-router)#`
`redistribute eigrp 10`
`metric 100 subnets`
	Redistributes routes learned from EIGRP autonomous system 10. A metric of 100 is assigned to all routes. Subnets will also be redistributed
	
	NOTE: Without the **subnets** keyword, no subnets will be redistributed into the OSPF domain. (Only routes that are in the routing table with the default classful mask will be redistributed.) The **subnets** keyword is only necessary for OSPFv2. OSPFv3 automatically redistributes all classless prefixes

Assigning E1 or E2 Routes in OSPF

`Router(config)# router ospf 1`	Starts the OSPF routing process

`Router(config-router)#`
`redistribute eigrp 1`
`metric-type 1`
	Redistributes routes learned from EIGRP autonomous system 1. Routes will be advertised as E1 routes
	
	NOTE: If the **metric-type** argument is not used, routes will be advertised by default in OSPF as E2 routes. E2 routes have a default fixed cost of 20 associated with them, but this value can be changed with the **metric** keyword. For E2 routes, the metric will not change as the route is propagated throughout the OSPF area. E1 routes will have internal area costs added to the seed metric

TIP: Use external type 1 (E1) routes when there are multiple Autonomous System Border Routers (ASBRs) advertising an external route to the same autonomous system to avoid suboptimal routing (see Figure 6-1).

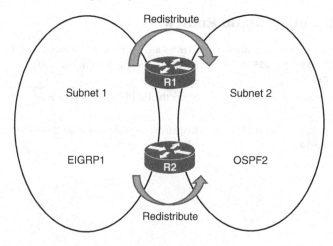

Figure 6-1   Network Topology with Two ASBRs

TIP: Use external type 2 (E2) routes if only one ASBR is advertising an external route to the AS (see Figure 6-2).

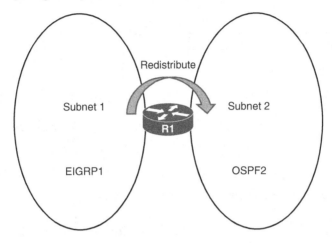

Figure 6-2   Network Topology with One ASBR

Redistributing OSPF Internal and External Routes

Router(config)# **router eigrp 10**	Starts the EIGRP routing process for autonomous system 10
Router(config-router)# **redistribute ospf 1 match internal external 1**	Redistributes internal and external type 1 routes learned from OSPF process ID 1. Available keywords are **match internal**, **external 1**, and **external 2**. These instruct EIGRP to only redistribute internal, external type 1 and type 2 OSPF routes
	NOTE: The default behavior when redistributing OSPF routes is to redistribute all routes—internal, external 1, and external 2. The keywords **match internal external 1** and **external 2** are required only if router behavior is to be modified

Configuration Example: Route Redistribution for IPv4

Figure 6-3 shows the network topology for the configuration that follows, which demonstrates how to implement single-point two-way basic redistribution between EIGRP and OSPF for IPv4, using the commands covered in this chapter. For this configuration example, assume that EIGRP and OSPF routing has been configured correctly on all four routers.

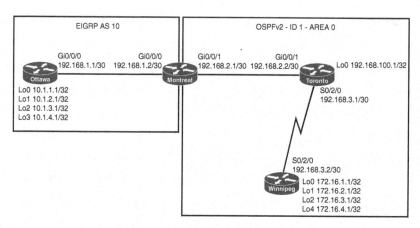

Figure 6-3   Network Topology for IPv4 Route Redistribution

`Montreal(config)# router` `eigrp 10`	Enters EIGRP configuration mode

`Montreal(config-router)#`
`redistribute ospf 1 metric`
`1500 10 255 1 1500`
	Redistributes routes from OSPF process ID 1 into EIGRP AS 10 and assigns a seed metric to these routes

`Montreal(config-router)# exit`	Returns to global configuration mode
`Montreal(config)# router` `ospf 1`	Enters OSPF configuration mode
`Montreal(config-router)#` `redistribute eigrp 10 subnets`	Redistributes classless routes from EIGRP AS 10 into OSPF process ID 1 as external type 2 (E2) with a metric of 20, which is fixed and does not change across the OSPF domain **NOTE:** Omitting the **subnets** keyword is a common configuration error. Without this keyword, only networks in the routing table with a classful mask will be redistributed. Subnets will not be redistributed

`Montreal(config-router)#`
`redistribute eigrp 10`
`metric-type 1 subnets`
	Redistributes classless routes from EIGRP AS 10 into OSPF process ID 1 as external type 1 (E1). Type 1 external routes calculate the cost by adding the external cost (20) to the internal cost of each link that the packet crosses

Configuration Example: Route Redistribution for IPv6

Figure 6-4 shows the network topology for the configuration that follows, which demonstrates how to implement single-point two-way basic redistribution between EIGRP using named mode configuration and OSPFv3 for IPv6, with the commands covered in this chapter. For this configuration example, assume that EIGRP and OSPF routing for IPv6 has been configured correctly on all four routers.

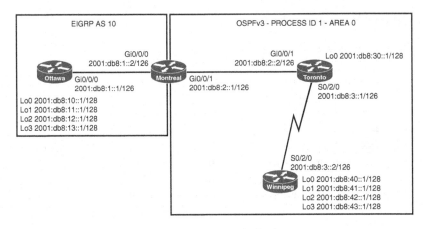

Figure 6-4 Network Topology for IPv6 Route Redistribution

Montreal(config)# **router eigrp DEMO**	Enters EIGRP using named mode configuration
Montreal(config-router)# **address-family ipv6 unicast autonomous-system 10**	Enables the IPv6 unicast address family for AS 10
Montreal(config-router-af)# **topology base**	Enters EIGRP address-family topology subconfiguration mode
Montreal(config-router-af-topology)# **redistribute ospf 1 metric 1500 10 255 1 1500 include-connected**	Redistributes IPv6 routes from OSPF process ID 1 into EIGRP AS 10 and assigns a seed metric to these routes **NOTE:** The **include-connected** keywords instruct the source routing protocol to redistribute the connected interfaces if the source routing protocol is running on them
Montreal(config-router-af-topology)# **router ospfv3 1**	Enters OSPFv3 process ID 1 configuration mode
Montreal(config-router)# **address-family ipv6 unicast**	Enters the OSPFv3 IPv6 unicast address family
Montreal(config-router-af)# **redistribute eigrp 10 include-connected**	Redistributes IPv6 routes from EIGRP AS 10 into OSPFv3 process ID 1 as external type 2 (E2) with a metric of 20, which is fixed and does not change across the OSPF domain
Montreal(config-router-af)# **redistribute eigrp 10 metric-type 1 include-connected**	Redistributes IPv6 routes from EIGRP AS 10 into OSPFv3 process ID 1 as external type 1 (E1). Type 1 external routes calculate the cost by adding the external cost (20) to the internal cost of each link that the packet crosses **NOTE:** The **subnets** keyword does not exist in OSPFv3 redistribution configuration

Verifying Route Redistribution

Router# **show ip route** Router# **show ipv6 route**	Displays the current state of the routing table
Router# **show ip eigrp topology** Router# **show ipv6 eigrp topology**	Displays the EIGRP topology table
Router# **show ip protocols** Router# **show ipv6 protocols**	Displays parameters and the current state of any active routing process
Router# **show ip rip database** Router# **show ipv6 rip database**	Displays summary address entries in the RIP routing database
Router# **show ip ospf database** Router# **show ospfv3 database**	Displays the link-state advertisement (LSA) types within the link-state database (LSDB)

Route Filtering Using the distribute-list Command

Router(config)# **router eigrp 10**	Starts the EIGRP routing process for autonomous system 10 **NOTE:** If using EIGRP named mode configuration with address families, the **distribute-list** command is entered under the topology subconfiguration mode: Router(config-router-af-topology)# **NOTE:** If using OSPFv3 with address families, the **distribute-list** command is entered under the specific address family in use on the router: Router(config-router-af)#
Router(config-router)# **distribute-list 1 in**	Creates an incoming global distribute list that refers to access control list (ACL) 1
Router(config-router)# **distribute-list 2 out**	Creates an outgoing global distribute list that refers to ACL 2
Router(config-router)# **distribute-list 3 in** **gigabitethernet 0/0/0**	Creates an incoming distribute list for interface GigabitEthernet 0/0/0 and refers to ACL 3
Router(config-router)# **distribute-list 4 out serial** **0/2/0**	Creates an outgoing distribute list for interface Serial 0/2/0 and refers to ACL 4
Router(config-router)# **distribute-list 5 out ospf 1**	Filters updates redistributed from OSPF process ID 1 into EIGRP AS 10 according to ACL 5

Configuration Example: Inbound and Outbound Distribute List Route Filters

Figure 6-5 shows the network topology for the configuration that follows, which demonstrates how to configure inbound and outbound route filters to control routing updates using the commands covered in this chapter. Assume that all basic configurations and EIGRP routing have been configured correctly.

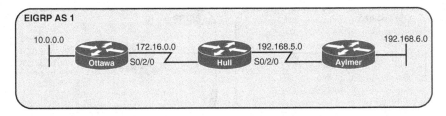

Figure 6-5   Network Topology for Inbound and Outbound Distribute List Route Filters

The first objective is to prevent router Aylmer from learning the 10.0.0.0/8 network using an outbound distribute list on router Hull.

`Hull(config)# ` **`access-list 10 deny 10.0.0.0 0.255.255.255`**	Creates a standard ACL number 10 and explicitly denies the 10.0.0.0/8 network
`Hull(config)# ` **`access-list 10 permit any`**	Adds a second line to ACL 10 which permits all other networks
`Hull(config)# ` **`router eigrp 1`**	Enters EIGRP AS 1 routing process
`Hull(config-router)# ` **`distribute-list 10 out`** Or `Hull(config-router)# ` **`distribute-list 10 out serial 0/2/0`**	Creates an outbound global distribute list that refers to ACL 10 Creates an outgoing distribute list for interface Serial 0/2/0 that refers to ACL 10

The second objective is to prevent router Ottawa from learning the 192.168.6.0/24 network using an inbound distribute list on router Ottawa.

`Ottawa(config)# ` **`access-list 20 deny 192.168.6.0 0.0.0.255`**	Creates a standard ACL number 20 and explicitly denies the 192.168.6.0/24 network
`Ottawa(config)# ` **`access-list 20 permit any`**	Adds a second line to ACL 20 which permits all other networks
`Ottawa(config)# ` **`router eigrp 1`**	Enters EIGRP AS 1 routing process
`Ottawa(config-router)#` **`distribute-list 20 in`** Or `Ottawa(config-router)#` **`distribute-list 20 in serial 0/2/0`**	Creates an inbound global distribute list that refers to ACL 20 Creates an inbound distribute list for interface Serial 0/2/0 that refers to ACL 20

Configuration Example: Controlling Redistribution with Outbound Distribute Lists

Figure 6-6 shows the network topology for the configuration that follows, which demonstrates how to control redistribution with an outbound distribute list using the commands covered in this chapter. Assume that all basic configurations and routing have been configured correctly. This example uses OSPFv3 with address families.

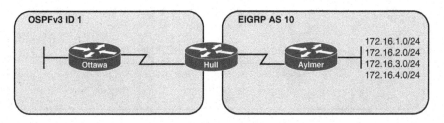

Figure 6-6   Network Topology for Controlling Redistribution with Outbound Distribute
Lists

The objective is to prevent networks 172.16.3.0/24 and 172.16.4.0/24 from being redistributed into the OSPF domain.

`Hull(config)# `**`access-list 30`**` `**`permit 172.16.1.0 0.0.0.255`**	Creates a standard ACL number 30 and explicitly permits the 172.16.1.0/24 network
`Hull(config)# `**`access-list 30`**` `**`permit 172.16.2.0 0.0.0.255`**	Adds a second line to ACL 30 that explicitly permits the 172.16.2.0/24 network
`Hull(config)# `**`router ospfv3 1`**	Enters OSPFv3 process ID 1 routing process
`Hull(config-router)#` **`address-family ipv4 unicast`**	Enters the OSPFv3 IPv4 address family
`Hull(config-router-af)#` **`redistribute eigrp 10`**	Redistributes all EIGRP networks into OSPFv3
`Hull(config-router-af)#` **`distribute-list 30 out eigrp 10`**	Creates an outbound distribute list to filter routes being redistributed from EIGRP into OSPFv3 **NOTE:** The implicit "deny any" statement at the end of the access list prevents routing updates about any other network from being advertised. As a result, networks 172.16.3.0/24 and 172.16.4.0/24 will not be redistributed into OSPFv3

Verifying Route Filters

`Router# `**`show ip protocols`**
 	
`Routing Protocol is "eigrp 10"`
`   Outgoing update filter list for all`
`interfaces is 2`
`    Redistributed ospf 1 filtered by 5`
`    Serial 0/2/0 filtered by 4`
`   Incoming update filter list for all`
`interfaces is 1`
`    GigabitEthernet 0/0/0 filtered by 3`
	Displays the parameters and current state of active routing protocols

NOTE: For each interface and routing process, Cisco IOS permits the following:

- One incoming global distribute list
- One outgoing global distribute list
- One incoming interface distribute list
- One outgoing interface distribute list
- One outgoing redistribution distribute list

CAUTION: For OSPF, route filters have *no* effect on LSAs or the LSDB. A basic requirement of link-state routing protocols is that routers in an area must have identical LSDBs.

NOTE: OSPF routes *cannot* be filtered from entering the OSPF database. The **distribute-list in** command filters routes only from entering the routing table, but it doesn't prevent link-state packets (LSPs) from being propagated.

NOTE: The command **distribute-list out** works only on the routes being redistributed by the ASBR into OSPF. It can be applied to external type-2 and external type-1 routes but *not* to intra-area and interarea routes.

Route Filtering Using Prefix Lists

The general syntax for configuring IPv4 and IPv6 prefix lists is as follows:

```
Router(config)# ip prefix-list list-name [seq seq-value]
{deny | permit} network/len [ge ge-value] [le le-value]

Router(config)# ipv6 prefix-list list-name [seq seq-value]
{deny | permit} network/len [ge ge-value] [le le-value]
```

The table that follows describes the parameters for this command.

Parameter	Description
list-name	The name of the prefix list
seq	(Optional) Applies a sequence number to the entry being created or deleted
seq-value	(Optional) Specifies the sequence number
deny	Denies access to matching conditions
permit	Permits access for matching conditions
network/len	(Mandatory) The IPv4 or IPv6 network number and length (in bits) of the netmask
ge	(Optional) Applies *ge-value* to the range specified
ge-value	(Optional) Specifies the lesser value of a range (the "from" portion of the range description)
le	(Optional) Applies *le-value* to the range specified
le-value	(Optional) Specifies the greater value of a range (the "to" portion of the range description)

TIP: You must define a prefix list before you can apply it as a route filter.

TIP: There is an implicit deny statement at the end of each prefix list.

TIP: The range of sequence numbers that can be entered is from 1 to 4 294 967 294. If a sequence number is not entered when configuring this command, a default sequence numbering is applied to the prefix list. The number 5 is applied to the first prefix entry, and subsequent unnumbered entries are incremented by 5.

A router tests for prefix list matches from the lowest sequence number to the highest. By numbering your **prefix-list** statements, you can add new entries at any point in the list.

The following examples show how you can use the **prefix-list** command to filter networks using some of the more commonly used options.

`Router(config)# ip prefix-list` `ROSE permit 192.0.0.0/8 le 24`	Creates a prefix list where the prefix length to be permitted needs to be between /8 and /24, inclusive, and where the first octet is 192. Because no sequence number is identified, the default number of 5 is applied
`Router(config)# ip prefix-list` `ROSE deny 192.0.0.0/8 ge 25`	Creates a prefix list where the prefix length to be denied needs to be between 25 and 32, inclusive, and where the first octet is 192. Because no sequence number is identified, the number 10 is applied—an increment of 5 over the previous statement **NOTE:** This configuration will permit routes such as 192.2.0.0/16 or 192.2.20.0/24 but will deny a more specific subnet such as 192.168.10.128/25

`Router(config)# ip prefix-list`
`TOWER permit 10.0.0.0/8 ge 16`
`le 24`
	Creates a prefix list that permits all prefixes that have a length between 16 and 24 bits (greater than or equal to 16 bits, and less than or equal to 24 bits), and where the first octet is 10

`Router(config)# ip prefix-list` `TEST seq 5 permit 0.0.0.0/0`	Creates a prefix list and assigns a sequence number of 5 to a statement that permits only the default route 0.0.0.0/0

`Router(config)# ip prefix-list`
`TEST seq 10 permit 0.0.0.0/0`
`ge 30 le 30`
	Creates a prefix list and assigns a sequence number of 10 to a statement that permits any prefix with a length of exactly 30 bits

`Router(config)# ip prefix-list`
`TEST seq 15 permit 0.0.0.0/0`
`le 32`
	Creates a prefix list and assigns a sequence number of 15 to a statement that permits any address or subnet (permit any)

`Router(config)# no ip prefix-`
`list TEST seq 10 0.0.0.0/0 ge`
`30 le 30`
	Removes sequence number 10 from the prefix list

`Router(config)# ipv6 prefix-` `list V6TEST seq 5 permit ::/0`	Creates a prefix list and assigns a sequence number of 5 to a statement that permits only the default route

`Router(config)# ipv6 prefix-list` `V6TEST seq 10 permit ::/0 le 128`	Creates a prefix list and assigns a sequence number of 10 to a statement that permits any address or prefix length (permit any)

Configuration Example: Using a Distribute List That References a Prefix List to Control Redistribution

Figure 6-7 shows the network topology for the configuration that follows, which demonstrates how to control redistribution with a prefix list using the commands covered in this chapter. Assume that all basic configurations and EIGRP and OSPF routing have been configured correctly.

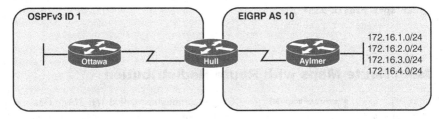

Figure 6-7 Network Topology for Distribute List Configuration with Prefix Lists

The objective is to prevent networks 172.16.3.0/24 and 172.16.4.0/24 from being redistributed into the OSPF domain.

`Hull(config)# ip prefix-`
`list FILTER seq 5 permit`
`172.16.1.0/24`
	Creates a prefix list called *FILTER* with a first sequence number of 5 that explicitly permits the 172.16.1.0/24 network

`Hull(config)# ip prefix-`
`list FILTER seq 10 permit`
`172.16.2.0/24`
	Adds a second line to the *FILTER* prefix list that explicitly permits the 172.16.2.0/24 network

`Hull(config)# router ospf 1`	Enters OSPF process ID 1 routing process
`Hull(config-router)#` `redistribute eigrp 10 subnets`	Redistributes all EIGRP networks into OSPF. The **subnets** keyword is required for accurate OSPFv2 redistribution of subnets learned from the Aylmer router

`Hull(config-router)#`
`distribute-list prefix FILTER`
`out eigrp 10`
	Creates an outbound distribute list to filter routes being redistributed from EIGRP into OSPF that references the prefix list

	NOTE: The implicit deny any statement at the end of the prefix list prevents routing updates about any other network from being advertised. As a result, networks 172.16.3.0/24 and 172.16.4.0/24 will not be redistributed into OSPF

TIP: You can attach prefix lists to the redistribution process either via a distribute list or via a route map.

Verifying Prefix Lists

`show ip prefix-list [detail | summary]`
 	
`show ipv6 prefix-list [detail | summary]`
	Displays information on all prefix lists. Specifying the **detail** keyword includes the description and the hit count (the number of times the entry matches a route) in the display

`clear ip prefix-list prefix-list-name [network/length]`
 	
`clear ipv6 prefix-list prefix-list-name [network/length]`
	Resets the hit count shown on prefix list entries

Using Route Maps with Route Redistribution

`Router(config)# route-map MY_MAP permit 10`	Creates a route map called *MY_MAP*. This **route-map** statement will be used to permit redistribution based on subsequent criteria. A sequence number of 10 is assigned
`Router(config-route-map)# match ip address 5`	Specifies the match criteria (the conditions that should be tested); in this case, match addresses filtered using a standard access list number 5
`Router(config-route-map)# set metric 500`	Specifies the set action (what action is to be performed if the match criteria is met); in this case, set the external metric to 500 (instead of the default value of 20 for OSPF)
`Router(config-route-map)# set metric-type type-1`	Specifies a second set action for the same match criteria. In this case, set the external OSPF network type to E1
`Router(config-route-map)# route-map MY_MAP deny 20`	Adds a second statement to the *MY_MAP* route map that will deny redistribution based on subsequent criteria
`Router(config-route-map)# match ip address prefix-list MY_PFL`	Specifies the match criteria (the conditions that should be tested); in this case, match addresses filtered using a prefix list named *MY_PFL*
`Router(config-route-map)# route-map MY_MAP permit 30`	Adds a third statement to the *MY_MAP* route map that will permit redistribution based on subsequent criteria **NOTE:** When no "match" criteria are explicitly specified, all other routes will be redistributed with the following "set" criteria applied

`Router(config-route-map)# set` `metric 5000`	Specifies the set action (what action is to be performed if the match criteria is met); in this case, since no match criteria is defined, it sets the external metric to 5000 (instead of the default value of 20) for all other routes
`Router(config-route-map)# set` `metric-type type-2`	Specifies a second set action for the same match criteria; in this case, set the external OSPF network type to E2. This is optional since the default type for redistributed routes into OSPF is external type 2
`Router(config-route-map)#` `router ospf 10`	Enters OSPF process ID 10 routing process

`Router(config-router)#`
`redistribute eigrp 1 route-map`
`MY_MAP subnets`
	Redistributes only EIGRP routes into OSPF that are permitted by route map *MY_MAP*

NOTE: When used to filter redistribution, route map **permit** or **deny** statements determine whether the route will be redistributed. Routes without a match will not be redistributed. Like an access list or prefix list, a route map stops processing at the first match and there is also an implicit deny statement at the end.

Configuration Example: Route Maps

Figure 6-8 shows the network topology for the configuration that follows, which demonstrates how to control redistribution with a route map using the commands covered in this chapter. Assume that all basic configurations and EIGRP and OSPF routing have been configured correctly.

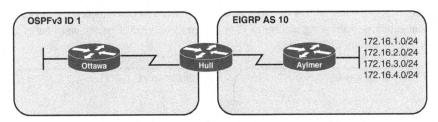

Figure 6-8   Network Topology for Route Map Configuration

The objective is to only redistribute networks 172.16.1.0/24 and 172.16.2.0/24 into OSPF and advertise them as external type 1 (E1) routes with an external metric of 50.

`Hull(config)# access-list 5` `permit 172.16.1.0 0.0.0.255`	Creates a standard ACL number 5 and explicitly permits the 172.16.1.0/24 network
`Hull(config)# access-list 5` `permit 172.16.2.0 0.0.0.255`	Adds a second line to ACL 5 that explicitly permits the 172.16.2.0/24 network
`Hull(config)# route-map FILTER` `permit 10`	Creates a route map called *FILTER*. This route map will permit traffic based on subsequent criteria. A sequence number of 10 is assigned

`Hull(config-route-map)# match ip address 5`	Specifies the match criteria; match addresses filtered from ACL 5
`Hull(config-route-map)# set metric 50` `Hull(config-route-map)# set metric-type type-1`	Specifies the set actions (what actions are to be performed if the match criterion is met); in this case, sets the external metric to 50 *and* sets the type to external type 1 (E1)
`Hull(config-route-map)# router ospf 1`	Enters OSPF process ID 1 routing process
`Hull(config)# redistribute eigrp 10 subnets route-map FILTER`	Redistributes only those EIGRP networks into OSPF that match the route map **NOTE:** Networks 172.16.2.0/24 and 172.16.3.0/24 will not be redistributed because of the implicit deny any at the end of the route map

Manipulating Redistribution Using Route Tagging

There are several ways redistribution can be enabled, including one-way one-point, two-way one-point, one-way multipoint, and two-way multipoint redistribution. Two-way multipoint redistribution can introduce routing loops in the network. One option to prevent redistribution of already redistributed routes is to use route tagging. In two-way multipoint redistribution scenarios, route tags must be applied and filtered in *both* directions and on *both* routers performing redistribution.

Figure 6-9 shows the network topology for the configuration that follows, which demonstrates how to control redistribution with route tags using the commands covered in this chapter. Assume that all basic configurations and EIGRP and OSPF routing have been configured correctly. A tag number of 11 is used to identify OSPF routes, and a tag of 22 is used to identify EIGRP routes.

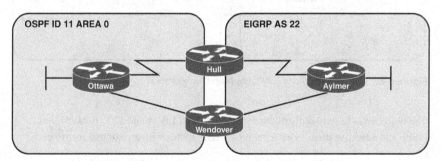

Figure 6-9 Network Topology for Redistribution Using Route Tagging

The following configuration only shows the commands entered on the Hull router. For filtering using route tags, the following configuration would need to be entered on *both* the Hull and Wendover routers.

`Hull(config)# route-map`
`EIGRPtoOSPF deny 10`
 	
`Hull(config-route-map)# match`
`tag 11`
	Creates a route map named *EIGRPtoOSPF* and denies redistribution for all routes tagged with the value 11

`Hull(config-route-map)# route-`
`map EIGRPtoOSPF permit 20`
 	
`Hull(config-route-map)# set tag`
`22`
	Creates a second statement for route map *EIGRPtoOSPF* permitting all other routes to be redistributed with a tag of 22

`Hull(config-route-map)# route-`
`map OSPFtoEIGRP deny 10`
 	
`Hull(config-route-map)# match`
`tag 22`
	Creates a route map named *OSPFtoEIGRP* and denies redistribution for all routes tagged with the value 22

`Hull(config-route-map)# route-`
`map OSPFtoEIGRP permit 20`
 	
`Hull(config-route-map)# set tag`
`11`
	Creates a second statement for route map *OSPFtoEIGRP* permitting all other routes to be redistributed with a tag of 11

`Hull(config-route-map)# router` `ospf 11`	Enters OSPF configuration mode

`Hull(config-router)#`
`redistribute eigrp 22 subnets`
`route-map EIGRPtoOSPF`
	Redistributes all EIGRP routes with a tag of 22 into the OSPF domain

`Hull(config-router)# router` `eigrp 22`	Enters EIGRP configuration mode

`Hull(config-router)#`
`redistribute ospf 11 metric`
`1500 1 255 1 1500 route-map`
`OSPFtoEIGRP`
	Redistributes all OSPF routes with a tag of 11 into the EIGRP domain
	
	NOTE: The result here is to ensure that only routes originating in the OSPF domain are redistributed into EIGRP, while only routes originating in the EIGRP domain are redistributed into the OSPF domain. This avoids a scenario where a route is redistributed back into the domain from which it originated

Changing Administrative Distance

The commands to change the administrative distance (AD) for internal and external routes are as follows.

`Router(config)# router ospf 1`	Starts the OSPF routing process

`Router(config-router)# distance`
`ospf intra-area 105 inter-area`
`105 external 125`
	Changes the AD to 105 for intra-area and interarea routes, and changes the AD to 125 for external routes

`Router(config)# router eigrp 100`	Starts the EIGRP routing process

Router(config-router)# **distance eigrp 80 105**	Changes the AD to 80 for internal EIGRP routes and to 105 for EIGRP external routes
Router(config)# **router bgp 65001**	Starts the BGP routing process
Router(config-router)# **distance bgp 30 200 220**	Changes the AD to 30 for external BGP routes, 200 for internal BGP routes, and 220 for local BGP routes

It is also possible to change the AD for certain routes learned from specific neighbors. These commands can be used for all routing protocols.

Router(config-router)# **distance 50**	Sets an AD of 50 for all routes learned through a specific routing protocol
Router(config-router)# **distance 255**	Sets an AD of 255 for all routes learned through a specific routing protocol. This instructs the router to ignore all routing updates from networking devices for which an explicit distance has not been set
Router(config-router)# **distance 85 192.168.40.0 0.0.0.255**	Sets the AD to 85 for all routes learned from neighbors on network 192.168.40.0/24
Router(config-router)# **distance 125 172.16.200.5 0.0.0.0 10**	Sets the AD to 125 for all routes specifically from neighbor 172.16.200.5/32 that match ACL 10

Path Control with Policy-Based Routing

Path control is the mechanism that changes default packet forwarding across a network. It is not quality of service (QoS) or MPLS Traffic Engineering (MPLS-TE). Path control is a collection of tools or a set of commands that gives you more control over routing by extending and complementing the existing mechanisms provided by routing protocols. Bypassing the default packet forwarding decision may be required to obtain better resiliency, performance, or availability in your network.

Configuring Policy Based Routing (PBR) is a two-step process. First, a route map is created that specifies the new forwarding decision to be implemented. Second, the route map is applied to an incoming interface.

Router(config)# **route-map ISP1 permit 10**	Creates a route map named *ISP1*. This route map will permit traffic based on subsequent criteria. A sequence number of 10 is assigned
	NOTE: In route maps, the default action is to permit
	NOTE: The *sequence-number* is used to indicate the position the route map statement is to have within the route map. A route map is composed of route map statements with the same route map name. If no sequence number is given, the first statement in the route map is automatically numbered as 10

`Router(config-route-map)# match ip address 1`	Specifies the match criteria (the conditions that should be tested); in this case, match addresses using ACL 1
`Router(config-route-map)# set ip next-hop 209.165.201.1`	Specifies the set action (what action is to be performed if the match criteria are met); in this case, output packets to the router at IP address 209.165.201.1
`Router(config-route-map)# set interface serial 0/2/0`	Specifies the set action (what action is to be performed if the match criteria are met); in this case, forward packets out interface Serial 0/2/0 **NOTE:** If no explicit route exists in the routing table for the destination network address of the packet (that is, the packet is a broadcast packet or destined to an unknown address), the **set interface** command has no effect and is ignored **NOTE:** A default route in the routing table will not be considered an explicit route for an unknown destination address
`Router(config-route-map)# set ip default next-hop 209.165.201.1`	Defines where to output packets that pass a match clause of a route map for policy routing and for which the router has no explicit route to the destination address
`Router(config-route-map)# set default interface serial 0/2/0`	Defines where to output packets that pass a match clause of a route map for policy routing and for which the router has no explicit route to the destination address **NOTE:** This is recommended for point-to-point links only
`Router(config-route-map)# exit`	Returns to global configuration mode
`Router(config)# interface gigabitethernet 0/0/0`	Moves to interface configuration mode
`Router(config-if)# ip policy route-map ISP1`	Specifies a route map to use for policy routing on an incoming interface that is receiving the packets that need to be policy routed
`Router(config-if)# exit`	Returns to global configuration mode
`Router(config)# ip local policy route-map ISP1`	Specifies a route map to use for policy routing on all packets originating on the router

TIP: Packets that are generated by the router are not normally policy routed. Using the **ip local policy route-map** [*map-name*] command will make these packets adhere to a policy. For example, you may want packets originating from the router to take a route other than the best path according to the routing table.

Verifying Policy-Based Routing

`Router# show ip policy`	Displays route maps that are configured on the interfaces
`Router# show route-map [map-name]`	Displays route maps

Router# **debug ip policy**	Enables the display of IP policy routing events
Router# **traceroute**	Enables the extended **traceroute** command, which allows the specification of the source address
Router# **ping**	Enables the extended **ping** command, which allows for the specification of the source address

Configuration Example: PBR with Route Maps

Figure 6-10 shows the network topology for the configuration that follows, which demonstrates how to configure PBR with route maps using the commands covered in this chapter.

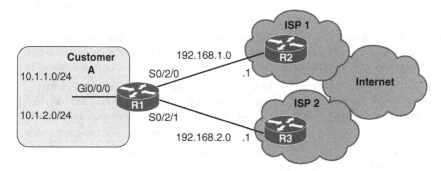

Figure 6-10   Network Topology for PBR with Route Maps

The objective is to forward Internet traffic sourced from the 10.1.1.0/24 network to ISP 1 and traffic sourced from the 10.1.2.0/24 network to ISP 2. Assume that all basic configurations and routing have been configured.

R1(config)# **access-list 11 permit 10.1.1.0 0.0.0.255**	Creates a standard access list that matches traffic originating from network 10.1.1.0/24. The number 11 is used for this ACL
R1(config)# **access-list 12 permit 10.1.2.0 0.0.0.255**	Creates a standard access list that matches traffic originating from network 10.1.2.0/24. The number 12 is used for this ACL
R1(config)# **route-map PBR permit 10**	Creates a route map named *PBR*. This route map will permit traffic based on subsequent criteria. A sequence number of 10 is assigned
R1(config-route-map)# **match ip address 11**	Specifies the match criteria—match addresses permitted by ACL 11

R1(config-route-map)# **set ip next-hop 192.168.1.1**	Specifies the set action (what action is to be performed if the match criteria are met); in this case, forward packets to the router at 192.168.1.1 (ISP1)
R1(config-route-map)# **route-map PBR permit 20**	Adds a second statement to the PBR route map. A sequence number of 20 is assigned
R1(config-route-map)# **match ip address 12**	Specifies the match criteria; match addresses permitted by ACL 12
R1(config-route-map)# **set ip next-hop 192.168.2.1**	Specifies the set action (what action is to be performed if the match criteria are met); in this case, forward packets to the router at 192.168.2.1 (ISP 2)
R1(config-route-map)# **route-map PBR permit 30**	Adds a third statement to the PBR route map. A sequence number of 30 is assigned
R1(config-route-map)# **set default interface null0**	Specifies that all other traffic not matching ACL 11 or ACL 12 will be sent to the Null0 interface (traffic is dropped)
R1(config-route-map)# **exit**	Exits the route map configuration mode
R1(config)# **interface gigabitethernet 0/0/0**	Enters GigabitEthernet 0/0/0 interface configuration mode
R1(config-if)# **ip policy route-map PBR**	Applies the PBR route map to the interface. This is the incoming interface receiving the packets to be policy-routed

Cisco IOS IP SLA

Cisco IOS IP service level agreements (SLAs) send data across the network to measure performance between multiple network locations or network paths. They simulate network data and IP services and collect network performance information in real time. IP SLAs can also send SNMP traps that are triggered by events such as these:

- Connection loss
- Timeout
- Round-trip time threshold
- Average jitter threshold
- One-way packet loss
- One-way jitter
- One-way mean opinion score (MOS)
- One-way latency

Cisco IOS IP SLAs can also test the following services:

- DNS
- HTTP
- DHCP
- FTP

NOTE: Cisco IOS IP SLAs are used to perform network performance measurements within Cisco Systems devices using active traffic monitoring.

TIP: SLAs use time-stamp information to calculate performance metrics such as jitter, latency, network and server response times, packet loss, and mean opinion score.

Figure 6-11 is the network topology for the IP SLA commands.

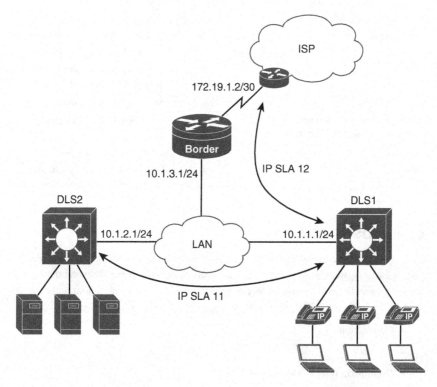

Figure 6-11   IP SLA Network Topology

DLS1# `configure terminal`	Enters global configuration mode
DLS1(config)# `ip sla 11`	Creates an IP SLA operation and enters IP SLA configuration mode
DLS1(config-ip-sla)# `icmp-echo` `10.1.2.1 source-ip 10.1.1.1`	Configures the IP SLA as an ICMP echo operation and enters ICMP echo configuration mode **NOTE:** The ICMP echo operation does not require the IP SLA responder to be enabled

`DLS1(config-ip-sla-echo)#` `frequency 5`	Sets the rate at which the IP SLA operation repeats. Frequency is measured in seconds. The default value is 60 seconds
`DLS1(config-ip-sla-echo)# exit`	Exits IP SLA configuration mode
`DLS1(config)# ip sla schedule` `11 start-time now life forever`	Configures the IP SLA operation scheduling parameters to start now and continue forever **NOTE:** The start time for the SLA can be set to a particular time and day, to be recurring, to be activated after a threshold is passed, and kept as an active process for a configurable number of seconds
`DLS2(config)# ip sla responder`	Enables IP SLA responder functionality in response to control messages from the source. This command is entered on the target device
`DLS1(config)# ip sla 12`	Creates an IP SLA operation and enters IP SLA configuration mode

`DLS1(config-ip-sla)# path-`
`jitter 172.19.1.2 source-ip`
`10.1.1.1 [targetOnly]`
	Configures the IP SLA as an ICMP path-jitter operation and enters path-jitter configuration mode. ICMP path jitter provides hop-by-hop jitter, packet loss, and delay measurement statistics in an IP network. Adding the **targetOnly** keyword bypasses the hop-by-hop measurements and echo probes are sent to the destination only
	
	NOTE: The ICMP path-jitter SLA sends 10 packets per operation with a 20-ms time interval between them by default. These values are configurable

`DLS1(config-ip-sla-path-` `jitter)# frequency 5`	Sets the rate at which the IP SLA operation repeats. The default value is 60 seconds
`DLS1(config-ip-sla-path-` `jitter)# exit`	Exits path-jitter configuration mode

`DLS1(config)# ip sla schedule`
`12 recurring start-time 07:00`
`life 3600`
	Configures the IP SLA operation scheduling parameters to start at 7 a.m. and continue for 1 hour every day. 3600 seconds is the default life time for an IP SLA. The switch will require accurate time and date to implement the SLA schedule

TIP: When using **udp-echo**, **udp-jitter**, or **tcp-connect** IP SLA operations, you must configure the target device as an IP SLA responder with either the **udp-echo** or **tcp-connect** commands.

Configuring Authentication for IP SLA

`Router(config)# key chain Juliet`	Identifies a key chain
`Router(config-keychain)# key 1`	Identifies the key number
`Router(config-keychain)#` `key-string Shakespeare`	Identifies the key string

`Router(config-keychain)# exit`	Returns to global configuration mode
`Router(config)# ip sla key-chain Juliet`	Applies the key chain to the IP SLA process **NOTE:** This must also be done on the responder

Monitoring IP SLA Operations

`Router# show ip sla application`	Displays global information about Cisco IOS IP SLAs **NOTE:** The **show ip sla application** command displays supported SLA operation types and supported SLA protocols
`Router# show ip sla configuration 11`	Displays configuration values including all defaults for SLA 11 **NOTE:** The use of a number in this command is optional
`Router# show ip sla statistics`	Displays current or aggregated operational status and statistics

PBR with Cisco IOS IP SLA

Figure 6-12 shows the network topology for the configuration that follows, which shows the use of PBR with Cisco IOS IP SLA functionality for path control. Assume that all basic configurations have been configured.

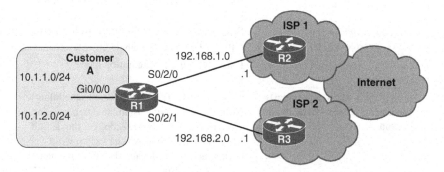

Figure 6-12   Network Topology for PBR with IOS IP SLA

Customer requirements:

- Customer A is multihoming to ISP 1 and ISP 2.

- The link to ISP 1 is the primary link for all traffic.

- Customer A is using default routes to the Internet service providers (ISPs).

- Customer A is using these default routes with different administrative distances to make ISP 1 the preferred route.

Potential problem: If ISP 1 is having uplink connectivity problems to the Internet, Customer A will still be sending all its traffic to ISP 1, only to have that traffic get dropped by the ISP.

Possible solutions: (1) IOS IP SLA can be used to conditionally announce the default route, *or* (2) the IP SLA can be used to verify availability for PBR.

Follow these steps to configure Cisco IOS IP SLA functionality:

   1. Define probe(s).

   2. Define tracking object(s).

  3a. Define the action on the tracking object(s).

      or

  3b. Define policy routing using the tracking object(s).

   4. Verify IP SLA operations.

NOTE: Only the configuration on R1 for neighbor ISP 1 is shown. Typically, in a multi-homing scenario, R1 would be configured with two SLAs, two tracking objects, and two default routes (one for each ISP) with different AD values.

Step 1: Define Probe(s)

`R1(config)# ip sla 1`	Begins configuration for an IP SLA operation and enters SLA configuration mode. 1 is the operation number and can be a number between 1 and 2 147 483 647
`R1(config-ip-sla)# icmp-echo 192.168.1.1 source-interface gigabitethernet 0/0/0`	Defines an ICMP echo operation to destination address 192.168.1.1 using a source interface of GigabitEthernet 0/0/0 and enters ICMP echo configuration mode **TIP:** Typically, the address tested is farther within the ISP network instead of the next hop
`R1(config-ip-sla-echo)# frequency 10`	Sets the rate at which the operation repeats. Measured in seconds from 1 to 604 800 (7 days)
`R1(config-ip-sla-echo)# timeout 5000`	Length of time the operation waits to receive a response from its request packet, in milliseconds. Range is 0 to 604 800 000 **TIP:** It is recommended that the timeout value be based on the sum of both the maximum round-trip time (RTT) value for the packets and the processing time of the IP SLAs operation
`R1(config-ip-sla-echo)# exit`	Exits IP SLA ICMP echo configuration mode and returns to global configuration mode
`R1(config)# ip sla schedule 1 start-time now life forever`	Sets a schedule for IP SLA monitor 1. Packets will be sent out immediately and will continue forever

Step 2: Define Tracking Object(s)

R1(config)# **track 11 ip sla 1 reachability**	Configures a tracking object to track the reachability of IP SLA 1
R1(config-track)# **exit**	Returns to global configuration mode

Step 3a: Define the Action on the Tracking Object(s)

R1(config)# **ip route 0.0.0.0 0.0.0.0 192.168.1.1 2 track 11**	Adds a default route with a next hop of 192.168.1.1 with an AD of 2 to the routing table if tracking object 11 is up

OR

Step 3b: Define Policy Routing Using the Tracking Object(s)

R1(config)# **route-map IPSLA permit 10**	Creates a route map that will use the tracking object. No match criteria is specified so all traffic will be policy routed
R1(config-route-map)# **set ip next-hop verify-availability 192.168.1.1 10 track 11**	Configures policy routing to verify the reachability of the next hop 192.168.1.1 before the router performs policy routing to that next hop. A sequence number of 10 is used and tracking object 11 is referenced
	NOTE: The sequence number is used when tracking the availability of multiple addresses. Each address tracked would get its own sequence number (for example, 10, 20, 30). If the first tracking objects fails, the next one in the sequence is used. If all tracking objects fail, the policy routing fails, and the packets are routed according to the routing table
R1(config-route-map)# **interface gigabitethernet 0/0/0**	Enters interface configuration mode
R1(config-if)# **ip policy route-map IPSLA**	Applies the IPSLA route map to the interface. This is the incoming interface receiving the packets to be policy routed

Step 4: Verify IP SLA Operations

R1# **show ip sla configuration**	Displays configuration values including all defaults for all SLAs
R1# **show ip sla statistics**	Displays the current operational status and statistics of all SLAs
R1# **show track**	Displays information about objects that are tracked by the tracking process

NOTE: Effective with Cisco IOS Releases 12.4(4)T, 12.2(33)SB, and 12.2(33)SXI, the **ip sla monitor** command is replaced by the **ip sla** command.

NOTE: Effective with Cisco IOS Releases 12.4(4)T, 12.2(33)SB, and 12.2(33)SXI, the **type echo protocol ipIcmpEcho** command is replaced by the **icmp-echo** command.

NOTE: Effective with Cisco IOS Releases 12.4(20)T, 12.2(33)SXI1, and 12.2(33)SRE and Cisco IOS XE Release 2.4, the **track rtr** command is replaced by the **track ip sla** command.

NOTE: Effective with Cisco IOS Releases 12.4(20)T, 12.2(33)SXI1, and 12.2(33)SRE and Cisco IOS XE Release 2.4, the **show ip sla monitor configuration** command is replaced by the **show ip sla configuration** command.

NOTE: Effective with Cisco IOS Releases 12.4(20)T, 12.2(33)SXI1, and 12.2(33) SRE and Cisco IOS XE Release 2.4, the **show ip sla monitor statistics** command is replaced by the **show ip sla statistics** command.

This chapter provides information about the following topics:

- Configuring BGP: classic configuration
- Configuring Multiprotocol BGP (MP-BGP)
- Configuring BGP: address families
- Configuration example: using MP-BGP address families to exchange IPv4 and IPv6 routes
- BGP support for 4-byte AS numbers
- BGP timers
- BGP and **update-source**
- IBGP next-hop behavior
- EBGP multihop
- Attributes
    - Route selection decision process—the BGP best path algorithm
    - Weight attribute
    - Using AS path access lists to manipulate the weight attribute
    - Using prefix lists and route maps to manipulate the weight attribute
    - Local preference attribute
    - Using AS path access lists and route maps to manipulate the local preference attribute
    - AS Path attribute prepending
    - AS Path: removing private autonomous systems
    - Multi-exit Discriminator (MED) attribute
- Verifying BGP
- Troubleshooting BGP
- Default routes
- Route aggregation
- Route reflectors
- Regular expressions
- Regular expressions: examples
- BGP route filtering using access lists and distribute lists

- Configuration example: using prefix lists and AS path access lists

- BGP peer groups

- Authentication for BGP

  - Configuring authentication between BGP peers

  - Verifying BGP authentication

Configuring BGP: Classic Configuration

`Router(config)# router` `bgp 100`	Starts BGP routing process 100 **NOTE:** Cisco IOS Software permits only one Border Gateway Protocol (BGP) process to run at a time; therefore, a router cannot belong to more than one autonomous system (AS)

`Router(config-router)#`
`neighbor 192.31.7.1`
`remote-as 200`
	Identifies a peer router with which this router will establish a BGP session. The AS number will determine whether the neighbor router is an external BGP (EBGP) or internal BGP (IBGP) neighbor
	
	TIP: If the AS number configured in the **router bgp** command is identical to the AS number configured in the **neighbor** statement, BGP initiates an internal session (IBGP). If the field values differ, BGP builds an external session (EBGP)
	
	TIP: **neighbor** statements must be symmetrical for a neighbor relationship to be established

`Router(config-router)#` `network 192.135.250.0`	Tells the BGP process what locally learned networks to advertise **NOTE:** The networks can be connected routes, static routes, or routes learned via a dynamic routing protocol, such as Open Shortest Path First (OSPF) **NOTE:** Configuring just a **network** statement will not establish a BGP neighbor relationship **NOTE:** The networks must also exist in the local router's routing table; otherwise, they will not be sent out in updates

`Router(config-router)#`
`network 128.107.0.0 mask`
`255.255.255.0`
	Used to specify an individual subnet that must be present in the routing table or it will not be advertised by BGP

TIP: Routes learned by the BGP process are propagated by default but are often filtered by a routing policy.

CAUTION: If you misconfigure a **network** command, such as the example **network 192.168.1.1 mask 255.255.255.0**, BGP will look for exactly 192.168.1.1/24 in the routing table. It may find 192.168.1.0/24 or 192.168.1.1/32; however, it may never find 192.168.1.1/24. Because there is no exact match for the 192.168.1.1/24 network, BGP does not announce it to any neighbors.

TIP: If you issue the command **network 192.168.0.0 mask 255.255.0.0** to advertise a CIDR block, BGP will look for 192.168.0.0/16 in the routing table. It may find 192.168.1.0/24 or 192.168.1.1/32; however, it may never find 192.168.0.0/16. Because there is no exact match for the 192.168.0.0/16 network, BGP does not announce it to any neighbors. In this case, you can configure a static route towards the Null interface so BGP can find an exact match in the routing table:

```
ip route 192.168.0.0 255.255.0.0 null0
```

After finding this exact match in the routing table, BGP will announce the 192.168.0.0/16 network to any neighbors.

Configuring Multiprotocol BGP (MP-BGP)

Original BGP was designed to carry only IPv4-specific information. A recent extension was defined to also support other protocols like IPv6. This extension is called MP-BGP (Multiprotocol BGP). MP-BGP is the supported Exterior Gateway Protocol (EGP) for IPv6. IPv6 enhancements to MP-BGP include support for IPv6 address family configuration. You can run MP-BGP over IPv4 or IPv6 transport and can exchange routes for IPv4, IPv6, or both. BGP uses TCP for peering, and this has no relevance to the routes carried inside the BGP exchanges. Both IPv4 and IPv6 can be used to transport a TCP connection on the network layer.

R1(config)# **ipv6 unicast-routing**	Enables the forwarding of IPV6 unicast datagrams globally on the router
R1(config)# **router bgp 65500**	Starts the BGP routing process
R1(config-router)# **bgp router-id 192.168.99.70**	Configures a fixed 32-bit router ID as the identifier of the local device running BGP **NOTE:** Configuring a router ID using the **bgp router-id** command resets all active BGP peering sessions, if any are already established
R1(config-router)# **no bgp default ipv4-unicast**	Disables the IPv4 unicast address family for the current BGP routing process **NOTE:** Routing information for the IPv4 unicast address family is advertised by default for each BGP routing session configured with the **neighbor remote-as** command unless you configure the **no bgp default ipv4-unicast** command before configuring the **neighbor remote-as** command. This command is optional and only required if the router is only routing for IPv6
R1(config-router)# **neighbor 2001:0db8:12::2 remote-as 65501**	Configures an IPv6 BGP neighbor

NOTE: When configuring BGP on a device that is enabled only for IPv6 (that is, the device does not have an IPv4 address), you must manually configure the BGP router ID for the device. The BGP router ID, which is represented as a 32-bit value using an IPv4 address syntax, must be unique to the BGP peers of the device.

Configuring BGP: Address Families

`Router(config)# router bgp 100`	Starts BGP routing process 100
`Router(config)# neighbor 10.0.0.44 remote-as 200`	Adds the IPv4 address of the neighbor in the specified AS to the IPv4 multiprotocol BGP neighbor table of the local device
`Router(config)# neighbor 2001:db8:0:cc00::1 remote-as 200`	Adds the IPv6 address of the neighbor in the specified AS to the IPv6 multiprotocol BGP neighbor table of the local device
`Router(config-router)# address-family ipv4`	Enters into address-family configuration mode for IPv4. By default, the device is placed in configuration mode for the IPv4 unicast address family if a keyword is not specified
`Router(config-router)# address-family ipv4 multicast`	Enters into address-family configuration mode and specifies only multicast address prefixes for the IPv4 address family
`Router(config-router)# address-family ipv4 unicast`	Enters into address-family configuration mode and specifies only unicast address prefixes for the IPv4 address family
`Router(config-router)# address-family ipv4 vrf CustomerA`	Enters into address-family configuration mode and specifies CustomerA as the name of the VRF instance to associate with subsequent IPv4 address-family configuration mode commands **NOTE:** Use this form of the command, which specifies a VRF, only to configure routing exchanges between provider edge (PE) and customer edge (CE) devices
`Router(config-router-af)# neighbor 10.0.0.44 activate`	Enables the exchange of information with a BGP neighbor
`Router(config-router-af)# no neighbor 2001:db8:1:1::1 activate`	Disables the exchange of information with the specified IPv6 neighbor
`Router(config-router-af)# network 10.108.0.0 mask 255.255.0.0`	Specifies the network to be advertised by the BGP routing process
`Router(config-router-af)# exit`	Exits the IPv4 unicast address family
`Router(config-router)# address-family ipv6`	Enters into address-family configuration mode for IPv6 **NOTE:** By default, the device is placed into configuration mode for the IPv6 unicast address family. The keyword **multicast** is also a valid entry here, just like in IPv4
`Router(config-router-af)# neighbor 2001:db8:0:cc00::1 activate`	Enables the neighbor to exchange prefixes for the IPv6 address family with the local device

| Router(config-router-af)#
network 2001:db8:1:1::/64 | Specifies the network to be advertised by the BGP routing process |

Configuration Example: Using MP-BGP Address Families to Exchange IPv4 and IPv6 Routes

In this example, MP-BGP is used to exchange both IPv4 and IPv6 routes. The IPv4 routes will use an IPv4 TCP connection, and the IPv6 routes will use an IPv6 TCP connection.

Figure 7-1 shows the network topology for the configuration that follows, which demonstrates how to configure MP-BGP using address families to exchange both IPv4 and IPv6 routes. Assume that all basic configurations are accurate.

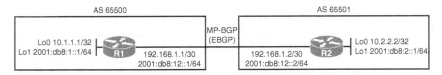

Figure 7-1   Configuring MP-BGP Using Address Families to Exchange IPv4 and IPv6 Routes

R1(config)# **ipv6 unicast-routing**	Enables the forwarding of IPv6 unicast datagrams globally on the router
R1(config)# **router bgp 65500**	Starts the BGP routing process
R1(config-router)# **neighbor 2001:db8:12::2 remote-as 65501**	Configures R2 as an IPv6 BGP neighbor
R1(config-router)# **neighbor 192.168.1.2 remote-as 65501**	Configures R2 as an IPv4 BGP neighbor
R1(config-router)# **address-family ipv4 unicast**	Enters IPv4 address-family configuration mode for unicast address prefixes **TIP:** Unicast address prefixes are the default when IPv4 address prefixes are configured
R1(config-router-af)# **neighbor 192.168.1.2 activate**	Enables the exchange of IPv4 BGP information with R2. The IPv4 neighbors will be automatically activated, so this command is optional
R1(config-router-af)# **network 10.1.1.1 mask 255.255.255.255**	Advertises an IPv4 network into BGP
R1(config-router-af)# **exit**	Exits the IPv4 address-family configuration mode
R1(config-router)# **address-family ipv6 unicast**	Enters IPv6 address-family configuration mode for unicast address prefixes **TIP:** Unicast address prefixes are the default when IPv6 address prefixes are configured

R1(config-router-af)# **neighbor** **2001:db8:12::2 activate**	Enables the exchange of IPv6 BGP information with R2
R1(config-router-af)# **network** **2001:db8:1::1/64**	Advertises an IPv6 network into BGP
R2(config)# **ipv6 unicast-routing**	Enables the forwarding of IPv6 unicast datagrams globally on the router
R2(config)# **router bgp 65501**	Starts the BGP routing process
R2(config-router)# **neighbor** **2001:db8:12::1 remote-as 65500**	Configures R1 as an IPv6 BGP neighbor
R2(config-router)# **neighbor** **192.168.1.1 remote-as 65500**	Configures R1 as an IPv4 BGP neighbor
R2(config-router)# **address-family** **ipv4 unicast**	Enters IPv4 address-family configuration mode for unicast address prefixes
R2(config-router-af)# **neighbor** **192.168.1.1 activate**	Enables the exchange of IPv4 BGP information with R1. The IPv4 neighbors will be automatically activated, so this command is optional
R2(config-router-af)# **network** **10.2.2.2 mask 255.255.255.255**	Advertises an IPv4 network into BGP
R2(config-router-af)# **exit**	Exits the IPv4 address-family configuration mode
R2(config-router)# **address-family** **ipv6 unicast**	Enters IPv6 address-family configuration mode for unicast address prefixes
R2(config-router-af)# **neighbor** **2001:db8:12::1 activate**	Enables the exchange of IPv6 BGP information with R1
R2(config-router-af)# **network** **2001:db8:2::1/64**	Advertises an IPv6 network into BGP

BGP Support for 4-Byte AS Numbers

Prior to January 2009, BGP autonomous system (AS) numbers that were allocated to companies were two-octet numbers in the range from 1 to 65 535 as described in RFC 4271. Due to increased demand for AS numbers, the Internet Assigned Number Authority (IANA) started to allocate four-octet AS numbers in the range from 65 536 to 4 294 967 295.

Cisco has implemented the following two methods:

- **Asplain:** Decimal value notation where both 2-byte and 4-byte AS numbers are represented by their decimal value. For example, 65 526 is a 2-byte AS number and 234 567 is a 4-byte AS number.

- **Asdot:** Autonomous system dot notation where 2-byte AS numbers are represented by their decimal value and 4-byte AS numbers are represented by a dot notation. For example, 65 526 is a 2-byte AS number and 1.169031 is a 4-byte AS number (this is dot notation for the 234 567 decimal number).

Cisco implementation of 4-byte autonomous system (AS) numbers uses asplain—65 538, for example—as the default regular expression match and output display format for AS numbers, but you can configure 4-byte AS numbers in both the asplain format and the asdot format as described in RFC 5396.

Router(config-router)# **bgp asnotation dot**	Changes the default output format of BGP 4-byte AS numbers from asplain (decimal values) to dot notation. Use the **no** keyword with this command to revert to the asplain format
	NOTE: 4-byte AS numbers can be configured using either asplain format or asdot format. This command affects only the output displayed for show commands or the matching of regular expressions
Router# **clear ip bgp ***	Clears and resets all current BGP sessions
	A hard reset is performed to ensure that the 4-byte AS number format change is reflected in all BGP sessions

BGP Timers

| Router(config-router)#
timers bgp 70 120 | Sets BGP network timers. BGP keepalives will be sent every 70 seconds and the holdtime for declaring a BGP peer as dead is set to 120 seconds |
| | **NOTE:** By default, the keepalive timer is set to 60 seconds and the holdtime timer is set to 180 seconds |

BGP and update-source

Router(config)# **router bgp 100**	Starts the BGP routing process
Router(config-router)# **neighbor 172.16.1.2 update-source loopback 0**	The **update-source** keyword informs the router to use any operational interface as the source IP address for TCP connections. The loopback interface is commonly selected because it never goes down, which adds stability to the configuration
	TIP: Without the **neighbor update-source** command, BGP will use the closest IP interface to the peer. This command provides BGP with a more robust configuration, because BGP will still operate in the event the link to the closest interface fails
	NOTE: You can use the **neighbor update-source** command with either EBGP or IBGP sessions. In the case of a point-to-point EBGP session, this command is not needed because there is only one path for BGP to use

IBGP Next-Hop Behavior

The EBGP next-hop attribute is the IP address that is used to reach the advertising router. For EBGP peers, the next-hop address is, in most cases, the IP address of the connection between the peers. For IBGP, the EBGP next-hop address is carried into the local AS.

Figure 7-2 shows the network topology for the configuration that follows, which demonstrates how to configure the next-hop attribute. The objective here is to allow R3 to learn the correct next-hop address when trying to reach networks outside its AS. Assume that all basic and OSPF configurations are accurate.

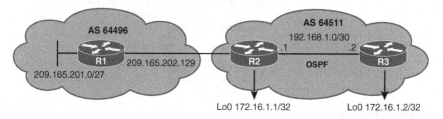

Figure 7-2   IBGP Next-Hop Behavior

`R2(config)# router bgp 64511`	Starts the BGP routing process
`R2(config-router)# neighbor 209.165.202.129 remote-as 64496`	Identifies R1 as an EBGP neighbor
`R2(config-router)# neighbor 172.16.1.2 remote-as 64511`	Identifies R3 as an IBGP neighbor
`R2(config-router)# neighbor 172.16.1.2 update-source loopback 0`	Informs R2 to use the Loopback 0 IP address (172.16.1.1) as the source IP address for all BGP TCP packets sent to R3
`R2(config-router)# neighbor 172.16.1.2 next-hop-self`	Allows R2 to advertise itself as the next hop to its IBGP neighbor for networks learned from AS 64496. R3 will then use 172.16.1.1 as the next hop to reach network 209.165.201.0/27 instead of using the EBGP next hop of 209.165.202.129

EBGP Multihop

By default, EBGP neighbors exchange packets with a TTL (Time To Live) set to 1. If you attempt to establish an EBGP session between loopbacks, BGP packets will be dropped due to an expired TTL.

Figure 7-3 shows the network topology for the configuration that follows, which demonstrates how to configure EBGP multihop. Assume that all basic configurations are accurate.

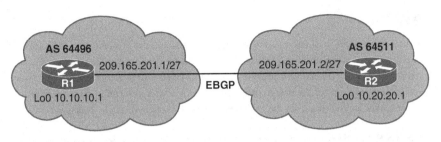

Figure 7-3 EBGP Multihop

R1(config)# **ip route** 10.20.20.1 255.255.255.255 209.165.201.2	Defines a static route to the Loopback 0 address on R2
R1(config)# **router bgp 64496**	Starts the BGP routing process
R1(config-router)# **neighbor** 10.20.20.1 **remote-as 64511**	Identifies a peer router at 10.20.20.1
R1(config-router)# **neighbor** 10.20.20.1 **update-source loopback 0**	Informs R1 to use the Loopback 0 IP address as the source IP address for all BGP TCP packets sent to R2
R1(config-router)# **neighbor** 10.20.20.1 **ebgp-multihop 2**	Allows for two routers that are not directly connected to establish an EBGP session. A TTL value of 2 is defined
R2(config)# **ip route** 10.10.10.1 255.255.255.255 209.165.201.1	Defines a static route to the Loopback 0 address on R1
R2(config)# **router bgp 64511**	Starts the BGP routing process
R2(config-router)# **neighbor** 10.10.10.1 **remote-as 64496**	Identifies a peer router at 10.10.10.1
R2(config-router)# **neighbor** 10.10.10.1 **update-source loopback 0**	Informs R2 to use the Loopback 0 IP address as the source IP address for all BGP TCP packets sent to R1
R2(config-router)# **neighbor** 10.10.10.1 **ebgp-multihop 2**	Allows for two routers that are not directly connected to establish an EBGP session. A TTL value of 2 is defined

NOTE: The **ebgp-multihop** keyword is a Cisco IOS option. It must be configured on each peer. The **ebgp-multihop** keyword is only used for EBGP sessions, not for IBGP. EBGP neighbors are usually directly connected (over a WAN connection, for example) to establish an EBGP session. However, sometimes one of the directly connected routers is unable to run BGP. The **ebgp-multihop** keyword allows for a logical connection to be made between peer routers, even if they are not directly connected. The **ebgp-multihop** keyword allows for an EBGP peer to be up to 255 hops away and still create an EBGP session.

NOTE: If redundant links exist between two EBGP neighbors and loopback addresses are used, you must configure **ebgp-multihop**. Otherwise, the router decrements the TTL before giving the packet to the loopback interface, meaning that the normal IP forwarding logic discards the packet.

Attributes

Routes learned via BGP have associated properties that are used to determine the best route to a destination when multiple paths exist to a particular destination. These properties are referred to as *BGP attributes*, and an understanding of how BGP attributes influence route selection is required for the design of robust networks. After describing the route selection process, this section describes the attributes that BGP uses in the route selection process.

Route Selection Decision Process—The BGP Best Path Algorithm

Border Gateway Protocol routers typically receive multiple paths to the same destination. The BGP best path algorithm decides which is the best path to install in the IP routing table and to use for traffic forwarding.

Initially, a path is *not considered if its next hop cannot be reached*. Afterward, the decision process for determining the best path to reach a destination is based on the following:

1. Prefer the path with the *highest weight* (local to the router).

2. If the weights are the same, prefer the path with the *highest local preference* (global within the AS).

3. If the local preferences are the same, prefer the path that was *originated by the local router* (next hop = 0.0.0.0).

4. If no route was originated, prefer the route that has the *shortest autonomous system path*.

5. If all paths have the same AS path length, prefer the path with the *lowest origin code* (where IGP is lower than EGP, and EGP is lower than Incomplete).

6. If the origin codes are the same, prefer the path with the *lowest Multi-exit Discriminator (MED) attribute*.

7. If the paths have the same MED, prefer the *external path* (EBGP) over the internal path (IBGP).

8. If the paths are still the same, prefer the path through the *lowest IGP metric* to the BGP next hop.

9. Determine if multiple paths require installation in the routing table for *BGP Multipath*.

10. For EBGP paths, select the *oldest route* to minimize the effects of route flapping.

11. Prefer the route with the *lowest neighbor BGP router ID value*.

12. If the originator or router ID is the same for multiple paths, prefer the path with the *minimum cluster list length*.

13. If the BGP router IDs are the same, prefer the router with the *lowest neighbor IP address*.

Weight Attribute

Weight is a Cisco-specific parameter. The weight is configured locally on a router and is not propagated to any other routers. This attribute applies when one router is used with multiple exit points out of an AS, as opposed to the local preference attribute, which is used when two or more routers provide multiple exit points.

Figure 7-4 shows the network topology for the configuration that follows, which demonstrates how to configure the weight attribute. Assume that all basic configurations are accurate.

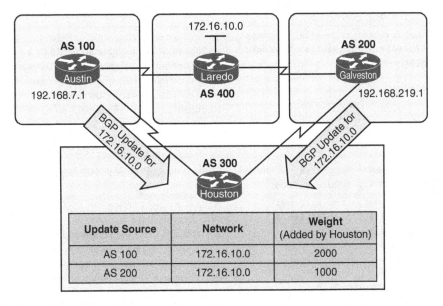

Figure 7-4   Weight Attribute

`Houston(config)# router bgp 300`	Starts the BGP routing process
`Houston(config-router)# neighbor 192.168.7.1 remote-as 100`	Identifies a peer router at 192.168.7.1
`Houston(config-router)# neighbor 192.168.7.1 weight 2000`	Sets the weight of all route updates from neighbor 192.168.7.1 to 2000
`Houston(config-router)# neighbor 192.168.219.1 remote-as 200`	Identifies a peer router at 192.168.219.1
`Houston(config-router)# neighbor 192.168.219.1 weight 1000`	Sets the weight of all route updates from neighbor 192.168.219.1 to 1000

The result of this configuration will have Houston forward traffic to the 172.16.10.0 network through AS 100, because the route entering AS 300 from AS 100 has a higher weight attribute set compared to that same route advertised from AS 200.

NOTE: The weight attribute is local to the router and not propagated to other routers. By default, the weight attribute is 32 768 for paths that the router originates, and 0 for other paths. Routes with a *higher weight are preferred* when there are multiple routes to the same destination.

Using AS Path Access Lists to Manipulate the Weight Attribute

Refer to Figure 7-4 for the configuration that follows, which demonstrates how to configure the weight attribute using AS path access lists.

`Houston(config)# router bgp 300`	Starts the BGP routing process
`Houston(config-router)# neighbor 192.168.7.1 remote-as 100`	Identifies a peer router at 192.168.7.1
`Houston(config-router)# neighbor 192.168.7.1 filter-list 5 weight 2000`	Assigns a weight attribute of 2000 to updates from the neighbor at 192.168.7.1 that are permitted by access list 5. Access list 5 is defined in the **ip as-path access-list 5** command listed below in global configuration mode. Filter list 5 refers to the **ip as-path access-list 5** command that defines which path will be used to have this weight value assigned to it
`Houston(config-router)# neighbor 192.168.219.1 remote-as 200`	Identifies a peer router at 192.168.219.1
`Houston(config-router)# neighbor 192.168.219.1 filter-list 6 weight 1000`	Assigns a weight attribute of 1000 to updates from the neighbor at 192.168.219.1 that are permitted by access list 6. Access list 6 is defined in the **ip as-path access-list 5** command listed below in global configuration mode
`Houston(config-router)# exit`	Returns to global configuration mode
`Houston(config)# ip as-path access-list 5 permit _100_`	Permits updates whose AS path attribute shows the update passing through AS 100 **NOTE:** The _ symbol is used to form regular expressions. See the section "Regular Expressions" in this chapter (after the sections on the different attributes) for more examples
`Houston(config)# ip as-path access-list 6 permit _200_`	Permits updates whose AS path attribute shows the update passing through AS 200

The result of this configuration will have Houston forward traffic for the 172.16.10.0 network through AS 100, because it has a higher weight attribute set as compared to the weight attribute set for the same update from AS 200. Adding the AS path access list allows you to filter prefixes based on (1) their originating AS, (2) the AS they pass through, or (3) the identity of the connected neighbor AS.

Using Prefix Lists and Route Maps to Manipulate the Weight Attribute

Refer to Figure 7-4 for the configuration that follows, which demonstrates how to configure the weight attribute using prefix lists and route maps. The objective here is for Houston to prefer the path through Austin to reach the 172.16.10.0/24 network.

Houston(config)# `ip prefix-list AS400_ROUTES permit 172.16.10.0/24`	Creates a prefix list that matches the 172.16.10.0/24 network belonging to AS 400
Houston(config)# `route-map SETWEIGHT permit 10`	Creates a route map called SETWEIGHT. This route map will permit traffic based on the subsequent criteria. A sequence number of 10 is assigned
Houston(config-route-map)# `match ip address prefix-list AS400_ROUTES`	Specifies the condition under which policy routing is allowed, matching the AS400_ROUTES prefix list
Houston(config-route-map)# `set weight 200`	Assigns a weight of 200 to any route update that meets the condition of prefix list AS400_ROUTES
Houston(config-route-map)# `route-map SETWEIGHT permit 20`	Creates the second statement for the route map named SETWEIGHT. This route map will permit traffic based on subsequent criteria. A sequence number of 20 is assigned
Houston(config-route-map)# `set weight 100`	Assigns a weight of 100 to all other route updates/networks learned
Houston(config-route-map)# `exit`	Returns to global configuration mode
Houston(config)# `router bgp 300`	Starts the BGP routing process
Houston(config-router)# `neighbor 192.168.7.1 route-map SETWEIGHT in`	Uses the route map SETWEIGHT to filter all routes learned from neighbor 192.168.7.1

Local Preference Attribute

Local preference is a BGP attribute that provides information to routers in the AS about the path that is preferred for exiting the AS. A path with a higher local preference is preferred. The local preference is an attribute that is configured on a router and exchanged among routers within the same AS only.

R1(config-router)# `bgp default local-preference 150`	Changes the default local preference value from 100 to 150

> **NOTE:** The local preference value can be a number between 0 and 429 496 729. Higher is preferred. If a **local-preference** value is not set, the default is 100.

> **NOTE:** The local preference attribute is local to the AS; it is exchanged between IBGP peers but not advertised to EBGP peers. Use the local preference attribute to force BGP routers to prefer one exit point over another.

Using AS Path Access Lists with Route Maps to Manipulate the Local Preference Attribute

Route maps provide more flexibility than the **bgp default local-preference** router configuration command.

Figure 7-5 shows the network topology for the configuration that follows, which demonstrates how to configure the local-preference attribute using AS path access lists with route maps. The objective here is to prefer Galveston as the exit point out of AS 256 for all networks originating in AS 300.

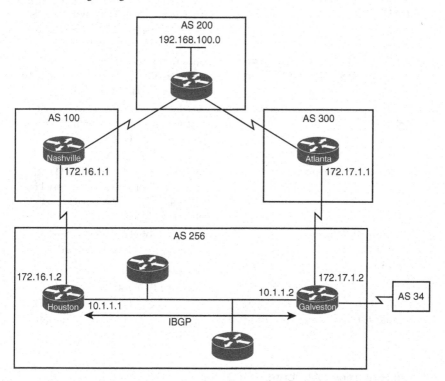

Figure 7-5 Using AS Path Access Lists with Route Maps to Manipulate the Local Preference Attribute

`Galveston(config)# `**`router bgp`**` 256`	Starts the BGP routing process
`Galveston(config-router)#` **`neighbor 172.17.1.1 remote-`** **`as 300`**	Identifies a peer router at 172.17.1.1
`Galveston(config-router)#` **`neighbor 172.17.1.1 route-map`** **`SETLOCAL in`**	Refers to a route map called SETLOCAL. All network updates received from neighbor 172.17.1.1 will be processed by the route map
`Galveston(config-router)#` **`neighbor 10.1.1.1 remote-as`** **`256`**	Identifies a peer router at 10.1.1.1
`Galveston(config-router)# `**`exit`**	Returns to global configuration mode
`Galveston(config)# ip` **`as-path access-list 7 permit`** **`^300$`**	Permits updates whose AS path attribute starts with 300 (represented by the ^) and ends with 300 (represented by the $)

`Galveston(config)# route-map` `SETLOCAL permit 10`	Creates a route map called SETLOCAL. This route map will permit traffic based on subsequent criteria. A sequence number of 10 is assigned
`Galveston(config-route-map)#` `match as-path 7`	Specifies the condition under which policy routing is allowed, matching the BGP ACL 7
`Galveston(config-route-map)#` `set local-preference 200`	Assigns a local preference of 200 to any update originating from AS 300, as defined by ACL 7
`Galveston(config-route-map)#` `route-map SETLOCAL permit 20`	Creates the second statement of the route map SETLOCAL. This instance will accept all other routes **NOTE:** Forgetting a **permit** statement at the end of the route map is a common mistake that prevents the router from learning any other routes

AS Path Attribute Prepending

AS paths can be manipulated by prepending AS numbers to the existing AS paths. Assuming that the values of all other attributes are the same, routers will pick the shortest AS path attribute; therefore, prepending numbers to the path will manipulate the decision as to the best path. Normally, AS path prepending is performed on outgoing EBGP updates over the undesired return path.

Refer to Figure 7-6 for the configuration that follows, which demonstrates the commands necessary to configure the **as-path prepend** option. Assume that all basic configurations are accurate.

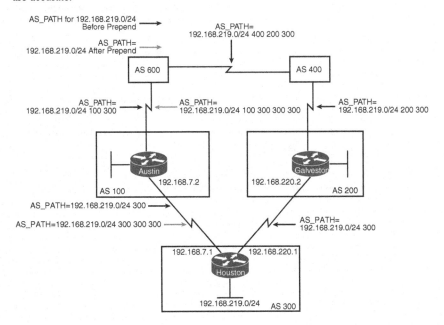

Figure 7-6   AS Path Attribute Prepending

In this scenario, you want to use the configuration on Houston to influence the choice of paths in AS 600. Currently, the routers in AS 600 have reachability information to the 192.168.219.0/24 network via two routes: (1) via AS 100 with an AS path attribute of (100, 300), and (2) via AS 400 with an AS path attribute of (400, 200, 300). Assuming that the values of all other attributes are the same, the routers in AS 600 will pick the shortest AS path attribute: the route through AS 100. You will prepend, or add, extra AS numbers to the AS path attribute for routes that Houston advertises to AS 100 to have AS 600 select AS 400 as the preferred path of reaching the 192.168.219.0/24 network.

`Houston(config)# router bgp 300`	Starts the BGP routing process
`Houston(config-router)# network 192.168.219.0`	Tells the BGP process what locally learned networks to advertise
`Houston(config-router)# neighbor 192.168.220.2 remote-as 200`	Identifies a peer router at 192.168.220.2
`Houston(config-router)# neighbor 192.168.7.2 remote-as 100`	Identifies a peer router at 192.168.7.2
`Houston(config-router)# neighbor 192.168.7.2 route-map SETPATH out`	Read this command to say, "All routes sent to neighbor 192.168.7.2 will have to follow the conditions laid out by the *SETPATH* route map"
`Houston(config-router)# exit`	Returns to global configuration mode
`Houston(config)# route-map SETPATH permit 10`	Creates a route map named *SETPATH*. This route map will permit traffic based on subsequent criteria. A sequence number of 10 is assigned
`Houston(config-route-map)# set as-path prepend 300 300`	Read this command to say, "The local router will add (prepend) the AS number 300 twice to the AS path attribute before sending updates out to its neighbor at 192.168.7.2"

The result of this configuration is that the AS path attribute of updates for network 192.168.219.0 that AS 600 receives via AS 100 will be (100, 300, 300, 300), which is longer than the value of the AS path attribute of updates for network 192.168.219.0 that AS 600 receives via AS 400 (400, 200, 300).

AS 600 will choose AS 400 (400, 200, 300) as the better path. This is because BGP is a path vector routing protocol that chooses the path with the least number of ASs that it must cross.

AS Path: Removing Private Autonomous Systems

Private AS numbers (64,512 to 65,535) cannot be passed on to the Internet because they are not unique. Cisco has implemented a feature, **remove-private-as**, to strip private AS numbers out of the AS path list before the routes get propagated to the Internet.

Figure 7-7 shows the network topology for the configuration that follows, which demonstrates the **remove-private-as** option. Assume that all basic configurations are accurate.

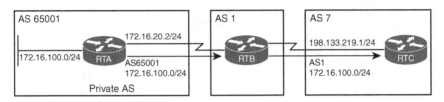

Figure 7-7   AS Path: Removing Private Autonomous Systems

`RTB(config)# router bgp 1`	Starts the BGP routing process
`RTB(config-router)# neighbor` `172.16.20.2 remote-as 65001`	Identifies a peer router at 172.16.20.2
`RTB(config-router)# neighbor` `198.133.219.1 remote-as 7`	Identifies a peer router at 198.133.219.1
`RTB(config-router)# neighbor` `198.133.219.1 remove-private-as`	Removes private AS numbers from the path in outbound routing updates **NOTE:** The **remove-private-as** command is available for EBGP neighbors only

Multi-Exit Discriminator (MED) Attribute

The MED attribute, also called the BGP metric, can be used to indicate to EBGP neighbors what the preferred path is into an AS. Unlike local preference, the MED is exchanged between ASs. The MED is sent to EBGP peers. By default, a router compares the MED attribute only for paths from neighbors in the same AS. The **metric** command is used to configure the MED attribute.

Figure 7-8 shows the commands necessary to configure the MED attribute. Assume that all basic configurations are accurate. The objective here is to influence Mazatlan to choose Houston as the entry point for AS 300 to reach network 192.168.100.0.

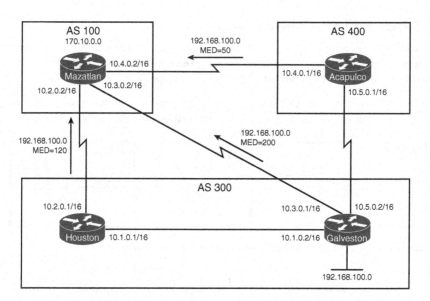

Figure 7-8   MED Attribute

`Mazatlan(config)# router bgp 100`	Starts the BGP routing process
`Mazatlan(config-router)# neighbor` `10.2.0.1 remote-as 300`	Identifies a peer router at 10.2.0.1
`Mazatlan(config-router)# neighbor` `10.3.0.1 remote-as 300`	Identifies a peer router at 10.3.0.1
`Mazatlan(config-router)# neighbor` `10.4.0.1 remote-as 400`	Identifies a peer router at 10.4.0.1
`Acapulco(config)# router bgp 400`	Starts the BGP routing process
`Acapulco(config-router)# neighbor` `10.4.0.2 remote-as 100`	Identifies a peer router at 10.4.0.2
`Acapulco(config-router)# neighbor` `10.4.0.2 route-map SETMEDOUT out`	Refers to a route map named *SETMEDOUT*
`Acapulco(config-router)# neighbor` `10.5.0.2 remote-as 300`	Identifies a peer router at 10.5.0.2
`Acapulco(config-router)# exit`	Returns to global configuration mode
`Acapulco(config)# route-map` `SETMEDOUT permit 10`	Creates a route map named *SETMEDOUT*. This route map will permit traffic based on subsequent criteria. A sequence number of 10 is assigned
`Acapulco(config-route-map)# set` `metric 50`	Sets the metric value for BGP
`Houston(config)# router bgp 300`	Starts the BGP routing process
`Houston(config-router)# neighbor` `10.2.0.2 remote-as 100`	Identifies a peer router at 10.2.0.1

Houston(config-router)# **neighbor** **10.2.0.2 route-map SETMEDOUT out**	Refers to a route map named *SETMEDOUT*
Houston(config-router)# **neighbor** **10.1.0.2 remote-as 300**	Identifies a peer router at 10.1.0.2
Houston(config-router)# **exit**	Returns to global configuration mode
Houston(config)# **route-map SETMEDOUT** **permit 10**	Creates a route map named *SETMEDOUT*. This route map will permit traffic based on subsequent criteria. A sequence number of 10 is assigned
Houston(config-route-map)# **set** **metric 120**	Sets the metric value for BGP
Galveston(config)# **router bgp 300**	Starts the BGP routing process
Galveston(config-router)# **neighbor** **10.3.0.2 remote-as 100**	Identifies a peer router at 10.3.0.2
Galveston(config-router)# **neighbor** **10.3.0.2 route-map SETMEDOUT out**	Refers to a route map named *SETMEDOUT*
Galveston(config-router)# **neighbor** **10.1.0.1 remote-as 300**	Identifies a peer router at 10.1.0.1
Galveston(config-router)# **neighbor** **10.5.0.1 remote-as 400**	Identifies a peer router at 10.5.0.1
Galveston(config-router)# **exit**	Returns to global configuration mode
Galveston(config)# **route-map** **SETMEDOUT permit 10**	Creates a route map named *SETMEDOUT*. This route map will permit traffic based on subsequent criteria. A sequence number of 10 is assigned
Galveston(config-route-map)# **set** **metric 200**	Sets the metric value for BGP

- A lower MED value is preferred over a higher MED value. The default value of the MED is 0. It is possible to change the default value of the MED using the **default-metric** command under the BGP process.

- Unlike local preference, the MED attribute is exchanged between autonomous systems, but a MED attribute that comes into an AS does not leave the AS.

- Unless otherwise specified, the router compares MED attributes for paths from external neighbors that are in the same AS.

- If you want MED attributes from neighbors in other ASs to be compared, you must configure the **bgp always-compare-med** command.

NOTE: By default, BGP compares the MED attributes of routes coming from neighbors in the same external AS (such as AS 300). Mazatlan can only compare the MED attribute coming from Houston (120) to the MED attribute coming from Galveston (200) even though the update coming from Acapulco has the lowest MED value. Mazatlan will choose Houston as the best path for reaching network 192.168.100.0.

To force Mazatlan to include updates for network 192.168.100.0 from Acapulco in the comparison, use the **bgp always-compare-med** router configuration command on Mazatlan:

```
Mazatlan(config)# router bgp 100
Mazatlan(config-router)# neighbor 10.2.0.1 remote-as 300
Mazatlan(config-router)# neighbor 10.3.0.1 remote-as 300
Mazatlan(config-router)# neighbor 10.4.0.1 remote-as 400
Mazatlan(config-router)# bgp always-compare-med
```

Assuming that all other attributes are the same, Mazatlan will choose Acapulco as the best next hop for reaching network 192.168.100.0.

NOTE: The most recent IETF decision about BGP MED assigns a value of infinity to the missing MED, making the route that is lacking the MED variable the least preferred. The default behavior of BGP routers that are running Cisco IOS Software is to treat routes without the MED attribute as having a MED of 0, making the route that is lacking the MED variable the most preferred. To configure the router to conform to the IETF standard, use the **bgp bestpath missing-as-worst** command.

Verifying BGP

Router# **show bgp all community**	Displays routes for all address families belonging to a particular BGP community
Router# **show bgp all neighbors**	Displays information about BGP connections to neighbors of all address families
Router# **show bgp ipv6 unicast**	Displays entries in the IPv6 BGP routing table
Router# **show bgp ipv6 unicast rib-failure**	Displays the IPv6 BGP routes that fail to install in the Routing Information Base (RIB) table
Router# **show ip bgp**	Displays entries in the BGP table
Router# **show ip bgp neighbors**	Displays information about the BGP and TCP connections to neighbors
Router# **show ip bgp rib-failure**	Displays networks that are not installed in the RIB and the reason that they were not installed
Router# **show ip bgp summary**	Displays the status of all IPv4 BGP connections
Router# **show bgp ipv6 unicast summary**	Displays the status of all IPv6 BGP connections
Router# **show ip route bgp**	Displays the IPv4 BGP entries from the routing table
Router# **show ipv6 route bgp**	Displays the IPv6 BGP entries from the routing table

Troubleshooting BGP

Whenever the routing policy changes due to a configuration change, BGP peering sessions must be reset by using the **clear ip bgp** command. Cisco IOS Software supports the following three mechanisms to reset BGP peering sessions:

- **Hard reset:** A hard reset tears down the specified peering sessions, including the TCP connection, and deletes routes coming from the specified peer.

- **Soft reset:** A soft reset uses stored prefix information to reconfigure and activate BGP routing tables without tearing down existing peering sessions. Soft reconfiguration can be configured for inbound or outbound sessions.

- **Dynamic inbound soft reset:** The route refresh capability, as defined in RFC 2918, allows the local device to reset inbound routing tables dynamically by exchanging route refresh requests to supporting peers. To determine if a BGP device supports this capability, use the **show ip bgp neighbors** command. This is the preferred method of refreshing BGP information.

`Router# clear ip bgp *`	Forces BGP to clear its table and resets all BGP sessions
`Router# clear ip bgp ipv4` `unicast autonomous-system-number`	Resets BGP connections for the IPv4 unicast address family session for the specified *autonomous-system-number*
`Router# clear ip bgp ipv6` `unicast autonomous-system-number`	Resets BGP connections for the IPv6 unicast address family session for the specified *autonomous-system-number*
`Router# clear ip bgp 10.1.1.1`	Resets the specific BGP session with the neighbor at 10.1.1.1
`Router# clear ip bgp 10.1.1.2` `soft out`	Forces the remote router to resend all BGP information to the neighbor without resetting the connection. Routes from this neighbor are not lost **TIP:** The **clear ip bgp w.x.y.z soft out** command is highly recommended when you are changing an outbound policy on the router. The **soft out** option does not help if you are changing an inbound policy **TIP:** The **soft** keyword of this command is optional; **clear ip bgp out** will do a soft reset for all outbound updates

`Router(config-router)#`
`neighbor 10.1.1.2`
`soft-reconfiguration inbound`
	Causes the router to store all updates from this neighbor in case the inbound policy is changed
	
	CAUTION: The **soft-reconfiguration inbound** command is memory intensive

`Router# clear ip bgp 10.1.1.2` `soft in`	Uses the stored information to generate new inbound updates

`Router# clear ip bgp {* | 10.1.1.2} [soft in | in]`	Creates a dynamic soft reset of inbound BGP routing table updates. Routes are not withdrawn. Updates are not stored locally. The connection remains established. See the notes that follow for more information on when this command can be used
`Router# debug ip bgp`	Displays all information related to BGP
`Router# debug ip bgp events`	Displays all BGP event information
`Router# debug ip bgp updates`	Displays information about the processing of BGP update
`Router# debug ip bgp ipv4 unicast`	Displays all IPv4 unicast address family information
`Router# debug ip bgp ipv6 unicast`	Displays all IPv6 unicast address family information

NOTE: Beginning with Cisco IOS Releases 12.0(2)S and 12.0(6)T, Cisco introduced a BGP soft reset enhancement feature known as *route refresh*. Route refresh is not dependent on stored routing table update information. This method requires no pre-configuration and requires less memory than previous soft methods for inbound routing table updates.

NOTE: To determine whether a BGP router supports route refresh capability, use the **show ip bgp neighbors** command. The following message is displayed in the output when route refresh is supported:

```
Received route refresh capability from peer
```

NOTE: When a BGP session is reset and soft reconfiguration is used, several commands enable you to monitor BGP routes that are received, sent, or filtered:

```
Router# show ip bgp
Router# show ip bgp neighbor address advertised
Router# show ip bgp neighbor address received
Router# show ip bgp neighbor address routes
```

CAUTION: The **clear ip bgp *** command is both processor and memory intensive and should be used only in smaller environments. A more reasonable approach is to clear only a specific network or a specific session with a neighbor with the **clear ip bgp** *specific-network* command. However, you can use this command whenever the following changes occur:

- Additions or changes to the BGP-related access lists
- Changes to BGP-related weights
- Changes to BGP-related distribution lists
- Changes in the BGP timer's specifications
- Changes to the BGP administrative distance
- Changes to BGP-related route maps

Default Routes

Router(config)# **router bgp** 100	Starts the BGP routing process
Router(config-router)# **neighbor** 192.168.100.1 **remote-as** 200	Identifies a peer router at 192.168.100.1
Router(config-router)# **neighbor** 192.168.100.1 **default-originate**	States that the default route of 0.0.0.0 will only be sent to 192.168.100.1

NOTE: If you want your BGP router to advertise a default to all peers and the 0.0.0.0 route exists in the routing table, use the **network** command with an address of 0.0.0.0:

```
R1(config)# router bgp 100
R1(config-router)# neighbor 172.16.20.1 remote-as 150
R1(config-router)# neighbor 172.17.1.1 remote-as 200
R1(config-router)# network 0.0.0.0
```

Route Aggregation

R1(config-router)# **aggregate-address** 172.16.0.0 255.255.0.0	Creates an aggregate entry in the BGP routing table if any more-specific BGP routes are available that fall within the specified range. The aggregate route will be advertised as coming from your AS and will have the atomic aggregate attribute set. More specific routes will also be advertised unless the **summary-only** keyword is added at the end of the command
R1(config-router)# **aggregate-address** 172.16.0.0 255.255.0.0 **summary-only**	Creates the aggregate route but also suppresses advertisements of more-specific routes to all neighbors. Specific AS path information to the individual subnets that fall within the summary is lost
R1(config-router)# **aggregate-address** 172.16.0.0 255.255.0.0 **as-set**	Creates an aggregate entry but the path advertised for this route will be a list of AS paths from where the individual subnets originated

Route Reflectors

By default, a router that receives an EBGP route advertises it to its EBGP and IBGP peers. However, if it receives it through IBGP, it does not advertise it to its IBGP peers, as a loop-prevention mechanism (split horizon). Because of this behavior, the only way for all IBGP routers to receive a route after it is originated into the AS is to have a full mesh of IBGP peers. This can get complex with a large number of peers. A route reflector allows a topology to get around the IBGP limitation of having to have a full mesh.

Figure 7-9 shows the commands necessary to configure BGP route reflectors. Assume that basic BGP configurations are accurate. The objective is to allow R2 to advertise to

R1 the 209.165.201.0/27 network learned from R3. Without these commands, R1 will never learn the 209.165.201.0/27 network unless a full-mesh IBGP topology is built.

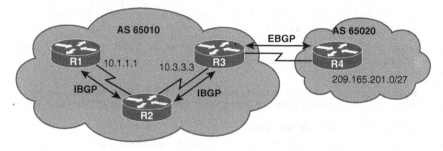

Figure 7-9   Route Reflectors

R2(config)# **router bgp 65010**	Enters BGP routing configuration mode
R2(config-router)# **neighbor 10.1.1.1 route-reflector-client**	Configures the local router as a BGP route reflector and the specified neighbor as a client
R2(config-router)# **neighbor 10.3.3.3 route-reflector-client**	Configures the local router as a BGP route reflector and the specified neighbor as a client

Regular Expressions

A *regular expression* is a pattern to match against an input string, such as those listed in the following table.

Character	Description
^	Matches the beginning of the input string
$	Matches the end of the input string
_	Matches a space, comma, left brace, right brace, the beginning of an input string, or the ending of an input stream
.	Matches any single character
*	Matches 0 or more single- or multiple-character patterns

For example, in the case of the **ip as-path access-list** command, the input string is the AS path attribute.

Router(config)# **ip as-path access-list 1 permit 2150**	Matches any AS path that includes the pattern of 2150
Router# **show ip bgp regexp 2150**	Matches any AS path that includes the pattern of 2150
	NOTE: In both previous commands, not only will AS 2150 be a match, but so will AS 12 150 or 21 507

Router(config)# **ip as-path access-list 6 deny ^200$**	Denies updates whose AS path attribute starts with 200 (represented by the ^) and ends with 200 (represented by the $)
Router(config)# **ip as-path access-list 1 permit .***	Permits updates whose AS path attribute starts with any character—represented by the period (.) symbol—and repeats that character—the asterisk (*) symbol means a repetition of that character **NOTE:** The argument of .* will match any value of the AS path attribute

Regular Expressions: Examples

Refer to the following **show ip bgp** output to see how different examples of regular expressions can help filter specific patterns:

```
R1# show ip bgp
    Network          Next Hop    Metric LocPrf Weight Path
* i172.16.0.0       172.20.50.1   100            0 65005 65004 65003 i
*>i                 192.168.28.1  100            0 65002 65003 i
*>i172.24.0.0       172.20.50.1   100            0 65005 i
*  i                192.168.28.1  100            0 65002 65003 65004
                                                   65005 i
*>i172.30.0.0       172.20.50.1   100            0 65005 65004 i
*  i                192.168.28.1  100            0 65002 65003 65004 i
*>i192.168.3.3/32   0.0.0.0         0         32768 i
```

To find all subnets originating from AS 65004 (AS path ends with 65004):

```
R1# show ip bgp regexp _65004$
    Network          Next Hop    Metric LocPrf Weight Path
*>i172.30.0.0       172.20.50.1   100            0 65005 65004 i
*  i                192.168.28.1  100            0 65002 65003 65004 i
```

To find all subnets reachable via AS 65002 (AS path begins with 65002):

```
R1# show ip bgp regexp ^65002_
    Network          Next Hop    Metric LocPrf Weight Path
*>i172.16.0.0       192.168.28.1  100            0 65002 65003 i
*  i172.24.0.0       192.168.28.1  100            0 65002 65003 65004
                                                   65005 i
*  i172.30.0.0       192.168.28.1  100            0 65002 65003
                                                   65004 i
```

To find all routes transiting through AS 65005:

```
R1# show ip bgp regexp _65005_
   Network          Next Hop    Metric LocPrf Weight Path
* i172.16.0.0       172.20.50.1   100              0 65005 65004
                                                     65003 i

*>i172.24.0.0       172.20.50.1   100              0 65005 i
* i                 192.168.28.1  100              0 65002 65003 65004
                                                     65005 i

*>i172.30.0.0       172.20.50.1   100              0 65005 65004 i
```

To find subnets that originate from R1's AS (AS path is blank):

```
R1# show ip bgp regexp ^$
   Network          Next Hop    Metric LocPrf Weight Path
*>i192.168.3.3/32   0.0.0.0        0          32768 i
```

BGP Route Filtering Using Access Lists and Distribute Lists

Figure 7-10 shows the commands necessary to configure route filters using access lists and distribute lists.

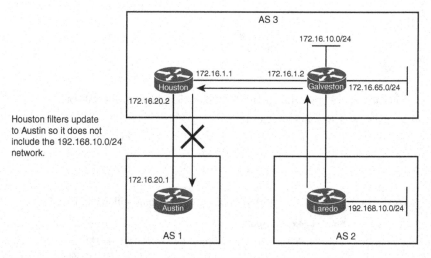

Figure 7-10   BGP Route Filtering Using Access Lists and Distribute Lists

In this scenario, we want to have Houston filter updates to Austin so that it does not include the 192.168.10.0/24 network.

`Houston(config)# router bgp 3`	Starts the BGP routing process
`Houston(config-router)# neighbor 172.16.1.2 remote-as 3`	Identifies a peer router at 172.16.1.2

Houston(config-router)# **neighbor** **172.16.20.1 remote-as 1**	Identifies a peer router at 172.16.20.1
Houston(config-router)# **neighbor** **172.16.20.1 distribute-list 1 out**	Applies a filter of ACL 1 to updates sent to neighbor 172.16.20.1
Houston(config-router)# **exit**	Returns to global configuration mode
Houston(config)# **access-list 1** **deny 192.168.10.0 0.0.0.255**	Creates the filter to prevent the 192.168.10.0/24 network from being part of the routing update
Houston(config)# **access-list 1** **permit any**	Creates the filter that allows all other net-works to be part of the routing update

TIP: A standard ACL offers limited functionality. If you want to advertise the aggregate address of 172.16.0.0/16 but not the individual subnet, a standard ACL will not work. You need to use an extended ACL.

When you are using extended ACLs with BGP route filters, the extended ACL will first match the network address and *then* match the subnet mask of the prefix. To do this, both the network and the netmask are paired with their own wildcard bitmask:

```
Router(config)# access-list 101 permit ip 172.16.0.0 0.0.255.255
255.255.0.0 0.0.0.0
```

To help overcome the confusing nature of this syntax, Cisco IOS Software introduced the **ip prefix-list** command in Cisco IOS Release 12.0.

Configuration Example: Using Prefix Lists and AS Path Access Lists

Figure 7-11 shows the network topology for the configuration that follows, which demonstrates how to configure prefix lists and AS path access lists. Assume that all BGP and basic configurations are accurate. There are two objectives here. The first is to allow CE1 and CE2 to only learn ISP routes with a mask greater than /15 (ge 16) and less than /25 (le 24). The second is to ensure that AS 65 000 does not become a transit AS for ISP1 to reach ISP2 (and vice versa).

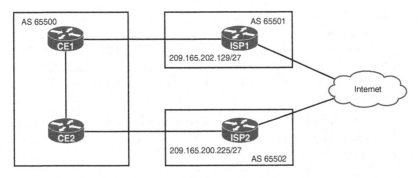

Figure 7-11 Configuration Example: Using Prefix Lists and AS Path Access Lists

CE1(config)# **ip prefix-list ISP1 permit 0.0.0.0 ge 16 le 24**	Creates a prefix list that only permits routes with a mask between 16 and 24
CE1(config)# **ip as-path access-list 1 permit ^$**	Creates an AS path access list matching routes that originate only from within AS 65 500
CE1(config)# **router bgp 65000**	Starts the BGP routing process
CE1(config-router)# **neighbor 209.165.202.129 prefix-list ISP1 in**	Assigns the ISP1 prefix list to neighbor 209.165.202.129 (ISP1) for all routes learned from that neighbor
CE1(config-router)# **neighbor 209.165.202.129 filter-list 1 out**	Assigns the AS path access list to neighbor 209.165.202.129 (ISP1) for all routes sent to that neighbor
CE2(config)# **ip prefix-list ISP2 permit 0.0.0.0 ge 16 le 24**	Creates a prefix list that only permits routes with a mask between 16 and 24
CE2(config)# **ip as-path access-list 1 permit ^$**	Creates an AS path access list matching routes that originate only from within AS 65 500
CE2(config)# **router bgp 65000**	Starts the BGP routing process
CE2(config-router)# **neighbor 209.165.200.225 prefix-list ISP2 in**	Assigns the ISP2 prefix list to neighbor 209.165.200.225 (ISP2) for all routes learned from that neighbor
CE2(config-router)# **neighbor 209.165.200.225 filter-list 1 out**	Assigns the AS path access list to neighbor 209.165.200.225 (ISP2) for all routes sent to that neighbor

BGP Peer Groups

To ease the burden of configuring a large number of neighbors with identical or similar parameters (for example, route maps, filter lists, or prefix lists), the concept of peer groups was introduced. The administrator configures the peer group with all the BGP parameters that are to be applied to multiple BGP peers. Actual BGP neighbors are bound to the peer group, and the network administrator applies the peer group configuration on each of the BGP sessions.

Figure 7-12 shows the network topology for the configuration that follows, which demonstrates how to configure peer groups. Assume that all BGP, OSPF, and basic configurations are accurate.

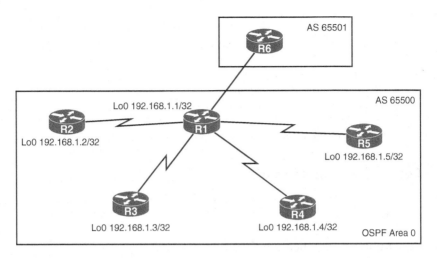

Figure 7-12   BGP Peer Groups

R1(config)# **router bgp 65500**	Starts the BGP routing process
R1(config-router)# **neighbor INTERNAL peer-group**	Creates a BGP peer group called *INTERNAL*
R1(config-router)# **neighbor INTERNAL remote-as 65500**	Assigns a first parameter to the peer group
R1(config-router)# **neighbor INTERNAL next-hop-self**	Assigns a second parameter to the peer group
R1(config-router)# **neighbor INTERNAL update-source loopback 0**	Assigns a third parameter to the peer group
R1(config-router)# **neighbor INTERNAL route-reflector-client**	Assigns a fourth parameter to the peer group
R1(config-router)# **neighbor 192.168.1.2 peer-group INTERNAL**	Assigns the peer group to neighbor R2
R1(config-router)# **neighbor 192.168.1.3 peer-group INTERNAL**	Assigns the peer group to neighbor R3
R1(config-router)# **neighbor 192.168.1.4 peer-group INTERNAL**	Assigns the peer group to neighbor R4
R1(config-router)# **neighbor 192.168.1.5 peer-group INTERNAL**	Assigns the peer group to neighbor R5

The result here is that all four IBGP neighbors have the same basic BGP configuration assigned to them.

TIP: A peer group can be, among others, configured to do the following:

- Use the IP address of a specific interface as the source address when opening the TCP session or use the next-hop-self feature
- Use, or not use, the EBGP multihop function
- Use, or not use, MD5 authentication on the BGP sessions
- Filter out any incoming or outgoing routes using a prefix list, a filter list, and a route map
- Assign a specific weight value to the routes that are received

Authentication for BGP

Authentication for routers using BGP relies on the use of predefined passwords and uses MD5.

Configuring Authentication Between BGP Peers

`Router(config)# router bgp 65100`	Enters routing protocol configuration mode
`Router(config-router) neighbor 209.165.202.130 remote-as 65000`	Defines a BGP peer at IP address 209.165.202.130
`Router(config-router)# neighbor 209.165.202.130 password P@55word`	Enables MD5 authentication on a TCP connection with peer at IP address 209.165.202.130. The password is **P@55word**
`Router(config-router)# neighbor 2001:db8:0:10::1 password P@55word`	Enables MD5 authentication on a TCP connection with peer at IPv6 address 2001:db8:0:10::1. The password is **P@55word** **NOTE:** To avoid losing your peer relationship, the same password must be configured on your remote peer before the hold-down timer expires, which has a default setting of 180 seconds

Verifying BGP Authentication

`Router# show ip bgp summary`	Displays summary of BGP neighbor status
`Router# show ip bgp neighbors`	Displays detailed information on TCP and BGP neighbor connections
`Router# show bgp ipv6 unicast summary`	Displays the status of all IPv6 BGP connections
`Router# show bgp ipv6 unicast neighbors`	Displays information about IPv6 BGP connections to neighbors

This chapter provides information and commands concerning the following topics:

- Network Address Translation (NAT)
    - Private IP addresses: RFC 1918
    - Configuring static NAT
    - Configuring dynamic NAT
    - Configuring Port Address Translation (PAT)
    - Configuring a NAT virtual interface
    - Verifying NAT and PAT configurations
    - Troubleshooting NAT and PAT configurations
    - Configuration example: PAT
    - Configuration example: NAT virtual interfaces and static NAT
- First-hop redundancy protocols
    - Hot Standby Router Protocol (HSRP)
        - Default HSRP configuration settings
        - Configuring HSRP
        - Verifying HSRP
        - HSRP optimization options
            - Preempt
            - HSRP message timers
            - Authentication
            - Interface tracking
        - Multiple HSRP groups
        - HSRP IP SLA tracking
        - HSRPv2 for IPv6
        - Debugging HSRP

- Virtual Router Redundancy Protocol (VRRP)
  - Configuring VRRP
  - VRRP optimization options
    - Interface tracking
  - Verifying VRRP
  - Debugging VRRP
- IPv4 configuration example: HSRP on L3 switch
  - IP SLA tracking: switch DLS1 VLAN 10
- IPv4 configuration example: VRRP on router and L3 switch with IP SLA tracking
- IPv6 configuration example: HSRPv2 on router and L3 switch

- Dynamic Host Control Protocol (DHCP)
  - Implementing DHCP for IPv4
    - Configuring a DHCP server on a Cisco IOS router
    - Configuring DHCP manual assignment
    - Configuring DHCP replay
    - Configuring a DHCP client on a Cisco IOS Software Ethernet interface
    - Verifying and troubleshooting DHCP configuration
  - Implementing DHCP for IPv6
    - Using SLAAC and configuring a router as a stateless DHCPv6 server
    - Configuring a router as a stateful DHCPv6 server
    - Configuring a DHCPv6 client
    - Configuring a DHCPv6 relay agent
    - Verifying and troubleshooting DHCPv6
  - Configuration example: DHCP for IPv4
  - Configuration example: DHCP for IPv6

Network Address Translation (NAT)

Private IP Addresses: RFC 1918

Table 8-1 lists the RFC 1918 private address ranges available to use within a private network. These will be your "inside-the-LAN" addresses that will have to be translated into public addresses that can be routed across the Internet. Any network can use these addresses; however, these addresses are not allowed to be routed onto the public Internet.

TABLE 8-1 RFC 1918 Private Address Ranges

Internal Address Range	CIDR Prefix	Traditional Class
10.0.0.0–10.255.255.255	10.0.0.0/8	A
172.16.0.0–172.31.255.255	172.16.0.0/12	B
192.168.0.0–192.168.255.255	192.168.0.0/16	C

Configuring Static NAT

Figure 8-1 shows the network topology for the configuration that follows, which demonstrates how to configure static Network Address Translation (NAT). The objective here is to statically translate the address of the server to a public IP address.

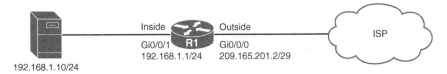

192.168.1.10/24

Figure 8-1 Configuring Static NAT

`R1(config)# interface gigabitgethernet 0/0/0`	Enters GigabitEthernet 0/0/0 interface configuration mode
`R1(config-if)# ip address 209.165.201.2 255.255.255.248`	Assigns a public IP address to the outside interface
`R1(config-if)# ip nat outside`	Defines which interface is the outside interface for NAT
`R1(config-if)# interface gigabitethernet 0/0/1`	Enters GigabitEthernet 0/0/1 interface configuration mode
`R1(config-if)# ip address 192.168.1.1 255.255.255.0`	Assigns a private IP address to the inside interface
`R1(config-if)# ip nat inside`	Defines which interface is the inside interface for NAT. You can have multiple NAT inside interfaces on a router
`R1(config-if)# exit`	Returns to global configuration mode
`R1(config)# ip nat inside source static 192.168.1.10 209.165.201.5`	Permanently translates the inside address of 192.168.1.10 to a public address of 209.165.201.5 Use the command for each of the private IP addresses you want to statically map to a public address

Configuring Dynamic NAT

Figure 8-2 shows the network topology for the configuration that follows, which demonstrates how to configure dynamic NAT. The objective here is to dynamically translate the addresses of the PCs to a range of public IP addresses.

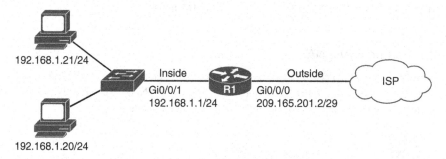

Figure 8-2 Configuring Dynamic NAT

R1(config)# **access-list 1 permit** **192.168.1.0 0.0.0.255**	Defines an access list that identifies the private network that will be translated
R1(config)# **ip nat pool R1_POOL** **209.165.201.8 209.165.201.15** **netmask 255.255.255.248**	Creates a pool of eight public addresses named *R1_POOL* that will be used for translation On certain IOS devices, you can include the **add-route** keyword at the end of the command to automatically add a static route in the routing table that points to the NAT virtual interface (NVI)
R1(config)# **interface** **gigabitethernet 0/0/0**	Enters GigabitEthernet 0/0/0 interface configuration mode
R1(config-if)# **ip address** **209.165.201.2 255.255.255.248**	Assigns a public IP address to the outside interface
R1(config-if)# **ip nat outside**	Defines which interface is the outside interface for NAT
R1(config-if)# **interface** **gigabitethernet 0/0/1**	Enters GigabitEthernet 0/0/1 interface configuration mode
R1(config-if)# **ip address** **192.168.1.1 255.255.255.0**	Assigns a private IP address to the inside interface
R1(config-if)# **ip nat inside**	Defines which interface is the inside interface for NAT. There can be multiple inside interfaces
R1(config-if)# **exit**	Returns to global configuration mode
R1(config)# **ip nat inside source** **list 1 pool R1_POOL**	Enables translation of addresses permitted by ACL number 1 to the addresses in pool *R1_POOL*

Configuring Port Address Translation (PAT)

Figure 8-3 shows the network topology for the configuration that follows, which demonstrates how to configure NAT overload or Port Address Translation (PAT). The objective here is to translate the PC's addresses to the address of the router's public interface.

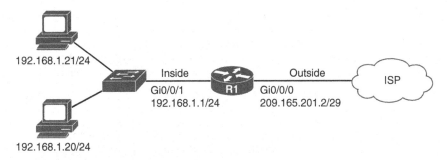

Figure 8-3 Configuring Port Address Translation (PAT)

`R1(config)# access-list 1 permit 192.168.1.0 0.0.0.255`	Defines an access list that identifies the private network that will be translated
`R1(config)# interface gigabitethernet 0/0/0`	Enters GigabitEthernet 0/0/0 interface configuration mode
`R1(config-if)# ip address 209.165.201.2 255.255.255.248`	Assigns a public IP address to the outside interface
`R1(config-if)# ip nat outside`	Defines which interface is the outside interface for NAT
`R1(config-if)# interface gigabitethernet 0/0/1`	Enters GigabitEthernet 0/0/1 interface configuration mode
`R1(config-if)# ip address 192.168.1.1 255.255.255.0`	Assigns a private IP address to the inside interface
`R1(config-if)# ip nat inside`	Defines which interface is the inside interface for NAT. There can be multiple inside interfaces
`R1(config-if)# exit`	Returns to global configuration mode
`R1(config)# ip nat inside source list 1 interface gigabitethernet 0/0/0 overload`	Enables translation of addresses permitted by ACL number 1 and uses the interface GigabitEthernet 0/0/0 IP address for the NAT process. The keyword **overload** allows multiple inside devices to share a single public IP address while keeping track of port numbers to ensure sessions remain unique

NOTE: It is possible to overload a dynamic pool instead of an interface. This allows the inside private devices to share multiple public IP address instead of only one. Use the command **ip nat inside source list** *acl* **pool** *pool* **overload** to achieve this. Also, instead of a pool of multiple addresses, the pool used for overloading could be a pool of only one public address. For example, the command **ip nat pool MyPool 203.0.113.1 203.0.113.1 netmask 255.255.255.0** creates a pool of one public address that can be overloaded.

Configuring a NAT Virtual Interface

A NAT virtual interface, or NVI, removes the requirements to configure an interface as either inside or outside. Also, because NVI performs routing, translation, and routing again, it is possible to route packets from inside to inside interfaces successfully.

R1(config-if)# **ip nat enable**	Allows the interface to participate in NVI translation processing
R1# **show ip nat nvi translations**	Displays the list of active NVI translations **NOTE:** Legacy NAT terminology does not apply because there are no "inside" or "outside" interfaces. Instead, NVI uses the source global, source local, destination global, and destination local terminology
R1# **show ip nat nvi statistics**	Displays the interfaces participating in NVI translation processing, as well as Hit and Miss counters

NOTE: NAT virtual interfaces are not supported in the Cisco IOS XE software.

Verifying NAT and PAT Configurations

Router# **show access-list**	Displays access lists
Router# **show ip nat translations**	Displays the translation table
Router# **show ip nat statistics**	Displays NAT statistics
Router# **clear ip nat translation inside** *1.1.1.1 2.2.2.2* **outside** *3.3.3.3 4.4.4.4*	Clears a specific translation from the table before it times out: 1.1.1.1 = Global IP address 2.2.2.2 = Local IP address 3.3.3.3 = Local IP address 4.4.4.4 = Global IP address
Router# **clear ip nat translation** *	Clears the entire translation table before entries time out

NOTE: The default timeout for a translation entry in a NAT table is 24 hours.

Troubleshooting NAT and PAT Configurations

`Router# debug ip nat`	Displays information about every packet that is translated **CAUTION:** Using this command can potentially generate a tremendous amount of output and overwhelm the router
`Router# debug ip nat detailed`	Displays greater detail about packets being translated

Configuration Example: PAT

Figure 8-4 shows the network topology for the PAT configuration that follows using the commands covered in this chapter.

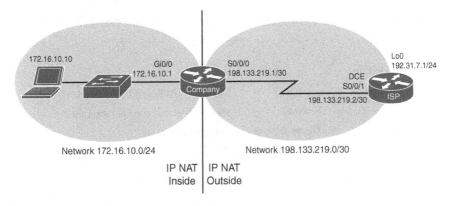

Network 172.16.10.0/24   Network 198.133.219.0/30

IP NAT | IP NAT
Inside | Outside

Figure 8-4 Port Address Translation Configuration

ISP Router

`Router> enable`	Moves to privileged EXEC mode
`Router# configure terminal`	Moves to global configuration mode
`Router(config)# hostname ISP`	Sets the host name
`ISP(config)# no ip domain-lookup`	Turns off Domain Name System (DNS) resolution to avoid wait time due to DNS lookup of spelling errors
`ISP(config)# enable secret cisco`	Sets the encrypted password to *cisco*
`ISP(config)# line console 0`	Moves to line console mode
`ISP(config-line)# password cisco`	Sets the console line password to *class*
`ISP(config-line)# login`	Requires user to log in to be able to access the console port
`ISP(config-line)# logging synchronous`	Displays unsolicited messages and debug output on a separate line than user input.
`ISP(config-line)# exit`	Returns to global configuration mode
`ISP(config)# interface serial 0/0/1`	Moves to interface configuration mode

`ISP(config-if)# ip address 198.133.219.2 255.255.255.252`	Assigns an IP address and netmask
`ISP(config-if)# clock rate 4000000`	Assigns the clock rate to the DCE cable on this side of the link
`ISP(config-if)# no shutdown`	Enables the interface
`ISP(config-if)# interface loopback 0`	Creates loopback interface 0 and moves to interface configuration mode
`ISP(config-if)# ip address 192.31.7.1 255.255.255.255`	Assigns an IP address and netmask
`ISP(config-if)# exit`	Returns to global configuration mode
`ISP(config)# exit`	Returns to privileged EXEC mode
`ISP# copy running-config startup-config`	Saves the configuration to NVRAM

Company Router

`Router> enable`	Moves to privileged EXEC mode
`Router# configure terminal`	Moves to global configuration mode
`Router(config)# hostname Company`	Sets the host name
`Company(config)# no ip domain-lookup`	Turns off DNS resolution to avoid wait time due to DNS lookup of spelling errors
`Company(config)# enable secret cisco`	Sets the secret password to *cisco*
`Company(config)# line console 0`	Moves to line console mode
`Company(config-line)# password class`	Sets the console line password to *class*
`Company(config-line)# login`	Requires user to log in to be able to access the console port
`Company(config-line)# logging synchronous`	Causes commands to be appended to a new line
`Company(config-line)# exit`	Returns to global configuration mode
`Company(config)# interface gigabitethernet 0/0`	Moves to interface configuration mode
`Company(config-if)# ip address 172.16.10.1 255.255.255.0`	Assigns an IP address and netmask
`Company(config-if)# no shutdown`	Enables the interface
`Company(config-if)# interface serial 0/0/0`	Moves to interface configuration mode
`Company(config-if)# ip address 198.133.219.1 255.255.255.252`	Assigns an IP address and netmask
`Company(config-if)# no shutdown`	Enables the interface
`Company(config-if)# exit`	Returns to global configuration mode
`Company(config)# ip route 0.0.0.0 0.0.0.0 198.133.219.2`	Sends all packets not defined in the routing table to the ISP router

Company(config)# **access-list 1 permit 172.16.10.0 0.0.0.255**	Defines which addresses are permitted through; these addresses are those that will be allowed to be translated with NAT
Company(config)# **ip nat inside source list 1 interface serial 0/0/0 overload**	Creates NAT by combining list 1 with the interface Serial 0/0/0. Overloading will take place
Company(config)# **interface gigabitethernet 0/0**	Moves to interface configuration mode
Company(config-if)# **ip nat inside**	Specifies location of private inside addresses
Company(config-if)# **interface serial 0/0/0**	Moves to interface configuration mode
Company(config-if)# **ip nat outside**	Specifies location of public outside addresses
Company(config-if)# **end**	Returns to privileged EXEC mode
Company# **copy running-config startup-config**	Saves the configuration to NVRAM

Configuration Example: NAT Virtual Interfaces and Static NAT

Figure 8-5 shows the network topology for the configuration that follows, which demonstrates how to configure NAT virtual interfaces with dynamic NAT and static NAT, using the commands covered in this chapter. Assume that all basic configurations are accurate. Recall that this configuration example will not work on a Cisco IOS XE router.

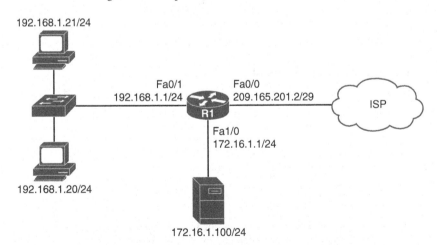

Figure 8-5 Configuration Example: NAT Virtual Interfaces and Static NAT

R1(config)# **access-list 1 permit 192.168.1.0 0.0.0.255**	Defines an access list that identifies the private network that will be translated
R1(config)# **ip nat pool R1_POOL 209.165.201.8 209.165.201.15 netmask 255.255.255.248**	Creates a pool of eight public addresses named *R1_POOL* that will be used for translation

`R1(config)# ip nat source list 1` `pool R1_POOL`	Enables translation of addresses permitted by ACL number 1 to the addresses in pool *R1_POOL*
`R1(config)# ip nat source static` `172.16.1.100 209.165.201.5`	Permanently translates the inside address of 172.16.1.100 to a public address of 209.165.201.5
`R1(config)# interface` `fastethernet 0/0`	Enters FastEthernet 0/0 interface configuration mode
`R1(config-if)# ip nat enable`	Enables NVI processing on the interface
`R1(config-if)# interface` `fastethernet 0/1`	Enters FastEthernet 0/1 interface configuration mode
`R1(config-if)# ip nat enable`	Enables NVI processing on the interface
`R1(config-if)# interface` `fastethernet 1/0`	Enters FastEthernet 1/0 interface configuration mode
`R1(config-if)# ip nat enable`	Enables NVI processing on the interface

First-Hop Redundancy Protocols

A first-hop redundancy protocol (FHRP) is a networking protocol that is designed to protect the default gateway by allowing two or more routers or Layer 3 switches to provide backup for that address. If one first-hop device fails, the backup router will take over the address, by default, within a few seconds. FHRPs are equally at home on routers as Layer 3 (L3) switches. Hot Standby Router Protocol (HSRP) and Virtual Router Redundancy Protocol (VRRP) are implemented for both IPv4 and IPv6 environments. Platform IOS matrices should be consulted for next-hop redundancy protocol support.

Hot Standby Router Protocol

HSRP provides network redundancy for IP networks, ensuring that user traffic immediately and transparently recovers from first-hop failures in network-edge devices or access circuits.

When configuring HSRP on a switch platform, the specified interface must be a Layer 3 interface and Layer 3 functions must be enabled:

- **Routed port:** A physical port configured as a Layer 3 port by entering the **no switchport** interface configuration command

- **SVI:** A VLAN interface created by using the **interface vlan** *vlan_id* global configuration command and by default a Layer 3 interface

- **EtherChannel port channel in Layer 3 mode:** A port-channel logical interface created by using the **interface port-channel** *port-channel-number* global configuration command and binding the Ethernet interface into the channel group

Default HSRP Configuration Settings

Feature	Default Setting
HSRP version	Version 1 **NOTE:** HSRPv1 and HSRPv2 have different packet structures. The same HSRP version must be configured on all devices of an HSRP group
HSRP groups	None configured
Standby group number	0
Standby MAC address	System assigned as 0000.0c07.ac*XX*, where *XX* is the HSRP group number. For HSRPv2, the MAC address will be 0000.0c9f.f*XXX*
Standby priority	100
Standby delay	0 (no delay)
Standby track interface priority	10
Standby hello time	3 seconds
Standby holdtime	10 seconds

Configuring Basic HSRP

`Switch(config)# interface vlan10`	Moves to interface configuration mode on the switch virtual interface (SVI)
`Switch(config-if)# ip address 172.16.0.10 255.255.255.0`	Assigns IP address and netmask
`Switch(config-if)# standby 1 ip 172.16.0.1`	Activates HSRP group 1 on the interface and creates a virtual IP address of 172.16.0.1 for use in HSRP **NOTE:** The group number can be from 0 to 255. The default is 0
`Switch(config-if)# standby 1 priority 120`	Assigns a priority value of 120 to standby group 1 **NOTE:** The priority value can be from 1 to 255. The default is 100. A higher priority will result in that switch being elected the active switch. If the priorities of all switches in the group are equal, the switch with the *highest IP address* becomes the active switch

NOTE: HSRP configuration commands for a router are the same as HSRP configuration commands on a Layer 3 switch platform.

Verifying HSRP

`Switch# show standby`	Displays HSRP information
`Switch# show standby brief`	Displays a single-line output summary of each standby group
`Switch# show standby vlan 1`	Displays HSRP information on the VLAN 1 group

HSRP Optimization Options

Options are available that make it possible to optimize HSRP operation in the campus network. The next sections explain four of these options: standby preempt, message timers, authentication, and interface tracking.

Preempt

`Switch(config)# interface vlan10`	Moves to interface configuration mode
`Switch(config-if)# standby 1 preempt`	Configures this switch to preempt, or take control of, the active switch if the local priority is higher than the priority of the active switch
`Switch(config-if)# standby 1 preempt delay minimum 180 reload 140`	Causes the local switch to postpone taking over as the active switch for 180 seconds since the HSRP process on that switch was last restarted or 140 seconds since the switch was last reloaded
`Switch(config-if)# no standby 1 preempt delay`	Disables the preemption delay, but preemption itself is still enabled. Use the **no standby** *x* **preempt** command to eliminate preemption **NOTE:** If the **preempt** argument is not configured, the local switch assumes control as the active switch only if the local switch receives information indicating that there is no switch currently in the active state

HSRP Message Timers

`Switch(config)# interface vlan10`	Moves to interface configuration mode
`Switch(config-if)# standby 1 timers 5 15`	Sets the hello timer to 5 seconds and sets the hold timer to 15 seconds **NOTE:** The hold timer is normally set to be greater than or equal to three times the hello timer **NOTE:** The hello timer can be from 1 to 254; the default is 3. The hold timer can be from 1 to 255; the default is 10. The default unit of time is seconds
`Switch(config-if)# standby 1 timers msec 200 msec 600`	Sets the hello timer to 200 milliseconds and sets the hold timer to 600 milliseconds **NOTE:** If the **msec** argument is used, the timers can be an integer from 15 to 999

Authentication

`Switch(config)#` **`key chain`** **`MyHSRPChain`**	Creates an authentication key chain called *MyHSRPChain*
`Switch(config-keychain)#` **`key 1`**	Adds a first key to the key chain
`Switch(config-keychain-key)#` **`key-string australia`**	Configures a key string of *australia*
`Switch(config-keychain-key)#` **`interface vlan10`**	Moves to interface configuration mode
`Switch(config-if)#` **`standby 1 authentication text canada`**	Configures *canada* as the plain-text authentication string used by group 1
`Switch(config-if)#` **`standby 2 authentication md5 key-string england`**	Configures *england* as the MD5 authentication key string used by group 2
`Switch(config-if)#` **`standby 3 authentication md5 key-chain MyHSRPChain`**	Configures MD5 authentication using key chain *MyHSRPChain*. HSRP queries the key chain to obtain the current live key and key ID

Interface Tracking.

`Switch(config)#` **`interface vlan10`**	Moves to interface configuration mode
`Switch(config-if)#` **`standby 1 track gigabitethernet 1/0/1 25`**	Causes HSRP to track the availability of interface GigabitEthernet 1/0/1. If GigabitEthernet 1/0/1 goes down, the priority of the switch in group 1 will be decremented by 25
	NOTE: The default value of the **track** argument is 10
	TIP: The **track** argument does not assign a new priority if the tracked interface goes down. The **track** argument assigns a value that the priority will be decreased if the tracked interface goes down. Therefore, if you are tracking GigabitEthernet 1/0/1 with a track value of 25 (**standby 1 track gigabitethernet 1/0/1 25**) and GigabitEthernet 1/0/1 goes down, the priority will be decreased by 25; assuming a default priority of 100, the new priority will now be 75

Multiple HSRP Groups

Figure 8-6 shows the network topology for the configuration that follows, which demonstrates how to configure multiple HSRP groups using the commands covered in this chapter. Note that only the commands specific to HSRP and STP are shown in this example.

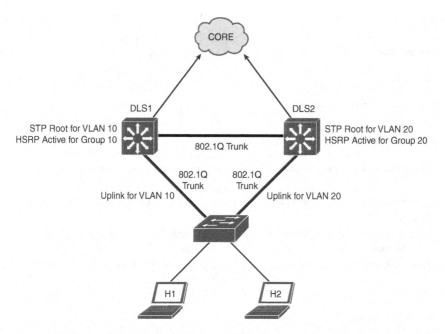

Figure 8-6   Network Topology for Multigroup HSRP Configuration Example

Multigroup HSRP enables switches to simultaneously provide redundant backup and perform load sharing across different IP subnets. The objective here is to configure DLS1 as STP root and HSRP active for VLAN 10, while DLS2 is configured as STP root and HSRP active for VLAN 20. DLS1 is also configured as backup root and HSRP standby for VLAN 20, while DLS2 is configured as backup root and HSRP standby for VLAN 10. Only the configuration for DLS1 is shown here. DLS2 would be configured in the opposite way. Host H1 is in VLAN 10 and host H2 is in VLAN 20.

`DLS1(config)# spanning-tree vlan 10 root primary`	Configures spanning-tree root primary for VLAN 10
`DLS1(config)# spanning-tree vlan 20 root secondary`	Configures spanning-tree root secondary for VLAN 20
	NOTE: Load balancing can be accomplished by having one switch be the active HSRP L3 switch forwarding for half of the VLANs and the standby L3 switch for the remaining VLANs. The second HSRP L3 switch would be reversed in its active and standby VLANs. Care must be taken to ensure that spanning tree is forwarding to the active L3 switch for the correct VLANs by making that L3 switch the spanning-tree primary root for those VLANs
`DLS1(config)# interface vlan 10`	Moves to interface configuration mode
`DLS1(config-if)# ip address 10.1.10.2 255.255.255.0`	Assigns IP address and netmask

`DLS1(config-if)# standby 10 ip 10.1.10.1`	Activates HSRP group 10 on the interface and creates a virtual IP address of 10.1.10.1 for use in HSRP
`DLS1(config-if)# standby 10 priority 110`	Assigns a priority value of 110 to standby group 10. This will be the active forwarded for VLAN 10
`DLS1(config-if)# standby 10 preempt`	Configures this switch to preempt, or take control of, VLAN 10 forwarding if the local priority is higher than the active switch VLAN 10 priority
`DLS1(config-if)# interface vlan20`	Moves to interface configuration mode
`DLS1(config-if)# ip address 10.1.20.2 255.255.255.0`	Assigns IP address and netmask
`DLS1(config-if)# standby 20 ip 10.1.20.1`	Activates HSRP group 20 on the interface and creates a virtual IP address of 10.1.20.1 for use in HSRP
`DLS1(config-if)# standby 20 priority 90`	Assigns a priority value of 90 to standby group 20. This switch will be the standby device for VLAN 20
`DLS1(config-if)# standby 20 preempt`	Configures this switch to preempt, or take control of, VLAN 20 forwarding if the local priority is higher than the active switch VLAN 20 priority

HSRP IP SLA Tracking

See Chapter 6, "Redistribution and Path Control," for a more detailed explanation of IP service level agreement (SLA) objects. The objective here is to associate an IP SLA to the HSRP process, allowing failover to occur by decrementing the HSRP priority if the object fails.

`Switch(config)# ip sla 10`	Creates SLA process 10
`Switch(config-ip-sla)# icmp-echo 172.19.10.1`	Configures the SLA as an ICMP echo operation to destination 172.19.10.1
`Switch(config-ip-sla)# exit`	Exits SLA configuration mode
`Switch(config)# ip sla schedule 10 start-time now life forever`	Configures the scheduling for SLA 10 to start now and continue forever
`Switch(config)# track 90 ip sla 10 state`	Creates an object, 90, to track the state of SLA process 10
`Switch(config-track)# interface vlan 10`	Moves to interface configuration mode
`Switch(config-if)# ip address 192.168.10.1 255.255.255.0`	Assigns IP address and netmask

`Switch(config-if)# standby 10 ip 192.168.10.254`	Activates HSRP group 10 on the interface and creates a virtual IP address of 192.168.10.254 for use in HSRP
`Switch(config-if)# standby 10 priority 110`	Assigns a priority value of 110 to standby group 10
`Switch(config-if)# standby 10 preempt`	Configures this switch to preempt, or take control of, the active switch if the local priority is higher than the active switch
`Switch(config-if)# standby 10 track 90 decrement 20`	Tracks the state of object 90 and decrements the device priority if the object fails

HSRPv2 for IPv6

HSRP Version 2 must be enabled on an interface before HSRP for IPv6 can be configured.

`Switch(config-if)# standby version 2`	Enables HSRPv2 on an interface
`Switch(config-if)# standby 1 ipv6 autoconfig`	Enables HSRP for IPv6 using a virtual link-local address that will be generated automatically from the link-local prefix and a modified EUI-64 format interface identifier, where the EUI-64 interface identifier is created from the relevant HSRP virtual MAC address
`Switch(config-if)# standby 1 ipv6 fe80::1:1`	Enables HSRP for IPv6 using an explicitly configured link-local address to be used as the virtual IPv6 address for group 1
`Switch(config-if)# standby 1 ipv6 2001::db8:2/64`	Enables HSRP for IPv6 using a global IPv6 address as the virtual address for group 1

NOTE: All other relevant HSRP commands (preempt, priority, authentication, tracking, and so on) are identical in HSRPv1 and HSRPv2.

NOTE: When configuring the IPv6 virtual address, if an IPv6 global address is used, it must include an IPv6 prefix length. If a link-local address is used, it does not have a prefix.

Debugging HSRP

`Switch# debug standby`	Displays all HSRP debugging information, including state changes and transmission/reception of HSRP packets
`Switch# debug standby errors`	Displays HSRP error messages
`Switch# debug standby events`	Displays HSRP event messages
`Switch# debug standby events terse`	Displays all HSRP events except for hellos and advertisements

Switch# `debug standby events track`	Displays all HSRP tracking events
Switch# `debug standby packets`	Displays HSRP packet messages
Switch# `debug standby terse`	Displays all HSRP errors, events, and packets, except for hellos and advertisements

Virtual Router Redundancy Protocol

NOTE: HSRP is Cisco proprietary. Virtual Router Redundancy Protocol (VRRP) is an IEEE standard.

NOTE: VRRP might not be completely supported on platforms such as the Catalyst 3750-E, 3750, 3560, or 3550. For example, the Catalyst 3560 supports VRRP for IPv4, but not for IPv6. The IPv4 implementation supports text authentication, but not message digest 5 (MD5) authentication key-chain implementation. Also, the Switch Database Management (SDM) should prefer the **routing** option for IPv4 or the **dual-ipv4-and-ipv6** option for dual-stack or IPv6 implementations. Only VRRP Version 3 (VRRPv3) is supported on the Catalyst 3650 and Catalyst 9200/9300 platforms. Verify VRRP capabilities by platform datasheets and appropriate Cisco IOS command and configuration guides.

NOTE: The VRRPv3 Protocol Support feature provides the capability to support IPv4 and IPv6 address families, while VRRPv2 only supports IPv4 addresses. To enable VRRPv3, use the **fhrp version vrrp v3** command in global configuration mode. When VRRPv3 is in use, VRRPv2 is disabled by default.

VRRP is an election protocol that dynamically assigns responsibility for one or more virtual switches to the VRRP switches on a LAN, allowing several switches on a multi-access link to use the same virtual IP address. A VRRP switch is configured to run VRRP in conjunction with one or more other switches attached.

Configuring VRRPv2

Switch(config)# `interface vlan10`	Moves to interface configuration mode
Switch(config-if)# `ip address 172.16.100.5 255.255.255.0`	Assigns IP address and netmask
Switch(config-if)# `vrrp 10 ip 172.16.100.1`	Enables VRRP for group 10 on this interface with a virtual IP address of 172.16.100.1. The group number can be from 1 to 255 **NOTE:** VRRP supports using the real interface IP address as the virtual IP address for the group. If this is done, the router with that address becomes the master
Switch(config-if)# `vrrp 10 description Engineering Group`	Assigns a text description to the group
Switch(config-if)# `vrrp 10 priority 110`	Sets the priority level for this VLAN. The range is from 1 to 254. The default is 100

`Switch(config-if)# vrrp 10 preempt`	Configures this switch to preempt, or take over, as the virtual switch master for group 10 if it has a higher priority than the current virtual switch master **NOTE:** The switch that is the IP address owner will preempt, regardless of the setting of this command **NOTE:** The **preempt** VRRP option is enabled by default
`Switch(config-if)# vrrp 10 preempt delay minimum 60`	Configures this switch to preempt, but only after a delay of 60 seconds **NOTE:** The default delay period is 0 seconds
`Switch(config-if)# vrrp 10 timers advertise 15`	Configures the interval between successful advertisements by the virtual switch master **NOTE:** The default interval value is 1 second **NOTE:** All switches in a VRRP group must use the same timer values. If switches have different timer values set, the VRRP group will not communicate with each other **NOTE:** The range of the advertisement timer is 1 to 255 seconds. If you use the **msec** argument, you change the timer to measure in milliseconds. The range in milliseconds is 50 to 999
`Switch(config-if)# vrrp 10 timers learn`	Configures the switch, when acting as a virtual switch backup, to learn the advertisement interval used by the virtual switch master
`Switch(config-if)# vrrp 10 shutdown`	Disables VRRP on the interface, but configuration is still retained
`Switch(config-if)# no vrrp 10 shutdown`	Reenables the VRRP group using the previous configuration
`Switch(config-if) vrrp 10 authentication text ottawa`	Configures plain-text authentication for group 10 using the key **ottawa**
`Switch(config-if)# vrrp 10 authentication md5 key-string winnipeg`	Configures MD5 authentication for group 10 using the key **winnipeg**

Configuring VRRPv3

`Switch(config)# fhrp version vrrp v3`	Enables the ability to configure VRRPv3
`Switch(config)# interface vlan 10`	Moves to interface configuration mode
`Switch(config-if)# vrrp 10 address-family ipv4`	Creates a VRRP group number 10 and enters VRRP configuration mode for IPV4

`Switch(config-if-vrrp)#` `address 10.0.1.10`	Specifies an IPv4 address for the VRRP group
`Switch(config-if-vrrp)#` `priority 150`	Specifies the priority value of the VRRP group. The priority of a VRRP group is 100 by default
`Switch(config-if-vrrp)# preempt` `delay minimum 30`	Enables preemption of lower priority master device with a 30 second delay Preemption is enabled by default
`Switch(config-if-vrrp)# timers` `advertise 5000`	Sets the advertisement timer to 5000 milliseconds. The advertisement timer is set to 1000 milliseconds by default
`Switch(config-if-vrrp)# vrrpv2`	Enables support for VRRPv2 simultaneously, so as to interoperate with devices that only support VRRP v2. VRRPv2 is disabled by default

VRRP Optimization Options

Interface Tracking

VRRP does not have a native interface tracking mechanism. Instead, it has the ability to track objects. This allows the VRRP master to lose its status if a tracked object (interface, IP SLA, and so on) fails.

`Switch(config)# track 10`
`interface gigabitethernet 1/0/1`
`line-protocol`
	Creates a tracked object, where the status of the uplink interface is tracked

`Switch(config-track)# interface` `vlan 10`	Moves to interface configuration mode
`Switch(config-if)# vrrp 1` `track 10 decrement 30`	Configures VRRP to track the previously created object and decrease the VRRP priority by 30 should the uplink interface fail

Verifying VRRP

NOTE: The VRRP verification commands are the same for IPv6 and IPv4.

`Switch# show vrrp`	Displays VRRP information
`Switch# show vrrp brief`	Displays a brief status of all VRRP groups
`Switch# show vrrp 10`	Displays detailed information about VRRP group 10
`Switch# show vrrp` `interface vlan10`	Displays information about VRRPv2 as enabled on interface VLAN 10
`Switch# show vrrp` `interface vlan10 brief`	Displays a brief summary about VRRPv2 on interface VLAN 10
`Switch# show vrrp` `ipv4 vlan 10`	Displays information about VRRPv3 as enabled on interface VLAN 10
`Switch# show vrrp brief` `vlan 10`	Displays a brief summary about VRRPv3 on interface VLAN 10

Debugging VRRP

Switch# **debug vrrp all**	Displays all VRRP messages
Switch# **debug vrrp error**	Displays all VRRP error messages
Switch# **debug vrrp events**	Displays all VRRP event messages
Switch# **debug vrrp packet**	Displays messages about packets sent and received
Switch# **debug vrrp state**	Displays messages about state transitions

IPv4 Configuration Example: HSRP on L3 Switch

Figure 8-7 shows the network topology for the configuration that follows, which demonstrates how to configure HSRP using the commands covered in this chapter. Note that only the commands specific to HSRP are shown in this example.

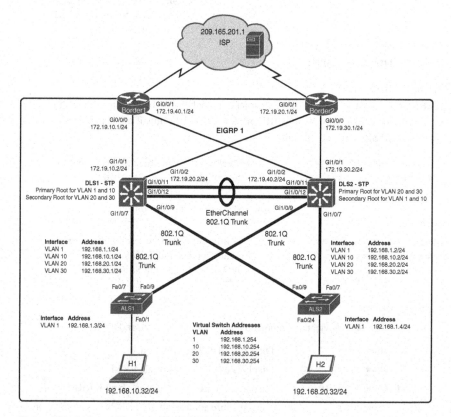

Figure 8-7   Network Topology for HSRP Configuration Example

The network devices are configured as follows:

- DLS1 and DLS2 are configured as Layer 3 devices; ALS1 and ALS2 are configured as Layer 2 devices.

- Border1, Border2, DLS1, and DLS2 run Enhanced Interior Gateway Routing Protocol (EIGRP). Border1 and Border2 also provide default routing into the cloud.

- The links from DLS1 and DLS2 to Border1 and Border2 are routed links using the **no switchport** command on DLS1 and DLS2.

- Four VLANs are configured on DLS1. DLS1 is the VTP server for DLS2, ALS1, and ALS2.

- A Layer 2 EtherChannel trunk connects DLS1 and DLS2.

- All connections towards the access layer are 802.1Q trunks.

- DLS1 is the spanning-tree primary root for VLANs 1 and 10 and DLS1 is the secondary root for VLANs 20 and 30.

- DLS2 is the spanning-tree primary root for VLANs 20 and 30 and DLS1 is the secondary root for VLANs 1 and 10.

- DLS1 is to be HSRP active for VLANs 1 and 10, and HSRP standby for VLANs 20 and 30.

- DLS2 is to be HSRP active for VLANs 20 and 30, and HSRP standby for VLANs 1 and 10.

- Interface tracking is configured to allow for HSRP failover to occur if an uplink fails.

Switch DLS1

`DLS1(config)#` `interface vlan 1`	Moves to interface configuration mode
`DLS1(config-if)#` **standby 1** `ip 192.168.1.254`	Activates HSRP group 1 on the interface and creates a virtual IP address of 192.168.1.254 for use in HSRP
`DLS1(config-if)#` **standby 1** `priority 105`	Assigns a priority value of 105 to standby group 1
`DLS1(config-if)#` **standby 1** `preempt`	Configures this switch to preempt, or take control of, VLAN 1 forwarding if the local priority is higher than the active switch VLAN 1 priority
`DLS1(config-if)#` **standby 1 track gigabitethernet 1/0/1 20**	HSRP will track the availability of interface GigabitEthernet 1/0/1. If GigabitEthernet 1/0/1 goes down, the priority of the switch in group 1 will be decremented by 20
`DLS1(config-if)#` **standby 1 track gigabitethernet 1/0/2**	HSRP will track the availability of interface GigabitEthernet 1/0/2. If GigabitEthernet 1/0/2 goes down, the priority of the switch in group 1 will be decremented by the default value of 10
`DLS1(config-if)#` **exit**	Moves to global configuration mode
`DLS1(config)#` **interface vlan 10**	Moves to interface configuration mode
`DLS1(config-if)#` **standby 10 ip 192.168.10.254**	Activates HSRP group 10 on the interface and creates a virtual IP address of 192.168.10.254 for use in HSRP
`DLS1(config-if)#` **standby 10 priority 105**	Assigns a priority value of 105 to standby group 10

DLS1(config-if)# standby 10 preempt	Configures this switch to preempt, or take control of, VLAN 10 forwarding if the local priority is higher than the active switch VLAN 10 priority
DLS1(config-if)# standby 10 track gigabitethernet 1/0/1 20	HSRP will track the availability of interface GigabitEthernet 1/0/1. If GigabitEthernet 1/0/1 goes down, the priority of the switch in group 10 will be decremented by 20
DLS1(config-if)# standby 10 track gigabitethernet 1/0/2	HSRP will track the availability of interface GigabitEthernet 1/0/2. If GigabitEthernet 1/0/2 goes down, the priority of the switch in group 10 will be decremented by the default value of 10
DLS1(config-if)# exit	Moves to global configuration mode
DLS1(config)# interface vlan20	Moves to interface configuration mode
DLS1(config-if)# standby 20 ip 192.168.20.254	Activates HSRP group 20 on the interface and creates a virtual IP address of 192.168.20.254 for use in HSRP
DLS1(config-if)# standby 20 priority 100	Assigns a priority value of 100 to standby group 20
DLS1(config-if)# standby 20 track gigabitethernet 1/0/1 20	HSRP will track the availability of interface GigabitEthernet 1/0/1. If GigabitEthernet 1/0/1 goes down, the priority of the switch in group 20 will be decremented by 20
DLS1(config-if)# standby 20 track gigabitethernet 1/0/2	HSRP will track the availability of interface GigabitEthernet 1/0/2. If GigabitEthernet 1/0/2 goes down, the priority of the switch in group 20 will be decremented by the default value of 10
DLS1(config-if)# exit	Moves to global configuration mode
DLS1(config)# interface vlan30	Moves to interface configuration mode
DLS1(config-if)# standby 30 ip 192.168.30.254	Activates HSRP group 30 on the interface and creates a virtual IP address of 192.168.30.254 for use in HSRP
DLS1(config-if)# standby 30 priority 100	Assigns a priority value of 100 to standby group 30
DLS1(config-if)# standby 30 track gigabitethernet 1/0/1 20	HSRP will track the availability of interface GigabitEthernet 1/0/1. If GigabitEthernet 1/0/1 goes down, the priority of the switch in group 30 will be decremented by 20
DLS1(config-if)# standby 30 track gigabitethernet 1/0/2	HSRP will track the availability of interface GigabitEthernet 1/0/2. If GigabitEthernet 1/0/2 goes down, the priority of the switch in group 30 will be decremented by the default value of 10
DLS1(config-if)# exit	Moves to global configuration mode

Switch DLS2

`DLS2(config)# interface vlan1`	Moves to interface configuration mode
`DLS2(config-if)# standby 1` `ip 192.168.1.254`	Activates HSRP group 1 on the interface and creates a virtual IP address of 192.168.1.254 for use in HSRP
`DLS2(config-if)# standby 1` `priority 100`	Assigns a priority value of 100 to standby group 1
`DLS2(config-if)# standby 1` `track gigabitethernet 1/0/1 20`	HSRP will track the availability of interface GigabitEthernet 1/0/1. If GigabitEthernet 1/0/1 goes down, the priority of the switch in group 1 will be decremented by 20
`DLS2(config-if)# standby 1` `track gigabitethernet 1/0/2`	HSRP will track the availability of interface GigabitEthernet 1/0/2. If GigabitEthernet 1/0/2 goes down, the priority of the switch in group 1 will be decremented by the default value of 10
`DLS2(config-if)# exit`	Moves to global configuration mode
`DLS2(config)# interface` `vlan10`	Moves to interface configuration mode
`DLS2(config-if)# standby 10` `ip 192.168.10.254`	Activates HSRP group 10 on the interface and creates a virtual IP address of 192.168.10.254 for use in HSRP
`DLS2(config-if)# standby 10` `priority 100`	Assigns a priority value of 100 to standby group 10
`DLS2(config-if)# standby 10` `track gigabitethernet 1/0/1 20`	HSRP will track the availability of interface GigabitEthernet 1/0/1. If GigabitEthernet 1/0/1 goes down, the priority of the switch in group 10 will be decremented by 20
`DLS2(config-if)# standby 10` `track gigabitethernet 1/0/2`	HSRP will track the availability of interface GigabitEthernet 1/0/2. If GigabitEthernet 1/0/2 goes down, the priority of the switch in group 10 will be decremented by the default value of 10
`DLS2(config-if)# exit`	Moves to global configuration mode
`DLS2(config)# interface` `vlan20`	Moves to interface configuration mode
`DLS2(config-if)# standby 20` `ip 192.168.20.254`	Activates HSRP group 20 on the interface and creates a virtual IP address of 192.168.20.254 for use in HSRP
`DLS2(config-if)# standby 20` `priority 105`	Assigns a priority value of 105 to standby group 20
`DLS2(config-if)# standby 20` `preempt`	Configures this switch to preempt, or take control of, VLAN 20 forwarding if the local priority is higher than the active switch VLAN 20 priority
`DLS2(config-if)# standby 20` `track gigabitethernet 1/0/1 20`	HSRP will track the availability of interface GigabitEthernet 1/0/1. If GigabitEthernet 1/0/1 goes down, the priority of the switch in group 20 will be decremented by 20

DLS2(config-if)# **standby 20 track gigabitethernet 1/0/2**	HSRP will track the availability of interface GigabitEthernet 1/0/2. If GigabitEthernet 1/0/2 goes down, the priority of the switch in group 20 will be decremented by the default value of 10
DLS2(config-if)# **exit**	Moves to global configuration mode
DLS2(config)# **interface vlan30**	Moves to interface configuration mode
DLS2(config-if)# **standby 30 ip 192.168.30.254**	Activates HSRP group 30 on the interface and creates a virtual IP address of 192.168.30.254 for use in HSRP
DLS2(config-if)# **standby 30 priority 105**	Assigns a priority value of 105 to standby group 30
DLS2(config-if)# **standby 30 preempt**	Configures this switch to preempt, or take control of, VLAN 30 forwarding if the local priority is higher than the active switch VLAN 30 priority
DLS2(config-if)# **standby 30 track gigabitethernet 1/0/1 20**	HSRP will track the availability of interface GigabitEthernet 1/0/1. If GigabitEthernet 1/0/1 goes down, the priority of the switch in group 30 will be decremented by 20
DLS2(config-if)# **standby 30 track gigabitethernet 1/0/2**	HSRP will track the availability of interface GigabitEthernet 1/0/2. If GigabitEthernet 1/0/2 goes down, the priority of the switch in group 30 will be decremented by the default value of 10
DLS2(config-if)# **exit**	Moves to global configuration mode

IP SLA Tracking: Switch DLS1 VLAN 10

Refer to Figure 8-7. The objective here is to probe the availability of a web server hosted in the ISP cloud at address 209.165.201.1. If the server does not respond to the IP SLA ping, the HSRP priority on interface VLAN 10 will be decremented by 20. This configuration could be applied to all other VLANs where the HSRP Active device resides (DLS1 for VLANs 1 and 10; DLS2 for VLANs 20 and 30).

DLS1(config)# **ip sla 10**	Creates SLA process 10
DLS1(config-ip-sla)# **icmp-echo 209.165.201.1**	Configures the SLA as an ICMP echo operation to destination 209.165.201.1
DLS1(config-ip-sla-echo)# **exit**	Exits SLA configuration mode
DLS1(config)# **ip sla schedule 10 start-time now life forever**	Configures the scheduling for SLA 10 process to start now and continue forever
DLS1(config)# **track 90 ip sla 10 state**	Creates an object, 90, to track the state of SLA process 10
DLS1(config-track)# **exit**	Moves to global configuration mode

DLS1(config)# **interface vlan 10**	Moves to interface configuration mode
DLS1(config-if)# **standby 10 track 90 decrement 20**	Tracks the state of object 90 and decrements the device priority by 20 if the object fails
DLS1(config-if)# **exit**	Moves to global configuration mode

IPv4 Configuration Example: VRRPv2 on Router and L3 Switch with IP SLA Tracking

Figure 8-8 shows the network topology for the configuration that follows, which shows how to configure VRRPv2 using the commands covered in this chapter. Note that only the commands specific to VRRPv2 are shown in this example. Full routing and connectivity are assumed. R1 and DLS-2 are the participating devices in VRRPv2.

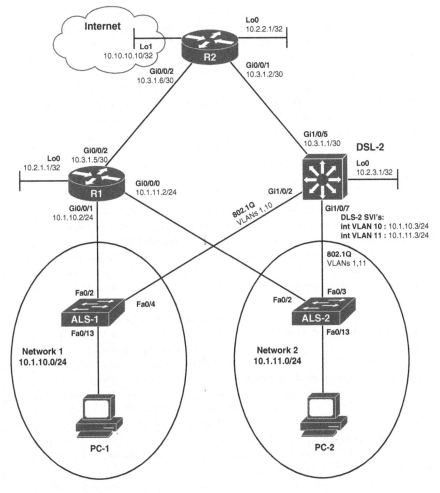

Figure 8-8   VRRP for IPv4 Using Router and L3 Switch

The network devices are configured as follows:

- R1 and DLS-2 are VRRP partners.

- ALS-1 and ALS-2 are Layer 2 switches, where ALS-1 is the network switch for 10.1.10.0/24 and ALS-2 is the network switch for 10.1.11.0/24.

- R1, R2, and DLS-2 are OSPF neighbors; GigabitEthernet 1/0/5 on DLS-2 is a routed port.

- VLAN 10 is configured on ALS-1; VLAN 11 is configured on ALS-2; DLS-2 has both VLAN 10 and 11 configured.

- All lines connecting DLS-2, ALS-1, and ALS-2 are 802.1Q trunks.

- R1 is the preferred forwarder for network 10.1.10.0/24 and DLS-2 is the preferred forwarder for network 10.1.11.0/24.

R1

`R1(config)# ip sla 10`	Enters SLA programming mode
`R1(config-ip-sla)# icmp-echo 10.10.10.10`	Has the SLA ping 10.10.10.10
`R1(config-ip-sla-echo)# frequency 5`	Pings 10.10.10.10 every 5 seconds
`R1(config-ip-sla-echo)# exit`	Exits SLA programming mode
`R1(config)# ip sla schedule 10 life forever start-time now`	Specifies the SLA start time and duration
`R1(config)# track 100 ip sla 10`	Creates tracking object 100 calling SLA 10
`R1(config)# track 2 interface gigabitethernet 0/0/2 line-protocol`	Creates tracking object 2 to monitor line protocol up/down status of interface GigabitEthernet 0/0/2
`R1(config-track)# exit`	Exits tracking configuration mode
`R1(config)# interface gigabitethernet 0/0/0`	Enters interface configuration mode for GigabitEthernet 0/0/0
`R1(config-if)# ip address 10.1.11.2 255.255.255.0`	Assigns the physical interface address of 10.1.11.2/24
`R1(config-if)# vrrp 11 ip 10.1.11.1`	Assigns the VRRP virtual IP address of 10.1.11.1 for VRRP group 11
`R1(config-if)# vrrp 11 authentication text CISCO123`	Uses the string *CISCO123* for authentication between group 11 members **NOTE:** Authentication by key chain is not available on some L3 switch platforms
`R1(config-if)# vrrp 11 track 2`	Has VRRP group 11 watch tracking object 2, line protocol up/down on interface GigabitEthernet 0/0/2
`R1(config-if)# interface gigabitethernet 0/0/1`	Enters interface configuration mode
`R1(config-if)# ip address 10.1.10.2 255.255.255.0`	Assigns the physical interface address of 10.1.10.2/24

`R1(config-if)# vrrp 10` `ip 10.1.10.1`	Assigns the VRRP virtual IP address of 10.1.10.1 for VRRP group 10
`R1(config-if)# vrrp 10` `priority 105`	Assigns group 10 virtual forwarder priority of 105. The default is 100
`R1(config-if)# vrrp 10 track 2`	Has VRRP group 10 watch tracking object 2, line protocol up/down on interface GigabitEthernet 0/0/2
`R1(config-if)# vrrp 10` `track 100 decrement 6`	Has VRRP group 10 watch a second tracking object. Object 100 looks for ICMP ping connectivity to 10.10.10.10 every 5 seconds
`R1(config-if)# end`	Returns to privileged EXEC mode

DLS-2

`DLS-2(config)# ip sla 10`	Enters SLA 10 programming mode
`DLS-2(config-ip-sla)# icmp-echo` `10.10.10.10`	Has the SLA ping 10.10.10.10
`DLS-2(config-ip-sla-echo)#` `frequency 5`	Pings 10.10.10.10 every 5 seconds
`DLS-2(config-ip-sla-echo)# exit`	Exits SLA programming mode
`DLS-2(config)# ip sla schedule 10` `life forever start-time now`	Specifies SLA 10 start time and duration
`DLS-2(config)# track 100 ip sla 10`	Creates tracking object 100, which calls SLA 10
`DLS-2(config)# track 2 interface` `gigabitethernet 1/0/5 line-protocol`	Creates tracking object 2 to monitor line protocol up/down status of interface GigabitEthernet 1/0/5 (routed port to R2)
`DLS-2(config-if)# interface` `gigabitethernet 1/0/5`	Enters interface configuration mode
`DLS-2(config-if)# no switchport`	Changes GigabitEthernet 1/0/5 to a Layer 3 port
`DLS-2(config-if)# ip address` `10.3.1.1 255.255.255.252`	Assigns IPv4 address 10.3.1.1/30
`DLS-2(config)# interface` `gigabitethernet 1/0/2`	Enters interface configuration mode
`DLS-2(config-if)# switchport` `mode trunk`	Forces trunk mode
`DLS-2(config-if)# switchport trunk` `allowed vlan 1,10`	Limits VLAN traffic on this trunk to VLANs 1 and 10
`DLS-2(config-if)# interface` `gigabitethernet 1/0/7`	Enters interface configuration mode
`DLS-2(config-if)# switchport mode` `trunk`	Forces trunk mode

`DLS-2(config-if)# ` **`switchport trunk`** `allowed vlan 1,11`	Limits VLAN traffic on this trunk to VLANs 1 and 11
`DLS-2(config-if)# ` **`interface vlan 10`**	Enters switched virtual interface configuration mode for VLAN 10
`DLS-2(config-if)# ` **`ip address`** `10.1.10.3 255.255.255.0`	Assigns IPv4 address 10.1.10.3/24
`DLS-2(config-if)# ` **`vrrp 10`** `ip 10.1.10.1`	Assigns the VRRP virtual IP address of 10.1.10.1 for VRRP group 10
`DLS-2(config-if)# ` **`vrrp 10 track 2`**	Has VRRP group 10 watch tracking object 2, line protocol up/down on interface GigabitEthernet 1/0/5
`DLS-2(config-if)# ` **`interface vlan 11`**	Enters switched virtual interface configuration mode for VLAN 11
`DLS-2(config-if)# ` **`ip address`** `10.1.11.3 255.255.255.0`	Assigns IPv4 address 10.1.11.3/24
`DLS-2(config-if)# ` **`vrrp 11`** `ip 10.1.11.1`	Assigns the VRRP virtual IP address of 10.1.11.1 for VRRP group 11
`DLS-2(config-if)# ` **`vrrp 11`** **`priority 105`**	Assigns group 11 virtual forwarder priority of 105. The default is 100
`DLS-2(config-if)# ` **`vrrp 11`** **`authentication text CISCO123`**	Uses the string *CISCO123* for authentication between group 11 members
`DLS-2(config-if)# ` **`vrrp 11 track 2`**	Has VRRP group 11 watch tracking object 2, line protocol up/down on interface GigabitEthernet 1/0/5
`DLS-2(config-if)# ` **`vrrp 11 track`** **`100 decrement 6`**	Has VRRP group 11 watch a second tracking object. Object 100 looks for ICMP ping connectivity to 10.10.10.10 every 5 seconds
`DLS-2(config-if)# ` **`exit`**	Returns to privileged EXEC mode

IPv6 Configuration Example: HSRPv2 on Router and L3 Switch

Figure 8-9 shows the network topology for the IPv6 HSRPv2 configuration that follows. Router R1 and L3 switch DLS-2 are the HSRP pair.

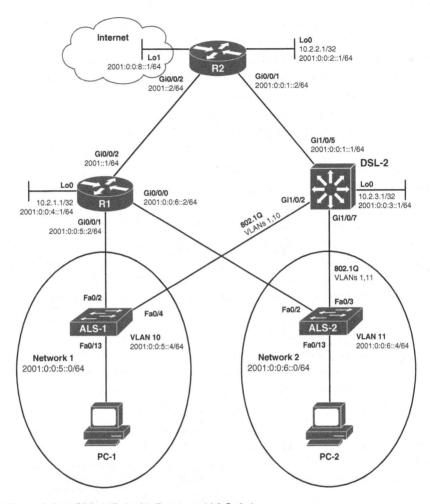

Figure 8-9   HSRPv2 IPv6 with Router and L3 Switch

R1

The network devices are configured similar to those in the previous example:

- R1 and DLS-2 are HSRPv2 partners.

- ALS-1 and ALS-2 are Layer 2 switches, where ALS-1 is the network switch for 2001:0:0:5::0/64 and ALS-2 is the network switch for 2001:0:0:6::0/64.

- R1, R2, and DLS-2 are OSPFv3 neighbors; GigabitEthernet 1/0/5 on DLS-2 is a routed port.

- VLAN 10 is configured on ALS-1; VLAN 11 is configured on ALS-2; DLS-2 has both VLANs 10 and 11 configured.

- All lines connecting DLS-2, ALS-1, and ALS-2 are 802.1Q trunks.

- R1 is the preferred forwarder for network 2001:0:0:5::0/64 and DLS-2 is the preferred forwarder for network 2001:0:0:6::0/64.

R1(config)# **ipv6 unicast-routing**	Enables IPv6 forwarding
R1(config)# **ip sla 11**	Enters SLA programming mode for process 11
R1(config-ip-sla)# **icmp-echo 2001:0:0:8::1 source-interface gigabitethernet 0/0/2**	Has the SLA ping 2001:0:0:8::1
R1(config-ip-sla-echo)# **frequency 5**	Pings every 5 seconds
R1(config-ip-sla-echo)# **exit**	Exits SLA programming mode
1(config)# **ip sla schedule 11 life forever start-time now**	Defines the start and duration for SLA 11
R1(config)# **track 111 ip sla 11**	Creates tracking object 111 that uses SLA 11
R1(config-track)# **exit**	Exits tracking
R1(config)# **interface gigabitethernet 0/0/0**	Enters interface configuration mode
R1(config-if)# **ipv6 address 2001:0:0:6::2/64**	Assigns IPv6 unicast address
R1(config-if)# **standby version 2**	Enables HSRPv2 **NOTE:** HSRPv2 is required for IPv6 implementation
R1(config-if)# **standby 11 ipv6 autoconfig**	Creates IPv6 HSRP virtual address **NOTE:** When you enter the **standby ipv6** command, a modified EUI-64 format interface identifier is generated in which the EUI-64 interface identifier is created from the relevant HSRP virtual MAC address **NOTE:** The **standby group ipv6** interface command can offer different options when using different platforms. For example, a 3560 L3 switch will allow an IPv6 **prefix** argument, whereas a 2911G2 router will not
R1(config-if)# **standby 11 preempt**	Configures this device to preempt, or take control of, the active forwarding if the local priority is higher than any of the other members of the HSRP group **NOTE:** The same preempt command arguments are available for IPv6 as in IPv4

`R1(config-if)# standby 11 track gigabitethernet 0/0/2 12`	Instructs HSRPv2 to follow the line protocol of GigabitEthernet 0/0/2 and decrement the interface group priority by 12 when the interface goes down **NOTE:** When the preceding tracking command is entered, the router creates the following line protocol tracking object: **track x interface GigabitEthernet 0/0/2 line-protocol**, where **x** is the next available number available for a tracking object. The IOS then substitutes the tracking command **standby 11 track x decrement 12** at the interface (as seen below)
`R1(config-if)# standby 11 track 1 decrement 12`	Has HSRP group 11 watch tracking object 1, line protocol up/down on interface GigabitEthernet 0/0/2
`R1(config-if)# interface gigabitethernet 0/0/1`	Enters interface configuration mode
`R1(config-if)# ipv6 address 2001:0:0:5::2/64`	Assigns an IPv6 unicast address
`R1(config-if)# standby version 2`	Selects HSRPv2
`R1(config-if)# standby 10 ipv6 autoconfig`	Creates IPv6 HSRP virtual address
`R1(config-if)# standby 10 priority 105`	Sets a priority of 105 for standby group 10 on this interface
`R1(config-if)# standby 10 preempt`	Configures this device to preempt, or take control of, the active forwarding if the local priority is higher than any of the other members of the HSRP group
`R1(config-if)# standby 10 track 1 decrement 12`	Links tracking object 1 to this HSRP group and decreases this device's priority by 12 when tracking object 1 is asserted
`R1(config-if)# standby 10 track 111 decrement 7`	Links a second tracking object to this HSRP group and decreases the device's priority by 7 when asserted

DLS-2

`DLS-2(config)# ip routing`	Enables IOS Layer 3 functionality
`DLS-2(config)# ipv6 unicast-routing`	Enables IOS IPv6 Layer 3 functionality
`DLS-2(config)# sdm prefer dual-ipv4-and-ipv6`	Configures the Switching Database Manager on the switch to optimize memory and operating system for both IPv4 and IPv6 Layer 3 forwarding **CAUTION:** This command requires a reload of the switch to take effect and is not available on the Catalyst 3650

`DLS-2(config)# ip sla 11`	Creates and enters SLA 11 **NOTE:** The SLAs are added only as an illustration of capability **NOTE:** There seems to be no distinction between IPv4 and IPv6 in the **ip sla** command
`DLS-2(config-ip-sla)#` `icmp-echo 2001:0:0:8::1`	Assigns 2001:0:0:8::1 as the ICMP ping destination for this SLA
`DLS-2(config-ip-sla-echo)#` `frequency 5`	Sends pings every 5 seconds
`DLS-2(config-ip-sla-echo)#` `exit`	Exits SLA configuration mode
`DLS-2(config)# ip sla schedule` `11 life forever start-time now`	Assigns the start time and duration for SLA 11
`DLS-2(config)# track 101` `ip sla 11`	Creates tracking object 101, which uses SLA 11
`DLS-2(config-track)# exit`	Exits tracking configuration mode
`DLS-2(config)# interface` `loopback 0`	Enters interface configuration mode
`DLS-2(config-if)# ipv6 address` `2001:0:0:3::1/64`	Assigns an IPv6 unicast address
`DLS-2(config-if)# interface` `gigabitethernet 1/0/5`	Enters interface configuration mode
`DLS-2(config-if)# no` `switchport`	Changes Layer 2 switch port to a Layer 3 routed port
`DLS-2(config-if)# ipv6 address` `2001:0:0:1::1/64`	Assigns an IPv6 address to this L3 forwarding port
`DLS-2(config-if)# interface` `gigabitethernet 1/0/2`	Enters interface configuration mode for L2 interface
`DLS-2(config-if)# switchport` `trunk allowed vlan 1,10`	Permits traffic from VLANs 1 and 10 on the trunk
`DLS-2(config-if)# switchport` `mode trunk`	Sets the port to trunk unconditionally
`DLS-2(config-if)# interface` `gigabitfastethernet 0/7`	Enters interface configuration mode
`DLS-2(config-if)# switchport` `trunk allowed vlan 1,11`	Permits traffic from VLANs 1 and 11 on the trunk
`DLS-2(config-if)# switchport` `mode trunk`	Sets the port to trunk unconditionally
`DLS-2(config-if)# interface` `vlan 10`	Enters interface programming mode for VLAN 10 SVI
`DLS-2(config-if)# standby` `version 2`	Specifies HSRPv2
`DLS-2(config-if)# ipv6 address` `2001:0:0:5::3/64`	Assigns IPv6 unicast address

`DLS-2(config-if)#` **`standby 10`** `ipv6 autoconfig`	Creates IPv6 HSRP virtual address
`DLS-2(config-if)#` **`standby 10`** `preempt`	Enables this group's HSRP forwarder to become active at any time when its group priority is the highest
`DLS-2(config-if)#` **`standby 10`** `track 111 decrement 10`	Links tracking object 111 to this standby group and decreases this device's priority by 10 when tracking object 111 is asserted
`DLS-2(config-if)#` **`interface`** `vlan 11`	Enters interface configuration mode for VLAN 11 SVI
`DLS-2(config-if)#` **`ipv6 address`** `2001:0:0:6::3/64`	Assigns IPv6 unicast address
`DLS-2(config-if)#` **`standby`** `version 2`	Specifies HSRPv2
`DLS-2(config-if)#` **`standby 11`** `ipv6 autoconfig`	Creates IPv6 HSRP virtual address
`DLS-2(config-if)#` **`standby 11`** `priority 105`	Sets a priority of 105 for standby group 11 on this interface
`DLS-2(config-if)#` **`standby 11`** `preempt`	Enables this group's HSRP forwarder to transition to active at any time when its group priority is the highest
`DLS-2(config-if)#` **`standby 11`** `track 111 decrement 10`	Links tracking object 111 to HSRP group 11 and decreases this device's priority by 10 when tracking object 111 is asserted

NOTE: HSRP verification and **debug** commands are the same for IPv4 and IPv6.

Dynamic Host Control Protocol (DHCP)

DHCP is a network management protocol used on UDP/IP networks whereby a DHCP server dynamically assigns an IP address and other network configuration parameters to each device on a network so that the devices can communicate with other IP networks.

Implementing DHCP for IPv4

DHCP was first defined in RFC 1531 in October 1993, but due to errors in the editorial process was almost immediately reissued as RFC 1541.

Configuring a DHCP Server on a Cisco IOS Router

`Router(config)#` **`ip dhcp pool`** `INTERNAL`	Creates a DHCP pool named INTERNAL. The name can be anything of your choosing
`Router(dhcp-config)#` **`network`** `172.16.10.0 255.255.255.0`	Defines the range of addresses to be leased
`Router(dhcp-config) #` **`default-router 172.16.10.1`**	Defines the address of the default router for the client. One IP address is required; however, you can specify up to eight IP addresses in the command line, listed in order of precedence

Router(dhcp-config)# **dns-server 172.16.10.10**	Defines the address of the DNS server for the client
Router(dhcp-config)# **netbios-name-server** **172.16.10.10**	Defines the address of the NetBIOS server for the client
Router(dhcp-config)# **domain-name fakedomainname.com**	Defines the domain name for the client
Router(dhcp-config)# **lease** **14 12 23**	Defines the lease time to be 14 days, 12 hours, 23 minutes
Router(dhcp-config)# **lease** **infinite**	Sets the lease time to infinity; the default time is 1 day
Router(dhcp-config)# **exit**	Returns to global configuration mode
Router(config)# **ip dhcp** **excluded-address 172.16.10.1** **172.16.10.10**	Specifies the range of addresses not to be leased out to clients
Router(config)# **service dhcp**	Enables the DHCP service and relay features on a Cisco IOS router
Router(config)# **no service dhcp**	Turns off the DHCP service, which is on by default in Cisco IOS Software

Configuring DHCP Manual IP Assignment

It is sometimes desirable to link a specific network device with a specific IPv4 address using a Cisco device's DHCP service. The Cisco device uses a "client ID" to identify a DHCP client device and is programmed into the DHCP pool.

NOTE: The DHCP client device ID can be determined using the **show ip dhcp binding** command after the client has successfully obtained the next available IP address from the DHCP pool.

The DHCP pool programming must also include any other required programming such as default router IP, DNS, or WINS addresses, and so on.

Router(config)# **ip dhcp pool POOL1**	Creates a DHCP pool named POOL1
Router(dhcp-config)# **host** **172.22.12.88/24**	Defines the single IP address for the DHCP pool in dotted decimal with subnet mask or CIDR notation
Router(dhcp-config)# **client-identifier 0063.6973.636f.2d** **30.3030.362e.6636.3962.2e65.3331.31** **2d.4769.302f.31**	Specifies the client ID of the network device that should receive the specific IP
Router(dhcp-config)# **default-router** **172.22.12.1**	Specifies the gateway router for the DHCP clients
Router(dhcp-config)# **dns-server** **192.168.22.11**	Specifies the IP address of the DNS service
Router(dhcp-config)# **lease 1 0 0**	Specifies the DHCP lease length in "days hours minutes"
Router(dhcp-config)# **exit**	Leaves DHCP configuration mode

Configuring DHCP Relay

DHCP services can reside anywhere within the network. The DHCP relay service translates a client broadcast DHCP service request to a unicast DHCP request directed to the DHCP server IP address. The command is added to the Layer 3 interface on the IP segment from which the DHCP broadcast request originates.

`Router(config)# interface gigabitethernet 0/0`	Moves to interface configuration mode
`Router(config-if)# ip helper-address 172.16.20.2`	Forwards DHCP broadcast messages as unicast messages to this specific address instead of having them be dropped by the router

NOTE: The **ip helper-address** command forwards broadcast packets as a unicast to eight different UDP ports by default:

- TFTP (port 69)
- DNS (port 53)
- Time service (port 37)
- NetBIOS name server (port 137)
- NetBIOS datagram server (port 138)
- Boot Protocol (BOOTP) client and server datagrams (ports 67 and 68)
- TACACS service (port 49)

If you want to close some of these ports, use the **no ip forward-protocol udp** x command at the global configuration prompt, where x is the port number you want to close. Services not forwarded by **ip helper-address** can be added using the **ip forward-protocol** global command.

`Router(config-if)# ip helper-address 10.1.1.1`	Forwards the DHCP traffic to the DHCP server at 10.1.1.1
`Router(config)# no ip forward-protocol udp 37`	Prevents forwarding of traffic for UDP time services using port 37
`Router(config)# ip forward-protocol udp 5858`	Forwards traffic for UDP services using port 5858

Configuring a DHCP Client on a Cisco IOS Software Ethernet Interface

Figure 8-10 shows the network topology for the configuration that follows, which demonstrates how to configure provider-assigned IPv4 DHCP address.

Figure 8-10 Configure a Provider-Assigned DHCP IPv4 Address

`EDGE(config)# interface` `gigabitethernet 0/0`	Enters GigabitEthernet 0/0 interface configuration mode
`EDGE(config-if)# ip address dhcp`	Allows the interface to obtain an address dynamically from the ISP
`EDGE(config-if)# no shutdown`	Enables the interface

NOTE: If the default gateway optional parameter is contained within the DHCP reply packet, the router will install a static default route in its routing table, with the default gateway's IP address as the next hop. The default route is installed with the administrative distance of 254, which makes it a floating static route. To disable this feature, use the interface-level command **no ip dhcp client request router.**

Verifying and Troubleshooting DHCP Configuration

`Router# show ip dhcp binding`	Displays a list of all bindings created
`Router# show ip dhcp binding` `w.x.y.z`	Displays the bindings for a specific DHCP client with an IP address of *w.x.y.z*
`Router# clear ip dhcp binding` `a.b.c.d`	Clears an automatic address binding from the DHCP server database
`Router# clear ip dhcp binding *`	Clears all automatic DHCP bindings
`Router# show ip dhcp conflict`	Displays a list of all address conflicts that the DHCP server recorded
`Router# clear ip dhcp conflict` `a.b.c.d`	Clears an address conflict from the database
`Router# clear ip dhcp conflict *`	Clears conflicts for all addresses
`Router# show ip dhcp database`	Displays recent activity on the DHCP database
`Router# show ip dhcp pool`	Displays information about DHCP address pools
`Router# show ip dhcp pool` *name*	Displays information about the DHCP pool named *name*
`Router# show ip dhcp interface`	Displays interface on which DHCP is enabled
`Router# show ip dhcp server` `statistics`	Displays a list of the number of messages sent and received by the DHCP server
`Router# clear ip dhcp server` `statistics`	Resets all DHCP server counters to 0
`Router# debug ip dhcp server` `{events	packet	linkage |` `class}`	Displays the DHCP process of addresses being leased and returned
`Router# debug ip dhcp server` `events`	Report address assignments, lease expirations, and so on
`Router# debug ip dhcp server` `packets`	Decodes DHCP server message receptions and transmissions

Implementing DHCP for IPv6

DHCPv6 can deliver both stateful and stateless information. Stateful, or centrally managed, information is used to provide parameters not available through stateless address autoconfiguration (SLAAC) or neighbor discovery. SLAAC means that the client picks their own address based on the router prefix being advertised. Additional parameters such as a DNS server address must be provided by stateless DHCPv6 services.

DHCPv6 clients and servers are identified to each other by a DHCP unique identifier (DUID) using the lowest number interface MAC address. DHCPv6 exchanges are either normal four-message (solicit, advertise, request, reply) exchanges or the rapid commit two-message (solicit, reply) exchanges.

The DHCPv6 server maintains a binding table in RAM that maintains configuration parameters.

> **NOTE:** Unlike DHCPv4, the DHCPv6 service does not give out IP addresses; instead, it gives out prefixes. The client creates the remaining bits for a valid IPv6 address. The duplicate address detection (DAD) mechanism ensures the uniqueness of the address. There is no DHCPv6 **excluded-address** command.

There are three methods for dynamically allocating IPv6 addressing and configuration information:

1. SLAAC (no DHCPv6 server required)

2. SLAAC and a stateless DHCPv6 server

3. Stateful DHCPv6 server

Using SLAAC and Configuring a Router as a Stateless DHCPv6 Server

A stateless DHCPv6 server doesn't allocate or maintain IPv6 global unicast addressing information. A stateless server only provides common network information that is available to all devices on the network, such as a list of DNS server addresses or a domain name.

The SLAAC with stateless DHCPv6 method involves setting the Other Configuration flag (O flag) to 1. With this method the device creates its own global unicast address (GUA) using SLAAC. It also needs to use information from other sources, such as the link MTU contained in the router advertisement (RA). In this scenario, the three RA flags are as follows:

- A flag = 1 – Use SLAAC to create a global unicast address

- O flag = 1 – Communicate with a stateless DHCPv6 server for other addressing information

- M flag = 0 – Do not need to communicate with a stateful DHCPv6 server

Router# **configure terminal**	Enters global configuration mode
Router(config)# **ipv6 dhcp pool STATELESS**	Creates a DHCPv6 pool named *STATELESS*

`Router(config-dhcp)# domain-name` `nodomain.com`	Configures a domain name for a DHCPv6 client
`Router(config-dhcp)# dns-server` `2001:db8:3000:3000::42`	Specifies the DNS server address for the DHCPv6 clients
`Router(config-dhcp)# exit`	Leaves DHCPv6 configuration mode
`Router(config)# interface` `gigabitethernet 0/0`	Specifies an interface type and number, and enters interface configuration mode
`Router(config-if)# ipv6 nd` `other-config-flag`	Sets the router advertisement Other Configuration flag (O flag) to 1 **NOTE:** The default setting of the O flag is 0 **NOTE:** To set the O flag back to the default setting of 0, use the **no ipv6 nd other-config-flag** command **NOTE:** When the O flag is set to 1, this tells the end client device that other information is available from a stateless DHCPv6 server
`Router(config-if)# ipv6 dhcp` `server STATELESS`	Enables DHCPv6 on an interface for the appropriate IPv6 address pool
`Router(config-if)# end`	Moves to privileged EXEC mode

Configuring a Router as a Stateful DHCPv6 Server

Unlike the other methods used to assign IPv6 addresses to clients, stateful DHCPv6 does not utilize SLAAC to generate a global unicast address. Stateful DHCPv6 is similar to the DHCP services provided for IPv4.

A stateful DHCPv6 server provides IPv6 GUA addresses to clients and keeps track of which devices have been allocated IPv6 addresses.

The stateful DHCPv6 method involves modifying two flags: the Managed Address Configuration flag (M flag) and the Address Autoconfiguration flag (A flag). In this scenario, the three RA flags are as follows:

- A flag = 0 – Do not use SLAAC to create a global unicast address

- O flag = 0 – No need to communicate with a stateless DHCPv6 server

- M flag = 1 – Obtain the global unicast address and other information from a stateful DHCPv6 server

`Router# configure terminal`	Enters global configuration mode
`Router(config)# ipv6 dhcp pool` `STATEFUL-DHCPv6`	Creates a DHCPv6 pool named *STATEFUL-DHCPv6*
`Router(config-dhcp)# address` `prefix 2001:db8:cafe:1::/64`	Causes the router to be a stateful DHCPv6 server and to allocate addresses. The prefix length indicates the number of available address in the pool

`Router(config-dhcp)#` `domain-name nodomain.com`	Configures a domain name for a DHCPv6 client
`Router(config-dhcp)# dns-` `server 2001:db8:cafe:1::8888`	Specifies the DNS server address for the DHCPv6 clients
`Router(config-dhcp)# exit`	Leaves DHCPv6 configuration mode
`Router(config)# interface` `gigabitethernet 0/0`	Specifies an interface type and number, and enters interface configuration mode
`Router(config-if)# ipv6 nd` `managed-config-flag`	Sets the Managed Configuration flag (M flag) to 1 **NOTE:** The default setting of the M flag is 0 **NOTE:** To set the M flag back to the default setting of 0, use the **no ipv6 nd managed-config-flag** command

`Router(config-if)# ipv6 nd`
`prefix 2001:db8:cafe:1::/64`
`no-autoconfig`
	Assigns an IPv6 address to the interface
	
	The **no-autoconfig** keyword sets the A flag to 0. This ensures that the interface won't use SLAAC in its RA messages to clients

`Router(config-if)# ipv6 dhcp` `server STATEFUL-DHCPv6`	Enables the DHCPv6 service on the client-facing interface and associates it with the pool *STATEFUL-DHCPv6* **NOTE:** You can add the **rapid-commit** keyword at the of this command to enable the use of the two-message exchange between server and client
`Router(config-if)# end`	Moves to privileged EXEC mode

Configuring DHCPv6 Client

`Router# configure terminal`	Enters global configuration mode
`Router(config)# interface` `interface-id`	Enters interface configuration mode, and specifies the interface to configure
`Router(config-if)# ipv6` `address dhcp`	Enables the interface to acquire an IPv6 address using the four-message exchange from the DHCPv6 server
`Router(config-if)# ipv6` `address dhcp rapid-commit`	Enables the interface to acquire an IPv6 address using the two-message exchange from the DHCPv6 server

Configuring DHCPv6 Relay Agent

`Router# configure terminal`	Enters global configuration mode
`Router(config)# interface` `gigabitethernet 0/0`	Specifies an interface type and number, and enters interface configuration mode

`Router(config-if)#`
`ipv6 dhcp relay destination`
`fe80::250:a2ff:febf:a056`
`gigabitethernet 0/1`
	Specifies a destination address to which client packets are forwarded and enables DHCPv6 relay service on the interface
	
	NOTE: It is possible to use a global unicast IPv6 address as the relay destination instead of a link-local address

`Router(config-if)# end`	Return to privileged EXEC mode

Verifying and Troubleshooting DHCPv6

`Router# show ipv6 dhcp binding`	Displays the IPv6 to MAC address bindings
`Router# show ipv6 dhcp pool`	Displays DHCPv6 pool statistics
`Router# show ipv6 dhcp interface`	Displays interface on which DHCPv6 is enabled
`Router# debug ipv6 dhcp [detail]`	Enables DHCPv6 debugging
`Router# debug ipv6 dhcp relay`	Enables DHCPv6 relay agent debugging

Configuration Example: DHCP for IPv4

Figure 8-11 illustrates the network topology for the configuration that follows, which shows how to configure DHCP services on a Cisco IOS router using the commands covered in this chapter.

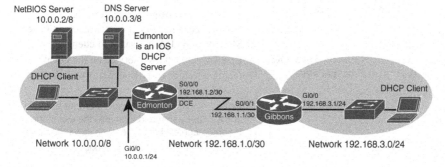

Figure 8-11 Network Topology for DHCP Configuration

Edmonton Router

`Router> enable`	Moves to privileged EXEC mode
`Router# configure terminal`	Moves to global configuration mode
`Router(config)# hostname Edmonton`	Sets the host name
`Edmonton(config)# interface gigabitethernet 0/0`	Moves to interface configuration mode
`Edmonton(config-if)# description LAN Interface`	Sets the local description of the interface
`Edmonton(config-if)# ip address 10.0.0.1 255.0.0.0`	Assigns an IP address and netmask
`Edmonton(config-if)# no shutdown`	Enables the interface
`Edmonton(config-if)# interface serial 0/0/0`	Moves to interface configuration mode
`Edmonton(config-if)# description Link to Gibbons Router`	Sets the local description of the interface

Edmonton(config-if)# **ip address** **192.168.1.2 255.255.255.252**	Assigns an IP address and netmask
Edmonton(config-if)# **clock rate** **4000000**	Assigns the clock rate to the DCE cable on this side of link
Edmonton(config-if)# **no shutdown**	Enables the interface
Edmonton(config-if)# **exit**	Returns to global configuration mode
Edmonton(config)# **ip route** **192.168.3.0 255.255.255.0** **serial 0/0/0**	Creates a static route to the destination network
Edmonton(config)# **service dhcp**	Verifies that the router can use DHCP services and that DHCP is enabled. This command is enabled by default in Cisco IOS and will not appear in the running configuration
Edmonton(config)# **ip dhcp pool** **10NETWORK**	Creates a DHCP pool called *10NETWORK*
Edmonton(dhcp-config)# **network** **10.0.0.0 255.0.0.0**	Defines the range of addresses to be leased
Edmonton(dhcp-config)# **default-router 10.0.0.1**	Defines the address of the default router for clients
Edmonton(dhcp-config)# **netbios-name-server 10.0.0.2**	Defines the address of the NetBIOS server for clients
Edmonton(dhcp-config)# **dns-server** **10.0.0.3**	Defines the address of the DNS server for clients
Edmonton(dhcp-config)# **domain-name fakedomainname.com**	Defines the domain name for clients
Edmonton(dhcp-config)# **lease 12 14 30**	Sets the lease time to be 12 days, 14 hours, 30 minutes
Edmonton(dhcp-config)# **exit**	Returns to global configuration mode
Edmonton(config)# **ip dhcp** **excluded-address 10.0.0.1** **10.0.0.5**	Specifies the range of addresses not to be leased out to clients
Edmonton(config)# **ip dhcp pool** **192.168.3NETWORK**	Creates a DHCP pool called *192.168.3NETWORK*
Edmonton(dhcp-config)# **network** **192.168.3.0 255.255.255.0**	Defines the range of addresses to be leased
Edmonton(dhcp-config)# **default-router 192.168.3.1**	Defines the address of the default router for clients
Edmonton(dhcp-config)# **netbios-name-server 10.0.0.2**	Defines the address of the NetBIOS server for clients
Edmonton(dhcp-config)# **dns-server** **10.0.0.3**	Defines the address of the DNS server for clients
Edmonton(dhcp-config)# **domain-name fakedomainname.com**	Defines the domain name for clients

`Edmonton(dhcp-config)# ` **`lease`** **`12 14 30`**	Sets the lease time to be 12 days, 14 hours, 30 minutes
`Edmonton(dhcp-config)# ` **`exit`**	Returns to global configuration mode
`Edmonton(config)# ` **`exit`**	Returns to privileged EXEC mode
`Edmonton# ` **`copy running-config startup-config`**	Saves the configuration to NVRAM

Gibbons Router

`Router> ` **`enable`**	Moves to privileged EXEC mode
`Router# ` **`configure terminal`**	Moves to global configuration mode
`Router(config)# ` **`hostname Gibbons`**	Sets the host name
`Gibbons(config)# ` **`interface gigabitethernet 0/0`**	Moves to interface configuration mode
`Gibbons(config-if)# ` **`description LAN Interface`**	Sets the local description of the interface
`Gibbons(config-if)# ` **`ip address 192.168.3.1 255.255.255.0`**	Assigns an IP address and netmask
`Gibbons(config-if)# ` **`ip helper-address 192.168.1.2`**	Forwards DHCP broadcast messages as unicast messages to this specific address instead of having them be dropped by the router
`Gibbons(config-if)# ` **`no shutdown`**	Enables the interface
`Gibbons(config-if)# ` **`interface serial 0/0/1`**	Moves to interface configuration mode
`Gibbons(config-if)# ` **`description Link to Edmonton Router`**	Sets the local description of the interface
`Gibbons(config-if)# ` **`ip address 192.168.1.1 255.255.255.252`**	Assigns an IP address and netmask
`Gibbons(config-if)# ` **`no shutdown`**	Enables the interface
`Gibbons(config-if)# ` **`exit`**	Returns to global configuration mode
`Gibbons(config)# ` **`ip route 0.0.0.0 0.0.0.0 serial 0/0/1`**	Creates a default static route to the destination network
`Gibbons(config)# ` **`exit`**	Returns to privileged EXEC mode
`Gibbons# ` **`copy running-config startup-config`**	Saves the configuration to NVRAM

Configuration Example: DHCP for IPv6

Figure 8-12 illustrates the network topology for the configuration that follows, which shows how to configure DHCP for IPv6 services on a Cisco IOS router using the commands covered in this chapter. For this lab, the DHCPv6 clients are simulated as IOS routers to show the interface configuration required for stateless and stateful DHCPv6 to be operational.

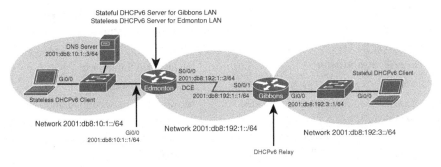

Figure 8-12 Network Topology for DHCPv6 Configuration

Edmonton Router

Router> **enable**	Moves to privileged EXEC mode
Router# **configure terminal**	Moves to global configuration mode
Router(config)# **hostname Edmonton**	Sets the host name
Edmonton(config)# **ipv6 unicast-routing**	Enables IPv6 routing
Edmonton(config)# **ipv6 dhcp pool EDMONTONLAN**	Creates a DHCPv6 pool for the Edmonton LAN. Since this pool is used for stateless DHCPv6, no prefix is configured
Edmonton(config-dhcpv6)# **dns-server 2001:db8:10:1::3**	Sets the DNS server address
Edmonton(config-dhcpv6)# **domain-name cisco.com**	Sets the domain name
Edmonton(config-dhcpv6)# **exit**	Exits the *EDMONTONLAN* pool
Edmonton(config)# **ipv6 dhcp pool GIBBONSLAN**	Creates a DHCPv6 pool for the Gibbons LAN
Edmonton(config-dhcpv6)# **address prefix 2001:db8:192:3::/64**	Defines a prefix for the DHCP pool
Edmonton(config-dhcpv6)# **dns-server 2001:db8:10:1::3**	Sets the DNS server address
Edmonton(config-dhcpv6)# **domain-name cisco.com**	Sets the domain name
Edmonton(config-dhcpv6)# **exit**	Exits the *GIBBONSLAN* pool
Edmonton(config)# **interface gigabitethernet 0/0**	Moves to interface configuration mode
Edmonton(config-if)# **description LAN Interface**	Sets the local description of the interface
Edmonton(config-if)# **ipv6 enable**	Enables IPv6 functions
Edmonton(config-if)# **ipv6 address 2001:db8:10:1::1/64**	Assigns an IPv6 address and prefix length

Edmonton(config-if)# **ipv6 nd other-config-flag**	Sets the Other Configuration flag to 1 for stateless DHCPv6
Edmonton(config-if)# **ipv6 dhcp server EDMONTONLAN**	Assigns the *EDMONTONLAN* pool to the local LAN interface
Edmonton(config-if)# **no shutdown**	Enables the interface
Edmonton(config-if)# **interface serial 0/0/0**	Moves to interface configuration mode
Edmonton(config-if)# **description Link to Gibbons Router**	Sets the local description of the interface
Edmonton(config-if)# **ipv6 enable**	Enables IPv6 functions
Edmonton(config-if)# **ipv6 address 2001:db8:192:1::2/64**	Assigns an IP address and prefix length
Edmonton(config-if)# **ipv6 dhcp server GIBBONSLAN**	Assigns the *GIBBONSLAN* pool to the WAN interface since it will be receiving DHCPv6 relay messages from Gibbons
Edmonton(config-if)# **clock rate 4000000**	Assigns the clock rate to the DCE cable on this side of link
Edmonton(config-if)# **no shutdown**	Enables the interface
Edmonton(config-if)# **exit**	Returns to global configuration mode
Edmonton(config)# **ipv6 route 2001: db8:192:3::/64 2001:db8:192:1::1**	Creates a static route to the Gibbons LAN network
Edmonton# **copy running-config startup-config**	Saves the configuration to NVRAM

Gibbons Router

Router> **enable**	Moves to privileged EXEC mode
Router# **configure terminal**	Moves to global configuration mode
Router(config)# **hostname Gibbons**	Sets the host name
Gibbons(config)# **ipv6 unicast-routing**	Enables IPv6 routing
Gibbons(config)# **interface gigabitethernet 0/0**	Moves to interface configuration mode
Gibbons(config-if)# **description LAN Interface**	Sets the local description of the interface
Gibbons(config-if)# **ipv6 enable**	Enables IPv6 functions
Gibbons(config-if)# **ipv6 address 2001:db8:192:3::1/64**	Assigns an IP address and prefix length
Gibbons(config-if)# **ipv6 dhcp relay destination 2001:db8:192:1::2**	Forwards DHCPV6 multicast messages as unicast messages to this specific address instead of having them be dropped by the router

`Gibbons(config-if)# ipv6 nd managed-config-flag`	Sets the Managed Address Configuration flag to 1 for stateful DHCPv6
`Gibbons(config-if)# no shutdown`	Enables the interface
`Gibbons(config-if)# interface serial 0/0/1`	Moves to interface configuration mode
`Gibbons(config-if)# description Link to Edmonton Router`	Sets the local description of the interface
`Gibbons(config-if)# ipv6 enable`	Enables IPv6 functions
`Gibbons(config-if)# ipv6 address 2001:db8:192:1::1/64`	Assigns an IP address prefix length
`Gibbons(config-if)# no shutdown`	Enables the interface
`Gibbons(config-if)# exit`	Returns to global configuration mode
`Gibbons(config)# ipv6 route ::/0 2001:db8:192:1::2`	Creates an IPv6 default static route that points to the Edmonton router
`Gibbons(config)# exit`	Returns to privileged EXEC mode
`Gibbons# copy running-config startup-config`	Saves the configuration to NVRAM

EdmontonPC Stateless DHCPv6 Client (IOS Router)

`EdmontonPC(config)# interface gigabitethernet 0/0`	Moves to interface configuration mode
`EdmontonPC(config-if)# ipv6 enable`	Enables IPv6 functions
`EdmontonPC(config-if)# ipv6 address autoconfig default`	Sets the interface for SLAAC and installs an IPv6 default route to the Edmonton GigabitEthernet 0/0 interface link-local address
`EdmontonPC(config-if)# no shutdown`	Enables the interface
`EdmontonPC(config)# exit`	Returns to privileged EXEC mode
`EdmontonPC# copy running-config startup-config`	Saves the configuration to NVRAM

GibbonsPC Stateful DHCPv6 Client (IOS Router)

`GibbonsPC(config)# interface gigabitethernet 0/0`	Moves to interface configuration mode
`GibbonsPC(config-if)# ipv6 enable`	Enables IPv6 functions
`GibbonsPC(config-if)# ipv6 address dhcp`	Sets the interface for stateful DHCPv6
`GibbonsPC(config-if)# no shutdown`	Enables the interface
`GibbonsPC# copy running-config startup-config`	Saves the configuration to NVRAM

CHAPTER 9

Device Management

This chapter provides information about the following topics:

- Configuring passwords
- Cleartext password encryption
- Password encryption algorithm types
- Configuring SSH
- Verifying SSH
- Boot system commands
- The Cisco IOS File System
- Viewing the Cisco IOS File System
- Commonly used URL prefixes for Cisco network devices
- Deciphering IOS image filenames
- Backing up configurations to a TFTP server
- Restoring configurations from a TFTP server
- Backing up the Cisco IOS Software to a TFTP server
- Restoring/upgrading the Cisco IOS Software from a TFTP server
- Restoring the Cisco IOS Software using the ROM Monitor environmental variables and **tftpdnld** command
- Secure Copy Protocol (SCP)
  - Configuring an SCP server
  - Verifying and troubleshooting SCP
  - Configuration example: SCP
- Disabling unused services
- Useful device management options

Configuring Passwords

These commands work on both routers and switches.

Edmonton(config)# **enable password cisco**	Sets the enable password. This password is stored as cleartext
Edmonton(config)# **enable secret class**	Sets the enable secret password. This password is stored using a cryptographic hash function (MD5)

Edmonton(config)# enable algorithm-type sha256 secret class	Sets the enable secret password using the SHA-256 algorithm, which is a stronger hashing algorithm than MD5
Edmonton(config)# enable algorithm-type scrypt secret class	Sets the enable secret password using the scrypt algorithm, which is a stronger hashing algorithm than MD5
Edmonton(config)# line console 0	Enters console line configuration mode
Edmonton(config-line)# password cisco12345	Sets the console line mode password to *cisco12345*
Edmonton(config-line)# login	Enables password checking at login
Edmonton(config-line)# line vty 0 4	Enters vty line configuration mode for all five vty lines
Edmonton(config-line)# password cisco12345	Sets the vty password to *cisco12345*
Edmonton(config-line)# login	Enables password checking at login
Edmonton(config-line)# line aux 0	Enters auxiliary line configuration mode
Edmonton(config-line)# password backdoor	Sets the auxiliary line mode password to *backdoor*
Edmonton(config-line)# login	Enables password checking at login
Edmonton(config-line)# no exec	Disables access to the AUX port when it is not in use

CAUTION: The **enable secret** password is encrypted by default using the MD5 cryptographic hash function. The **enable password** password is not; it is stored as cleartext. For this reason, recommended practice is that you *never* use the **enable password** command. Use only the **enable secret** command in a router or switch configuration. The **enable secret** command password takes precedence over the **enable password** command password. For instance, if **enable secret class** and **enable password cisco** are both configured, Cisco IOS will only grant privileged EXEC mode access when the enable secret password **class** is entered.

TIP: You can set both **enable secret** password and **enable password** password to the same password. However, doing so defeats the use of encryption.

CAUTION: Line passwords are stored as cleartext. They should be encrypted using the **service password-encryption** command as a bare minimum. However, this encryption method is weak and easily reversible.

TIP: The best place to store passwords is an external AAA (authentication, authorization, and accounting) server.

Cleartext Password Encryption

Edmonton(config)# service password-encryption	Applies a Vigenère cipher (type 7) weak encryption to passwords
Edmonton(config)# no service password-encryption	Turns off password encryption

CAUTION: If you have turned on service password encryption, used it, and then turned it off, any passwords that you have encrypted will stay encrypted. New passwords will remain unencrypted.

TIP: The **service password-encryption** command will work on the following cleartext passwords:

- Username
- Authentication key
- Console
- Virtual terminal line access
- BGP neighbors
- Passwords using this encryption are shown as type 7 passwords in the router configuration:

Edmonton# **show run	include secret	line con 0	password	line vty 0	password**
					 no service password-encryption
					 enable secret 5
					 Rv4kArhts7yA2xd8BD2YTVbts
					 line con 0
					  password 7 00271A5307542A02D22842
					 line vty 0 4
					  password 7 00271A5307542A02D22842
						
						 5 signifies MD5 hash
						
						 7 signifies Vigenère cipher
						 7 signifies Vigenère cipher

Password Encryption Algorithm Types

There are different algorithm types available to hash a password in Cisco IOS:

- **Type 4:** Specified a SHA-256 encrypted secret string
  - Deprecated due to a software bug that allowed this password to be viewed in plaintext under certain conditions
- **Type 5:** Specifies a message digest algorithm 5 (MD5) encrypted secret
- **Type 8:** Specifies a Password-Based Key Derivation Function 2 with SHA-256 hashed secret (PBKDF2 with SHA-256)
- **Type 9:** Specifies a scrypt hashed secret (SCRYPT)

TIP: MD5 is no longer considered to be secure. Therefore, it is recommended that type 8 or type 9 always be configured.

Edmonton(config)# **username demo5 secret cisco** OR Edmonton(config)# **username demo5 algorithm-type md5 secret cisco**	Either option generates password encrypted with a type 5 algorithm
Edmonton(config)# **username demo8 algorithm-type sha256 secret cisco**	Generates password encrypted with a type 8 algorithm
Edmonton(config)# **username demo9 algorithm-type scrypt secret cisco**	Generates password encrypted with a type 9 algorithm

NOTE: Type 5, type 8, and type 9 passwords are not reversible.

CAUTION: If you configure type 8 or type 9 passwords and then downgrade to a Cisco IOS Software release that does not support type 8 and type 9 passwords, you must configure the type 5 passwords before downgrading. If not, you will be locked out of the device and a password recovery is required. Type 8 and type 9 passwords have been supported since 15.3(3)M.

Configuring SSH

Telnet and Secure Shell (SSH) are two remote access methods to connect to a device. Although popular, Telnet is not secure because Telnet traffic is forwarded in cleartext. Therefore, its content can easily be read if intercepted.

Secure Shell (SSH) encrypts all traffic between source and destination and is therefore the recommended remote access method. SSH should always be used if available.

CAUTION: SSH Version 1 implementations have known security issues. It is recommended to use SSH Version 2 whenever possible.

NOTE: SSH provides encryption services using private and public cryptographic keys that are created using the **crypto key generate rsa** global configuration command. However, the **crypto key** command requires that a device host name (i.e., **hostname** *name*) and a fully qualified domain name (i.e., **ip domain-name** *name*) first be configured. SSH cannot use the default host names (e.g., *Switch* or *Router*).

NOTE: The Cisco implementation of SSH requires Cisco IOS Software to support Rivest, Shamir, Adleman (RSA) authentication and minimum Data Encryption Standard (DES) encryption (a cryptographic software image).

Edmonton(config)# **username BabyYoda password mandalorian**	Creates a locally significant username/password combination. These are the credentials you must enter when connecting to the router with SSH client software
Edmonton(config)# **username BabyYoda privilege 15 secret mandalorian**	Creates a locally significant username of *BabyYoda* with privilege level 15. Assigns a secret password of *mandalorian*
Edmonton(config)# **ip domain-name test.lab**	Creates a host domain for the router
Edmonton(config)# **crypto key generate rsa modulus 2048**	Enables the SSH server for local and remote authentication on the router and generates an RSA key pair. The number of modulus bits on the command line is 2048 bits. The size of the key modulus is 360 to 4096 bits. If a crypto key already exists on the router, use the **crypto key zeroize rsa** command to remove it
Edmonton(config)# **ip ssh version 2**	Enables SSH version 2 on the device **NOTE:** To work, SSH requires a local username database, a local IP domain, and an RSA key to be generated

`Edmonton(config)# ip ssh authentication-retries 2`	Sets the maximum number of password prompts provided to the user to 2. The default is 3
`Edmonton(config)# ip ssh time-out 90`	Sets the time interval that the router waits for the SSH client to respond to 90 seconds. The default is 120
`Edmonton(config)# ip ssh source-interface loopback 1`	Forces the SSH client to use the IP address of the Loopback 1 interface as the source address for SSH packets
`Edmonton(config)# line vty 0 4`	Moves to vty configuration mode for all five vty lines of the router **NOTE:** Depending on the Cisco IOS Software release and platform, there may be more than 5 vty lines
`Edmonton(config-line)# login local`	Enables password checking on a per-user basis. Username and password will be checked against the data entered with the **username** global configuration command. Ensure that a local username database has been configured before entering this command
`Edmonton(config-line)# transport input ssh`	Limits remote connectivity to SSH connections only–disables Telnet. It is possible to specify other input methods, but the most common ones are SSH and Telnet

Verifying SSH

`Edmonton# show ip ssh`	Verifies that SSH is enabled
`Edmonton# show ssh`	Checks the SSH connection to the device

Boot System Commands

`Router(config)# boot system flash` *image-name*	Loads the Cisco IOS Software with *image-name*
`Router(config)# boot system tftp://172.16.10.3/`*image-name*	Loads the Cisco IOS Software with *image-name* from a TFTP server
`Router(config)# boot system rom`	Loads the Cisco IOS Software from ROM
`Router(config)# exit`	Returns to privileged EXEC mode
`Router# copy running-config startup-config`	Saves the running configuration to NVRAM. The router executes commands in their order on the next reload

TIP: If you enter **boot system flash** first, that is the first place the router goes to look for the Cisco IOS Software. If you want to go to a TFTP server first, make sure that the **boot system tftp** command is the first command you enter.

TIP: If the configuration has no **boot system** commands, the router defaults to loading the first valid Cisco IOS image in flash memory and running it. If no valid Cisco IOS image is found in flash memory, the router attempts to boot from a network TFTP server. After six unsuccessful attempts of locating a network TFTP server, the router loads into ROMmon mode.

The Cisco IOS File System

The Cisco IOS File System (IFS) provides a single interface to all the file systems available on a routing device, including the flash memory file system; network file systems such as TFTP, remote copy protocol (rcp), and FTP; and any other endpoint for reading and writing data, such as NVRAM, or the running configuration. The Cisco IFS minimizes the required prompting for many commands. Instead of entering in an EXEC-level **copy** command and then having the system prompt you for more information, you can enter a single command on one line with all necessary information.

Cisco IOS Software Commands	IFS Commands
`copy tftp running-config`	`copy tftp: system:running-config`
`copy tftp startup-config`	`copy tftp: nvram:startup-config`
`show startup-config`	`more nvram:startup-config`
`erase startup-config`	`erase nvram:`
`copy running-config startup-config`	`copy system:running-config nvram:startup-config`
`copy running-config tftp`	`copy system:running-config tftp:`
`show running-config`	`more system:running-config`

Viewing the Cisco IOS File System

`Router# show file systems`	Displays all the available file systems on the device

NOTE: The Cisco IOS File System uses a URL convention to specify files on network devices and the network. Many of the most commonly used URL prefixes are also available in the Cisco IOS File System.

Commonly Used URL Prefixes for Cisco Network Devices

The URL prefix specifies the file system. The list of available file systems differs by platform and operation. Refer to your product documentation or use the **show file systems** command in privileged EXEC mode to determine which prefixes are available on your platform. File system prefixes are listed in Table 9-1.

TABLE 9-1   File System Prefixes

Prefix	File System
bootflash:	Boot Flash memory
flash:	Flash memory. Available on all platforms. An alias for the flash: prefix is slot0
ftp: sftp:	FTP and secure FTP network server
http:	HTTP server
https:	HTTPS server
null:	Null destination for copies **NOTE:** You can copy a remote file to null to determine its size
nvram:	NVRAM
rcp:	Remote copy protocol network server
scp:	Secure Copy
system:	Contains system memory, including the current running configuration
tar:	For creating TAR files
tftp:	TFTP network server
xmodem:	Obtains the file from a network machine using the Xmodem protocol
ymodem:	Obtains the file from a network machine using the Ymodem protocol
usbflash0:, usbflash1:, usb0:, usb1:	Universal Serial Bus (USB) flash

Deciphering IOS Image Filenames

Although it looks long and complex, there is a reason that Cisco names its IOS images the way that it does. It is important to understand the meaning behind an IOS image name so that you can correctly choose which file to work with.

There are different parts to the image filename, as shown in the following example and described in the table:

isr4300-universalk9.16.09.04.SPA.bin

isr4300	Indicates the platform on which the image runs. In this case, it is a Cisco ISR 4300 series router
universal	Specifies the feature set. Universal on a 4300 would include IP Base, Security, Unified Communication, and Data feature sets. Each router is activated for IP Base; the others need software activation **NOTE:** k9 in an image name means that strong encryption, such as 3DES/AES, is included

16.09.04	Identifies the version number of the software. In this case, it is major release 16, minor release 9, new feature release 4
SPA	Indicates this software is digitally signed. There are two file extensions possible: SPA and SSA. The first character *S* stands for digitally signed software. The second character *P* in SPA means that this release is meant for production. A second character *S* in SSA means it is a special image and has limited use or special conditions. The third character *A* indicates the key version used to digitally sign the image
.bin	Represents the file extension. .bin shows that this file is a binary executable file

NOTE: The Cisco IOS naming conventions, meanings, content, and other details are subject to change.

Backing Up Configurations to a TFTP Server

Denver# `copy running-config` `startup-config`	Saves the running configuration from DRAM to NVRAM (locally)
Denver# `copy running-config tftp`	Copies the running configuration to the remote TFTP server
Address or name of remote host[ ]? **192.168.119.20**	The IP address of the TFTP server
Destination Filename [Denver-confg]?	The name to use for the file saved on the TFTP server
!!!!!!!!!!!!!!!!!	Each bang symbol (!) = 1 datagram of data
624 bytes copied in 7.05 secs	
Denver#	File has been transferred successfully

NOTE: You can also use the preceding sequence for a **copy startup-config tftp** command sequence.

Restoring Configurations from a TFTP Server

Denver# `copy tftp running-config`	Merges the configuration file from the TFTP server with the running-config file in DRAM
Address or name of remote host[ ]? **192.168.119.20**	The IP address of the TFTP server
Source filename [ ]? **Denver-confg**	Enter the name of the file you want to retrieve
Destination filename [running-config]? ⏎**Enter**	Pressing the Enter key will begin the copy process
Accessing tftp://192.168.119.20/ Denver-confg...	

`Loading Denver-confg from`
`192.168.119.02 (via GigabitEthernet`
`0/0):`	

`!!!!!!!!!!!!!!`	
`[OK-624 bytes]`	
`624 bytes copied in 9.45 secs`	
`Denver#`	File has been transferred successfully

NOTE: You can also use the preceding sequence for a **copy tftp startup-config** command sequence.

NOTE: When copying a file into a configuration file, the **no shutdown** command does not carry over into the configuration file. You must enable the interfaces with the **no shutdown** command.

Backing Up the Cisco IOS Software to a TFTP Server

`Denver# copy flash: tftp:`	Copies from flash to a remote TFTP server
`Source filename [ ]? isr4300-` `universalk9.16.09.04.SPA.bin`	Name of the Cisco IOS Software image
`Address or name of remote host [ ]?` `192.168.119.20`	Address of the TFTP server
`Destination filename [isr4300-` `universalk9.16.09.04.SPA.bin]?` ⏎Enter	The destination filename is the same as the source filename, so just press ⏎Enter

`!!!!!!!!!!!!!!!!!!!!!!!!!!!!!!!!!!!!!!!`
`!!!!!!!!!!!!!!!!!!!!!!!!!!!!!!!!!!!!!!!`
`!!!!!!!!!`	

`8906589 bytes copied in 263.68 seconds`	
`Denver#`	

Restoring/Upgrading the Cisco IOS Software from a TFTP Server

`Denver# copy tftp: flash:`	Copies from a remote TFTP server to flash
`Address or name of remote host [ ]?` `192.168.119.20`	
`Source filename [ ]? isr4300-` `universalk9.16.09.04.SPA.bin`	
`Destination filename [isr4300-` `universalk9.16.09.04.SPA.bin]?` ⏎Enter	

Accessing tftp://192.168.119.20/ **isr4300-universalk9.16.09.04.SPA.bin**	
Erase flash: before copying? [confirm] ⏎Enter	If flash memory is full, erase it first
Erasing the flash file system will remove all files	
Continue? [confirm] ⏎Enter	Press Ctrl-C if you want to cancel
Erasing device eeeeeeeeeeeeeeeeee... erased	Each *e* represents data being erased
Loading **isr4300-universalk9.16.09.04.** **SPA.bin from 192.168.119.20**	
(via GigabitEthernet 0/0): !!!!!!!!!! !!!!!!!!!!!!!!!!!!!!!!!!!!!!!!!!!!!!!!! !!!!!!!!!!!!!!!!!!!!!!!!!!!!!!!!!!!!!!! !!!!!!!!!!!	Each bang symbol (!) = 1 datagram of data
Verifying Check sum .... OK	
[OK - 8906589 Bytes]	
8906589 bytes copied in 277.45 secs	
Denver#	Success

Restoring the Cisco IOS Software Using the ROM Monitor Environmental Variables and tftpdnld Command

rommon 1> **IP_** **ADDRESS=192.168.100.1**	Indicates the IP address for this unit
rommon 2> **IP_SUBNET_** **MASK=255.255.255.0**	Indicates the subnet mask for this unit
rommon 3> **DEFAULT_** **GATEWAY=192.168.100.1**	Indicates the default gateway for this unit
rommon 4> **TFTP_** **SERVER=192.168.100.2**	Indicates the IP address of the TFTP server
rommon 5> **TFTP_FILE=** **c2900-universalk9-mz.SPA.** **152-4.M1.bin**	Indicates the filename to fetch from the TFTP server
rommon 6> **tftpdnld**	Starts the process
...<output cut>...	
Do you wish to continue? y/n: [n]:**y**	
...<output cut>...	
rommon 7> **i**	Resets the router. The *i* stands for initialize

CAUTION: Commands and environmental variables are case sensitive, so be sure that you do not accidentally add spaces between variables and answers.

Secure Copy Protocol (SCP)

The Secure Copy Protocol (SCP) feature provides a secure and authenticated method for copying device configurations or device image files. SCP relies on Secure Shell (SSH). SCP allows a user with appropriate authorization to copy any file that exists in the Cisco IOS File System (IFS) to and from a device by using the **copy** command.

NOTE: Before enabling SCP, you must correctly configure SSH, authentication, and authorization on the device and replace Telnet with SSH on the vty ports. See the section "Configuring SSH" earlier in this chapter for the commands needed to configure SSH.

NOTE: Because SCP relies on SSH for its secure transport, the device must have a Rivest, Shamir, and Adelman (RSA) key pair.

Configuring an SCP Server

Denver# **configure terminal**	Moves to global configuration mode
Denver(config)# **aaa new-model**	Sets AAA authentication at login
Denver(config)# **aaa authentication login default local**	Enables the AAA access control system. In this example, authentication comes from a local username
Denver(config)# **aaa authorization exec default local**	Sets parameters that restrict user access to a network. In this example, authorization comes from a local database
Denver(config)# **username superuser privilege 15 secret superpassword**	Creates a local username/password combination. In this example, the username is *superuser*, the privilege level is 15, and the MD5 password is *superpassword*
Denver(config)# **ip scp server enable**	Enables SCP server-side functionality

Verifying and Troubleshooting SCP

Denver# **show running-config**	Shows the current configuration in DRAM. The IP SCP server is enabled and visible in the running config
Denver# **debug ip scp**	Displays output related to SCP authentication problems

Configuration Example: SCP

The following example shows the commands for using SCP to transfer a Cisco IOS image from flash to a remote host that supports SSH.

NOTE: Your router does not need to be set up as an SCP server for this transfer to work. You only need to have SSH configured.

Denver# **copy flash: scp:**	Initiates secure copy from flash: to a remote host
Source filename []? **isr4300-universalk9.16.09.04.SPA.bin**	Enter the name of the file you want to transfer
Address or name of remote host[]? **192.168.119.20**	The IP address of the remote host
Destination username [Denver]? **superuser**	The username needed for the connection
Destination filename [**isr4300-universalk9.16.09.04.SPA.bin**]?	Press Enter, as the filename is already prompted
Writing **isr4300-universalk9.16.09.04.SPA.bin**	Connection is being created and verified
Password:	Enter the password when prompted
!!! !!!!!!	Each bang symbol (!) = 1 datagram of data
Denver#	File has been transferred successfully

NOTE: As with any use of the **copy** command, you can enter some of the specific details into the command itself:

```
Denver# copy flash:isr4300-universalk9.16.09.04.SPA.bin
scp://superuser@192.168.119.20/
```

Disabling Unneeded Services

Services that are not being used on a router can represent a potential security risk. If you do not need a specific service, you should disable it.

TIP: If a service is off by default, disabling it does not appear in the running configuration.

TIP: Do not assume that a service is disabled by default; you should explicitly disable all unneeded services, even if you think they are already disabled.

TIP: Depending on the Cisco IOS Software release, some services are on by default; some are off. Be sure to check the IOS configuration guide for your specific software release to determine the default state of the service.

Table 9-2 lists the services that you should disable if you are not using them.

TABLE 9-2   Disabling Unneeded Services

Service	Commands Used to Disable Service
DNS name resolution	Edmonton(config)# **no ip domain-lookup** Or Edmonton(config)# **no ip domain lookup**
Cisco Discovery Protocol (CDP) (globally)	Edmonton(config)# **no cdp run**
CDP (on a specific interface)	Edmonton(config-if)# **no cdp enable**
Network Time Protocol (NTP)	Edmonton(config-if)# **ntp disable**
BOOTP server	Edmonton(config)# **no ip bootp server**
DHCP	Edmonton(config)# **no service dhcp**
Proxy Address Resolution Protocol (ARP)	Edmonton(config-if)# **no ip proxy-arp**
IP source routing	Edmonton(config)# **no ip source-route**
IP redirects	Edmonton(config-if)# **no ip redirects**
HTTP service	Edmonton(config)# **no ip http server**
HTTPS service	Edmonton(config)# **no ip http secure-server**

Useful Device Management Options

The following commands are useful options available when using FTP and HTTP/HTTPS for device management.

Perth(config)# **ip ftp source-interface loopback 1**	Specifies the source IP address for FTP connections
Perth (config)# **ip ftp username admin**	Specifies the username to be used for FTP connections
Perth (config)# **ip ftp password cisco**	Specifies the password to be used for FTP connections
Perth (config)# **ip http authentication local**	Specifies the authentication method to be used for login when a client connects to the HTTP server. In this case, the local database is used for authentication
Perth (config)# **ip http access-class 10**	Specifies that access list 10 should be used to allow access to the HTTP server
Perth (config)# **ip http path flash:/GUI**	Sets the base HTTP path for HTML files
Router(config)# **ip http max-connections 10**	Sets the maximum number of allowed concurrent connections to the HTTP server. The default value is 5

CHAPTER 10

Infrastructure Security

This chapter provides information about the following topics:

- IPv4 access control lists (ACLs)
  - Configuring and applying standard IPv4 ACLs
  - Configuring and applying extended IPv4 ACLs
  - Configuring and applying time-based ACLs
  - Configuring and applying vty ACLs
- IPv6 ACLs
  - Configuring and applying IPv6 ACLs
  - Verifying IPv4 and IPv6 ACLs
- Implementing authentication methods
  - Simple local database authentication
  - AAA-based local database authentication
  - RADIUS authentication
    - Legacy configuration for RADIUS servers
    - Modular configuration for RADIUS servers
  - TACACS+ authentication
    - Legacy configuration for TACACS+ servers
    - Modular configuration for TACACS+ servers
  - Configuring authorization and accounting
    - Authorization
    - Accounting
  - Troubleshooting AAA
- Control Plane Policing (CoPP)
  - Define ACLs to identify permitted CoPP traffic flows
  - Define class maps for matched traffic
  - Define a policy map to police matched traffic
  - Assign a policy map to the control plane
  - Verifying CoPP

- Unicast Reverse Path Forwarding (uRPF)

  - Configuring uRPF

  - Verifying and troubleshooting uRPF

CAUTION: Your hardware platform or software release might not support all the commands documented in this chapter. Please refer to the Cisco website for specific platform and software release notes.

IPv4 Access Control Lists (ACLs)

When configuring IPv4 ACLs, many options are available. You can configure either standard (numbered or named) or extended (numbered or named) IPv4 ACLs, and you also can configure time-based or vty ACLs. These options are all explored in the following sections.

Configuring and Applying Standard IPv4 ACLs

It is possible to configure numbered or named standard IPv4 ACLs. Standard IPv4 ACLs, whether numbered (1 to 99 and 1300 to 1999) or named, filter packets that are based on a source address and mask, and they permit or deny the entire TCP/IP protocol suite.

Numbered Standard IPv4 ACL	
Router(config)# **access-list 1 permit host 192.168.1.5**	Permits traffic that matches the source address 192.168.1.5
Router(config)# **access-list 1 permit 192.168.2.0 0.0.0.255**	Permits traffic that matches any source address that starts with 192.168.2.*x*
Router(config)# **access-list 1 permit any**	Permits traffic that matches any source address
Router(config)# **access-list 1 deny 10.0.0.0 0.255.255.255**	Denies traffic that matches any source address that starts with 10.*x.x.x*
Router(config)# **no access-list 1**	Removes the entire numbered ACL 1
Router(config)# **interface gigabitethernet 0/0/0**	Moves to interface configuration mode
Router(config-if)# **ip access-group 1 in**	Applies ACL 1 on the interface as an inbound filter
Router(config-if)# **ip access-group 1 out**	Applies ACL 1 on the interface as an outbound filter
Named Standard IPv4 ACL	
Router(config)# **ip access-list standard MyFilter**	Creates a named standard ACL called *MyFilter* and moves to standard named ACL configuration mode
Router(config-std-nacl)# **deny host 172.16.50.12**	Denies traffic that matches the source address 172.16.50.12
Router(config-std-nacl)# **permit 172.16.50.0 0.0.0.255**	Permits traffic that matches any source address that starts with 172.16.50.*x*

`Router(config-std-nacl)# permit any`	Permits traffic that matches any source address
`Router(config-std-nacl)# interface gigabitethernet 0/0/0`	Moves to interface configuration mode
`Router(config-if)# ip access-group MyFilter in`	Applies ACL *MyFilter* on the interface as an inbound filter
`Router(config-if)# ip access-group MyFilter out`	Applies ACL *MyFilter* on the interface as an outbound filter
`Router(config)# no ip access-list standard MyFilter`	From global configuration mode, removes the entire named ACL *MyFilter*

Configuring and Applying Extended IPv4 ACLs

It is possible to configure numbered or named extended IPv4 ACLs. Extended IPv4 ACLs, whether numbered (100 to 199, or 2000 to 2699,) or named, provide a greater range of control. In addition to verifying packet source addresses, extended ACLs also check destination addresses, protocols, and port numbers.

Numbered Extended IPv4 ACL	
`Router(config)# access-list 120 permit tcp 192.168.1.0 0.0.0.255 any eq www`	Permits HTTP traffic that matches any source that starts with 192.168.1.*x* to any destination
`Router(config)# access-list 120 permit udp 192.168.1.0 0.0.0.255 any eq domain`	Permits DNS traffic that matches any source address that starts with 192.168.1.*x* to any destination
`Router(config)# access-list 120 permit ip any any`	Permits all IPv4 traffic that matches any source address to any destination address
`Router(config)# access-list 120 deny tcp any host 209.165.201.1 eq ftp`	Denies FTP traffic that matches any source address and is destined to address 209.165.201.1
`Router(config)# access-list 120 permit tcp any eq 443 10.0.0.0 0.0.0.255 established`	Permits HTTPS replies from any source to any destination in the 10.0.0.0/24 network. The **established** keyword option can be used with the TCP protocol only. It indicates an established connection
`Router(config)# no access-list 120`	Removes the entire numbered ACL 120
`Router(config)# interface gigabitethernet 0/0/0`	Moves to interface configuration mode
`Router(config-if)# ip access-group 120 in`	Applies ACL 120 on the interface as an inbound filter
`Router(config-if)# ip access-group 120 out`	Applies ACL 120 on the interface as an outbound filter

Named Extended IPv4 ACL	
`Router(config)# ip access-list extended MyExtFilter`	Creates a named extended ACL called *MyExtFilter* and moves to extended named ACL configuration mode
`Router(config-ext-nacl)# permit ip 192.168.1.0 0.0.0.255 any`	Permits all IPv4 traffic that matches any address in the 192.168.1.0/24 network to any destination
`Router(config-ext-nacl)# permit tcp any any eq 22`	Permits SSH traffic that matches any source address to any destination
`Router(config-ext-nacl)# permit udp any host 172.16.100.100 eq snmp`	Permits SNMP traffic that matches any source address destined to 172.16.100.100
`Router(config-ext-nacl)# interface gigabitethernet 0/0/0`	Moves to interface configuration mode
`Router(config-if)# ip access-group MyExtFilter in`	Applies ACL MyExtFilter on the interface as an inbound filter
`Router(config-if)# ip access-group MyFilter out`	Applies ACL MyExtFilter on the interface as an outbound filter
`Router(config)# no ip access-list extended MyExtFilter`	From global configuration mode, removes the entire named ACL MyExtFilter

NOTE: You may add the **log** keyword at the end of any standard or extended access list entry. Doing so causes an informational logging message about the packet matching the entry to be sent to the console.

Configuring and Applying Time-based ACLs

A time-based ACL permits or denies traffic based on a configurable time range. Therefore, access can be restricted selectively at different times, without any systems administrator action. Unlike most ACLs, which are always active, time-based ACLs allow the specification of periodic time ranges to enable or disable specific packet flows.

`Router(config)# time-range LUNCHACCESS`	Defines a time range called *LUNCHACCESS*
`Router(config-time-range)# periodic weekdays 12:00 to 13:00`	Defines a recurring period of time from 12:00 to 13:00 Monday to Friday (weekdays) **NOTE:** Other **periodic** keywords available include **daily, weekends, Monday, Tuesday, Wednesday, Thursday, Friday, Saturday,** and **Sunday**
`Router(config-time-range)# periodic Saturday 0:00 to Sunday 23:59`	Defines a recurring 48-hour period of time from midnight Saturday to 23:59 Sunday (weekend) **NOTE:** It is also possible to use the following with the same result: **periodic weekend 0:00 to 23:59**
`Router(config-time-range)# exit`	Exits time-range configuration mode

Router(config)# ip access-list extended MyTimeACL	Creates a named extended IPv4 access list called *MyTimeACL*
Router(config-ext-nacl)# permit tcp any any eq 80 time-range LUNCHACCESS	Permits HTTP traffic from any source to any destination according to the predefined time ranges **NOTE:** Outside the defined time ranges, this access list entry is ignored by the router when processing packets
Router(config-ext-nacl)# deny tcp any any eq 80	Denies HTTP traffic from any source to any destination
Router(config-ext-nacl)# permit ip any any	Permits all IP traffic from any source to any destination
Router(config-ext-nacl)# exit	Exits named ACL configuration mode
Router(config)# interface gigabitethernet 0/0/0	Enters interface configuration mode
Router(config-if)# ip access-group MyTimedACL out	Applies the time-based ACL outbound on the GigabitEthernet 0/0/0 interface

NOTE: The time period is based on the router's clock. Either manually set the correct time on the router or use a centralized NTP server to synchronize the router's clock to the correct time and date.

Configuring and Applying VTY ACLs

To control traffic into and out of the router (not through the router), you must protect the router virtual ports. A virtual port is called a *vty*. By default, the traditional virtual terminal lines are numbered vty 0 through vty 4. Note that some Cisco devices can even support up to 98 vty lines (0 to 97). The examples that follow will use the range from 0 to 4.

Restricting vty access is primarily a technique for increasing network security and defining which addresses are allowed remote terminal access to the router EXEC process.

Filtering Telnet or SSH traffic is typically considered an extended IP ACL function because it filters a higher-level protocol. Because you are filtering incoming or outgoing Telnet or SSH sessions by source addresses and applying the filter using the **access-class** command to the vty lines, you can use standard IP ACL statements to control vty access.

Router(config)# access-list 10 permit 172.16.100.0 0.0.0.255	Permits any traffic with a source address of 172.16.100.*x*
Router(config)# line vty 0 4	Enters vty line configuration mode

Router(config-line)# `access-class 10 in`	Applies the standard ACL number 10 to traffic entering (in) any of the five vty lines **NOTE:** Notice that identical restrictions have been set on every vty line (0 to 4) because you cannot control on which vty line a user will connect **NOTE:** The implicit **deny any** statement still applies to the ACL when it is used as an access class entry

IPv6 ACLs

In contrast to IPv4 ACLs, all IPv6 ACLs are named and extended. Some commands are slightly different, but all the basic concepts remain the same. Note that instead of a wildcard mask, IPv6 access list entries use the prefix length. Also, the implicit **deny ipv6 any any** at the end of the ACL has changed to permit critical ICMPv6 Neighbor Discovery (ND) messages. IPv6 ACLs can filter packets based on source and destination address, as well as port and protocol information. Also note that you can use IPv6 ACLs for time-based or vty ACL filtering.

Configuring and Applying IPv6 ACLs

Router(config)# `ipv6 access-list v6Filter`	Creates an IPv6 ACL called *v6Filter* and enters IPv6 ACL configuration mode

Router(config-ipv6-acl)#
 `permit tcp any eq www`
 `2001:db8:10:1::/64`
 `established`
	Permits HTTP traffic to return to the 2001:db8:10:1::/64 network from any source if that traffic was originally sourced from the 2001:db8:10:1::/64 network

Router(config-ipv6-acl)#
 `permit tcp any eq 443`
 `2001:db8:10:1::/64`
 `established`
	Permits HTTPS traffic to return to the 2001:db8:10:1::/64 network from any source if that traffic was originally sourced from the 2001:db8:10:1::/64 network

Router(config-ipv6-acl)# `permit udp any eq domain any`	Permits DNS responses from any source to any destination

Router(config-ipv6-acl)#
 `permit icmp any any`
 `echo-reply`
	Permits ICMP ping responses from any source to any destination

Router(config-ipv6-acl)#
 `sequence 5 deny ipv6 host`
 `2001:db8:10:1::100 any`
	Inserts a new ACL entry at line 5 that denies all IPv6 traffic from device 2001:db8:10:1::100 to any destination

Router(config-ipv6-acl)# `exit`	Returns to global configuration mode
Router(config)# `interface gigabitethernet 0/0/0`	Enters GigabitEthernet 0/0/0 interface configuration mode
Router(config-if)# `ipv6 traffic-filter v6Filter in`	Applies the IPv6 access list named *v6Filter* to the interface in the inbound direction

`Router(config)# no ipv6` `access-list v6Filter`	From global configuration mode, removes the entire named ACL *v6Filter*

NOTE: The implicit **deny ipv6 any any** rule has changed for IPv6 access lists to consider the importance of the Neighbor Discovery protocol. ND is to IPv6 what Address Resolution Protocol (ARP) is to IPv4, so naturally the protocol should not be disrupted. That is the reason two additional implicit statements have been added before the implicit **deny ipv6 any any** statement at the end of each IPv6 ACL.

These three new implicit rules are as follows:

```
permit icmp any any nd-na
permit icmp any any nd-ns
deny ipv6 any any
```

It is important to understand that any explicit **deny ipv6 any any** statement overrides all three implicit statements, which can lead to problems because ND traffic is blocked.

Verifying IPv4 and IPv6 ACLs

`Router# show ip interface`
`interface-type interface-`
`number`
	Displays any IPv4 ACL applied inbound or outbound to an interface

`Router# show ipv6 interface`
`interface-type interface-`
`number`
	Displays any IPv6 ACL applied inbound or outbound to an interface

`Router# show access-lists`	Displays the contents of all ACLs on the router, including any matches and sequence numbers
`Router# show ip access-lists`	Displays the contents of all IPv4 ACLs on the router, including any matches and sequence numbers
`Router# show ipv6 access-lists`	Displays the contents of all IPv6 ACLs on the router, including any matches and sequence numbers
`Router# show access-lists 1`	Displays the contents of ACL 1 only

TIP: Sequence numbers are used to allow for easier editing of your ACLs. Each entry in an ACL is automatically given a number, unless you specify one during configuration. Numbers start at 10 and increment by 10 for each line. This allows for simple editing of ACLs. You can add or remove an entry by referencing its line number. This applies to standard (numbered or named) and extended (numbered or named) IPv4 ACLs, as well as to IPv6 ACLs.

Implementing Authentication Methods

Authentication, authorization, and accounting (AAA) is a standards-based framework that you can implement to control who is permitted to access a network (authenticate), what they can do while they are there (authorize), and audit what actions they performed while accessing the network (accounting). AAA can be deployed in two models: local database authentication and sever-based authentication. Server-based authentication utilizes either RADIUS or TACACS+ protocols and offers a more scalable approach to network authentication.

Simple Local Database Authentication

`Router(config)# username ADMIN secret cisco123`	Creates an entry in the local database with a message digest 5 (MD5) authentication encrypted password
`Router(config)# line console 0`	Enters line console configuration mode
`Router(config-line)# login local`	Enables username and password checking from the local database when a user attempts to log into the router

NOTE: The preceding example demonstrates the use of a locally defined username database without enabling AAA.

AAA-based Local Database Authentication

`Router(config)# username ADMIN privilege 15 secret cisco123`	Creates an entry in the local database with a privilege level of 15 and a message digest 5 (MD5) authentication encrypted password
`Router(config)# aaa new-model`	Enables AAA access control mode
`Router(config)# aaa authentication login default local-case enable`	Defines the default authentication method list to authenticate to the case-sensitive local database first. If there are no entries, it should use the enable password second
`Router(config)# aaa authentication login VTY-Lines local line`	Defines the authentication method list *VTY-Lines* to authenticate to the local database first. If there are no entries, it should use the line configured password
`Router(config)# line vty 0 4`	Enters the vty line configuration mode
`Router(config-line)# login authentication VTY-Lines`	Specifies the AAA service to use the authentication method list VTY-Lines when a user logs in via the vty lines
`Router(config-line)# exit`	Returns to global configuration mode
`Router(config)# line console 0`	Enters Console 0 configuration mode
`Router(config-line)# login authentication default`	Specifies the AAA service to use the default method list when a user logs in via the console. This command is optional because the default list would automatically apply to the line

NOTE: A method list describes the sequence and authentication methods to be queried to authenticate a user. The software uses the first method listed to authenticate users; if that method fails to respond, the software selects the next authentication method in the method list. This process continues until there is successful communication with a listed authentication method or until all defined methods are exhausted. If authentication fails at any point in this cycle, the authentication process stops, and no other authentication methods are attempted.

RADIUS Authentication

RADIUS is a fully open standard protocol (RFCs 2865 and 2866). According to the RFCs, RADIUS uses UDP port 1812 for the authentication and authorization, and port 1813 for accounting. However, Cisco implementations default to UDP ports 1645 and 1646 (authentication and accounting, respectively).

Legacy Configuration for RADIUS Servers

The traditional approach to configure a RADIUS server on a Cisco IOS device would be with the **radius-server** global configuration command.

`Router(config)# username admin secret cisco`	Creates user with username *admin* and encrypted password *cisco*
`Router(config)# aaa new-model`	Enables AAA access control mode
`Router(config)# radius-server host 192.168.55.12 auth-port 1812 acct-port 1813 key S3CR3TKEY`	Specifies a RADIUS server at 192.168.55.12 with *S3CR3TKEY* as the authentication key using UDP port 1812 for authentication requests and UDP port 1813 for accounting requests
`Router(config)# aaa authentication login default group radius local line`	Sets login authentication for the default method list to authenticate to the RADIUS server first, locally defined users second, and use the line password as the last resort
`Router(config)# aaa authentication login NO_AUTH none`	Specifies the authentication method list *NO_AUTH* to require no authentication
`Router(config)# line vty 0 4`	Moves to vty line configuration mode
`Router(config-line)# login authentication default`	Specifies the AAA service to use the default method list when a user logs in via vty
`Router(config-line)# password S3cr3TwORd`	Specifies a vty line password on lines 0 through 4
`Router(config-line)# line console 0`	Moves to console 0 configuration mode
`Router(config-line)# login authentication NO_AUTH`	Specifies the AAA service to use the authentication method list *NO_AUTH* when a user logs in via the console port **NOTE:** If authentication is not specifically set for a line, the default is to deny access and no authentication is performed

Modular Configuration for RADIUS Servers

The legacy configuration method outlined in the previous section will soon be deprecated. The new approach brings modularity and consistency when configuring

RADIUS in both IPv4 and IPv6 environments. The new method is configured in three steps: (1) set the RADIUS server parameters, (2) define the RADIUS server group, and (3) define the AAA commands that use RADIUS.

Router(config)# **aaa new-model**	Enables AAA access control mode
Router(config)# **radius server RADSRV**	Specifies the name *RADSRV* for the RADIUS server configuration and enters RADIUS server configuration mode
Router(config-radius-server)# **address ipv4 192.168.100.100 auth-port 1812 acct-port 1813**	Configures the IPv4 address for the RADIUS server, as well as the accounting and authentication parameters
Router(config-radius-server)# **key C1sc0**	Defines the shared secret key configured on the RADIUS server. Depending on the Cisco IOS software release, this command might trigger a warning message: WARNING: Command has been added to the configuration using a type 0 password. However, type 0 passwords will soon be deprecated. Migrate to a supported password type. See the Note following this table for an explanation
Router(config-radius-server)# **exit**	Returns to global configuration mode
Router(config)# **ip radius source-interface gigabitethernet 0/0/0**	Forces RADIUS to use the IP address of a specified interface for all outgoing RADIUS packets
Router(config)# **aaa group server radius RADSRVGRP**	Defines a RADIUS server group called *RADSRVGRP*
Router(config-sg-radius)# **server name RADSRV**	Adds the RADIUS server RADSRV to the RADSRVGRP group
Router(config-sg-radius)# **exit**	Returns to global configuration mode
Router(config)# **aaa authentication login RAD_LIST group RADSRVGRP local**	Configures login authentication using a method list called *RAD_LIST*, which uses RADSRVGRP as the primary authentication option and local user database as a backup
Router(config)# **line vty 0 4**	Moves to vty line configuration mode
Router(config)# **authentication RAD_LIST**	Applies the RAD_LIST method list to the vty lines

NOTE: The warning message produced by the router appears after you enter a cleartext RADIUS or TACACS server key. This message says that at some point in the future Cisco IOS will no longer store plaintext passwords in either the running-config or startup-config. Instead, it will store only hashed passwords (MD5/SHA/scrypt) and securely encrypted passwords (AES). This requires either that the password is already hashed/encrypted at the time you enter it at the CLI or that the router is configured with strong password encryption so that after you enter the password in plaintext, IOS is immediately able to encrypt and store it in the configuration in the encrypted form. Although IOS will still accept plaintext passwords entered at the CLI, it will not store them as plaintext in the configuration. To enable strong password encryption using AES, you need to enter two commands. The first, **key config-key password-encryption** [*master key*], allows you to configure a master key that will be used to encrypt all other keys in the router configuration. The master key is not stored in the router configuration and cannot be seen or obtained in any way while connected to the router. The second command, **password encryption aes**, triggers the actual password encryption process.

For more on this security feature, see "Encrypt Pre-shared Keys in Cisco IOS Router Configuration Example" at https://www.cisco.com/c/en/us/support/docs/security-vpn/ipsec-negotiation-ike-protocols/46420-pre-sh-keys-ios-rtr-cfg.html.

TACACS+ Authentication

TACACS+ is a Cisco proprietary protocol that is not compatible with the older versions such as TACACS or XTACACS, which are now deprecated. TACACS+ allows for greater modularity, by total separation of all three AAA functions. TACACS+ uses TCP port 49, and thus reliability is ensured by the transport protocol itself. Entire TACACS+ packets are encrypted, so communication between Network Access Server (NAS) and the TACACS+ server is completely secure.

Legacy Configuration for TACACS+ Servers

The traditional approach to configure a TACACS+ server on a Cisco IOS device would be with the **tacacs-server** global configuration command.

`Router(config)# username admin secret cisco`	Creates user with username *admin* and encrypted password *cisco*
`Router(config)# aaa new-model`	Enables AAA access control mode
`Router(config)# tacacs-server host 192.168.55.13 single-connection key C1sc0`	Specifies a TACACS+ server at 192.168.55.13 with an encryption key of *C1sc0*. The **single-connection** keyword maintains a single open TCP connection between the switch and the server
`Router(config)# aaa authentication login TACSRV group tacacs+ local`	Sets login authentication for the *TACSRV* method list to authenticate to the TACACS+ server first, and the locally defined username and password second
`Router(config)# line console 0`	Moves to console 0 configuration mode
`Router(config-line)# login authentication TACSRV`	Specifies the AAA service to use the TACSRV authentication method list when users connect to the console port

Modular Configuration for TACACS+ Servers

Similar to the RADIUS modular configuration shown in the previous section, it is possible to use a modular approach when configuring TACACS+. The same three steps apply (define TACACS+ server parameters, define TACACS+ server group, and define AAA commands).

`Router(config)# aaa new-model`	Enables AAA access control mode
`Router(config)# tacacs server TACSRV`	Specifies the name *TACSRV* for the TACACS+ server configuration and enters TACACS+ server configuration mode
`Router(config-server-tacacs)# address ipv4 192.168.100.200`	Configures the IPv4 address for the TACACS+ server
`Router(config-server-tacacs)# key C1sc0`	Defines the shared secret key that is configured on the TACACS+ server
`Router(config-server-tacacs)# single-connection`	Enables all TACACS+ packets to be sent to the same server using a single TCP connection
`Router(config-server-tacacs)# exit`	Returns to global configuration mode
`Router(config)# aaa group server tacacs+ TACSRVGRP`	Defines a TACACS+ server group called *TACSRVGRP*
`Router(config-sg-tacacs+)# server name TACSRV`	Adds the TACACS+ server TACSRV to the TACSRVGRP group
`Router(config-sg-tacacs+)# exit`	Returns to global configuration mode
`Router(config)# aaa authentication login TAC_LIST group TACSRVGRP local`	Configures login authentication using a method list called *TAC_LIST*, which uses TACSRVGRP as the primary authentication option and the local user database as a backup
`Router(config)# line vty 0 4`	Moves to vty line configuration mode
`Router(config-line)# login authentication TAC_LIST`	Applies the TAC_LIST method list to the vty lines

Configuring Authorization and Accounting

After AAA has been enabled on a Cisco IOS device and AAA authentication has been configured, you can optionally configure AAA authorization and AAA accounting.

Authorization

Configuring authorization is a two-step process. First define a method list, and then apply it to a corresponding interface or line.

`Router(config)# aaa authorization exec default group radius group tacacs+ local`	Defines the default EXEC authorization method list, which uses the RADIUS servers first, the TACACS+ servers second, and the local user database as backup
`Router(config-line)# line vty 0 4`	Moves to vty line configuration mode

| Router(config-if)# **authorization exec default** | Applies the default authorization list to the vty lines |

Accounting

Configuring accounting is also a two-step process. First define a method list, and then apply it to a corresponding interface or line.

Router(config)# **aaa accounting exec default start-stop group radius**	Defines the default EXEC accounting method list to send to the RADIUS server, a start accounting notice at the beginning of the requested event, and a stop accounting notice at the end of the event
Router(config)# **line vty 0 4**	Moves to vty line configuration mode
Router(config-line)# **accounting exec default**	Applies the default accounting list to the vty lines

Troubleshooting AAA

Router# **debug aaa authentication**	Enables debugging of the AAA authentication process
Router# **debug aaa authorization**	Enables debugging of the AAA authorization process
Router# **debug aaa accounting**	Enables debugging of the AAA accounting process

Control Plane Policing (CoPP)

To prevent a Cisco device from denial of service (DoS) attacks to the control plane, Cisco IOS employs Control Plane Policing (CoPP). CoPP increases security on the device by protecting the system from unnecessary or DoS traffic and gives priority to important control-plane and management traffic. CoPP uses a dedicated control-plane configuration through Cisco Modular QoS CLI (MQC) to provide filtering and rate-limiting capabilities for control-plane packets. Configuring CoPP is a four-step process:

1. Define ACLs to identify permitted CoPP traffic flows
2. Define class maps for matched traffic
3. Define a policy map to police matched traffic
4. Assign a policy map to the control plane

In the CoPP configuration example that follows, routing protocols (OSPF, EIGRP, BGP), management traffic (Telnet, SSH, SNMP), and ICMP traffic destined to the router's control plane are policed.

Step 1: Define ACLs to Identify Permitted CoPP Traffic Flows

`Router(config)# ip access-list extended copp-routing-acl`	Creates an extended ACL called *copp-routing-acl*
`Router(config-ext-nacl)# permit ospf any host 224.0.0.5`	Permits OSPF traffic for CoPP inspection
`Router(config-ext-nacl)# permit ospf any host 224.0.0.6`	Permits OSPF traffic for CoPP inspection
`Router(config-ext-nacl)# permit eigrp any host 224.0.0.10`	Permits EIGRP traffic for CoPP inspection
`Router(config-ext-nacl)# permit tcp any any eq bgp`	Permits BGP traffic for CoPP inspection
`Router(config-ext-nacl)# permit tcp any eq bgp any`	Permits BGP traffic for CoPP inspection
`Router(config-ext-nacl)# exit`	Exits named ACL configuration mode
`Router(config)# ip access-list extended copp-management-acl`	Creates an extended ACL called *copp-management-acl*
`Router(config-ext-nacl)# permit tcp any any eq telnet`	Permits Telnet traffic for CoPP inspection
`Router(config-ext-nacl)# permit tcp any any eq 22`	Permits SSH traffic for CoPP inspection
`Router(config-ext-nacl)# permit udp any any eq snmp`	Permits SNMP traffic for CoPP inspection
`Router(config-ext-nacl)# exit`	Exits named ACL configuration mode
`Router(config)# ip access-list extended copp-icmp-acl`	Creates an extended ACL called *copp-icmp-acl*
`Router(config-ext-nacl)# permit icmp any any echo`	Permits ICMP echo request traffic for CoPP inspection
`Router(config-ext-nacl)# permit icmp any any echo-reply`	Permits ICMP echo reply traffic for CoPP inspection

Step 2: Define Class Maps for Matched Traffic

`Router(config)# class-map match-all copp-routing-map`	Creates a class map called *copp-routing-map*
`Router(config-cmap)# match access-group name copp-routing-acl`	Assigns the CoPP routing ACL to the CoPP routing class map
`Router(config-cmap)# class-map match-all copp-management-map`	Creates a class map called *copp-management-map*
`Router(config-cmap)# match access-group name copp-management-acl`	Assigns the CoPP management ACL to the CoPP management class map
`Router(config-cmap)# class-map match-all copp-icmp-map`	Creates a class map called *copp-icmp-map*

Router(config-cmap)# **match access-group name copp-icmp-acl**	Assigns the CoPP ICMP ACL to the CoPP ICMP class map

Step 3: Define a Policy Map to Police Matched Traffic

Router(config)# **policy-map copp-policy**	Creates a CoPP policy called *copp-policy*
Router(config-pmap)# **class copp-routing-map**	Assigns the CoPP routing class map to the policy map
Router(config-pmap-c)# **police 1000000 conform-action transmit exceed-action drop**	Polices up to 1 Mbps any routing protocol traffic sent to the control plane. Packets exceeding 1 Mbps are dropped
Router(config-pmap-c-police)# **class copp-management-map**	Assigns the CoPP management class map to the policy map
Router(config-pmap-c)# **police 100000 conform-action transmit exceed-action drop**	Polices up to 100 Kbps any management traffic sent to the control plane. Packets exceeding 100 Kbps are dropped
Router(config-pmap-c-police)# **class copp-icmp-map**	Assigns the CoPP ICMP class map to the policy map
Router(config-pmap-c)# **police 50000 conform-action transmit exceed-action drop**	Polices up to 50 Kbps any ICMP traffic sent to the control plane. Packets exceeding 50 Kbps are dropped
Router(config-pmap-c-police)# **class class-default**	Assigns the CoPP default class map to the policy map
Router(config-pmap-c)# **police 8000 conform-action transmit exceed-action drop**	Polices up to 8 Kbps any ICMP traffic sent to the control plane. Packets exceeding 8 Kbps are dropped

NOTE: When more than one class of traffic is defined within a policy map, the order of classes is important, as traffic is compared against successive classes, top-down, until a match is recorded. Once a packet has matched a class, no further comparisons are made. If no match is found after processing all classes, packets automatically match the always-defined class, **class-default**. The class **class-default** is special in MQC because it is always automatically placed at the end of every policy map. Match criteria cannot be configured for **class-default** because it automatically includes an implied match for all packets. Only a traffic policy can be configured for **class-default**.

Step 4: Assign a Policy Map to the Control Plane

Router(config)# **control-plane**	Enters control-plane configuration mode
Router(config-cp)# **service-policy input copp-policy**	Assigns the CoPP policy map to the input interface of the router's control plane

Verifying CoPP

Router# **show access-lists**	Displays all configured ACLs
Router# **show class-map**	Displays all configured class maps
Router# **show policy-map**	Displays all configured policy maps
Router# **show policy-map control-plane**	Displays the dynamic information about the actual policy applied, including rate information and the number of bytes (and packets) that conformed to or exceeded the configured policies

Unicast Reverse Path Forwarding (uRPF)

Network administrators can deploy Unicast Reverse Path Forwarding (uRPF) as an antispoofing mechanism to help limit malicious traffic on an enterprise network. This security feature works by enabling a router to verify the reachability of the source address in packets being forwarded. This capability can limit the appearance of spoofed addresses on a network. If the source IP address is not valid, the packet is discarded. uRPF works in one of two modes: *strict mode* or *loose mode*. When administrators use uRPF in strict mode, the packet must be received on the interface that the router would use to forward the return packet. When administrators use uRPF in loose mode, the source address must appear in the routing table.

Configuring uRPF

Router(config)# **interface gigabitethernet 0/0/0**	Moves to interface configuration mode
Router(config-if)# **ip verify unicast source reachable-via rx**	Enables uRPF strict mode
Router(config-if)# **ip verify unicast source reachable-via any**	Enables uRPF loose mode
Router(config-if)# **ip verify unicast source reachable-via rx 120**	Enables uRPF strict mode with ACL applied to bypass the drop function
Router(config-if)# **ip verify unicast source reachable-via rx allow-default**	Enables uRPF strict mode with permission to use a default route for the uRPF check **NOTE:** It is possible to add the **allow-self-ping** option, but this is not recommended by Cisco. It could lead to a DoS condition on the router

Verifying and Troubleshooting uRPF

Router# **debug ip cef drops rpf**	Displays information about dropped packets caused by uRPF
Router# **show ip traffic**	Displays information about uRPF drops
Router# **show cef interface**	Shows if uRPF is configured on an interface

CHAPTER 11

Network Assurance

This chapter provides information and commands concerning the following topics:

- Internet Control Message Protocol redirect messages
- The **ping** command
- Examples of using the **ping** and the extended **ping** commands
- The **traceroute** command
- The **debug** command
- Conditionally triggered debugs
- Configuring secure SNMP
  - Securing SNMPv1 or SNMPv2
  - Securing SNMPv3
  - Verifying SNMP
- Implementing logging
  - Configuring syslog
  - Syslog message format
  - Syslog severity levels
  - Syslog message example
- Configuring NetFlow
- Configuring Flexible NetFlow
- Verifying NetFlow
- Implementing port mirroring
  - Default SPAN and RSPAN configuration
  - Configuring local SPAN
  - Local SPAN guidelines for configuration
  - Configuration example: Local SPAN
  - Configuring remote SPAN
  - Remote SPAN guidelines for configuration
  - Configuration example: Remote SPAN
  - Configuring Encapsulated RSPAN (ERSPAN)
  - Verifying and troubleshooting local and remote SPAN

- Configuring Network Time Protocol
  - NTP configuration
  - NTP design
  - Securing NTP
  - Verifying and troubleshooting NTP
  - Setting the clock on a router
  - Using time stamps
  - Configuration example: NTP
- Tool Command Language (Tcl)
- Embedded Event Manager (EEM)
  - EEM configuration examples
  - EEM and Tcl scripts
  - Verifying EEM

Internet Control Message Protocol Redirect Messages

Internet Control Message Protocol (ICMP) is used to communicate to the original source the errors encountered while routing packets and to exercise control on the traffic. Routers use ICMP redirect messages to notify the hosts on the data link that a better route is available for a particular destination.

`Router(config-if)# no ip redirects`	Disables ICMP redirects from this specific interface
`Router(config-if)# ip redirects`	Reenables ICMP redirects from this specific interface

The ping Command

`Router# ping w.x.y.z`	Checks for Layer 3 connectivity with the device at IPv4 address *w.x.y.z*
`Router# ping aaaa:aaaa: aaaa:aaaa:aaaa:aaaa: aaaa:aaaa`	Checks for Layer 3 connectivity with the device at IPv6 address *aaaa:aaaa:aaaa:aaaa:aaaa:aaaa:aaaa:aaaa*
`Router# ping 172.16.20.1 source loopback 1`	Checks for Layer 3 connectivity with the device at IPv4 address 172.16.20.1 with the packets originating from source interface loopback 1
`Router# ping 2001::1 source loopback 1`	Checks for Layer 3 connectivity with the device at IPv6 address 2001::1 with the packets originating from source interface loopback 1
`Router# ping`	Enters extended ping mode, which provides more options

Table 11-1 describes the possible **ping** output characters.

TABLE 11-1   ping Output Characters

Character	Description
!	Each exclamation point indicates receipt of a reply
.	Each period indicates that the network server timed out while waiting for a reply
?	Unknown error
@	Unreachable for unknown reason
A	Administratively unreachable. Usually means that an access control list (ACL) is blocking traffic
B	Packet too big
H	Host unreachable
N	Network unreachable (beyond scope)
P	Port unreachable
R	Parameter problem
T	Time exceeded
U	No route to host

Examples of Using the ping and the Extended ping Commands

Router# **ping 172.16.20.1**	Performs a basic Layer 3 test to IPv4 address 172.16.20.1
Router# **ping paris**	Same as above but through the IP host name
Router# **ping 2001:db8:d1a5:c900::2**	Checks for Layer 3 connectivity with the device at IPv6 address 2001:db8:d1a5:c900::2
Router# **ping**	Enters extended ping mode; can now change parameters of ping test
Protocol [ip]: ⏎Return	Press ⏎Return to use **ping** for IP
Target IP address: **172.16.20.1**	Enter the target IP address
Repeat count [5]: **100**	Enter the number of echo requests you want to send. The default is 5
Datagram size [100]: ⏎Return	Enter the size of datagrams being sent. The default is 100
Timeout in seconds [2]: ⏎Return	Enter the timeout delay between sending echo requests
Extended commands [n]: **yes**	Allows you to configure extended commands

`Source address or interface:` `10.0.10.1`	Allows you to explicitly set where the pings are originating from. An interface name may also be used here
`Type of Service [0]`	Allows you to set the TOS field in the IP header
`Set DF bit in IP header [no]`	Allows you to set the DF bit in the IP header
`Validate reply data? [no]`	Allows you to set whether you want validation
`Data Pattern [0xABCD]`	Allows you to change the data pattern in the data field of the ICMP echo request packet
`Loose, Strict, Record,` `Timestamp, Verbose[none]:`	Offers IP header options. This prompt offers more than one of the following options to be selected: **Verbose** is automatically selected along with any other option **Record** is a very useful option because it displays the address(es) of the hops (up to nine) the packet goes through **Loose** allows you to influence the path by specifying the address(es) of the hop(s) you want the packet to go through **Strict** is used to specify the hop(s) that you want the packet to go through, but no other hop(s) are allowed to be visited **Timestamp** is used to measure roundtrip time to particular hosts
`Sweep range of sizes [no]:`	Allows you to vary the sizes of the echo packets that are sent
`Type escape sequence to` `abort` `Sending 100, 100-byte ICMP` `Echos to 172.16.20.1,` `timeout is 2 seconds:` `Packet sent with a source` `address of 10.0.10.1` `!!!!!!!!!!!!!!!!!!!!!!!!!!` `!!!!!!!!!!!!!!!!!!!!!!!!!!` `!!!!!!!!!!!!!!!!!!!!!!!!!!` `!!!!!!!!!!!!!!!!!!!!!!!!!!` `!!!!!!!!!!!!!!!!` `Success rate is 100 percent` `(100/100) round-trip min/` `avg/max = 1/1/4 ms`	

TIP: If you want to interrupt the **ping** operation, use the **Ctrl-Shift-6** keystroke combination. This ends the operation and returns you to the prompt.

The traceroute Command

The **traceroute** command (or **tracert** in Microsoft Windows) is a utility that allows observation of the path between two hosts.

Router# **traceroute** 172.16.20.1	Discovers the route taken to travel to the IPv4 destination of 172.16.20.1
Router# **traceroute** **paris**	Shows command with IP host name rather than IP address
Router# **traceroute** 2001:**db8**:**d1a5**:**c900**::**2**	Discovers the route taken to travel to the IPv6 destination of 2001:db8:d1a5:c900::2
Router# **trace** 172.16.20.1	Shows common shortcut spelling of the **traceroute** command

NOTE: In Microsoft Windows operating systems, the command to allow observation between two hosts is **tracert**:

```
C:\Windows\system32>tracert 172.16.20.1
C:\Windows\system32>tracert 2001:db8:c:18:2::1
```

The debug Command

The output from **debug** privileged EXEC commands provides diagnostic information that includes a variety of internetworking events related to protocol status and network activity in general.

CAUTION: Using the **debug** command may severely affect router performance and might even cause the router to reboot. Always exercise caution when using the **debug** command, and do not leave it on. Use **debug** long enough to gather needed information, and then disable debugging with the **undebug all** or **no debug all** command.

TIP: Send your **debug** output to a syslog server to ensure that you have a copy of it in case your router is overloaded and needs to reboot. Use the **no logging console** command to turn off logging to the console if you have configured a syslog server to receive **debug** output.

Router# **debug all**	Turns on all possible debugging **CAUTION:** This is just an example. Do not use this command in a production network
Router# **u all** (short form of **undebug all**)	Turns off all possible debugging
Router# **show debug**	Lists what debug commands are on
Router# **debug ip packet 10**	Turns on IPv4 packet debugging that matches the criteria defined in ACL 10 **NOTE:** The **debug ip packet** command helps you to better understand the IP packet forwarding process, but this command only produces information on packets that are process-switched by the router. Packets generated by a router or destined for a router are process-switched and are therefore displayed with the **debug ip packet** command

| Router# `terminal monitor` | Displays debug output through a Telnet/SSH (a vty line connection) session (default is to only send output on the console screen) |

Conditionally Triggered Debugs

When the Conditionally Triggered Debugging feature is enabled, the router generates debugging messages for packets entering or leaving the router on a specified interface; the router does not generate debugging output for packets entering or leaving through a different interface.

Use the **debug condition** command to restrict the debug output for some commands.

If any **debug condition** commands are enabled, output is generated only for interfaces associated with the specified keyword. In addition, this command enables debugging output for conditional debugging events. Messages are displayed as different interfaces meet specific conditions.

If multiple **debug condition** commands are enabled, output is displayed if at least one condition matches. All the conditions do not need to match. The **no** form of this command removes the debug condition specified by the condition identifier.

The condition identifier is displayed after you use a **debug condition** command or in the output of the **show debug condition** command. If the last condition is removed, debugging output resumes for all interfaces. You will be asked for confirmation before removing the last condition or all conditions.

Not all debugging output is affected by the **debug condition** command. Some commands generate output whenever they are enabled, regardless of whether they meet any conditions.

Router# **debug condition** **interface** *interface-type* *interface number*	Filters output on the basis of the specified interface
Router# **debug condition ip**	Filters output on the basis of the specified IP address
Router# **debug condition** **mac-address**	Filters messages on the specified MAC address
Router# **debug condition** **username**	Filters output on the basis of the specified username
Router# **debug condition vlan**	Filters output on the basis of the specified VLAN ID
Router# **show debug condition**	Displays which conditional debugs are enabled

Configuring Secure SNMP

Simple Network Management Protocol (SNMP) is the most commonly used network management protocol. It is important to restrict SNMP access to the routers on which it is enabled.

TIP: If SNMP is not required on a router, you should turn it off by using the **no snmp-server** global configuration command:

```
Edmonton(config)# no snmp-server
```

NOTE: Beginning with SNMPv3, methods to ensure the secure transmission of data between manager and agent were added. You can now define a security policy per group, or limit IP addresses to which its members can belong. You now have to define encryption and hashing algorithms and passwords for each user.

Table 11-2 shows the different SNMP security models.

TABLE 11-2 SNMP Security Models

SNMP Version	Access Mode	Authentication	Encryption
SNMPv1	noAuthNoPriv	Community string	No
SNMPv2c	noAuthNoPriv	Community string	No
SNMPv3	noAuthNoPriv	Username	No
	authNoPriv	MD5 or SHA-1	No
	authPriv	MD5 or SHA-1	DES, 3DES, or AES

TIP: The SNMP security levels are as follows:

- **noAuthNoPriv:** Authenticates SNMP messages using a community string. No encryption provided.
- **authNoPriv:** Authenticates SNMP messages using either HMAC with MD5 or SHA-1. No encryption provided.
- **authPriv:** Authenticates SNMP messages by using either HMAC-MD5 or SHA. Encrypts SNMP messages using DES, 3DES, or AES.
- **priv:** Does not authenticate SNMP messages. Encrypts only using either DES or AES.

TIP: SNMPv3 provides all three security level options. It should be used wherever possible.

TIP: If SNMPv3 cannot be used, then use SNMPv2c and secure it using uncommon, complex community strings and by enabling read-only access.

TIP: If community strings are also used for SNMP traps, they must be different from community strings for *get* and *set* methods. This is considered best practice.

Securing SNMPv1 or SNMPv2c

`Edmonton(config)# snmp-server` `community COmpl3xAdmin ro 98`	Sets a community string named *COmpl3xAdmin*. It is read-only and refers to ACL 98 to limit SNMP access to the authorized hosts **NOTE:** A named ACL can be used as well

`Edmonton(config)# access-list 98 permit host 192.168.10.3`	Creates an ACL that will limit the SNMP access to the specific host of 192.168.10.3
`Edmonton(config)# snmp-server host 192.168.10.3 AdminC0mpl3x`	Sets the Network Management System (NMS) IP address of 192.168.10.3 and the community string of *AdminC0mpl3x*, which will be used to protect the sending of the SNMP traps. The community string is also used to connect to the host

Securing SNMPv3

`Edmonton(config)# access-list 99 permit 10.1.1.0 0.0.0.255`	Creates an ACL that will be used to limit SNMP access to the local device from SNMP managers within the 10.1.1.0/24 subnet
`Edmonton(config)# snmp-server view MGMT sysUpTime included`	Defines an SNMP view named *MGMT* to include an OID name of *sysUpTime*
`Edmonton(config)# snmp-server view MGMT ifDescr included`	Defines an SNMP view named *MGMT* to include an OID name of *ifDescr*
`Edmonton(config)# snmp-server view MGMT ifAdminStatus included`	Defines an SNMP view named *MGMT* and an OID name of *ifAdminStatus*. This OID is included in the view
`Edmonton(config)# snmp-server view MGMT ifOperStatus included`	Defines an SNMP view named *MGMT* and an OID name of *ifOperStatus*. This OID is included in the view
`Edmonton(config)# snmp-server group groupAAA v3 priv read MGMT write MGMT access 99`	Defines an SNMPv3 group called *groupAAA* and configures it with the authPriv security level. SNMP read and write access to the MGMT view is limited to devices defined in ACL 99
`Edmonton(config)# snmp-server user userAAA groupAAA v3 auth sha itsa5ecret priv aes 256 another5ecret`	Configures a new user called *userAAA* to the SNMPv3 group *groupAAA* with authentication and encryption. Authentication uses SHA with a password of *itsa5ecret*. Encryption uses AES-256 with a password of *another5ecret*
`Edmonton(config)# snmp-server enable traps`	Enables SNMP traps
`Edmonton(config)# snmp-server host 10.1.1.50 traps version 3 priv userAAA cpu port-security`	Defines a receiving manager for traps at IP address 10.1.1.50. The user *userAAA* is used to authenticate the host. The traps sent relate to CPU and port security events

Edmonton(config)# snmp-server ifindex persist	Prevents index shuffle **NOTE:** SNMP does not identify object instances by names but by numeric indexes. Index number may change due to instance changes, such as a new interface being configured. This command will guarantee index persistence when changes occur

Verifying SNMP

Edmonton# show snmp	Provides basic information about SNMP configuration
Edmonton# show snmp view	Provides information about SNMP views
Edmonton# show snmp group	Provides information about configured SNMP groups
Edmonton# show snmp user	Provides information about configured SNMP users

Implementing Logging

It is important for network administrators to implement logging to get insight into what is occurring in their network. When a router reloads, all local logs are lost, so it is important to implement logging to an external destination. The following sections deal with the different mechanisms that you can use to configure logging to a remote location.

Configuring Syslog

Edmonton(config)# logging on	Enables logging to all supported destinations
Edmonton(config)# logging 192.168.10.53	Sends logging messages to a syslog server host at address 192.168.10.53
Edmonton(config)# logging sysadmin	Sends logging messages to a syslog server host named *sysadmin*
Edmonton(config)# logging trap *x*	Sets the syslog server logging level to value *x*, where *x* is a number between 0 and 7 or a word defining the level. Table 11-3 provides more details
Edmonton(config)# service sequence-numbers	Stamps syslog messages with a sequence number
Edmonton(config)# service timestamps log datetime	Causes a time stamp to be included in syslog messages

Syslog Message Format

The general format of syslog messages generated on Cisco IOS Software is as follows:

```
seq no:timestamp: %facility-severity-MNEMONIC:description
```

Item in Syslog Message	Definition
seq no	Sequence number. Stamped only if the **service sequence-numbers** global configuration command is configured
timestamp	Date and time of the message. Appears only if the **service timestamps log datetime** global configuration command is configured
facility	The facility to which the message refers (SNMP, SYS, and so on)
severity	Single-digit code from 0 to 7 that defines the severity of the message. See Table 11-3 for descriptions of the levels
MNEMONIC	String of text that uniquely defines the message
description	String of text that contains detailed information about the event being reported

Syslog Severity Levels

Table 11-3 outlines the eight levels of severity in logging messages.

TABLE 11-3 Syslog Severity Levels

Level #	Level Name	Description
0	Emergencies	System is unusable
1	Alerts	Immediate action needed
2	Critical	Critical conditions
3	Errors	Error conditions
4	Warnings	Warning conditions
5	Notifications	Normal but significant conditions
6	Informational	Informational messages (default level)
7	Debugging	Debugging messages

Setting a level means you will get that level and everything numerically below it; for example, setting level 6 means you will receive messages for levels 0 through 6.

Syslog Message Example

The easiest syslog message to use as an example is the one that shows up every time you exit from global configuration mode back to privileged EXEC mode. You have just finished entering a command and you want to save your work, but after you type **exit** you see something like this (your output will differ depending on whether you have sequence numbers and/or time/date stamps configured):

```
Edmonton(config)# exit
Edmonton#
```

```
*Oct 23:22:45:20.878: %SYS-5-CONFIG_I: Configured from console by
console
Edmonton#
```

So, what does this all mean?

- No sequence number is part of this message

- The message occurred on October 23, at 22:45:20.878 (or 10:45 PM, and 20.878 seconds)

- It is a SYS message, and it is level 5 (a notification)

- It is a CONFIG message, and the configuration occurred from the console

Configuring NetFlow

NetFlow is an application for collecting IP traffic information. It is used for network accounting and security auditing.

CAUTION: NetFlow consumes additional memory. If you have limited memory, you might want to preset the size of the NetFlow cache to contain a smaller amount of entries. The default cache size depends on the platform of the device.

`Edmonton(config)# interface` `gigabitethernet 0/0/0`	Moves to interface configuration mode
`Edmonton(config-if)# ip flow` `ingress`	Enables NetFlow on the interface. Captures traffic that is being received by the interface
`Edmonton(config-if)# ip flow` `egress`	Enables NetFlow on the interface. Captures traffic that is being transmitted by the interface
`Edmonton(config-if)# exit`	Returns to global configuration mode
`Edmonton(config)# ip flow-export` `destination` *ip_address udp_port*	Defines the IP address of the workstation to which you want to send the NetFlow information as well as the UDP port on which the workstation is listening for the information
`Edmonton(config)# ip flow-export` `version` *x*	Specifies the version format that the export packets used

NOTE: NetFlow exports data in UDP in one of five formats: 1, 5, 7, 8, 9. Version 9 is the most versatile, but is not backward compatible with versions 5 or 8. The default is version 1. Version 5 is the most commonly used format, but version 9 is the latest format and has some advantages for key technologies such as security, traffic analysis, and multicast.

Configuring Flexible NetFlow

Flexible NetFlow improves on original NetFlow by adding the capability to customize the traffic analysis parameters for your specific requirements. Flexible NetFlow facilitates the creation of more complex configurations for traffic analysis and data export through the use of reusable configuration components. Flexible NetFlow is an extension of NetFlow v9.

Configuring Flexible NetFlow is a four-step process:

Step 1.   Configure a flow record.

Step 2.   Configure a flow exporter.

Step 3.   Configure a flow monitor.

Step 4.   Apply the flow monitor to an interface.

Step 1: Configure a Flow Record

R1(config)# **flow record R1-FLOW-RECORD**	Creates a new flow record called *R1-FLOW-RECORD*
R1(config-flow-record)# **match ipv4 source address**	Includes the source IPv4 address to the flow record
R1(config-flow-record)# **match ipv4 destination address**	Includes the destination IPv4 address to the flow record
R1(config-flow-record)# **collect counter bytes**	Includes statistics on the number of bytes in the flow record

Step 2: Configure a Flow Exporter

R1(config)# **flow exporter R1-FLOW-EXPORTER**	Creates a flow exporter called *R1-FLOW-EXPORTER*
R1(config-flow-exporter)# **destination 10.250.250.25**	Specifies the IP address of the NetFlow collector

Step 3: Configure a Flow Monitor

R1(config)# **flow monitor R1-FLOW-MONITOR**	Creates a flow monitor called *R1-FLOW-MONITOR*
R1(config-flow-monitor)# **exporter R1-FLOW-EXPORTER**	Assigns the flow exporter to the flow monitor
R1(config-flow-monitor)# **record R1-FLOW-RECORD**	Assigns the flow record to the flow monitor

Step 4: Apply the Flow Monitor to an Interface

`R1(config)# interface gigabitethernet 0/0/0`	Enters interface configuration mode
`R1(config-if)# ip flow monitor R1-FLOW-MONITOR input`	Applies the flow monitor to the interface in the input direction

Verifying NetFlow

`Edmonton# show ip interface gigabitethernet 0/0/0`	Displays information about the interface, including NetFlow as being either ingress or egress enabled
`Edmonton# show ip flow export`	Verifies status and statistics for NetFlow accounting data export
`Edmonton# show ip cache flow`	Displays a summary of NetFlow statistics on a Cisco IOS router
`Edmonton# show flow monitor`	Displays a summary of the Flexible NetFlow configuration
`Edmonton# show flow exporter`	Displays information about the Flexible NetFlow exporter configuration
`Edmonton# show flow record`	Displays information about the configured Flexible NetFlow records

NOTE: The **show ip cache flow** command is useful for seeing which protocols use the highest volume of traffic and between which hosts this traffic flows.

Implementing Port Mirroring

Using a traffic sniffer can be a valuable tool to monitor and troubleshoot a network. In the modern era of switches, using the Switched Port Analyzer (SPAN) feature enables you to instruct a switch to send copies of packets seen on one port to another port on the same switch.

Default SPAN and RSPAN Configuration

Table 11-4 shows the default SPAN and remote SPAN (RSPAN) settings.

TABLE 11-4 SPAN and RSPAN Default Settings

Feature	Default Setting
SPAN state (SPAN and RSPAN)	Disabled
Source port traffic to monitor	Both received and sent traffic (both SPAN and RSPAN)
Encapsulation type (destination port)	Native form (untagged packets)
Ingress forwarding (destination port)	Disabled

Feature	Default Setting
VLAN filtering	On a trunk interface used as a source port, all VLANs are monitored
RSPAN VLANs	None configured

Configuring Local SPAN

Local SPAN supports a SPAN session entirely within one switch; all source ports or source VLANs and destination ports are in the same switch or switch stack. Local SPAN copies traffic from one or more source ports in any VLAN or from one or more VLANs to a destination port for analysis.

Local SPAN Guidelines for Configuration

When configuring SPAN, follow these guidelines:

- For SPAN sources, you can monitor traffic for a single port or VLAN or a series or range of ports or VLANs for each session. You cannot mix source ports and source VLANs within a single SPAN session.

- The destination port cannot be a source port; a source port cannot be a destination port.

- You cannot have two SPAN sessions using the same destination port.

- When you configure a switch port as a SPAN destination port, it is no longer a normal switch port; only monitored traffic passes through the SPAN destination port.

- Entering SPAN configuration commands does not remove previously configured SPAN parameters. You must enter the **no monitor session** {*session_number* | **all** | **local** | **remote**} global configuration command to delete configured SPAN parameters.

- For local SPAN, outgoing packets through the SPAN destination port carry the original encapsulation headers (untagged or IEEE 802.1Q) if the **encapsulation replicate** *keywords* are specified. If the keywords are not specified, the packets are sent in native form. For RSPAN destination ports, outgoing packets are not tagged.

- You can configure a disabled port to be a source or destination port, but the SPAN function does not start until the destination port and at least one source port or source VLAN are enabled.

- You can limit SPAN traffic to specific VLANs by using the **filter vlan** keywords. If a trunk port is being monitored, only traffic on the VLANs specified with these keywords are monitored. By default, all VLANs are monitored on a trunk port.

- You cannot mix source VLANs and filter VLANs within a single SPAN session.

Configuration Example: Local SPAN

Figure 11-1 is the network topology for local SPAN commands.

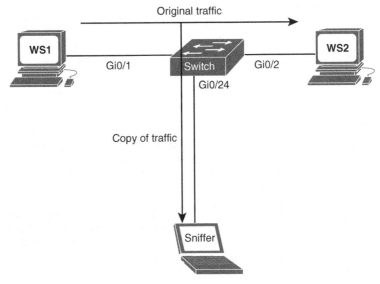

Figure 11-1   Local SPAN

`Switch(config)# ` **`no monitor`** **`session 1`**	Removes any existing SPAN configuration on session 1. The session number is a number between 1 and 66
`Switch(config)# ` **`no monitor`** **`session all`**	Removes all SPAN sessions
`Switch(config)# ` **`no monitor`** **`session local`**	Removes all local SPAN sessions
`Switch(config)# ` **`no monitor`** **`session remote`**	Removes all remote SPAN sessions
`Switch(config)# ` **`monitor`** **`session 1 source interface`** **`gigabitethernet 0/1`**	Sets a new SPAN session where the source of the traffic will be interface GigabitEthernet 0/1
`Switch(config)# ` **`monitor session 2`** **`source gigabitethernet 0/2 rx`**	Configures session 2 to monitor received traffic on interface GigabitEthernet 0/2
`Switch(config)# ` **`monitor session`** *`session_number`* **`source {interface`** *`interface-id`* | **`vlan`** *`vlan-id`*`}` `[,` | `-]` `[`**`both`** | **`rx`** | **`tx`**`]`	Options for this command include the following: *session_number*: Any number between 1 and 66 *interface-id*: Specifies the source port to monitor. Can be any valid physical interface or port channel logical interface *vlan-id*: Specifies the source VLAN to monitor. The range is 1 to 4094

	,	- (optional): To be used to help specify a series or ranges of interfaces. There must be a space both before and after the comma or hyphen
	both (optional): Monitors both received and sent traffic. This is the default setting
	rx (optional): Monitors received traffic
	tx (optional): Monitors sent traffic
	NOTE: A single session can include multiple sources (ports or VLANs), defined in a series of commands, but you cannot combine source ports and source VLANs in one session
	NOTE: You can use the **monitor session** *session_number* **source** command multiple times to configure multiple source ports
`Switch(config)# monitor session 1 filter vlan 6 - 10`	Limits the SPAN source traffic to VLANs 6 to 10
`Switch(config)# monitor session session_number filter vlan vlan-id [,	-]`	Options for this command include the following: *session_number*: Must match the session number used in the **monitor session source** command *vlan-id*: Specifies the source VLAN to monitor. The range is 1 to 4094 ,	- (optional): To be used to help specify a series or ranges of interfaces. There must be a space both before and after the comma or hyphen
`Switch(config)# monitor session 1 destination interface gigabitethernet 0/24 encapsulation replicate`	Sets a new SPAN session where the destination for the traffic will be interface GigabitEthernet 0/24. The encapsulation method will be retained
`Switch(config)# monitor session 2 destination interface gigabitethernet 0/24 encapsulation replicate ingress dot1q vlan 6`	Monitored traffic from session 2 will be sent to interface GigabitEthernet 0/24. It will have the same egress encapsulation type as the source port, and will enable ingress forwarding with IEEE 802.1Q encapsulation and VLAN 6 as the default ingress VLAN

`Switch(config)# monitor session` `session_number destination` `{interface interface-id [, |` `-] [encapsulation {dot1q |` `replicate}]} [ingress {dot1q vlan` `vlan-id	untaggedvlan vlan-id |` `vlan vlan-id}]}`	Options for this command include the following: *session_number*: Enter the session number used in the **source** command earlier in this example. For local SPAN, you *must* use the same session number for the source and destination interfaces *interface-id*: Specifies the destination port. This must be a physical port; it cannot be an EtherChannel, and it cannot be a VLAN , I - (optional): To be used to help specify a series or ranges of interfaces. There must be a space both before and after the comma or hyphen **encapsulation dot1q**: Specifies that the destination interface use the IEEE 802.1Q encapsulation method **encapsulation replicate**: Specifies that the destination interface replicate the source interface encapsulation method **NOTE:** If no encapsulation method is selected, the default is to send packets in native form (untagged) **ingress dot1q vlan** *vlan-id*: Accept incoming packets with IEEE 802.1Q encapsulation with the specified VLAN as the default VLAN **ingress untagged vlan** *vlan-id*: Accept incoming packets with untagged encapsulation with the specified VLAN as the default VLAN **ingress vlan** *vlan-id*: Accept incoming packets with untagged encapsulation with the specified VLAN as the default VLAN **NOTE:** You can use the **monitor session** *session_number* **destination** command multiple times to configure multiple destination ports

Configuring Remote SPAN

While local SPAN supports source and destination ports only on one switch, a remote SPAN supports source and destination ports on different switches. RSPAN consists of an RSPAN VLAN, an RSPAN source session, and an RSPAN destination session. You separately configure RSPAN source sessions and destination sessions on different switches.

Remote SPAN Guidelines for Configuration

When configuring RSPAN, follow these guidelines:

- All the items in the local SPAN guidelines for configuration apply to RSPAN.

- Because RSPAN VLANs have special properties, you should reserve a few VLANs across your network for use as RSPAN VLANs; do not assign access ports to these VLANs.

- You can apply an output access control list (ACL) to RSPAN traffic to selectively filter or monitor specific packets. Specify this ACL on the RSPAN VLAN in the RSPAN source switches.

- For RSPAN configuration, you can distribute the source ports and the destination ports across multiple switches in your network.

- RSPAN does not support bridge protocol data unit (BPDU) packet monitoring or other Layer 2 switch protocols.

- The RSPAN VLAN is configured only on trunk ports and not on access ports. To avoid unwanted traffic in RSPAN VLANs, make sure that the VLAN Remote SPAN feature is supported in all the participating switches.

- Access ports (including voice VLAN ports) on the RSPAN VLAN are put in the inactive state.

- RSPAN VLANs are included as sources for port-based RSPAN sessions when source trunk ports have active RSPAN VLANs. RSPAN VLANs can also be sources in SPAN sessions. However, because the switch does not monitor spanned traffic, it does not support egress spanning of packets on any RSPAN VLAN identified as the destination of an RSPAN source session on the switch.

- You can configure any VLAN as an RSPAN VLAN as long as these conditions are met:

    - The same RSPAN VLAN is used for an RSPAN session in all the switches.

    - All participating switches support RSPAN.

- Configure an RSPAN VLAN before you configure an RSPAN source or a destination session.

- If you enable VTP and VTP pruning, RSPAN traffic is pruned in the trunks to prevent the unwanted flooding of RSPAN traffic across the network for VLAN IDs that are lower than 1005.

Configuration Example: Remote SPAN

Figure 11-2 is the network topology for remote SPAN commands.

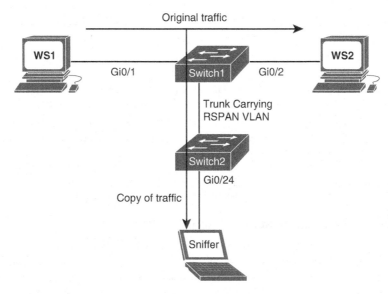

Figure 11-2 Remote SPAN

`Switch1(config)# vlan 901`	Creates VLAN 901 on Switch1
`Switch1(config-vlan)# remote span`	Makes this VLAN an RSPAN VLAN
`Switch1(config-vlan)# end`	Returns to global configuration mode
`Switch2(config)# vlan 901`	Creates VLAN 901 on Switch2
`Switch2(config-vlan)# remote span`	Makes this VLAN an RSPAN VLAN
`Switch2(config-vlan)# end`	Returns to global configuration mode

NOTE: You must create the RSPAN VLAN in all switches that will participate in RSPAN.

NOTE: If the RSPAN VLAN ID is in the normal range (lower than 1005) and VTP is enabled in the network, you can create the RSPAN VLAN in one switch, and VTP propagates it to the other switches in the VTP domain. For extended-range VLANs (greater than 1005), you must configure the RSPAN VLAN on both source and destination switches and any intermediate switches.

TIP: Use VTP pruning to get an efficient flow of RSPAN traffic, or manually delete the RSPAN VLAN from all trunks that do not need to carry the RSPAN traffic.

`Switch1(config)# no monitor session 1`	Removes any previous configurations for session 1
`Switch1(config)# monitor session 1 source interface gigabitethernet 0/1 tx`	Configures session 1 to monitor transmitted traffic on interface GigabitEthernet 0/1
`Switch1(config)# monitor session 1 source interface gigabitethernet 0/2 rx`	Configures session 1 to monitor received traffic on interface GigabitEthernet 0/2

Switch1(config)# **monitor session 1 destination remote vlan 901**	Configures session 1 to have a destination of RSPAN VLAN 901
Switch2(config)# **no monitor session 1**	Removes any previous configurations for session 1
Switch2(config)# **monitor session 1 source remote vlan 901**	Configures session 1 to have a source of VLAN 901
Switch2(config)# **monitor session 1 destination interface gigabitethernet 0/24**	Configures session 1 to have a destination interface of GigabitEthernet 0/24

NOTE: The commands to configure incoming traffic on a destination port and to filter VLAN traffic are the same for remote SPAN as they are for local SPAN.

Configuring Encapsulated RSPAN (ERSPAN)

The Cisco ERSPAN feature allows you to monitor traffic on one or more ports or one or more VLANs, and send the monitored traffic to one or more destination ports. ERSPAN sends traffic to a network analyzer such as a Switch Probe device or other Remote Monitoring (RMON) probe. ERSPAN supports source ports, source VLANs, and destination ports on different routers, which provides remote monitoring of multiple routers across a network. The traffic is encapsulated in Generic Routing Encapsulation (GRE) and is, therefore, routable across a Layer 3 network between the "source" switch and the "destination" switch. ERSPAN consists of an ERSPAN source session, routable ERSPAN GRE encapsulated traffic, and an ERSPAN destination session.

NOTE: ERSPAN is a Cisco proprietary feature and is available only to Catalyst 6500, 7600, 9200, 9300, Nexus, and ASR 1000 platforms to date. The ASR 1000 supports ERSPAN source (monitoring) only on FastEthernet, GigabitEthernet, and port-channel interfaces.

ERSPAN Source Configuration

Router-1(config)# **monitor session 1 type erspan-source**	Creates an ERSPAN source session
Router-1(config-mon-erspan-src)# **source interface gigabitethernet 0/0/1**	Assigns the GigabitEthernet 0/0/1 interface as the source interface for the ERSPAN session
Router-1(config-mon-erspan-src)# **destination**	Enters ERSPAN destination configuration mode
Router-1(config-mon-erspan-src-dst)# **erspan-id 1**	Assigns an ERSPAN ID of 1
Router-1(config-mon-erspan-src-dst)# **ip address 2.2.2.2**	Defines the ERSPAN destination IP address
Router-1(config-mon-erspan-src-dst)# **origin ip address 1.1.1.1**	Defines the ERSPAN source IP address

ERSPAN Destination Configuration

`Router-2(config)# monitor session 1 type erspan-destination`	Creates an ERSPAN destination session
`Router-2(config-mon-erspan-dst)# destination interface gigabitethernet 0/0/1`	Assigns the GigabitEthernet 0/0/1 interface as the destination interface for the ERSPAN session
`Router-2(config-mon-erspan-dst)# source`	Enters ERSPAN source configuration mode
`Router-2(config-mon-erspan-dst-src)# erspan-id 1`	Assigns an ERSPAN ID of 1
`Router-2(config-mon-erspan-dst-src)# ip address 2.2.2.2`	Defines the ERSPAN source IP address

Verifying and Troubleshooting Local and Remote SPAN

`Switch# show monitor session 1`	Displays output for SPAN session 1 **NOTE:** On some platforms the command is **show monitor**
`Switch# show running-config`	Displays configuration of sessions running in active memory
`Switch# show vlan remote-span`	Displays information about VLANs configured as RSPAN VLANs
`Switch# debug monitor all`	Displays all SPAN debugging messages
`Switch# debug monitor list`	Displays SPAN port and VLAN list tracing
`Switch# debug monitor requests`	Displays SPAN requests

Configuring Network Time Protocol

Most networks today are being designed with high performance and reliability in mind. Delivery of content is, in many cases, guaranteed by service level agreements (SLAs). Having your network display an accurate time is vital to ensuring that you have the best information possible when reading logging messages or troubleshooting issues.

NTP Configuration

`Edmonton(config)# ntp server 209.165.200.254`	Configures the Edmonton router to synchronize its clock to a public NTP server at address 209.165.200.254 **NOTE:** This command makes the Edmonton router an NTP client to the external NTP server **NOTE:** A Cisco IOS router can be both a client to an external NTP server and an NTP server to client devices inside its own internal network

	NOTE: When NTP is enabled on a Cisco IOS router, it is enabled on all interfaces
	CAUTION: NTP is slow to converge. It can take up to 5 minutes before an NTP client synchronizes with an NTP server
`Edmonton(config)# ntp server 209.165.200.234 prefer`	Specifies a preferred NTP server if multiple servers are configured
	TIP: It is recommended to configure more than one NTP server
`Edmonton(config-if)# ntp disable`	Disables the NTP server function on a specific interface. The interface will still act as an NTP client
	TIP: Use this command on interfaces connected to external networks
`Edmonton(config)# ntp master` *stratum*	Configures the router to be an NTP master clock to which peers synchronize when no external NTP source is available. The *stratum* is an optional number between 1 and 15. When enabled, the default stratum is 8
	NOTE: A reference clock (for example, an atomic clock) is said to be a stratum-0 device. A stratum-1 server is directly connected to a stratum-0 device. A stratum-2 server is connected across a network path to a stratum-1 server. The larger the stratum number (moving toward 15), the less authoritative that server is and the less accuracy it will have
`Edmonton(config)# ntp max-associations 200`	Configures the maximum number of NTP peer-and-client associations that the router will serve. The range is 0 to 4 294 967 295. The default is 100
`Edmonton(config)# access list 101 permit udp any host` *a.b.c.d* `eq ntp`	Creates an access list statement that will allow NTP communication for the NTP server at address *a.b.c.d*. This ACL should be placed in an inbound direction

NOTE: When a local device is configured with the **ntp master** command, it can be identified by a syntactically correct but invalid IP address. This address will be in the form of 127.127.*x.x*. The master will synchronize with itself and uses the 127.127.*x.x* address to identify itself. This address will be displayed with the **show ntp associations** command and must be permitted via an access list if you are authenticating your NTP servers.

NTP Design

You have two different options in NTP design: flat and hierarchical. In a flat design, all routers are peers to each other. Each router is both a client and a server with every other router. In a hierarchical model, there is a preferred order of routers that are servers and others that act as clients. You use the **ntp peer** command to determine the hierarchy. Figure 11-3 is a topology showing a hierarchical design.

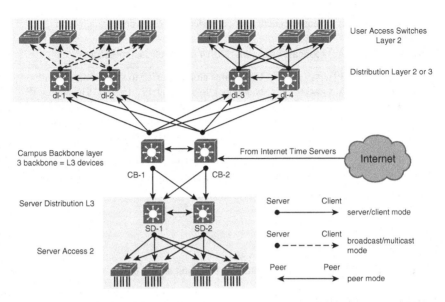

Figure 11-3   NTP Hierarchical Design

TIP: Do not use the flat model in a large network, because with many NTP servers it can take a long time to synchronize the time.

`Edmonton(config)# ntp` `source-interface loopback 0`	Configures the source interface for all NTP packets
`Edmonton(config)# ntp peer` `172.16.21.1`	Configures an IOS device to synchronize its software clock to a peer at 172.16.21.1
`Edmonton(config)# ntp peer` `172.16.21.1 version 2`	Configures an IOS device to synchronize its software clock to a peer at 172.16.21.1 using version 2 of NTP. There are three versions of NTP (versions 2–4)
`Edmonton(config-if)# ntp` `broadcast`	Configures the options for broadcasting or multicasting NTP traffic on a specified interface. You can include the authentication **key** and **version** options with this command
`Edmonton(config-if)# ntp` `broadcast client`	Configures a device to receive NTP broadcast or multicast messages on a specified interface. You can include the authentication **key** and **version** options with this command

NOTE: Although Cisco IOS recognizes three versions of NTP, versions 3 and 4 are most commonly used. Version 4 introduces support for IPv6 and is backward compatible with version 3. NTPv4 also adds DNS support for IPv6.

NOTE: NTPv4 has increased security support using public key cryptography and X.509 certificates.

NOTE: NTPv3 uses broadcast messages. NTPv4 uses multicast messages.

`Edmonton(config)# ntp`
`peer 172.16.21.1 source`
`loopback 0`
	Configures an IOS device to synchronize its software clock to a peer at 172.16.21.1. The source IP address is the address of interface Loopback 0
	
	TIP: Choose a loopback interface as your source for NTP, because it will never go down. ACL statements will also be easier to write as you will require only one line to allow or deny traffic

`Edmonton(config)# ntp`
`peer 172.16.21.1 source`
`loopback 0 prefer`
	Makes this peer the preferred peer that provides synchronization

Securing NTP

You can secure NTP operation using authentication and access lists.

Enabling NTP Authentication

`NTPServer(config)# ntp`
`authentication-key 1 md5`
`NTPpa55word`
	Defines an NTP authentication key
	
	1 = number of authentication key. Can be a number between 1 and 4 294 967 295
	
	md5 = using MD5 hash. This is the only option available on Cisco devices
	
	NTPpa55word = password associated with this key

`NTPServer(config)# ntp` `trusted-key 1`	Defines which keys are valid for NTP authentication. The key number here must match the key number you defined in the **ntp authentication-key** command
`NTPServer(config)# ntp` `authenticate`	Enables NTP authentication

`NTPClient(config)# ntp`
`authentication-key 1 md5`
`NTPpa55word`
	Defines an NTP authentication key

`NTPClient(config)# ntp` `server 192.168.200.1 key 1`	Defines the NTP server that requires authentication at address 192.168.200.1 and identifies the peer key number as key 1
`NTPClient(config)# ntp` `trusted-key 1`	Defines which keys are valid for NTP authentication. The key number here must match the key number you defined in the **ntp authentication-key** command
`NTPClient(config)# ntp` `authenticate`	Enables NTP authentication

NOTE: You can configure the device to authenticate the time sources to which the local clock is synchronized. When you enable NTP authentication, the device synchronizes to a time source only if the source carries one of the authentication keys specified by the **ntp trusted-key** command. The device drops any packets that fail the authentication check and prevents them from updating the local clock. NTP authentication is disabled by default.

You can also control access to NTP services by using access lists. Specifically, you can decide the types of requests that the device allows and the servers from which it accepts responses. If you do not configure any ACLs, NTP access is granted to all devices. If you configure ACLs, NTP access is granted only to the remote device whose source IP address passes the access list criteria.

NOTE: Once a device is synchronized to an NTP source, it becomes an NTP server to any device that requests synchronization.

Limiting NTP Access with Access Lists

`Edmonton(config)#` **access-list 1 permit 10.1.0.0 0.0.255.255**	Defines an access list that permits only packets with a source address of 10.1.*x.x*
`Edmonton(config)#` **ntp access-group peer 1**	Creates an access group to control NTP access and applies access list 1. The **peer** keyword enables the device to receive time requests and NTP control queries and to synchronize itself to servers specified in the access list
`Edmonton(config)#` **ntp access-group serve 1**	Creates an access group to control NTP access and applies access list 1. The **serve** keyword enables the device to receive time requests and NTP control queries from the servers specified in the access list but not to synchronize itself to the specified servers
`Edmonton(config)#` **ntp access-group serve-only 1**	Creates an access group to control NTP access and applies access list 1. The **serve-only** keyword enables the device to receive only time requests from servers specified in the access list
`Edmonton(config)#` **ntp access-group query-only 1**	Creates an access group to control NTP access and applies access list 1. The **query-only** keyword enables the device to receive only NTP control queries from the servers specified in the access list

NOTE: NTP access group options are scanned from least restrictive to most restrictive in the following order: **peer, serve, serve-only, query-only**. However, if NTP matches a deny ACL rule in a configured peer, ACL processing stops and does not continue to the next access group option.

Verifying and Troubleshooting NTP

Edmonton# **show ntp associations**	Displays the status of NTP associations
Edmonton# **show ntp associations detail**	Displays detailed information about each NTP association
Edmonton# **show ntp status**	Displays the status of the NTP configuration. This command shows whether the router's clock has synchronized with the external NTP server
Edmonton# **debug ip packets**	Checks to see whether NTP packets are received and sent
Edmonton# **debug ip packet 1**	Limits debug output to ACL 1
Edmonton# **debug ntp adjust**	Displays debug output for NTP clock adjustments
Edmonton# **debug ntp all**	Displays all NTP debugging output
Edmonton# **debug ntp events**	Displays all NTP debugging events
Edmonton# **debug ntp packet**	Displays NTP packet debugging; lets you see the time that the peer/server gives you in a received packet
Edmonton# **debug ntp packet detail**	Displays detailed NTP packet dump
Edmonton# **debug ntp packet peer** *a.b.c.d*	Displays debugging from NTP peer at address *a.b.c.d*

Setting the Clock on a Router

> **NOTE:** It is important to have your routers display the correct time for use with time stamps and other logging features.

If the system is synchronized by a valid outside timing mechanism, such as an NTP server, or if you have a router with a hardware clock, you do not need to set the software clock. Use the software clock if no other time sources are available.

Edmonton# **calendar set 16:30:00 23 October 2019**	Manually sets the system hardware clock. Time is set using military (24-hour) format. The hardware clock runs continuously, even if the router is powered off or rebooted
Edmonton# **show calendar**	Displays the hardware calendar
Edmonton(config)# **clock calendar-valid**	Configures the system as an authoritative time source for a network based on its hardware clock **NOTE:** Because the hardware clock is not as accurate as other time sources (it runs off of a battery), you should use this only when a more accurate time source (such as NTP) is not available
Edmonton# **clock read-calendar**	Manually reads the hardware clock settings into the software clock

Edmonton# `clock set` `16:30:00 23 October` `2019`	Manually sets the system software clock. Time is set using military (24-hour) format
Edmonton(config)# `clock summer-time` `zone` **recurring** [*week* *day month hh:mm week* *day month hh:mm* [*offset*]]	Configures the system to automatically switch to summer time (daylight saving time) **NOTE:** Summer time is disabled by default Arguments for the command are as follows: *zone*: Name of the time zone (see Tables 11-5 and 11-6 for alternative ways to specify the time zone)
Edmonton(config)# `clock summer-time` `zone` **date** *date month year hh:mm date month year hh:mm* [*offset*]	**recurring**: Indicates that summer time should start and end on the corresponding specified days every year **date**: Indicates that summer time should start on the first specific date listed in the command and end on the second specific date in the command
Edmonton(config)# `clock summer-time` `zone` **date** *month date year hh:mm month date year hh:mm* [*offset*]	*week*: (Optional) Week of the month (1 to 4 or **last**) *day*: (Optional) Day of the week (Sunday, Monday, and so on) *date*: Date of the month (1 to 31) *month*: (Optional) Month (January, February, and so on) *year*: Year (1993 to 2035) *hh:mm*: (Optional) Time (military format) in hours and minutes *offset*: (Optional) Number of minutes to add during summer time (default is 60)
Edmonton(config)# `clock timezone` *zone hours-offset* [*minutes-offset*]	Configures the time zone for display purposes. To set the time to Coordinated Universal Time (UTC), use the **no** form of this command *zone:* Name of the time zone to be displayed when standard time is in effect *hours-offset*: Hours difference from UTC *minutes-offset*: (Optional) Minutes difference from UTC
Edmonton(config)# `clock timezone` `PST -8`	Configures the time zone to Pacific Standard Time, which is 8 hours behind UTC
Edmonton(config)# `clock timezone` `NL -3 30`	Configures the time zone to Newfoundland time for Newfoundland, Canada, which is 3.5 hours behind UTC
Edmonton# `clock update-calendar`	Updates the hardware clock from the software clock
Edmonton# `show clock`	Displays the time and date from the system software clock
Edmonton# `show clock detail`	Displays the clock source (NTP, hardware) and the current summer-time setting (if any)

Table 11-5 shows the common acronyms used for setting the time zone on a router.

TABLE 11-5 Common Time Zone Acronyms

Region/Acronym	Time Zone Name and UTC Offset
Europe	
GMT	Greenwich Mean Time, as UTC
BST	British Summer Time, as UTC +1 hour
IST	Irish Summer Time, as UTC +1 hour
WET	Western Europe Time, as UTC
WEST	Western Europe Summer Time, as UTC +1 hour
CET	Central Europe Time, as UTC +1
CEST	Central Europe Summer Time, as UTC +2
EET	Eastern Europe Time, as UTC +2
EEST	Eastern Europe Summer Time, as UTC +3
MSK	Moscow Time, as UTC +3
MSD	Moscow Summer Time, as UTC +4
United States and Canada	
AST	Atlantic Standard Time, as UTC –4 hours
ADT	Atlantic Daylight Time, as UTC –3 hours
ET	Eastern Time, either as EST or EDT, depending on place and time of year
EST	Eastern Standard Time, as UTC –5 hours
EDT	Eastern Daylight Time, as UTC –4 hours
CT	Central Time, either as CST or CDT, depending on place and time of year
CST	Central Standard Time, as UTC –6 hours
CDT	Central Daylight Time, as UTC –5 hours
MT	Mountain Time, either as MST or MDT, depending on place and time of year
MST	Mountain Standard Time, as UTC –7 hours
MDT	Mountain Daylight Time, as UTC –6 hours
PT	Pacific Time, either as PST or PDT, depending on place and time of year
PST	Pacific Standard Time, as UTC –8 hours
PDT	Pacific Daylight Time, as UTC –7 hours
AKST	Alaska Standard Time, as UTC –9 hours
AKDT	Alaska Standard Daylight Time, as UTC –8 hours
HST	Hawaiian Standard Time, as UTC –10 hours

Region/Acronym	Time Zone Name and UTC Offset
Australia	
WST	Western Standard Time, as UTC +8 hours
CST	Central Standard Time, as UTC +9.5 hours
EST	Eastern Standard/Summer time, as UTC +10 hours (+11 hours during summer time)

Table 11-6 lists an alternative method for referring to time zones, in which single letters are used to refer to the time zone difference from UTC. Using this method, the letter Z is used to indicate the zero meridian, equivalent to UTC, and the letter *J* (Juliet) is used to refer to the local time zone. Using this method, the international date line is between time zones M and Y.

TABLE 11-6   Single-Letter Time Zone Designators

Letter Designator	Word Designator	Difference from UTC
Y	Yankee	UTC –12 hours
X	X-ray	UTC –11 hours
W	Whiskey	UTC –10 hours
V	Victor	UTC –9 hours
U	Uniform	UTC –8 hours
T	Tango	UTC –7 hours
S	Sierra	UTC –6 hours
R	Romeo	UTC –5 hours
Q	Quebec	UTC –4 hours
P	Papa	UTC –3 hours
O	Oscar	UTC –2 hours
N	November	UTC –1 hour
Z	Zulu	Same as UTC
A	Alpha	UTC +1 hour
B	Bravo	UTC +2 hours
C	Charlie	UTC +3 hours
D	Delta	UTC +4 hours
E	Echo	UTC +5 hours
F	Foxtrot	UTC +6 hours
G	Golf	UTC +7 hours
H	Hotel	UTC +8 hours
I	India	UTC +9 hours
K	Kilo	UTC +10 hours
L	Lima	UTC +11 hours
M	Mike	UTC +12 hours

Using Time Stamps

Edmonton(config)# **service timestamps**	Adds a time stamp to all system logging messages
Edmonton(config)# **service timestamps debug**	Adds a time stamp to all debugging messages
Edmonton(config)# **service timestamps debug uptime**	Adds a time stamp along with the total uptime of the router to all debugging messages
Edmonton(config)# **service timestamps debug datetime localtime**	Adds a time stamp displaying the local time and the date to all debugging messages
Edmonton(config)# **no service timestamps**	Disables all time stamps

Configuration Example: NTP

Figure 11-4 shows the network topology for the configuration that follows, which demonstrates how to configure NTP using the commands covered in this chapter.

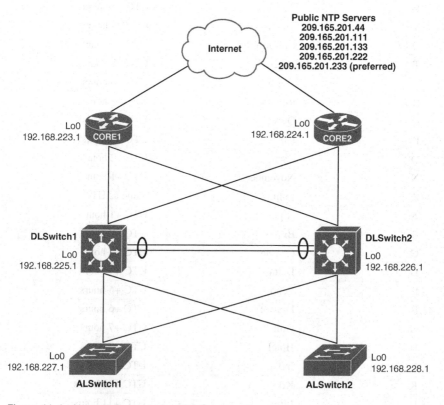

Figure 11-4   Network Topology for NTP Configuration

Core1 Router

Core1(config)# ntp server 209.165.201.44	Configures router to synchronize its clock to a public NTP server at address 209.165.201.44
Core1(config)# ntp server 209.165.201.111	Configures router to synchronize its clock to a public NTP server at address 209.165.201.111
Core1(config)# ntp server 209.165.201.133	Configures router to synchronize its clock to a public NTP server at address 209.165.201.133
Core1(config)# ntp server 209.165.201.222	Configures router to synchronize its clock to a public NTP server at address 209.165.201.222
Core1(config)# ntp server 209.165.201.233 prefer	Configures router to synchronize its clock to a public NTP server at address 209.165.201.233. This is the preferred NTP server
Core1(config)# ntp max-associations 200	Configures the maximum number of NTP peer-and-client associations that the router will serve
Core1(config)# clock timezone EST -5	Sets time zone to Eastern Standard Time
Core1(config)# clock summer-time EDT recurring 2 Sun Mar 2:00 1 Sun Nov 2:00	Configures the system to automatically switch to summer time and to repeat on the same day
Core1(config)# ntp master 10	Configures the router to serve as a master clock if the external NTP server is not available
Core1(config)# ntp source Loopback 0	Sets the source of all NTP packets to 192.168.223.1, which is the address of Loopback 0
Core1(config)# access-list 1 permit 127.127.1.1	Sets access 1 list to permit packets coming from 127.127.1.1
Core1(config)# access-list 2 permit 192.168.0.0 0.0.255.255	Sets access list 2 to permit packets coming from 192.168.*x.x*
Core1(config)# ntp access-group peer 1	Configures Core1 to peer with any devices identified in access list 1
Core1(config)# ntp access-group serve-only 2	Configures Core1 to receive only time requests from devices specified in the ACL

Core2 Router

`Core2(config)# ntp server` `209.165.201.44`	Configures router to synchronize its clock to a public NTP server at address 209.165.201.44
`Core2(config)# ntp server` `209.165.201.111`	Configures router to synchronize its clock to a public NTP server at address 209.165.201.111
`Core2(config)# ntp server` `209.165.201.133`	Configures router to synchronize its clock to a public NTP server at address 209.165.201.133
`Core2(config)# ntp server` `209.165.201.222`	Configures router to synchronize its clock to a public NTP server at address 209.165.201.222
`Core2(config)# ntp server` `209.165.201.233 prefer`	Configures router to synchronize its clock to a public NTP server at address 209.165.201.233. This is the preferred NTP server
`Core2(config)# ntp` `max-associations 200`	Configures the maximum number of NTP peer-and-client associations that the router will serve
`Core2(config)# clock timezone` `EST -5`	Sets time zone to Eastern Standard Time

`Core2(config)# clock summer-time`
`EDT recurring 2 Sun Mar 2:00 1`
`Sun Nov 2:00`
	Configures the system to automatically switch to summer time and to repeat on the same day

`Core2(config)# ntp master 10`	Configures the router to serve as a master clock if the external NTP server is not available
`Core2(config)# ntp source` `Loopback 0`	Sets the source of all NTP packets to 192.168.224.1, which is the address of Loopback 0
`Core2(config)# access-list 1` `permit 127.127.1.1`	Sets ACL 1 to permit packets coming from 127.127.1.1
`Core2(config)# access-list 2` `permit 192.168.0.0 0.0.255.255`	Sets ACL 2 to permit packets coming from 192.168.x.x
`Core2(config)# ntp access-group` `peer 1`	Configures Core2 to peer with any devices identified in ACL 1
`Core2(config)# ntp access-group` `serve-only 2`	Configures Core2 to receive only time requests from devices specified in the ACL

DLSwitch1

`DLSwitch1(config)# ntp source` `Loopback 0`	Sets the source of all NTP packets to 192.168.225.1, which is the address of Loopback 0
`DLSwitch1(config)# ntp server` `192.168.223.1`	Configures DLSwitch1 to synchronize its clock to an NTP server at address 192.168.223.1
`DLSwitch1(config)# ntp server` `192.168.224.1`	Configures DLSwitch1 to synchronize its clock to an NTP server at address 192.168.224.1
`DLSwitch1(config)# clock` `timezone EST -5`	Sets time zone to Eastern Standard Time

`DLSwitch1(config)# clock summer-`
`time EDT recurring 2 Sun Mar`
`2:00 1 Sun Nov 2:00`
	Configures the system to automatically switch to summer time and to repeat on the same day

DLSwitch2

`DLSwitch2(config)# ntp source` `Loopback 0`	Sets the source of all NTP packets to 192.168.226.1, which is the address of Loopback 0
`DLSwitch2(config)# ntp server` `192.168.223.1`	Configures DLSwitch2 to synchronize its clock to an NTP server at address 192.168.223.1
`DLSwitch2(config)# ntp server` `192.168.224.1`	Configures DLSwitch2 to synchronize its clock to an NTP server at address 192.168.224.1
`DLSwitch2(config)# clock` `timezone EST -5`	Sets time zone to Eastern Standard Time

`DLSwitch2(config)# clock summer-`
`time EDT recurring 2 Sun Mar`
`2:00 1 Sun Nov 2:00`
	Configures the system to automatically switch to summer time and to repeat on the same day

ALSwitch1

`ALSwitch1(config)# ntp source` `Loopback 0`	Sets the source of all NTP packets to 192.168.227.1, which is the address of Loopback 0
`ALSwitch1(config)# ntp server` `192.168.223.1`	Configures ALSwitch1 to synchronize its clock to an NTP server at address 192.168.223.1
`ALSwitch1(config)# ntp server` `192.168.224.1`	Configures ALSwitch1 to synchronize its clock to an NTP server at address 192.168.224.1

ALSwitch1(config)# **clock timezone EST -5**	Sets time zone to Eastern Standard Time
ALSwitch1(config)# **clock summer-time EDT recurring 2 Sun Mar 2:00 1 Sun Nov 2:00**	Configures the system to automatically switch to summer time and to repeat on the same day

ALSwitch2

ALSwitch2(config)# **ntp source Loopback 0**	Sets the source of all NTP packets to 192.168.228.1, which is the address of Loopback 0
ALSwitch2(config)# **ntp server 192.168.223.1**	Configures ALSwitch2 to synchronize its clock to an NTP server at address 192.168.223.1
ALSwitch2(config)# **ntp server 192.168.224.1**	Configures ALSwitch2 to synchronize its clock to an NTP server at address 192.168.224.1
ALSwitch2(config)# **clock timezone EST -5**	Sets time zone to Eastern Standard Time
ALSwitch2(config)# **clock summer-time EDT recurring 2 Sun Mar 2:00 1 Sun Nov 2:00**	Configures the system to automatically switch to summer time and to repeat on the same day

Tool Command Language (Tcl)

Tcl shell is a feature that is built into Cisco routers and switches that allows engineers to interact directly with the device by using various Tcl scripts. Tcl scripting has been around for quite some time and is a very useful scripting language. Tcl provides many ways to streamline different tasks that can help with day-to-day operations and monitoring of a network. Some of the following are tasks that can be automated by using these scripts:

- Verify IP and IPv6 reachability, using **ping**
- Verify IP and IPv6 reachability, using **traceroute**
- Check interface statistics
- Retrieve SNMP information by accessing Management Information Base (MIB) objects
- Send email messages containing CLI outputs from Tcl script

Most often, basic Tcl scripts are entered line by line within the Tcl shell, although, for some of the more advanced scripting methods, you can load the script into the flash of the device you are working on and execute the script from there using a command like **source flash:ping.tcl** from the Tcl shell.

A classic use case for Tcl scripting is when you need to perform network testing using **ping**. The following example shows the general syntax for a Tcl script:

``
Router# tclsh
Router(tcl)# foreach address {
+>(tcl)# 172.16.10.1
+>(tcl)# 172.16.10.2
+>(tcl)# 172.16.10.3
+>(tcl)# } { ping $address
+>(tcl)# }
Type escape sequence to abort.
Sending 5, 100-byte ICMP Echos to
172.16.10.1, timeout is 2 seconds:
!!!!!
Success rate is 100 percent (5/5),
round-trip min/avg/max = 1/2/6 ms
Type escape sequence to abort.
Sending 5, 100-byte ICMP Echos to
172.16.10.2 timeout is 2 seconds:
!!!!!
Success rate is 100 percent (5/5),
round-trip min/avg/max = 1/3/5 ms
Type escape sequence to abort.
Sending 5, 100-byte ICMP Echos to
172.16.10.3, timeout is 2 seconds:
!!!!!
Success rate is 100 percent (5/5),
round-trip min/avg/max = 1/2/6 ms
Router(tcl)# tclquit
Router#
``
	This simple Tcl script automates a ping test to the 172.16.10.1, 172.16.10.2, and 172.16.10.3 addresses. Notice that the test executes as soon as you enter the closing brace
	
	The **tclsh** command grants you access to the Tcl shell
	
	The **tclquit** command returns you to privileged EXEC mode

Embedded Event Manager (EEM)

Embedded Event Manager is a flexible system designed to customize Cisco IOS, XR, and NX-OS. EEM allows you to automate tasks, perform minor enhancements, and create workarounds. Applets and scripting are two pieces of EEM. *Applets* are a collection of CLI commands, while *scripts* are actions coded in Tcl. Event detectors are used by EEM, and actions provide notifications of the events. EEM event detectors include SNMP object monitoring, syslog message monitoring, interface counter monitoring, CLI event monitoring, and IP SLA and NetFlow event monitoring.

EEM actions can include sending an email, executing a CLI command, generating an SNMP trap, reloading a device, and generating specific syslog messages.

> **NOTE:** The following examples assume that the first command is typed in global configuration mode.

EEM Configuration Examples

EEM Example 1

The first EEM example shows an applet that monitors the GigabitEthernet 0/0/0 interface. If a syslog message indicates that its state has changed to administratively down, the applet is triggered, the interface is re-enabled, and an email is sent containing a list of users currently logged into the router.

Notice the use of the **$_cli_result** keyword in the email configuration. This means that the email body will include the output of any CLI commands that were issued in the applet. In this case, the output of the **show users** command will be included in the debug and the email message.

```
event manager applet interface_Shutdown
event syslog pattern "Interface GigabitEthernet 0/0/0, changed state
to administratively down"
action 1.0 cli command "enable"
action 1.5 cli command "config terminal"
action 2.0 cli command "interface gigabitethernet0/0/0"
action 2.5 cli command "no shutdown"
action 3.0 cli command "end"
action 3.5 cli command "show users"
action 4.0 mail server 209.165.201.1 to engineer@cisco.com from EEM@
cisco.com subject "ISP1 Interface GigabitEthernet0/0/0 SHUT." body
"Current users $_cli_result"
end
```

EEM Example 2

The second EEM example shows an applet that monitors the CLI for the **debug ip packet** command. When this pattern is matched, the applet will skip the command so that it does not take effect. The action list first enters the enabled mode and issues the **show users | append flash:Debug** command. This command will append the output from the **show users** command to the end of a file in flash called Debug. The next action will then append the current time stamp to the end of the file in flash named Debug_clock. By matching the order of the entries in both files you will have a list of the users that tried to enter the **debug** command and the date and time that the user attempted it.

```
event manager applet Stop_Debug
 event cli pattern "debug ip packet" sync no skip yes
 action 1.0 cli command "enable"
 action 2.0 cli command "show users | append flash:Debug"
 action 3.0 cli command "show clock | append flash:Debug_clock"
end
```

EEM Example 3

The third EEM example shows an applet that matches a CLI pattern that starts with
"wr". When a match is detected, the applet is triggered. Cisco IOS prompting is disabled
and a copy of the new startup-configuration file is backed up to a TFTP server. A syslog
message is triggered confirming a successful TFTP file transfer. Notice that two environment variables were created and are used within the applet, one for the file name and one
for the IP address.

```
event manager environment filename router.cfg
event manager environment tftpserver tftp://10.99.1.101/
event manager applet SAVE-to-TFTP
 event cli pattern "wr.*" sync yes
 action 1.0 cli command "enable"
 action 2.0 cli command "configure terminal"
 action 3.0 cli command "file prompt quiet"
 action 4.0 cli command "end"
 action 5.0 cli command "copy start $tftpserver$filename"
 action 6.0 cli command "configure terminal"
 action 7.0 cli command "no file prompt quiet"
 action 8.0 syslog priority informational msg "Running-config saved
to NVRAM! TFTP backup successful."
```

EEM Example 4

The final example is more complex but demonstrates how powerful EEM applets can
be. This example is based on the latest version of EEM (version 4). In this scenario,
an IP SLA is configured to send an ICMP echo request every 10 seconds to address
209.165.201.1. IP SLA reaction alerts are enabled, which allows the IP SLA to send an
alert after three consecutive timeouts. This triggers the EEM applet and a syslog message
is displayed. Notice the use of the **$_ipsla_oper_id** variable. This is a built-in environ-
ment variable and returns the IP SLA number, which in this case is 1.

```
ip sla 1
 icmp-echo 209.165.201.1
 frequency 10
ip sla schedule 1 life forever start-time now
ip sla reaction-configuration 1 react timeout threshold-type consecu-
tive 3
ip sla enable reaction-alerts
!
event manager applet IPSLA
 event ipsla operation-id 1 reaction-type timeout
 action 1.0 syslog priority emergencies msg "IP SLA operation
$_ipsla_oper_id to ISP DNS server has timed out"
```

EEM and Tcl Scripts

Using an EEM applet to call Tcl scripts is another very powerful aspect of EEM. This example shows how to manually execute an EEM applet that will, in turn, execute a Tcl script that is locally stored in the device's flash memory. It is important to understand that there are many ways to use EEM and that manually triggered applets are also a very useful tool. The following example depicts an EEM script that is configured with the **event none** command. This means that there is no automatic event that the applet is monitoring, and that this applet will only run when it is triggered manually. To manually run an EEM applet, the **event manager run** command must be used, as illustrated at the router prompt. In this example, the ping_script.tcl file is a Tcl script similar to the one described earlier in this chapter.

```
event manager applet myping
 event none
 action 1.0 cli command "enable"
 action 1.1 cli command "tclsh flash:/ping_script.tcl"

Router# event manager run myping
Router#
```

Verifying EEM

Router# **debug event manager action cli**	Displays actual actions taking place when an applet is running
Router# **show event manager policy registered**	Displays all configured applets, their triggers and actions
Router# **show event manager version**	Displays the version of EEM that is supported in the Cisco IOS software

CHAPTER 12

Wireless Security and Troubleshooting

This chapter provides information and commands concerning the following topics:

- Authenticating wireless clients
  - Open authentication
  - Authenticating with a pre-shared key
  - Authenticating with EAP
    - Configuring EAP-based authentication with external RADIUS servers
    - Configuring EAP-based authentication with local EAP
    - Verifying EAP-based authentication configuration
  - Authenticating with WebAuth
- Troubleshooting from the Wireless LAN Controller
  - Cisco AireOS Monitoring Dashboard GUI
  - Cisco AireOS Advanced GUI
  - Cisco IOS XE GUI
  - Cisco AireOS/IOS XE CLI
- Troubleshooting client connectivity problems
  - Cisco AireOS Monitoring Dashboard GUI
  - Cisco IOS XE GUI

Authenticating Wireless Clients

Before a wireless client device can communicate on your network through the access point, the client device must authenticate to the access point by using open or shared-key authentication. Networks can leverage many technologies and protocols to protect information sent wirelessly. This section explores different methods to authenticate wireless clients before they are granted access to the wireless network. Note that the figures used throughout this client authentication section are from the Cisco AireOS Advanced configuration GUI.

Open Authentication

Open authentication allows any device to authenticate and then attempt to communicate with the access point. Open authentication is true to its name; it offers open access to a WLAN. The only requirement is that a client must use an 802.11 authentication request before it attempts to associate with an AP. No other credentials are needed.

To create a WLAN with open authentication, first create a new WLAN. From the Advanced Monitor Summary screen, click **WLANs** in the top menu bar. You will see a list of already configured WLANs. Figure 12-1 shows one WLAN already created, named CCNPPCG. Click the **Go** button to create a new WLAN.

Figure 12-1   Creating a New WLAN

On the next screen, choose **WLAN** from the Type drop-down menu, enter the profile name and SSID, and choose your ID. The typical configuration, but not required, is to have the same profile name and SSID. Figure 12-2 shows this completed page, using 10 as the ID, to match with VLAN 10. Your choices for ID number range from 1 to 512. Click **Apply** when finished.

Figure 12-2   New WLAN Created

The next screen shows you what you entered on the previous screen. Verify that the information is correct and ensure that the **Enabled** check box for this new WLAN is checked, as shown in Figure 12-3.

NOTE: If you do not enable the WLAN, you will not be able to join the Cisco Wireless LAN Controller (WLC) from your wireless client.

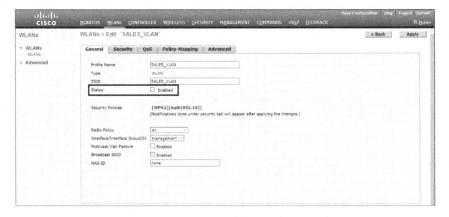

Figure 12-3 Enabling the New WLAN

Next, click the **Security** tab to configure the WLAN security and user authentication parameters. Click the **Layer 2** subtab, then choose **None** from the Layer 2 Security drop-down menu to configure open authentication, as shown in Figure 12-4.

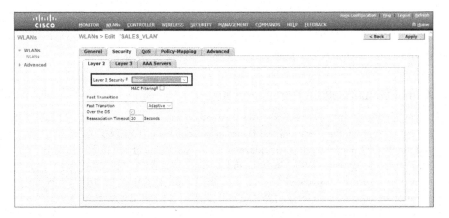

Figure 12-4 Configuring Open Authentication for a WLAN

When you are finished configuring the WLAN, click the **Apply** button. Return to the **General** tab and verify that the Security Policies field is set to None, as shown in Figure 12-5. Click the **Apply** button when finished. Figure 12-6 confirms that the new WLAN has been created and that there is no authentication set when showing the list of created WLANs.

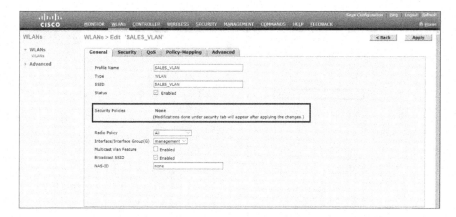

Figure 12-5 Verifying Open Authentication in the WLAN Configuration

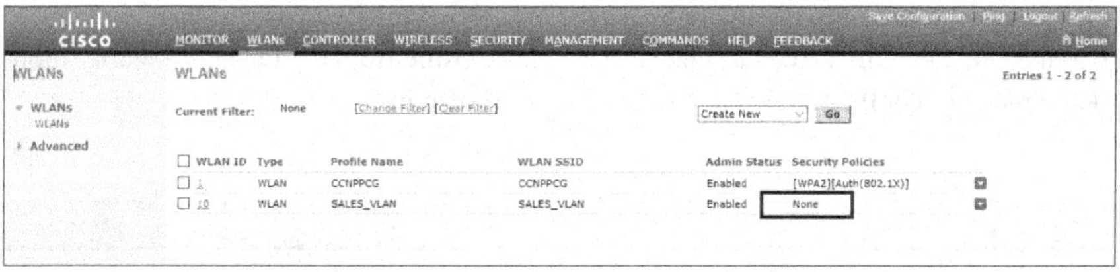

Figure 12-6 Verifying Open Authentication from the List of WLANs

Authenticating with a Pre-shared Key

When the Wired Equivalent Privacy (WEP) standard was found to be weak and easily breakable, both the Electrical and Electronics Engineers (IEEE) 802.11 committee and the Wi-Fi Alliance worked to replace it. Two generations of solutions emerged: Wi-Fi Protected Access (WPA) in 2003 and its successor, WPA2, in 2004. These solutions offer a security framework for authentication and encryption. In 2018, the Wi-Fi Alliance announced the release of WPA3 with several security improvements over WPA2.

WPA2 is the current implementation of the 802.11i security standard and deprecates the use of WEP and WPA. WPA2, being 802.11i compliant, is the current standard for enterprise networks. Unlike WPA, WPA2 provides support for IEEE 802.11n/ac. WPA2 provides either 802.1X or PSK authentication, and determines two modes of wireless protected access.

WPA2 Personal Mode

- Uses WPA2-PSK (Pre-Shared Key) authentication; a common key is statically configured on the client and the AP.

- Designed for environments where there is no RADIUS authentication server.

- Provides inadequate security for an enterprise wireless network; if attackers break the WPA2 PSK, they can access all device data.

WPA2 Enterprise Mode

- Uses IEEE 802.1X and EAP authentication; each user or device is individually authenticated.

- Incorporates a RADIUS authentication server for authentication and key management.

- Used by enterprise-class networks.

802.1X

You can configure WPA2 Personal mode and the pre-shared key in one step. Figures 12-7 and 12-8 show the screen in which this can occur. Click the **WLANs** tab and either click **Go** to create a new WLAN, or select the **WLAN ID** of an existing WLAN to edit. Make sure that the parameters on the **General** tab are set appropriately. Click the **Security** tab followed by the **Layer 2** subtab. Here you can choose the Layer 2 security option you require. Figure 12-7 shows WPA+WPA2 being selected for the WLAN named CCNPPCG. In the WPA+WPA2 Parameters section, WPA Policy is unchecked, leaving only WPA2 Policy and WPA2 Encryption AES selected.

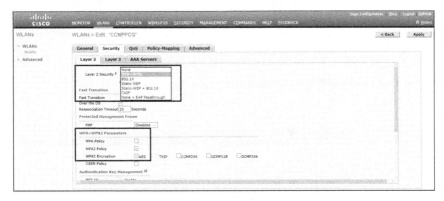

Figure 12-7   Selecting WPA2 Personal Security for a WLAN

The bottom portion of the **Layer 2** subtab is the Authentication Key Management section. Check the **Enable** check box to enable PSK, and then enter the pre-shared key string in the box next to PSK Format, as shown Figure 12-8.

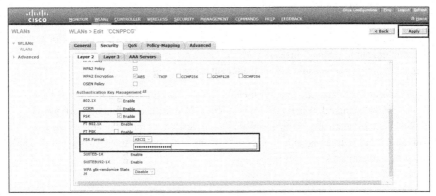

Figure 12-8   Selecting the Authentication Key Management Options

TIP: The controller will allow you to check both the WPA Policy and WPA2 Policy check boxes. You should do this only if you have legacy equipment that requires WPA support.

You can verify the security settings from the **General** tab for the WLAN. Click **Apply** to commit the changes. Figure 12-9 shows the Security Policies for the CCNPPCG WLAN have seen set to [WPA2][Auth(PSK)]. This is also shown in Figure 12-10.

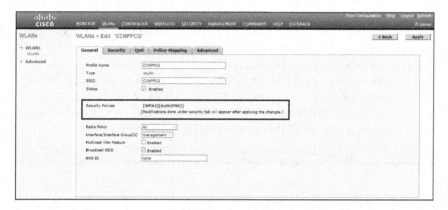

Figure 12-9   Verifying PSK Authentication in WLAN Configuration

Figure 12-10   Verifying PSK Authentication in WLAN Summary Page

Authenticating with EAP

Rather than build additional authentication methods into the 802.11 standard, the Extensible Authentication Protocol (EAP) offers a more flexible and scalable authentication framework. As its name implies, EAP is extensible and does not consist of any one authentication method. Instead, EAP defines a set of common functions that actual authentication methods can use to authenticate users.

EAP has another interesting quality: It can integrate with the IEEE 802.1X port-based access control standard. When 802.1X is enabled, it limits access to a network media until a client authenticates. This means that a wireless client might be able to associate with an AP, but will not be able to pass data to any other part of the network until it successfully authenticates.

With open and PSK authentication, wireless clients are authenticated locally at the AP without further intervention. The scenario changes with 802.1X; the client uses open authentication to associate with the AP, and then the actual client authentication process occurs at a dedicated authentication server.

The authentication server functionality in the EAP process can be provided by the following:

- Locally by a Cisco Wireless LAN Controller (referred to as local EAP)

  - Local EAP can use either the local user database or a Lightweight Directory Access Protocol (LDAP) database to authenticate users. Local EAP can also be used as a backup for RADIUS authentication. This approach allows wireless clients to authenticate even if the controller loses connectivity to the RADIUS server.

- Globally by a RADIUS server such as:

  - Cisco Identity Services Engine (ISE)

  - Microsoft Server that is configured for RADIUS-NPS

  - Any RADIUS-compliant server

802.1X and EAP address authentication but not encryption. 802.1X and EAP can be used with or without encryption. For 802.1X and EAP authentication, all packets must be relayed between the client and the authentication server. The content of the EAP messages is of no importance to the controller and AP, which simply relay the information.

There are multiple types of EAP. The three current most commonly used are EAP-TLS, PEAP, and EAP-FAST. PEAP is currently the most prominently used, as it is used with Microsoft servers; however, EAP-TLS is gaining in popularity because it can be supported by Cisco ISE.

Configuring EAP-based Authentication with External RADIUS Servers

Begin by configuring one or more external RADIUS servers on the controller. Navigate to **Security > AAA > RADIUS > Authentication**. Click the **New** button to define a new server or select the Server Index number to edit an existing server definition. In Figure 12-11, a new RADIUS server is being defined. Navigate to **Security > AAA > RADIUS > Authentication** and enter the appropriate information, and make sure the RADIUS port number is correct and that the Server Status is set to **Enabled**. Click **Apply** when you are finished.

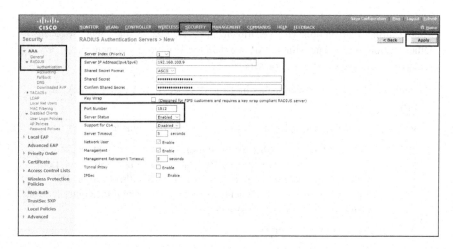

Figure 12-11 Defining a RADIUS Server for WPA2 Enterprise Authentication

Next, you need to enable 802.1X authentication on the WLAN. Navigate to **WLANs** and either click **Go** to create a new WLAN or click the number of an existing WLAN in the WLAN ID column to edit it. As an example, configure the WLAN security to use WPA2 Enterprise. Under the **Security > Layer 2** subtab, select **WPA+WPA2** and make sure that the **WPA2 Policy** check box is checked and that the WPA Policy check box is not checked. Beside WPA2 Encryption, check the box next to **AES** to use the most robust encryption. In the Authentication Key Management section, check the **Enable** check box next to 802.1X to enable the Enterprise mode. Make sure that the Enable check box next to PSK is not checked so that Personal mode will remain disabled. Figures 12-12 and 12-13 illustrate the settings that are needed to configure WPA2 Enterprise mode with 802.1X authentication.

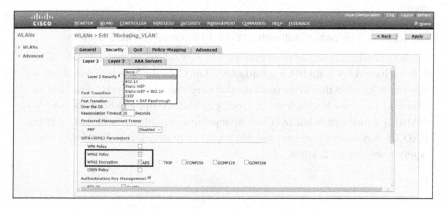

Figure 12-12 Enabling WPA2 Enterprise Mode with 802.1X Authentication

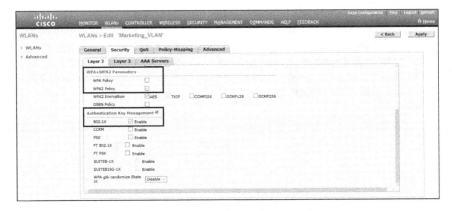

Figure 12-13   Enabling WPA2 Enterprise Mode with 802.1X Authentication, Part 2

By default, a controller will use the global list of RADIUS servers in the order you have defined under **Security > AAA > RADIUS > Authentication**. You can override that list from the **AAA Servers** tab, where you can define which RADIUS servers will be used for 802.1X authentication. You can define up to six RADIUS servers that will be tried in sequential order, designated as Server 1, Server 2, and so on. Choose a predefined server by clicking the drop-down menu next to one of the server entries. In Figure 12-14, the RADIUS server at 192.168.100.9 will be used as Server 1. After selecting your servers, you can edit other parameters or click **Apply** to make your configuration changes operational.

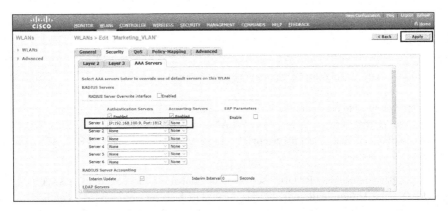

Figure 12-14   Selecting RADIUS Servers to Authenticate Clients in the WLAN

Configuring EAP-based Authentication with Local EAP

If your environment is relatively small or you do not have a RADIUS server in production, you can use an authentication server that is built in to the Wireless LAN Controller. This is called local EAP, which supports LEAP, EAP-FAST, PEAP, and EAP-TLS.

First, you need to define and enable the local EAP service on the controller. Navigate to **Security > Local EAP > Profiles** and click the **New** button. Enter a name for the local EAP profile, which will be used to define the authentication server methods. In Figure 12-15, a new profile called LocalEAP has been defined. Click the **Apply** button to create the profile. Now you should see the new profile listed, along with the authentication methods it supports, as shown in Figure 12-16. From this list, you can check or uncheck the boxes to enable or disable each method. In this example, LocalEAP has been configured to use PEAP.

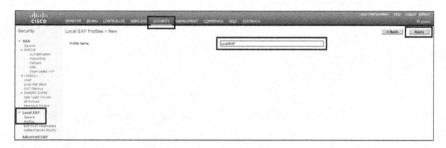

Figure 12-15   Defining a Local EAP Profile on a Controller

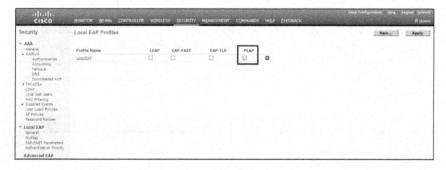

Figure 12-16   Displaying Configured Local EAP Profiles

Next, you need to configure the WLAN to use the local EAP server rather than a regular external RADIUS server. Navigate to **WLANs,** click the WLAN's number in the WLAN ID column, and then select the **Security > Layer 2** subtab and enable WPA2, AES, and 802.1X as before.

If you have defined any RADIUS servers in the global list under **Security > AAA > RADIUS > Authentication** or any specific RADIUS servers in the WLAN configuration, the controller will use those first. Local EAP will then be used as a backup method.

To make local EAP the primary authentication method, you must make sure that no RADIUS servers are defined on the controller. Click the **AAA Servers** tab and make sure that all three RADIUS servers are set to **None** in the drop-down menus, as shown in Figure 12-17.

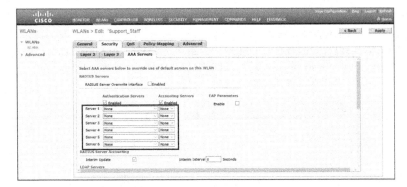

Figure 12-17   Removing RADIUS Servers for Authentication

On the bottom of the same screen, in the Local EAP Authentication section, check the **Enabled** check box to begin using the local EAP server. Select the EAP profile name that you have previously configured. In Figure 12-18, the local EAP authentication server is enabled and will use the LocalEAP profile, which was configured for PEAP.

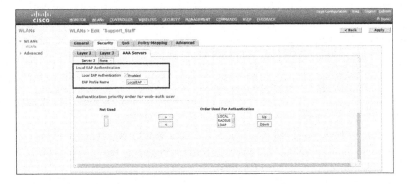

Figure 12-18   Enabling Local EAP Authentication for a WLAN

Because the local EAP server is local to the controller, you will have to maintain a local database of users or define one or more LDAP servers on the controller. You can create users by navigating to **Security > AAA > Local Net Users**. In Figure 12-19, a user named testuser has been defined and authorized for access to the Support_Staff WLAN.

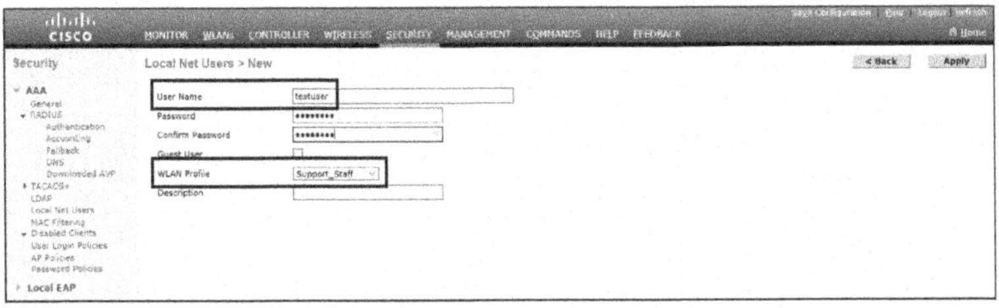

Figure 12-19   Creating a Local User for Local EAP Authentication

Verifying EAP-based Authentication Configuration

You can verify the WLAN and its security settings from the list of WLANs by selecting **WLANs > WLAN**, as shown in Figure 12-20. For EAP-based authentication, the Security Policies field should display [Auth(802.1X)]. You can also verify that the WLAN status is enabled and active.

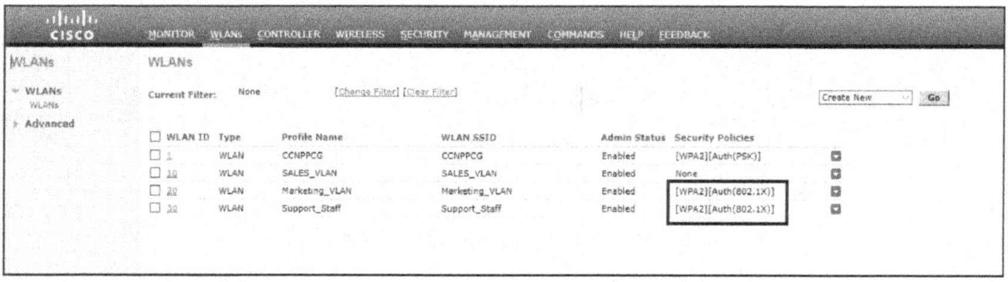

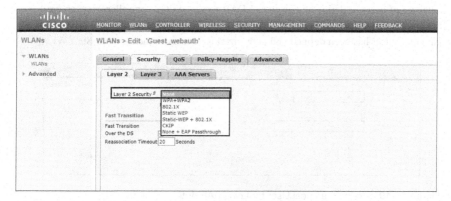

Figure 12-20 Verifying EAP Authentication on a WLAN

Authenticating with WebAuth

WebAuth is a process that allows users, typically guests, to authenticate to the network through a web portal via a browser interface. Clients that attempt to access the WLAN using HTTP are automatically redirected to a login page where they are prompted for their credentials. Their credentials are then passed to an authentication server, which then assigns the appropriate VLAN and ACLs for guest access to the Internet.

TIP: Web authentication can be handled locally on the WLC for smaller environments through local web authentication (LWA). When there are many controllers providing web authentication, it makes sense to use LWA with an external database on a RADIUS server such as Cisco ISE, keeping the user database centralized.

To configure WebAuth on a WLAN, first create the new WLAN and map it to the correct VLAN. Go to the **General** tab and enter the SSID string, apply the appropriate controller interface, and change the status to **Enabled**.

On the **Security** tab, click the **Layer 2** subtab to choose a wireless security scheme to be used on the WLAN. In Figure 12-21, the WLAN is named Guest_webauth, the SSID is Guest_webauth, and open authentication will be used because the **None** method has been selected.

Figure 12-21 Configuring Open Authentication for WebAuth

Next, click the **Security > Layer 3** subtab and choose the Layer 3 Security type **Web Policy**, as shown in Figure 12-22. When the **Authentication** radio button is selected (the default), web authentication will be performed locally on the WLC by prompting the user for credentials that will be checked against RADIUS, LDAP, or local EAP servers. In Figure 12-22, Passthrough has been selected, which will display web content such as an acceptable use policy to the user and prompt for acceptance. Through the other radio buttons, WebAuth can redirect the user to an external web server for content and interaction. Click the **Apply** button to apply the changes to the WLAN configuration.

Figure 12-22   Configuring WebAuth with Passthrough Authentication

You will need to configure the WLC's local web server with content to display during a WebAuth session. Navigate to **Security > Web Auth > Web Login Page**, as shown in Figure 12-23. By default, internal WebAuth is used. You can enter the web content that will be displayed to the user by defining a text string to be used as the headline, as well as a block of message text.

Figure 12-23   Configuring the WebAuth Page Content

Figure 12-24 shows the web content that is presented to a user that attempts to connect to the WLAN. The user must click the **Submit** button to be granted network access.

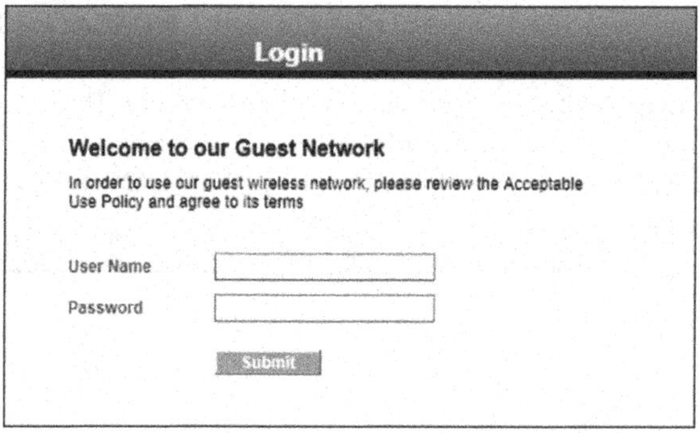

Figure 12-24 Example Web Content Presented by WebAuth Passthrough

You can verify the WebAuth security settings from the list of WLANs by selecting **WLANs > WLAN**. Figure 12-25 shows that WLAN 100 with SSID Guest_webauth uses the Web-Passthrough security policy. You can also verify that the WLAN status is enabled and active.

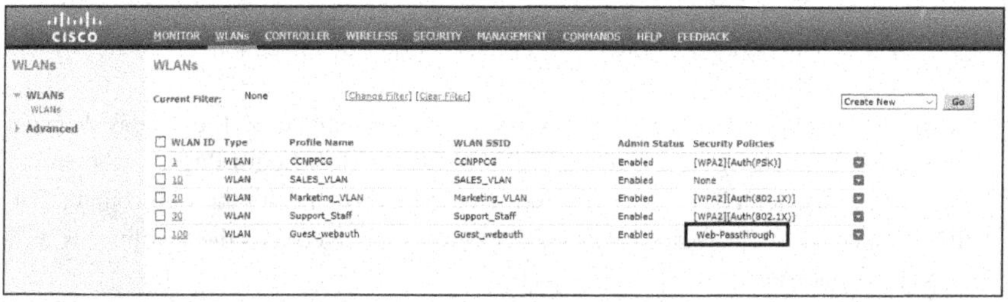

Figure 12-25 Verifying WebAuth Authentication on a WLAN

Troubleshooting from the Wireless LAN Controller

The Cisco Wireless LAN Controller (WLC) interface can be accessed using either of two modes: the command-line interface (CLI) or the graphical user interface (GUI). Unless you are using a network management system, the Cisco WLC GUI is where you will typically monitor your system. Here, you have access to overall health and specific issues in your WLAN. Depending on the model of WLC that you are using, you will see different GUIs. The following sections introduce, in turn, the Cisco AireOS Monitoring Dashboard GUI, the Cisco AireOS Advanced GUI, the Cisco IOS XE GUI, and the Cisco AireOS/IOS XE CLI.

Cisco AireOS Monitoring Dashboard GUI

The Cisco AireOS controller GUI has a new monitoring dashboard that gives a single-window overview of the network devices that are connected to the controller. The

Monitoring Dashboard screen is the default screen when you log in to the GUI of the AireOS controller. This screen is split into sections: numerical statistics and graphical widgets, as shown in Figure 12-26 and described next. From there it is possible to access the Advanced GUI (introduced in the next section) by clicking the **Advanced** menu item in the top right of the Monitoring Dashboard screen, as highlighted in Figure 12-26.

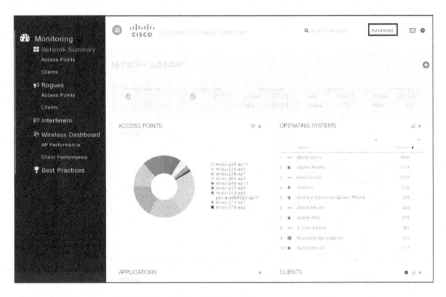

Figure 12-26 Cisco AireOS Monitoring Dashboard

Numerical Statistics

The top section of the dashboard (see Figure 12-27) is where you get a quick view of what is found on the network:

- **Wireless Networks:** Shows the number of WLANs enabled and disabled on this WLC

- **Wired Networks:** Shows the number of remote LANs and clients that are associated to the network (not displayed in Figure 12-27)

- **Access Points:** Shows the number of active Cisco APs in the network

- **Active Clients:** Shows the number of 2.4- and 5-GHz clients in the network

- **Rogues:** Shows the number of unauthorized/unclassified APs and clients found in your network

- **Interferers:** Shows the number of detected interference devices on the 2.4- and 5-GHz bands

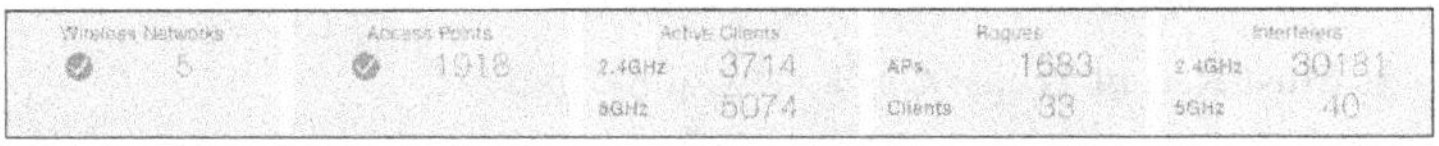

Figure 12-27 Cisco WLC Network Summary Statistics

Graphical Widgets

These graphical widgets (see Figure 12-28) present the numbers in the form of graphs. You can select the widgets to display from the available list:

- Access Points

- Operating Systems

- Clients

- Applications

- Top WLANs (not displayed in Figure 12-28)

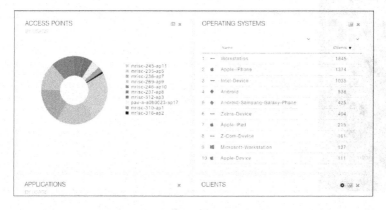

Figure 12-28   Cisco WLC Network Summary Widgets

From the Monitoring navigation pane along the left side of the dashboard (refer to Figure 12-26), you have the following options that are useful for troubleshooting:

- **Network Summary > Access Points:** Displays the list of Cisco APs connected to the controller

- **Network Summary > Clients:** Displays the list of clients connected to the controller (partially shown in Figure 12-28)

This Monitoring Dashboard is quite limited. For further troubleshooting options, access the Cisco AireOS Advanced GUI by clicking the **Advanced** button.

Cisco AireOS Advanced GUI

The Cisco AireOS WLC Advanced GUI includes the following troubleshooting options and menus:

- Monitor tab Summary screen (shown in Figure 12-29)

  - **Controller Summary:** Overall health of the WLC

  - **Most Recent Traps:** Quick view of the trap logs

  - **Access Point Summary:** How many APs or radios are up or down

  - **Client Summary:** How many clients (plus any issues)

- Wireless tab All APs screen

    - Displays the physical AP uptime and sorts by WLC associated time

    - Check the bottom of the AP list for any recent AP disruptions

    - Select the AP to see controller associated time (duration)

- Management tab

    - **Message Logs:** Message information on system conditions (for example, mobility group connection failure)

    - **Trap Logs:** Show rogues, AP and channel changes, and invalid settings

    - **Tech Support:** Information that the Cisco Technical Assistance Center (TAC) may require

- Monitor tab Cisco CleanAir screen

    - Check for interference devices per radio and AP (are they severe, and what is the duty cycle?)

    - Examine the Worst Air Quality Report to get a quick summary

    - Run the AQI report to get details on what the effect is to the WLAN

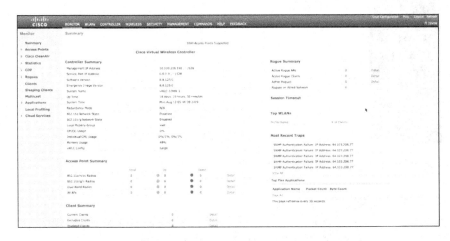

Figure 12-29   Cisco WLC Advanced GUI Page

Cisco IOS XE GUI

The Cisco IOS XE WLC GUI offers a new monitoring dashboard when you first log in. Like the AireOS GUI, it has a series of menus and widgets, as shown in Figure 12-30. The options available from the navigation pane on the left are as follows:

- **Dashboard:** This is the home screen for the IOS XE GUI. This page offers numerical information about WLANs, APs, Clients, Rogue APs, and Interferers, as well as graphical widgets relating to APs, clients, and system statistics. This is very similar to what is found in the AireOS Monitoring Dashboard GUI.

- **Monitoring:** This menu includes options to view information about general controller details, network services, and wireless APs and clients.

- **Configuration:** This menu includes options for configuring controller interfaces, routing protocols, security, RF, network services, tags, profiles, and WLANs.

- **Administration:** This menu includes options for accessing the CLI, and configuring DNS parameters, DHCP pools, licensing, software upgrades, and administrative users.

- **Troubleshooting:** This screen enables you to access troubleshooting tools such as syslog and debug, as well as packet capture, ping, and traceroute.

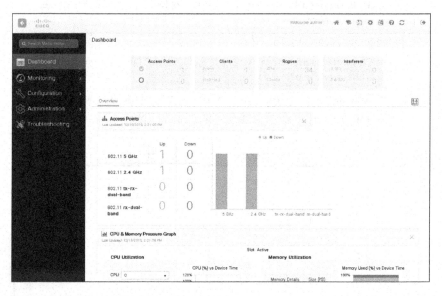

Figure 12-30   Cisco IOS XE GUI Dashboard

Cisco AireOS/IOS XE CLI

You may not always have access to the GUI of your Cisco Wireless LAN Controller, so it is good to know a few CLI commands to quickly access important troubleshooting information.

The Wireless LAN Controller CLI **show** commands to monitor the WLAN are listed in the following table. When the **show** commands differ between AireOS and IOS XE, both commands are listed in that order.

Clients	
(Cisco Controller) > **show client summary** [*ssid* | *ip* | *username* | *devicetype*]	Displays a summary of clients associated with a Cisco lightweight access point
IOSXE# **show wireless client summary**	

(Cisco Controller) > **show client detail** *mac-address* IOSXE# **show wireless client mac-address** *mac-address* **detail**	Displays client information learned through DNS snooping, including client username, associated AP, SSID, IP address, supported data rates, mobility state, security, and VLAN
(Cisco Controller) > **show client ap** {**802.11a** | **802.11b**} *ap-name* IOSXE# **show wireless client ap name** *ap-name* **dot11** {**24ghz** | **5ghz**}	Displays the clients on a radio for an AP
Logs	
(Cisco Controller) > **show traplog**	Displays the latest SNMP trap log information
(Cisco Controller) > **show logging**	Displays the syslog facility logging parameters, current log severity level, and buffer contents
Radios	
(Cisco Controller) > **show** {**802.11a** | **802.11b** | **802.11h**} IOSXE# **show ap dot11** {**24ghz** | **5ghz**} **network**	Displays radio networking settings (status, rates, supported, power, and channel)
WLANs	
(Cisco Controller) > IOSXE# **show wlan** {**apgroups** | **summary** | *wlan-id* | **foreignAp** | **lobby-admin-access**}	Displays WLAN information (name, security, status, and all settings). Keywords include **apgroups**: Displays access point group information **summary**: Displays a summary of all WLANs *wlan_id*: Displays the configuration of a WLAN. The WLAN identifier range is from 1 to 512 **foreignAp**: Displays the configuration for support of foreign access points **lobby-admin-access**: Displays all WLANs that have lobby-admin-access enabled
APs	
(Cisco Controller) > **show ap config** {**802.11a** | **802.11b**} [**summary**] *ap-name* IOSXE# **show ap dot11** {**24ghz** | **5ghz**} **summary**	Displays AP detailed configuration settings by radio

(Cisco Controller) > **show ap config general** *ap-name* IOSXE# **show ap name** *ap-name* **config general**	Displays general AP configuration information
(Cisco Controller) > **show ap** join **stats summary** *ap-mac* IOSXE# **show ap mac-address** *mac-address* **join stats** {**detailed** | **summary**} WLC# **show ap join stats summary**	Displays MAC, IP address, name, and join status of all APs joined
(Cisco Controller) > IOSXE# **show ap summary** [*ap-name*]	Displays APs (model, MAC, IP address, country, and number of clients)
(Cisco Controller) > **show ap wlan** {**802.11a** | **802.11b**} *ap-name* IOSXE# **show ap name** *ap-name* **wlan dot11** {**24ghz** | **5ghz** }	Displays WLAN IDs, interfaces, and BSSID

NOTE: When logging output from the Wireless LAN Controller, enter the **config paging disable** command first to stop page breaks.

Just as with routers and switches, **debug** commands are available on the Cisco WLC. One particular **debug** command that may be useful for troubleshooting wireless client connectivity is **debug client** *mac_address*. It is a macro that enables eight **debug** commands, plus a filter on the MAC address that is provided, so only messages that contain the specified MAC address are shown. The eight **debug** commands show the most important details about client association and authentication. The filter helps with situations where there are multiple wireless clients and too much output is generated, or the controller is overloaded when debugging is enabled without the filter.

Troubleshooting Wireless Client Connectivity

If clients are reporting problems, a good place to start troubleshooting is at the Cisco Wireless LAN Controller. This section shows the output from two different GUIs: the Cisco AireOS Monitoring Dashboard GUI and the Cisco IOS XE GUI.

Cisco AireOS Monitoring Dashboard GUI

From the **Monitoring** pane along the left side of the AireOS Dashboard GUI, select **Network Summary > Access Points** to check if the APs are functioning correctly.

The Access Point View page, shown in Figure 12-31, is displayed when an AP is selected. The AP details section provides tabs with information on the clients, RF Troubleshooting with neighboring and rogue APs (2.4 and 5 GHz) found in the surroundings, Clean Air with active interferers, and the tool tab to restart the AP.

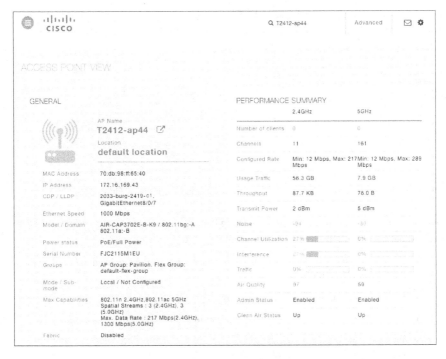

Figure 12-31 Cisco AireOS WLC Access Point View Details

Next, navigate to **Network Summary > Clients**. The Client View page is displayed when a client is selected. On this page, the client's general details are shown. There are two infographic representations on the Client View page. The first infographic (see Figure 12-32) shows the connection stage of the client.

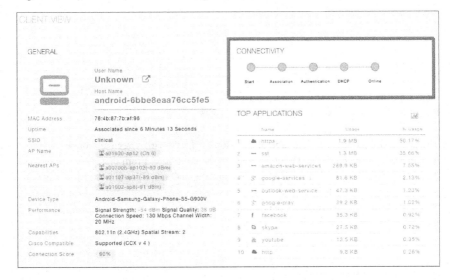

Figure 12-32 Cisco AireOS WLC Client View Details Connectivity Stage

The second infographic (see Figure 12-33) shows the connectivity roadmap between the controller and the client. It also shows the types of connection and the path that is used in the network from the controller to the client.

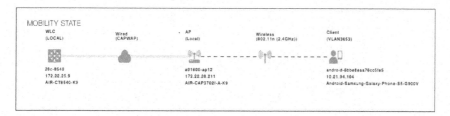

Figure 12-33   Cisco AireOS WLC Client View Details Connectivity Roadmap

The Client View page also offers the following debugging tools, as shown in Figure 12-34, to assess the connectivity from the client with the controller:

- **Ping Test:** Helps to determine the connectivity status and the latency between the two systems in a network

- **Connection:** Shows the connection logs for a client

- **Event Log:** Records the events and the option to save the logs to a spreadsheet

- **Packet Capture:** Provides various options to get precise information about the flow of packets to help resolve issues

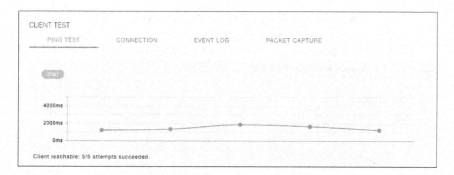

Figure 12-34   Cisco AireOS WLC Client Test Tools

You can also go to the top right side of the Monitor Dashboard screen and click **Advanced** to be taken to the Monitor screen in the controller. From there you can drill down on any of the issues from that screen and menus. Click **Clients** from the menu on the left to display a list of all wireless clients associated with the WLC. From there, clicking a MAC address displays detailed information for that client, as shown in Figure 12-35.

Figure 12-35   Verifying Client Details

The Clients > Detail page displays the IP address, the VLAN ID, the Policy Manager State, the type of security that client is using, the AP name and WLAN profile, as well as the client Reason Code and client Status Code.

The Policy Manager State will display one of these messages relating to the authentication state of the client:

- **START:** Initializing the authentication process

- **802.1X-REQD:** 802.1X (L2) authentication pending

- **DHCP_REQD:** IP learning state

- **WEBAUTH_REQD:** Web (L3) Authentication pending

- **RUN:** Client traffic forwarding

The client Reason Code can be one of the following:

no reason code (0)	Indicates normal operation
unspecified reason (1)	Indicates that the client associated but is no longer authorized
previousAuthNotValid (2)	Indicates that the client associated but was not authorized
deauthenticationLeaving (3)	Indicates that the AP went offline, deauthenticating the client
disassociationDueToInactivity (4)	Indicates that the client session was timeout exceeded

disassociationAPBusy (5)	Indicates that the AP is busy, for example, performing load balancing
class2FrameFromNonAuthStation (6)	Indicates that the client attempted to transfer data before it was authenticated
class2FrameFromNonAssStation (7)	Indicates that the client attempted to transfer data before it was associated
disassociationStaHasLeft (8)	Indicates that the operating system moved the client to another AP using nonaggressive load balancing
staReqAssociationWithoutAuth (9)	Indicates that the client is not authorized yet and is still attempting to associate with the AP
missingReasonCode (99)	Indicates that the client is momentarily in an unknown state

The client Status Code may be one of the following:

idle (0)	Indicates normal operation; no rejections of client association requests
aaaPending (1)	Indicates that a AAA transaction completed
authenticated (2)	Indicates that 802.11 authentication completed
associated (3)	Indicates that 802.11 association completed
powersave (4)	Indicates that the client is in power-save mode
disassociated (5)	Indicates that the 802.11 disassociation completed
tobedeleted (6)	Indicates that the client should be deleted after disassociation
probing (7)	Indicates that the client is not associated or authorized yet
disabled (8)	Indicates that the operating system automatically disabled the client for an operator-defined time

Cisco IOS XE GUI

When troubleshooting client connectivity from the IOS XE controller GUI, you can use the Monitoring menu. First, navigating to **Monitoring > AP Statistics** will list all APs associated with the WLC. Clicking a specific AP will display general information about that AP, including AP name, IP address, model, power status, number of clients, and RF utilization, as shown in Figure 12-36.

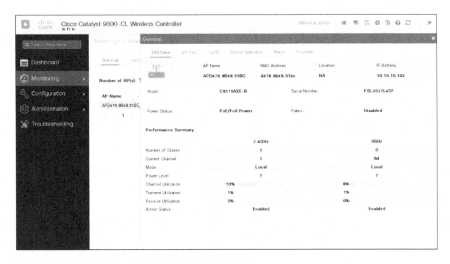

Figure 12-36 Verifying AP Details in IOS XE WLC

For specific client information, navigate to **Monitoring > Clients** and select a client from the list of all clients associated with the WLC. As shown in Figure 12-37, you can observe general client properties, AP properties, security information, and client statistics.

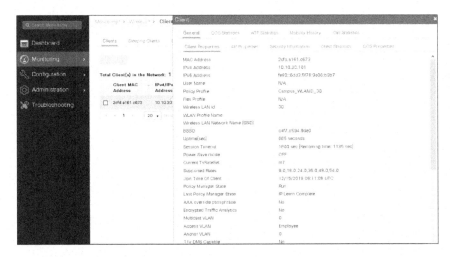

Figure 12-37 Verifying Client Details in IOS XE WLC

CHAPTER 13

Overlay Tunnels and VRF

This chapter provides information about the following topics:

- Generic Routing Encapsulation (GRE)
    - Configuring an IPv4 GRE tunnel
    - Configuring an IPv6 GRE tunnel
    - Verifying IPv4 and IPv6 GRE tunnels
    - Configuration example: IPv4 and IPv6 GRE tunnels with OSPFv3
- Site-to-site GRE over IPsec
    - GRE/IPsec using crypto maps
    - GRE/IPsec using tunnel IPsec profiles
    - Verifying GRE/IPsec
- Site-to-site virtual tunnel interface (VTI) over IPsec
- Cisco Dynamic Multipoint VPN (DMVPN)
    - Configuration example: Cisco DMVPN for IPv4
    - Verifying Cisco DMVPN
- VRF-Lite
    - Configuring VRF-Lite
    - Verifying VRF-Lite

CAUTION: Your hardware platform or software release might not support all the commands documented in this chapter. Please refer to Cisco.com for specific platform and software release notes.

Generic Routing Encapsulation (GRE)

GRE, defined in RFC 2784, is a carrier protocol that can be used with a variety of underlying transport protocols and that can carry a variety of passenger protocols. RFC 2784 also covers the use of GRE with IPv4 as the transport protocol and the passenger protocol. Cisco IOS Software supports GRE as the carrier protocol with many combinations of passenger and transport protocols such as:

- **GRE over IPv4 networks:** GRE is the carrier protocol, and IPv4 is the transport protocol. This is the most common type of GRE tunnel.
- **GRE over IPv6 networks:** GRE is the carrier protocol, and IPv6 is the transport protocol. Cisco IOS Software supports IPv4 and IPv6 as passenger protocols with GRE/IPv6.

Configuring an IPv4 GRE Tunnel

Perform the following configuration steps to configure a GRE tunnel. A tunnel interface is used to transport protocol traffic across a network that does not normally support the protocol. To build a tunnel, a tunnel interface must be defined on each of two routers and the tunnel interfaces must reference each other. At each router, the tunnel interface must be configured with a Layer 3 address. The tunnel endpoints, tunnel source, and tunnel destination must be defined, and the type of tunnel must be selected. Optional steps can be performed to customize the tunnel.

`Router(config)# interface tunnel 0`	Moves to interface configuration mode
`Router(config-if)# tunnel mode gre ip`	Specifies the encapsulation protocol to be used in the tunnel. By default, the tunnel protocol is GRE and the transport protocol is IPv4; therefore entering this command is optional and won't appear in the device's running configuration
`Router(config-if)# ip address 192.168.1.1 255.255.255.0`	Assigns an IP address and subnet mask to the tunnel interface
`Router(config-if)# tunnel source 209.165.201.1` Or `Router(config-if)# tunnel source gigabitethernet 0/0/0`	Identifies the local source of the tunnel. You can use either an interface name or the IP address of the interface that will transmit tunneled packets **NOTE:** The tunnel source can be a physical interface or a loopback interface
`Router(config-if)# tunnel destination 198.51.100.1`	Identifies the remote destination IP address
`Router(config-if)# bandwidth 8192`	Defines the tunnel bandwidth for use with a routing protocol or QoS in kilobits per second. In the example, the bandwidth is set to 8192 Kbps
`Router(config-if)# keepalive 3 5`	Sets the tunnel keepalives to 3 seconds and the number of retries to five to ensure that bidirectional communication exists between tunnel endpoints. The default timer is 10 seconds, with three retries
`Router(config-if)# ip mtu 1400`	Set the maximum transmission unit (MTU) size of IP packets sent on an interface to 1400 bytes. The default MTU is 1500 bytes **NOTE:** The GRE tunnel adds a minimum of 24 bytes to the packet size

Configuring an IPv6 GRE Tunnel

The same process that is described for IPv4 is used to configure an IPv6 GRE tunnel.

`Router(config)# interface tunnel 1`	Moves to interface configuration mode
`Router(config-if)# tunnel mode gre ipv6`	Specifies the encapsulation protocol to be used in the tunnel
`Router(config-if)# ip address 2001:db8:192:100::1/64`	Assigns an IPv6 address and subnet mask to the tunnel interface

`Router(config-if)# tunnel source 2001:db8:209:201::1`
Or
`Router(config-if)# tunnel source gigabitethernet 0/0/0`
	Identifies the local source of the tunnel. You can use either an interface name or the IPv6 address of the interface that will transmit tunneled packets
	NOTE: The tunnel source can be a physical interface or a loopback interface

`Router(config-if)# tunnel destination 2001:db8:198:51::1`	Identifies the remote destination IPv6 address
`Router(config-if)# bandwidth 4096`	Defines the tunnel bandwidth for use with a routing protocol or QoS in kilobits per second. In the example, the bandwidth is set to 4096 Kbps
`Router(config-if)# keepalive 3 5`	Sets the tunnel keepalives to 3 seconds and the number of retries to five to ensure that bidirectional communication exists between tunnel endpoints. The default timer is 10 seconds, with three retries
`Router(config-if)# ipv6 mtu 1400`	Set the maximum transmission unit (MTU) size of IPv6 packets sent on an interface to 1400 bytes. The default MTU is 1500 bytes **NOTE:** The GRE tunnel adds a minimum of 24 bytes to the packet size

Verifying IPv4 and IPv6 GRE Tunnels

`Router# show interfaces tunnel number`	Displays general information about the tunnel interface
`Router# show ip interface tunnel number`	Displays IPv4 information about the tunnel interface
`Router# show ipv6 interface tunnel number`	Displays IPv6 information about the tunnel interface

Configuration Example: IPv4 and IPv6 GRE Tunnels with OSPFv3

Figure 13-1 shows the network topology for the configuration that follows, which demonstrates how to configure IPv4 and IPv6 GRE tunnels to allow for OSPFv3 connectivity between two customer edge routers that peer with separate ISP routers. This example assumes that ISP1 and ISP2 are configured to route traffic across the underlay network between CE1 and CE2. Tunnel 0 is used for IPv4 and Tunnel 1 is used for IPv6.

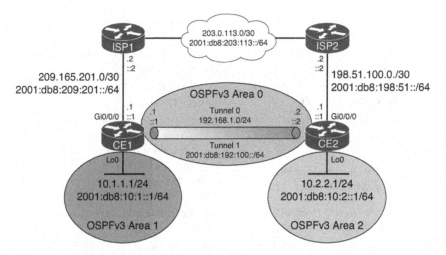

Figure 13-1   Network Topology for IPv4/IPv6 GRE Example

The example is built following these steps:

Step 1.   Underlay configuration (physical/logical interfaces, default routing).

Step 2.   Overlay configuration (tunnel interfaces).

Step 3.   Overlay routing with OSPFv3.

Step 1: Underlay Configuration

`CE1(config)# ipv6 unicast-routing`	Enables routing for IPv6 packets
`CE1(config)# interface gigabitethernet 0/0/0`	Enters interface configuration mode
`CE1(config-if)# ip address 209.165.201.1 255.255.255.252`	Applies an IPv4 address to the interface
`CE1(config-if)# ipv6 address 2001:db8:209:201::1/64`	Applies an IPv6 address to the interface
`CE1(config-if)# no shutdown`	Enables the interface
`CE1(config-if)# exit`	Exits interface configuration mode
`CE1(config)# interface loopback 0`	Enters interface configuration mode
`CE1(config-if)# ip address 10.1.1.1 255.255.255.0`	Applies an IPv4 address to the interface
`CE1(config-if)# ipv6 address 2001:db8:10:1::1/64`	Applies an IPv6 address to the interface
`CE1(config-if)# exit`	Exits interface configuration mode
`CE1(config)# ip route 0.0.0.0 0.0.0.0 209.165.201.2`	Defines an IPv4 default route to send all packets to ISP1
`CE1(config)# ipv6 route ::/0 2001:db8:209:201::2`	Defines an IPv6 default route to send all packets to ISP1

CE2(config)# **ipv6 unicast-routing**	Enables routing for IPv6 packets
CE2(config)# **interface gigabitethernet 0/0/0**	Enters interface configuration mode
CE2(config-if)# **ip address 198.51.100.1 255.255.255.252**	Applies an IPv4 address to the interface
CE2(config-if)# **ipv6 address 2001:db8:198:51::1/64**	Applies an IPv6 address to the interface
CE2(config-if)# **no shutdown**	Enables the interface
CE2(config-if)# **exit**	Exits interface configuration mode
CE2(config)# **interface loopback 0**	Enters interface configuration mode
CE2(config-if)# **ip address 10.2.2.1 255.255.255.0**	Applies an IPv4 address to the interface
CE2(config-if)# **ipv6 address 2001:db8:10:2::1/64**	Applies an IPv6 address to the interface
CE2(config-if)# **exit**	Exits interface configuration mode
CE2(config)# **ip route 0.0.0.0 0.0.0.0 198.51.100.2**	Defines an IPv4 default route to send all packets to ISP1
CE2(config)# **ipv6 route ::/0 2001:db8:198:51::2**	Defines an IPv6 default route to send all packets to ISP1

Step 2: Overlay Configuration

CE1(config)# **interface tunnel 0**	Enters interface configuration mode
CE1(config-if)# **ip address 192.168.1.1 255.255.255.0**	Applies an IPv4 address to the interface
CE1(config-if)# **tunnel source gigabitethernet 0/0/0**	Defines the physical source of the tunnel
CE1(config-if)# **tunnel destination 198.51.100.1**	Defines the tunnel destination across the underlay network
CE1(config-if)# **tunnel mode gre ip**	Enables GRE tunnel mode for IPv4. This is the default value and won't appear in the running configuration
CE1(config-if)# **ip mtu 1400**	Lowers the MTU to 1400 bytes from its default of 1500
CE1(config-if)# **ipv6 enable**	Enables IPv6 on the interface. This is required for OSPFv3 routing in the next step since there is no IPv6 address on Tunnel 0
CE1(config-if)# **interface tunnel 1**	Enters interface configuration mode
CE1(config-if)# **ipv6 address 2001:db8:192:100::1/64**	Applies an IPv6 address to the interface
CE1(config-if)# **tunnel source gigabitethernet 0/0/0**	Defines the physical source of the tunnel

CE1(config-if)# **tunnel destination** 2001:db8:198:51::1	Defines the tunnel destination across the underlay network
CE1(config-if)# **tunnel mode gre ipv6**	Enables GRE tunnel mode for IPv6
CE2(config)# **interface tunnel 0**	Enters interface configuration mode
CE2(config-if)# **ip address** 192.168.1.2 255.255.255.0	Applies an IPv4 address to the interface
CE2(config-if)# **tunnel source** gigabitethernet 0/0/0	Defines the physical source of the tunnel
CE2(config-if)# **tunnel destination** 209.165.201.1	Defines the tunnel destination across the underlay network
CE2(config-if)# **tunnel mode gre ip**	Enables GRE tunnel mode for IPv4. This is the default value and won't appear in the running configuration
CE2(config-if)# **ip mtu 1400**	Lowers the MTU to 1400 bytes from its default of 1500
CE2(config-if)# **ipv6 enable**	Enables IPv6 on the interface. This is required for OSPFv3 routing in the next step since there is no IPv6 address on Tunnel 0
CE2(config-if)# **interface tunnel 1**	Enters interface configuration mode
CE2(config-if)# **ipv6 address** 2001:db8:192:100::2/64	Applies an IPv6 address to the interface
CE2(config-if)# **tunnel source** gigabitethernet 0/0/0	Defines the physical source of the tunnel
CE2(config-if)# **tunnel destination** 2001:db8:209:201::1	Defines the tunnel destination across the underlay network
CE2(config-if)# **tunnel mode gre ipv6**	Enables GRE tunnel mode for IPv6

Step 3: Overlay Routing with OSPFv3

CE1(config)# **router ospfv3 1**	Starts OSPFv3 with a process ID of 1
CE1(config-router)# **address-family ipv4 unicast**	Creates the IPv4 unicast address family
CE1(config-router-af)# **router-id 1.1.1.1**	Defines a router ID of 1.1.1.1
CE1(config-router-af)# **address-family ipv6 unicast**	Creates the IPv6 unicast address family
CE1(config-router-af)# **router-id 1.1.1.1**	Defines a router ID of 1.1.1.1
CE1(config-router-af)# **interface tunnel 0**	Enters interface configuration mode
CE1(config-if)# **ospfv3 1 ipv4 area 0**	Assigns the Tunnel 0 interface to area 0 for the OSPFv3 IPv4 address family

CE1(config-if)# **interface tunnel 1**	Enters interface configuration mode
CE1(config-if)# **ospfv3 1 ipv6 area 0**	Assigns the Tunnel 1 interface to area 0 for the OSPFv3 IPv6 address family
CE1(config-router-af)# **interface loopback 0**	Enters interface configuration mode
CE1(config-if)# **ospfv3 1 ipv4 area 1**	Assigns the Loopback 0 interface to area 1 for the OSPFv3 IPv4 address family
CE1(config-if)# **ospfv3 1 ipv6 area 1**	Assigns the Loopback 0 interface to area 1 for the OSPFv3 IPv6 address family
CE2(config)# **router ospfv3 1**	Starts OSPFv3 with a process ID of 1
CE2(config-router)# **address-family ipv4 unicast**	Creates the IPv4 unicast address family
CE2(config-router-af)# **router-id 2.2.2.2**	Defines a router ID of 2.2.2.2
CE2(config-router-af)# **address-family ipv6 unicast**	Creates the IPv6 unicast address family
CE2(config-router-af)# **router-id 2.2.2.2**	Defines a router ID of 2.2.2.2
CE2(config-router-af)# **interface tunnel 0**	Enters interface configuration mode
CE2(config-if)# **ospfv3 1 ipv4 area 0**	Assigns the Tunnel 0 interface to area 0 for the OSPFv3 IPv4 address family
CE2(config-if)# **interface tunnel 1**	Enters interface configuration mode
CE2(config-if)# **ospfv3 1 ipv6 area 0**	Assigns the Tunnel 1 interface to area 0 for the OSPFv3 IPv6 address family
CE2(config-router-af)# **interface loopback 0**	Enters interface configuration mode
CE2(config-if)# **ospfv3 1 ipv4 area 2**	Assigns the Loopback 0 interface to area 2 for the OSPFv3 IPv4 address family
CE2(config-if)# **ospfv3 1 ipv6 area 2**	Assigns the Loopback 0 interface to area 2 for the OSPFv3 IPv6 address family

Site-to-Site GRE over IPsec

In GRE over IPsec (usually written GRE/IPsec for short), data packets are first encapsulated within GRE/IP, which results in a new IP packet being created inside the router. This packet is then selected for encryption (the traffic selector being GRE from local to remote endpoint IP address), and encapsulated into IPsec. Since a new IP header has already been added, IPsec transport mode is generally used to keep the overhead to a minimum. There are two different ways to encrypt traffic over a GRE tunnel:

- Using crypto maps (old method)
- Using tunnel IPsec profiles (newer method)

NOTE: Even though crypto maps are no longer recommended for tunnels, they are still widely deployed and should be understood.

The two GRE configuration scenarios that follow build on the previous GRE example but focus only on IPv4. You would configure one of the two scenarios, not both. Refer to Figure 13-1 for addressing information.

GRE/IPsec Using Crypto Maps

After the GRE tunnel has been configured, follow these steps to enable IPsec using crypto maps:

Step 1. Define a crypto ACL.

Step 2. Configure an ISAKMP policy for IKE SA.

Step 3. Configure pre-shared keys (PSKs).

Step 4. Create a transform set.

Step 5. Build a crypto map.

Step 6. Apply the crypto map to the outside interface.

Step 1: Define a Crypto ACL

CE1(config)# **access-list 101 permit gre host 192.168.1.1 host 192.168.1.2**	Defines the crypto ACL that identifies traffic entering the GRE tunnel. This traffic is encrypted by IPsec
CE2(config)# **access-list 101 permit gre host 192.168.1.2 host 192.168.1.1**	The crypto ACL on CE2 is a mirror image of the ACL on CE1

Step 2: Configure an ISAKMP Policy for IKE SA (repeat on CE2)

CE1(config)# **crypto isakmp policy 1**	Creates an ISAKMP policy number 1. Numbers range from 1 to 1000
CE1(config-isakmp)# **authentication pre-share**	Enables the use of PSKs for authentication. Option to use RSA signatures instead
CE1(config-isakmp)# **hash sha256**	Enables SHA-256 for hashing. Options are MD5, SHA, SHA-256, SHA-384, and SHA-512
CE1(config-isakmp)# **encryption aes 256**	Enables AES-256 for encryption. Options are DES, 3DES, and AES (128, 192, 256 bit)
CE1(config-isakmp)# **group 14**	Enables Diffie-Hellman group 14 for key exchange. Options are group 1, 2, 5, 14, 15, 16, 19, 20, 21, or 24

Step 3: Configure PSKs

CE1(config)# **crypto isakmp key secretkey address 198.51.100.1**	Defines a PSK for neighbor peer CE2
CE2(config)# **crypto isakmp key secretkey address 209.165.201.1**	Defines a PSK for neighbor peer CE1

Step 4: Create a Transform Set (repeat on CE2)

CE1(config)# **crypto ipsec transform-set GRE-SEC esp-aes 256 esp-sha256-hmac**	Defines an IPsec transform set called *GRE-SEC* that uses ESP with AES-256 for encryption and SHA-256 for authentication. Options are AH and MD5
CE1(cfg-crypto-trans)# **mode transport**	Enables transport mode to avoid double encapsulation from GRE and IPsec. The other option available is tunnel mode

Step 5: Build a Crypto Map (repeat on CE2 except for the peer configuration)

CE1(config)# **crypto map GREMAP 1 ipsec-isakmp**	Creates an IPsec crypto map called *GREMAP* with a sequence number of 1. Range is from 1 to 65535 **NOTE:** A message will appear at the console indicating that the crypto map will remain disabled until a peer and a valid ACL have been configured
CE1(config-crypto-map)# **match address 101**	Applies the previously configured crypto ACL to the crypto map
CE1(config-crypto-map)# **set transform-set GRE-SEC**	Applies the previously configured transform set to the crypto map
CE1(config-crypto-map)# **set peer 198.51.100.1**	Sets the remote peer, which in this case is CE2
CE2(config-crypto-map)# **set peer 209.165.201.1**	Sets the remote peer, which in this case is CE1

Step 6: Apply the Crypto Map to Outside Interface (repeat on CE2)

CE1(config)# **interface gigabitethernet 0/0/0**	Enters interface configuration mode
CE1(config-if)# **crypto map GREMAP**	Applies the crypto map to the outside interface connected to the ISP router

GRE/IPsec Using IPsec Profiles

After the GRE tunnel has been configured, follow these steps to enable IPsec using IPsec profiles:

Step 1.   Configure an ISAKMP policy for IKE SA.

Step 2.   Configure PSKs.

Step 3.   Create a transform set.

Step 4.   Create an IPsec profile.

Step 5.   Apply the IPsec profile to the tunnel interface.

Step 1: Configure an ISAKMP Policy for IKE SA (repeat on CE2)

`CE1(config)#` **`crypto isakmp`** `policy 1`	Creates an ISAKMP policy number 1. Numbers range from 1 to 1000
`CE1(config-isakmp)#` **`authentication pre-share`**	Enables the use of PSKs for authentication. Option to use RSA signatures instead
`CE1(config-isakmp)#` **`hash sha256`**	Enables SHA-256 for hashing Options are MD5, SHA, SHA-256, SHA-384, SHA-512
`CE1(config-isakmp)#` **`encryption aes 256`**	Enables AES-256 for encryption Options are DES, 3DES, and AES (128, 192, 256 bit)
`CE1(config-isakmp)#` **`group 14`**	Enables Diffie-Hellman group 14 for key exchange. Options are group 1, 2, 5, 14, 15, 16, 19, 20, 21, or 24

Step 2: Configure PSKs

`CE1(config)#` **`crypto isakmp key`** `secretkey address 198.51.100.1`	Defines a PSK for neighbor peer CE2
`CE2(config)#` **`crypto isakmp key`** `secretkey address 209.165.201.1`	Defines a PSK for neighbor peer CE1

Step 3: Create a Transform Set (repeat on CE2)

`CE1(config)#` **`crypto ipsec transform-set GRE-SEC esp-aes 256 esp-sha256-hmac`**	Defines an IPsec transform set called *GRE-SEC* that uses ESP with AES-256 for encryption and SHA-256 for authentication. Options are AH and MD5
`CE1(cfg-crypto-trans)#` **`mode transport`**	Enables transport mode to avoid double encapsulation from GRE and IPsec. The other option is available is tunnel mode

Step 4: Create an IPsec Profile (repeat on CE2)

`CE1(config)#` **`crypto ipsec profile GRE-PROFILE`**	Creates an IPsec profile named *GRE-PROFILE*
`CE1(ipsec-profile)#` **`set transform-set GRE-SEC`**	Applies the previously configured transform set to the IPsec profile

Step 5: Apply the IPsec Profile to Tunnel Interface (repeat on CE2)

CE1(config)# **interface tunnel 0**	Enters interface configuration mode
CE1(config-if)# **tunnel protection ipsec profile GRE-PROFILE**	Applies the IPsec profile to the tunnel interface, allowing IPsec to encrypt traffic flowing between CE1 and CE2

Verifying GRE/IPsec

CE1# **show crypto isakmp sa**	Displays current Internet Key Exchange (IKE) security associations (SAs)
CE1# **show crypto ipsec sa**	Displays the settings used by IPsec security associations

Site-to-Site Virtual Tunnel Interface (VTI) over IPsec

The use of IPsec virtual tunnel interfaces (VTIs) simplifies the configuration process when you must provide protection for site-to-site VPN tunnels. A major benefit of IPsec VTIs is that the configuration does not require a static mapping of IPsec sessions to a physical interface. The use of IPsec VTIs simplifies the configuration process when you must provide protection for site-to-site VPN tunnels and offers a simpler alternative to the use of Generic Routing Encapsulation (GRE) tunnels for encapsulation and crypto maps with IPsec.

The steps to enable a VTI over IPsec are very similar to those for GRE over IPsec configuration using IPsec profiles. The only difference is the addition of the command **tunnel mode ipsec {ipv4 | ipv6}** under the GRE tunnel interface to enable VTI on it and to change the packet transport mode to tunnel mode. To revert to GRE over IPsec, the command **tunnel mode gre {ip | ipv6}** is used.

Assuming that the GRE tunnel is already configured for IPsec using IPsec profiles as was described in the previous configuration example, you would need to make the following changes to migrate to a VTI over IPsec site-to-site tunnel using pre-shared keys:

CE1

CE1(config)# **crypto ipsec transform-set GRE-SEC esp-aes 256 esp-sha256-hmac**	Defines an IPsec transform set called *GRE-SEC* that uses ESP with AES-256 for encryption and SHA-256 for authentication. Options are AH and MD5
CE1(cfg-crypto-trans)# **mode tunnel**	Enables tunnel mode for VTI support
CE1(cfg-crypto-trans)# **exit**	Exits the transform set
CE1(config)# **interface tunnel 0**	Enters interface configuration mode
CE1(config-if)# **tunnel mode ipsec ipv4**	Enables IPsec for IPv4 on the tunnel interface

CE2

CE2(config)# **crypto ipsec transform-set GRE-SEC esp-aes 256 esp-sha256-hmac**	Defines an IPsec transform set called *GRE-SEC* that uses ESP with AES-256 for encryption and SHA-256 for authentication. Options are AH and MD5
CE2(cfg-crypto-trans)# **mode tunnel**	Enables tunnel mode for VTI support
CE2(cfg-crypto-trans)# **exit**	Exits the transform set
CE2(config)# **interface tunnel 0**	Enters interface configuration mode
CE2(config-if)# **tunnel mode ipsec ipv4**	Enables IPsec for IPv4 on the tunnel interface

Cisco Dynamic Multipoint VPN (DMVPN)

Cisco DMVPN is a solution that leverages IPsec and GRE to enable enterprises to establish a secure connection in a hub-and-spoke network or spoke-to-spoke network easily and effectively. All of the spokes in a DMVPN network are configured to connect to the hub and, when interesting traffic calls for it, each spoke can connect directly to another spoke as well.

DMVPN uses two primary technologies:

- Multipoint GRE (mGRE) with IPsec, which allows the routers in the solution to establish multiple GRE tunnels using only one configured tunnel interface

- Next Hop Resolution Protocol (NHRP), which is similar to ARP on Ethernet

There are three different deployment options for DMVPN, which are called phases:

- **Phase 1:** This phase can be deployed only as a hub-and-spoke tunnel deployment. In this deployment the hub is configured with an mGRE tunnel interface and the spokes have point-to-point GRE tunnel interface configurations. All traffic, including inter-spoke traffic, must traverse the hub.

- **Phase 2:** This phase improves on Phase 1 by establishing a mechanism for spokes to build dynamic spoke-to-spoke tunnels on demand. Spokes in this deployment type have mGRE tunnel interfaces and learn of their peer spoke addresses and specific downstream routes using a routing protocol.

- **Phase 3:** This phase is very similar to Phase 2, but the routing table must have the spoke address and all specific downstream routes propagated to all other spokes. This means that the hub cannot use summarization of routes in the routing protocol. The hub uses NHRP redirect messages to inform the spoke of a more effective path to the spoke's network, and the spoke will accept the "shortcut" and build the dynamic tunnel to the peer spoke.

Configuration Example: Cisco DMVPN for IPv4

Figure 13-2 shows the network topology for the configuration that follows, which demonstrates how to configure Cisco DMVPN for IPv4. The example shows you how to configure all three DMVPN phases and assumes that the physical interfaces are already configured with IP addresses.

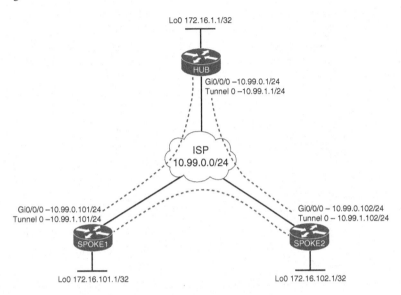

Figure 13-2 Network Topology for Cisco DMVPN for IPv4 Example

When configuring Cisco DMVPN, follow these steps:

1. Configure an ISAKMP policy for IKE SA.

2. Configure pre-shared keys (PSKs).

3. Create a transform set.

4. Create a crypto IPsec profile.

5. Define an mGRE tunnel interface.

6. Enable NHRP on the tunnel interface.

7. Apply the IPsec security profile to the tunnel interface.

8. Enable dynamic routing across the tunnel interface.

DMVPN Phase 1: Hub Router

`Hub(config)# `**`crypto isakmp`** **`policy 10`**	Creates an ISAKMP policy with the number 10
`Hub(config-isakmp)# `**`encryption`** **`aes 256`**	Enables AES-256 encryption
`Hub(config-isakmp)# `**`hash sha256`**	Enables SHA-256 hashing

`Hub(config-isakmp)#` `authentication pre-share`	Enables PSK authentication
`Hub(config-isakmp)# group 16`	Enables Diffie-Hellman group 16 (4096-bit)
`Hub(config-isakmp)# exit`	Exits the ISAKMP policy
`Hub(config)# crypto isakmp key` `CiscoDMVPNKey address 0.0.0.0`	Defines a PSK to be used for any ISAKMP neighbor

`Hub(config)# crypto ipsec`
`transform-set DMVPNset esp-aes`
`256 esp-sha256-hmac`
	Creates an IPsec transform set called *DMVPNset* that uses AES-256 and SHA-256 for ESP

`Hub(cfg-crypto-trans)# mode` `transport`	Enables tunnel mode for the IPsec tunnel
`Hub(cfg-crypto-trans)# exit`	Exits the transform set
`Hub(config)# crypto ipsec profile` `DMVPNprofile`	Creates an IPsec profile called *DMVPNprofile*
`Hub(ipsec-profile)# set` `transform-set DMVPNset`	Applies the DMVPNset transform set
`Hub(ipsec-profile)# exit`	Exits the IPsec profile
`Hub(config)# interface tunnel 0`	Enters interface configuration mode
`Hub(config-if)# ip address` `10.99.1.1 255.255.255.0`	Applies an IP address to the tunnel interface
`Hub(config-if)# no ip redirects`	Disables ICMP redirects, because NHRP will be responsible for sending redirect messages
`Hub(config-if)# ip mtu 1400`	Reduces the IP MTU from 1500 to 1400 bytes
`Hub(config-if)# ip tcp adjust-mss` `1360`	Reduces the TCP maximum segment size to 1360
`Hub(config-if)# ip nhrp` `authentication cisco`	Configures a password of *cisco* for NHRP authentication
`Hub(config-if)# ip nhrp map` `multicast dynamic`	Allows NHRP to automatically add spoke routers to the multicast NHRP mappings when these spoke routers initiate the mGRE tunnel and register their unicast NHRP mappings
`Hub(config-if)# ip nhrp network-` `id 123`	Defines an NHRP network ID
`Hub(config-if)# tunnel source` `gigabitethernet 0/0/0`	Specifies a tunnel source
`Hub(config-if)# tunnel mode gre` `multipoint`	Enables mGRE on the Hub router0
`Hub(config-if)# tunnel key 12345`	Uniquely identifies the tunnel within the router

Hub(config-if)# **tunnel protection ipsec profile DMVPNprofile**	Applies the IPsec security profile to secure the DMVPN packet exchange
Hub(config-if)# **exit**	Exits interface configuration mode
Hub(config)# **router eigrp CISCO**	Enables EIGRP using named mode configuration
Hub(config-router)# **address-family ipv4 unicast autonomous-system 10**	Creates an IPv4 address family for AS 10
Hub(config-router-af)# **network 172.16.1.1 0.0.0.0**	Advertises network 172.16.1.1/32
Hub(config-router-af)# **network 10.99.1.0 0.0.0.255**	Advertises network 10.99.1.0/24 (the tunnel interface network)
Hub(config-router-af)# **af-interface tunnel 0**	Enters address-family interface configuration mode for Tunnel 0
Hub(config-router-af-interface)# **no split-horizon**	Disables split horizon to allow the hub to retransmit routes learned from the peers to the other peers. Because all the routes are being learned through the tunnel interface, EIGRP will not by default advertise routes learned from an interface back out the same interface

DMVPN Phase 1: Spoke1 Router (similar configuration required on Spoke2)

Spoke1(config)# **crypto isakmp policy 10**	Creates an ISAKMP policy with the number 10
Spoke1(config-isakmp)# **encryption aes 256**	Enables AES-256 encryption
Spoke1(config-isakmp)# **hash sha256**	Enables SHA-256 hashing
Spoke1(config-isakmp)# **authentication pre-share**	Enables PSK authentication
Spoke1(config-isakmp)# **group 16**	Enables Diffie-Hellman group 16 (4096-bit)
Spoke1(config-isakmp)# **exit**	Exits the ISAKMP policy
Spoke1(config)# **crypto isakmp key CiscoDMVPNKey address 0.0.0.0**	Defines a PSK to be used for any ISAKMP neighbor
Spoke1(config)# **crypto ipsec transform-set DMVPNset esp-aes 256 esp-sha256-hmac**	Creates an IPsec transform set called *DMVPNset* that uses AES-256 and SHA-256 for ESP
Spoke1(cfg-crypto-trans)# **mode transport**	Enables tunnel mode for the IPsec tunnel

`Spoke1(cfg-crypto-trans)# exit`	Exits the transform set
`Spoke1(config)# crypto ipsec profile DMVPNprofile`	Creates an IPsec profile called *DMVPNprofile*
`Spoke1(ipsec-profile)# set transform-set DMVPNset`	Applies the DMVPNset transform set
`Spoke1(ipsec-profile)# exit`	Exits the IPsec profile
`Spoke1(config)# interface tunnel 0`	Enters interface configuration mode
`Spoke1(config-if)# ip address 10.99.1.101 255.255.255.0`	Applies an IP address to the tunnel interface
`Spoke1(config-if)# no ip redirects`	Disables ICMP redirects, because NHRP will be responsible for sending redirect messages
`Spoke1(config-if)# ip mtu 1400`	Reduces the IP MTU from 1500 to 1400 bytes
`Spoke1(config-if)# ip tcp adjust-mss 1360`	Reduces the TCP maximum segment size to 1360
`Spoke1(config-if)# ip nhrp authentication cisco`	Configures a password of *cisco* for NHRP authentication
`Spoke1(config-if)# ip nhrp map 10.99.1.1 10.99.0.1`	Maps the hub tunnel interface and physical interface together. This instructs the router that NHRP messages to the Hub router should be sent to the physical IP address
`Spoke1(config-if)# ip nhrp map multicast 10.99.0.1`	Maps NHRP multicast traffic to the physical address of the Hub router
`Spoke1(config-if)# ip nhrp network-id 123`	Defines an NHRP network ID
`Spoke1(config-if)# ip nhrp nhs 10.99.1.1`	Defines the NHRP server address
`Spoke1(config-if)# tunnel source gigabitethernet 0/0/0`	Specifies a tunnel source
`Spoke1(config-if)# tunnel destination 10.99.0.1`	Defines the Hub router's physical address as the tunnel destination
`Spoke1(config-if)# tunnel mode gre ip`	Enables standard GRE on the Spoke1 router
`Spoke1(config-if)# tunnel key 12345`	Uniquely identifies the tunnel within the router
`Spoke1(config-if)# tunnel protection ipsec profile DMVPNprofile`	Applies the IPsec security profile to secure the DMVPN packet exchange
`Spoke1(config-if)# exit`	Exits interface configuration mode
`Spoke1(config)# router eigrp CISCO`	Enables EIGRP using named mode configuration

Spoke1(config-router)# **address-family ipv4 unicast autonomous-system 10**	Creates an IPv4 address family for AS 10
Spoke1(config-router-af)# **network 172.16.101.1 0.0.0.0**	Advertises network 172.16.101.1/32
SPOKE1(config-router-af)# **network 10.99.1.0 0.0.0.255**	Advertises network 10.99.1.0/24 (the tunnel interface network)

For DMVPN Phase 2, you need to change the tunnel mode on the spokes and modify the routing configuration on the hub. Contrary to Phase 1, this configuration will allow the routers to build dynamic spoke-to-spoke tunnels based on traffic needs. The tunnel to the hub will be persistent.

DMVPN Phase 2: Hub Router

Hub(config)# **router eigrp CISCO**	Enters EIGRP using named mode configuration
Hub(config-router)# **address-family ipv4 unicast autonomous-system 10**	Enters the IPv4 address family for AS 10
Hub(config-router-af)# **af-interface tunnel 0**	Enters address-family interface configuration mode for Tunnel 0
Hub(config-router-af-interface)# **no next-hop-self**	Disables the EIGRP next-hop self feature. By default, the router will insert its IP address as the next hop on the updates sent to the peers. In Phase 2 DMVPN the spokes must see the tunnel interface IP address of the other spokes as the next hop for the remote networks, instead of the hub

DMVPN Phase 2: Spoke1 Router (identical configuration required on Spoke2)

Spoke1(config)# **interface tunnel 0**	Enters interface configuration mode
Spoke1(config-if)# **no tunnel destination 10.99.0.1**	Removes the **tunnel destination** command
Spoke1(config-if)# **tunnel mode gre multipoint**	Changes the tunnel mode to mGRE

Phase 3 DMVPN is designed for the hub to only advertise a summary address to the spokes, and only when there is a better route to the destination network will the hub tell the spoke about it. This is done using an NHRP traffic indication message to signal the spoke that a better path exists. To do this, you need to make a few configuration changes.

DMVPN Phase 3: Hub Router

Hub(config)# **interface tunnel 0**	Enters interface configuration mode
Hub(config-if)# **ip nhrp redirect**	NHRP Redirect is configured on the hub, instructing it to send the NHRP traffic indication message if a better route exists
Hub(config-if)# **exit**	Exits interface configuration mode
Hub(config)# **router eigrp CISCO**	Enters EIGRP using named mode configuration
Hub(config-router)# **address-family ipv4 unicast autonomous-system 10**	Enters the IPv4 address family for AS 10
Hub(config-router-af)# **af-interface tunnel 0**	Enters address-family interface configuration mode for Tunnel 0
Hub(config-router-af-interface)# **summary-address 0.0.0.0 0.0.0.0**	Advertises a summary address. In this case the summary advertised is an EIGRP default route (D*)

DMVPN Phase 3: Spoke1 Router (identical configuration required on Spoke2)

Spoke1(config)# **interface tunnel 0**	Enters interface configuration mode
Spoke1(config-if)# **ip nhrp shortcut**	Enables NHRP shortcut switching on the interface. This allows the spoke router to discover shorter paths to a destination network after receiving an NHRP redirect message from the hub. The spokes can then communicate directly with each other without the need for an intermediate hop

Verifying Cisco DMVPN

Router# **show dmvpn**	Displays DMVPN-specific session information
Router# **show ip nhrp**	Displays NHRP mapping information
Router# **show ip nhrp nhs detail**	Displays NHRP NHS information
Router# **debug dmvpn**	Displays real-time information about DMVPN sessions
Router# **debug nhrp**	Displays real-time information about NHRP

NOTE: Running OSPF over a DMVPN network has some of the same challenges as running OSPF over other types of networks. Because only the hub is in direct communication with all of the branches, it should be configured as the designated router (DR) on the DMVPN subnet. There is not typically a backup DR (BDR) for this type of configuration. A BDR is possible if a second hub is placed on the same subnet.

In strict hub-and-spoke DMVPNs, you should include the tunnel interface in the OSPF routing process and configure the tunnel interface as a point-to-multipoint OSPF network type on the hub router, and as a point-to-point network type on the branch routers. In this case, there is no need to elect a DR on the DMVPN subnet.

To create a partially meshed or fully meshed DMVPN, configure the mGRE tunnel on the hub router as an OSPF broadcast network. Each spoke router should be configured with an OSPF priority of 0 to prevent a spoke from becoming a DR or BDR.

VRF-Lite

Virtual routing and forwarding (VRF) is a technology that creates separate virtual routers on a physical router. Router interfaces, routing tables, and forwarding tables are completely isolated between VRFs, preventing traffic from one VRF from forwarding into another VRF. All router interfaces belong to the global VRF until they are specifically assigned to a user-defined VRF. The global VRF is identical to the regular routing table of non-VRF routers.

The use of Cisco VRF-Lite technology has the following advantages:

- Allows for true routing and forwarding separation

- Simplifies the management and troubleshooting of the traffic belonging to the specific VRF, because separate forwarding tables are used to switch that traffic

- Enables the support for alternate default routes

Configuring VRF-Lite

Follow these steps when configuring a Cisco router for VRF-Lite support:

Step 1. Create the VRF(s).

Step 2. Assign interface(s) to the VRF.

Step 3. Enable routing for the VRF.

Step 1: Create the VRFs

`Router(config)# ip vrf GUEST`	Creates an IPv4 VRF called *GUEST* using the old VRF CLI format
`Router(config-vrf)# exit`	Exits VRF configuration mode
`Router(config)# vrf definition STAFF`	Creates a VRF called *STAFF* using the new VRF CLI format
`Router(config-vrf)# address-family ipv4`	Enables the IPv4 address family for the STAFF VRF using the new VRF CLI format
`Router(config-vrf-af)# exit`	Exits the IPv4 address family
`Router(config-vrf)# address-family ipv6`	Enables the IPv6 address family for the STAFF VRF using the new VRF CLI format

| `Router(config-vrf-af)# exit` | Exits the IPv6 address family |
| `Router(config-vrf)# exit` | Exits VRF configuration mode |

Step 2: Assign an Interface to the VRF

`Router(config)# interface gigabitethernet 0/0/0`	Enters interface configuration mode
`Router(config-if)# ip vrf forwarding GUEST`	Assigns the GigabitEthernet 0/0/0 interface to the GUEST VRF using the old CLI format
`Router(config-if)# interface gigabitethernet 0/0/1`	Enters interface configuration mode
`Router(config-if)# vrf forwarding STAFF`	Assigns the GigabitEthernet 0/0/1 interface to the STAFF VRF using the new CLI format

Step 3: Enable Routing for the VRF

The following configuration examples demonstrate how IPv4 VRFs can be associated with a routing process. The same commands would apply for IPv6 VRFs.

`Router(config)# ip route vrf GUEST 0.0.0.0 0.0.0.0 172.16.16.2`	Defines a default route for the GUEST VRF
`Router(config)# router ospf 1 vrf STAFF`	Enables OSPFv2 for the STAFF VRF
`Router(config)# router ospfv3 1`	Enables OSPFv3
`Router(config-router)# address-family ipv4 unicast vrf STAFF`	Assigns the STAFF VRF to the IPv4 unicast address family
`Router(config)# router eigrp CISCO`	Enables EIGRP using named mode configuration
`Router(config-router)# address-family ipv4 unicast vrf GUEST autonomous-system 100`	Assigns the GUEST VRF to the IPv4 unicast address family for AS 100
`Router(config)# router bgp 65001`	Enables BGP for AS 65001
`Router(config-router)# address-family ipv4 vrf STAFF`	Assigns the STAFF VRF to the IPv4 address family

NOTE: Cisco IOS supports the old and new VRF CLI formats. Old Cisco IOS VRF configuration style supports IPv4 only. New multiprotocol VRF CLI now supports both IPv4 and IPv6. Cisco IOS offers a migration tool that upgrades a VRF instance or all VRFs configured on the router to support multiple address families under the same VRF. The **vrf upgrade-cli multi-af-mode {common-policies | non-common-policies}** [**vrf** *vrf-name*] command is issued in global configuration mode.

Verifying VRF-Lite

`Router# `**`show vrf`**	Displays a list of all configured VRFs, their address families, and their interfaces
`Router# `**`show vrf detail`**` vrf-name`	Provides detailed information about a specific VRF

Create Your Own Journal Here

Index

E

J - K

L

Q - R

REGISTER YOUR PRODUCT at CiscoPress.com/register

Access Additional Benefits and SAVE 35% on Your Next Purchase

- Download available product updates.
- Access bonus material when applicable.
- Receive exclusive offers on new editions and related products.
  (Just check the box to hear from us when setting up your account.)
- Get a coupon for 35% for your next purchase, valid for 30 days.
  Your code will be available in your Cisco Press cart. (You will also find
  it in the Manage Codes section of your account page.)

Registration benefits vary by product. Benefits will be listed on your account
page under Registered Products.

CiscoPress.com – Learning Solutions for Self-Paced Study, Enterprise, and the Classroom
Cisco Press is the Cisco Systems authorized book publisher of Cisco networking technology,
Cisco certification self-study, and Cisco Networking Academy Program materials.

At **CiscoPress.com** you can

- Shop our books, eBooks, software, and video training.
- Take advantage of our special offers and promotions (ciscopress.com/promotions).
- Sign up for special offers and content newsletters (ciscopress.com/newsletters).
- Read free articles, exam profiles, and blogs by information technology experts.
- Access thousands of free chapters and video lessons.

Connect with Cisco Press – Visit CiscoPress.com/community
Learn about Cisco Press community events and programs.

Cisco Press

ALWAYS LEARNING   PEARSON